Early Settlers of Tidewater Virginia

Volume 1

Elise Greenup Jourdan

HERITAGE BOOKS
2018

HERITAGE BOOKS

AN IMPRINT OF HERITAGE BOOKS, INC.

Books, CDs, and more—Worldwide

For our listing of thousands of titles see our website
at
www.HeritageBooks.com

Published 2018 by
HERITAGE BOOKS, INC.
Publishing Division
5810 Ruatan Street
Berwyn Heights, Md. 20740

International Standard Book Number
Paperbound: 978-16-8034-900-9

CONTENTS

INTRODUCTION

On 10 Apr 1606 King James I of England signed the first patents for the development of the Colony of Virginia and by the next year a small group of adventurers, under the auspices of the privately owned Virginia Company of London, were exploring the upper reaches of the Powhatan's River, later renamed the James River.

Some 4 years later in 1611, Sir Thomas Dale and his men went upriver from Jamestown seeking to establish a settlement less vulnerable to Indian attacks which were plaguing Jamestown. There on a peninsula on the north bank of the river they established the second settlement in the Virginia Colony called Henricus or Henrico Town in honor of Henry, Prince of Wales, eldest son of King James I, which later became known as Farrar's Island.

The settlements grew rapidly as more adventurers and settlers arrived in the new world and by 1619 a General Assembly was held in Jamestown attended by representatives from each of the plantations. After the Indian uprising of 1622, relative peace was established and by 1624 the British government assumed responsibility for the colony, laying out the boundaries for eight original colonies in 1634.

From the vast lands of the original Henrico County which extended from the junction of the Appomattox and the James Rivers to the Blue Ridge Mountains, many new counties were formed in the 18th century: Goochland, 1728; Albemarle, 1744; Chesterfield & Cumberland, 1749; Amherst & Buckingham, 1761; Powhatan & Fluvanna, 1777; etc. Today all or part of 10 counties cover the area which was once Henrico.

The people who settled this land were from all walks of life. Younger sons of upper class families came seeking their fortunes, bonded servants came for the free land, the merchants and traders came to establish new markets and the oppressed came for freedom of religion. Then there were those who were sent by the Crown to clear the city streets and clean out the prisons of Great Britain.

The first settlers wasted no time in establishing the Anglican Church. Henrico was the first parish and in 1611 Appomattox Church was built in southern Charles City County. Later Dale, Bristol, King William and other parishes were formed to serve the growing needs of the settlements.

By 1699 the Quakers had established what became known as the Henrico Monthly Meeting which was first known as Curles, later by various names such as New Kent, Upper, Upland, White Oak Swamp, Weyanoke, Cedar Creek, etc.

Elise Greenup Jourdan
Knoxville, Tennessee
elisejourdan@att.net
September 2005

REFERENCES

The sources used to reconstruct the families in this volume are many and varied from unpublished manuscripts, published family histories, magazine and newspaper articles, history books, biographies, abstracts of the record, as well as some original records of Henrico and the various counties which evolved from and adjoined the original county

Some records were found in 2 or more locations and, in some cases, both references are given. The same reference system was not followed throughout, thus any researcher desiring to go to the source used should familiarize themselves with the meaning of the references:

County abbreviations:

Ac	Accomack County
Al	Albemarle County
Am	Amelia County
Br	Brunswick County
Ch	Chesterfield County
Cu	Cumberland County
EC	Elizabeth City County
Fl	Fluvanna County
GC	Goochland County
Ha	Halifax County
HC	Henrico County
Lu	Lunenburg County
Me	Mecklenburg County
No	Nottoway County
PC	Prince Charles County
PE	Prince Edward County
PG	Prince George County
Po	Powhatan County
Su	Sussex County

Document abbreviations:

DB	Deed Book
OB	Order Book
PB	Patent Book
RB	Record Book
WA	Wills & Administrations
WB	Will Book
WD	Wills & Deeds

Example: (AcDB 1.11) identifies the source as Accomack County Deed Book Volume 1, page 11 of the original record

The following 10 books by Benjamin B. Weisiger, III, Iberian Publishing Company, Athens, GA, and the microfilm of Will Book 1 are referenced in a different manner:
Example: (GCWD-1 p. 8) identifies the source as page 8 of the Weisiger book

GCWD-1	Goochland County Virginia Wills & Deeds 1728-1736
GCWD-2	Goochland County Virginia Wills & Deeds 1736-1742
GCWD-3	Goochland County Virginia Wills & Deeds 1742-1749
HCVD-1	Henrico County Virginia Deeds, 1677-1705
HCVD-2	Henrico County Virginia Deeds, 1706-1737
HCVD-3	Henrico County Virginia Deeds, 1737-1750
HCVD-4	Henrico County Virginia Deeds, 1750-1767
HCVD-5	Henrico County Virginia Deeds, 1767-1774
HCVW-1	Henrico County Virginia Wills, 1677-1737
HCVW-2	Henrico County Virginia Wills, 1737-1781
HCVW-3	Henrico County Virginia Will Book 1, 1781-1787 (microfilm)

Other sources:

APP   Adventurers of Purse and Person, 1607-1624/5

ChDB   Chesterfield County Virginia Deeds; 3 volumes; Books 1 & 2, 1749-1756; Books 3 & 4, 1756-1764; Book 5, 1764-1768; Benjamin B. Weisiger, III, Iberian Publishing Company, Athens, GA

ChWB   Chesterfield County Virginia Wills; 2 volumes; Books 1 & 2, 1749-1774; Books 3 & 4, 1774-1802; Benjamin B. Weisiger, III, Iberian Publishing Company, Athens, GA

CPYC   Charles Parish York County, Virginia History and Registers; Births 1648-1789; Deaths 1665-1787; Landon C. Bell

CRHC   Colonial Records Henrico County

DR   The Douglas Register by William Douglas; J. W. Fergusson & Sons, Richmond, VA, 1928

LF&C   The Ligon Family and Connections, William D. Ligon, Hartford, Conn.: Printed by the Bond Press, 1947

LOG   Index to Land Office Grants, Library of Virginia

LOP   Index to Land Office Patents, Library of Virginia

LOV   Index to Wills and Administrations, Library of Virginia

MCC   Marriages of Chesterfield County, Virginia, 1771-1815, Catherine Lindsay Knorr; published by author

MHC   Marriages of Henrico County, Virginia, 1680-1808; Joyce H. Lindsay; published by author

QRH   Quaker Records of Henrico Monthly Meeting and Other Church Records of Henrico, New Kent and Charles City Counties, F. Edward Wright, Colonial Roots, Lewes, DE

PB   Cavaliers and Pioneers, 1623-1776, 7 volumes; Nell Marion Nugent; Genealogical Publishing Co., Baltimore, MD

TVF   Tidewater Virginia Families; A Magazine of History and Genealogy, Virginia Lee Hutcheson Davis, Editor; 12 volumes 1993-2004

VAWA   Virginia Wills and Administrations

VBHP   Vestry Book of Henrico Parish, Virginia, 1730-1773; Southern Historical Press, Inc., 1904

VP   The Edward Pleasants Valentine Papers, Genealogical Publishing Co., Baltimore, 1979

Other sources of information not referenced in the text:

Annals of Henrico Parish, Diocese of Virginia and especially of St. John's Church by Lewis W. Burton; Williams Printing Company, Richmond, VA, 1904

Marriage records & will indexes of the various counties

Some Prominent Virginia Families, Louise Pecquet du Bellet, Lynchburg, VA; J. P. Bell, 1907

The William and Mary Quarterly, published by the Omohundro Institute of Early American History and Culture

Tyler's Quarterly Historical and Genealogical Magazine, 33 volumes; published Richmond, VA 1919-1952; reprints Periodicals Service Company, 11 Maine Street, Germantown NY 12526

Virginia Magazine of History and Biography, 428 North Boulevard, Richmond, Virginia

Numbering System

The custom of using and re-using given names in these early families is both a help and hindrance in identifying the various generations. The following system has been devised to distinguish between generations:

> 3747-1   Thomas Batte (p. 39), only child listed of
> 374-7   Chamberlayne Batte (p. 39), 7th child listed of
> 37-4   Henry Batte (p. 38), 4th child listed of
> 3-7   William Batte (p. 37), 7th child listed of
> 3.   Henry Batte (p.36), 3rd child listed of
> John Batte (p. 33)

Abbreviations

?	this event or person may not belong in this place	(f)	female
		FH	family history
£	British Pound Sterling	(m)	male
adj.	adjoining	m.	married
admn.	administrator	mb	marriage bond
adms.	administrators	mc	marriage contract
admx.	administratrix	m/c	marriage consent
appt.	appointed	ml	marriage license
b.	born	mo.	month
ca	about the time of	mos.	months
chr.	christened	n.	north
dec'd	deceased	nok	next of kin
d.	died	p.	page
d/o	daughter of	re	regarding
e.	east	s.	south
est.	estimated	s/o	son of
ex.	executor	w.	west
exs.	executors	w/o	wife of
extx.	executrix		

JAMES AKIN

James Akin, Sr., b. ca 1632-3 Henrico Co., age 46 on Apr 1678; age 45 on 1 Aug 1678 (HCVD-1 p. 147, 156); d. by 1 Feb 1713; m. est. by ca 1661 **Sarah** ____; d. by 2 Aug 1714 Henrico Co.; James was charged with 2 tithables in 1679 Henrico Co. and the 1705 rent rolls of Henrico showed he held 200 ac.; children from James' will:

1. James Akin, Jr., b. est. ca 1662
2. Mary Akin, b. est. ca 1664
3. Elizabeth Akin, b. est. ca 1666
4. Sarah Akin, b. est. ca 1668

20 Oct 1665; James Akin granted 250 ac. on n. side of Appamattock River; adj. Thomas Webb's land (LOP 5.517)

26 May 1673; James Akin and Richard Womack granted 335 ac. on n. side of Appamattock; adj. Thomas Wells' land (LOP 5.517)

2 Dec 1682; 2 Apr 1683; James Aken, Sr. and Sarah his wife, assign land on e. side of *Cobbs Slash* in Bristol Parish to Eben Bellange (HCVD-1 p. 19)

15 Jun 1696; 20 Aug 1696; from James Eakin, Sr. and James Eakin, Jr. to John Farley, Jr.; 80 ac. in Varina Parish; bounded by *Flintons, Butterwood Bottom, Cobbs Slash*, etc. (HCVD-1 p. 95)

Will of James Akin, Sr., Varina Parish; Henrico Co.; 21 Apr 1712; 1 Feb 1713
To wife Sarah for life, plantation, Indian woman and her 2 children; then to son James Akin
Ex.: Sarah, all the rest of the estate
Codicil: To 4 child. James Akin, Mary Womeck, Elizabeth Farlow & Sarah Nunnoly, each 12p
Wit: Thomas Chamberlayne, Richard Oglesby, Chas. Roberts (HCVW-1 p. 126)
[James Akin, Sr.; Henrico County Wills and Administrations (1662-1800) p. 240. Will pro. 1 Feb. 1713. Records, 1710-1714 (Reel 6) (LOV)]

Will of Sarah Akin, widow; Henrico Co.; 2 Feb 1713/4; 2 Aug 1714
To son James Aiken, slaves, items
To grandson Daniel Nunnoly, feather bed
To dau. Elizabeth Farlow, feather bed
To dau. Sarah Nunnoly, items
To son in law John Womack, 1s
Remainder equally to children James, Elizabeth & Sarah
Ex: son James
Wit: Thomas Chamberlayne, William Baugh, Chas. Roberts (HCVW-1 p. 128)
[Sarah Akin; Henrico County Wills and Administrations (1662-1800) p. 283. Will pro. 2 Aug. 1714. p. 284. Inv. & appr. rec. 7 Sept. 1714. Records, 1710-1714 (Reel 6) (LOV)]

1. **James Akin, Jr.**, b. ca 1662, age 26 on Oct 1688 (HCVD-1 p. 152); d. by May 1744 Henrico Co.; m. est. ca 1683 **Anne** ____, b. est. ca 1667; d. bef. 29 Nov 1743 Henrico Co.; the rent roll of 1705 shows James held 218 ac. in Henrico Co. and he is found in the St. James Parish records of 1733; his father's will

left him the family plantation at the death of his mother; his mother's will left him slaves & items; children:

    1-1 William Akin, b. est. ca 1684
    1-2 Thomas Akin, b. est. ca 1686
    1-3 James Akin, b. est. ca 1688
    1-4 John Akin, b. est. ca 1690
    1-5 Elizabeth Akin, b. est. ca 1692
    1-6 Ann Akin, b. est. ca 1694

1 Dec 1636 (sic); [filed with 1687]; Anne, w/o James Eakins, Jr., relinquished dower right in land sold by her husband and James Eakins, Sr. to Bartholomew Roberts (HCVD-1 p. 43)

4 Oct 1717; 7 Oct 1717; deed of gift from James Aken to dau. Elizabeth, w/o John Baugh; 50 ac. in Bristol Parish next to James Baugh, *Cobs Slash*, etc.; Anne, w/o Aken, relinquished dower right (HCVD-2 p. 67)

12 Jul 1718; James Aken, Sr. granted 340 ac. Henrico Co. in forks of *Proctors*, near head of *Cold Water Run* (LOP 10.378)

11 Jul 1719; James Aken, Sr. granted 480 ac. Henrico Co. on s. side of *Swift Creek* (LOP 10.420)

Jan Ct. 1722; from James Aken to Edward Hill, deed; Anne, w/o James relinquished dower rights (HCVD-2 p. 197)

26 Jun 1731; James Akin granted 1,000 ac. Goochland Co. on n. side of Appomattock River; adj. *Halcoate Pride* (LOP 14.195)

8 May 1738; from James Akin of Henrico Co. to John Watkins of Goochland Co.; for £15; 250 ac on n. side of Appomattox River, easternmost part of 1,000 ac. patented by sd. Akin; /s/ James Akin, Anne Akin (GCWD-2 p. 20)

20 Aug 1739; 19 Feb 1739; from James Akin to John Farmer, Jr., both of Henrico Co.; for £16; 250 ac. on branch of *Butterwood Creek*; part of 1,000 ac. granted Akin; /s/ James Akin, Ann Akin (GCWD-2 p. 36)

Will of James Akin; Henrico Co.; 29 Nov 1743; May 1744
To grandson Thomas Moor, 200 ac. at *Butterwood*, Goochland Co., if he pay £4 to
    executor
To son William, 300 ac. remainder of land at *Butterwood*
To son Thomas, all my land in his possession and my land in Dale Parish
To grandson Isham Akin, items, negro
To granddau. Frances Akin, items & negro; if she die without issue to Thomas and her
    bro. James Akin
To dau. Baugh, negro
To son James, a cane & gallon pot
To son John, 40s credit
To son Thomas, ex., mulattoes for life, then to his sons Joseph, Thomas & James; and
    remainder of estate
Wit: William Moore, Thomas Poullan, Henry Poullan (HCVW-1 p. 113)

May Ct. 1744; Thomas Aken presented will of James Aken, dec'd; granted probate (HCVW-2 p. 22)
[James Akin; Henrico County Wills and Administrations (1662-1800) p. 1287-1290. Will pro. May 1744. Misc. Court Records, Vol. 4, [1738-1746] (Reel 2) (LOV)]

1-1 William Akin, Sr., b. est. ca 1684; d. by 4 Jun 1761 Chesterfield Co.; m. aft. Aug 1717 **Elizabeth Ashbrook**, b. ca 1700; d. by 4 Oct 1771; d/o Peter & Jennett Ashbrook; William inherited 300 ac. of *Butterwood*, Goochland Co., from the 1744 will of his father; Elizabeth was unmarried when her grandmother Jennett Ashbrook wrote her will in 1717 and called Elizabeth Akin in the 1756 will of her father; a Chesterfield deed made 18 Aug 1763 mentions bounded by Elizabeth Akin and others (ChDB 4.450); children:

> 11-1   William Akin
> 11-2   James Akin
> 11-3   Peter Akin
> 11-4   Joseph Akin
> 11-5   Isham Akin
> 11-6   Jean Akin
> 11-7   Mary Akin
> 11-8   Elizabeth Akin

[Note: This appears to have been the William who m. Elizabeth Ashbrook based on the names of these three sons in the will of Elizabeth Akin: William (her husband), James (her father in law) & Peter (her father). Her will shows that son William was alive in 1771 which means that the William Akin, Jr. who d. in 1767 in Chesterfield Co. was probably the s/o one of her husband's brothers called "Jr." to distinguish him from an older William in the same area. Nothing was found to positively identify him, so he is in the unplaced section at the end of this family.]

5 Aug 1728; 5 Aug 1728; from William Brown to William Akin, both of Henrico Co.; for £15; 150 ac. on 2nd branch of *Swift Creek* (HCVD-2 p. 111)

Mar Ct. 1739; from William Aken to Daniel Brown, deed; Elizabeth, w/o William, relinquished dower (HCVD-3 p. 84)

7 Apr 1753; Chesterfield Co.; William Akin and son William among those appointed to appraise estate of William Locket (ChOB 2.394)

<u>Will of William Akin, Sr. of Dale Parish; Chesterfield Co.; 26 Aug 1757; 4 Jun 1761</u>
To wife Elizabeth, 3 negroes, livestock, ½ household goods
To son James, 80 ac. land on s. side of *Swift Creek*, joining plantation where I live, negro, livestock, ½ household goods
To dau. Elizabeth Akin, negro, items
Exs: wife and son James
Wit: Henry Turpin, Robert Haskins, John Pride, Jr. (ChWB 1.325)
4 Jun 1761; inventory of William Akin, Sr.; no value given; by Elizabeth Akin and James Akin, exs. (ChWB 1.326); 5 Jun 1761; Will of William Akin presented by Elizabeth and James Akin, exs. (ChOB 3.126); 7 Aug 1761; inventory of William Akin returned (ChOB 3.168)

Will of Elizabeth Akin; Chesterfield Co.; 31 Jul 1771; 4 Oct 1771
To son Peter Akin, 1s
To sons Joseph & Isham Akin, 1 negro each
To son James Akin, 1 Indian fellow
To daus. Jean Farmer, Mary Pleasants & Elizabeth Cheatham, 1 negro each
Remainder divided between sons Wm. Akin and James Akin
Ex: James Akin
Wit: John Watkins, Richard Lockett, Currell Keen (ChWB 2.20)
4 Oct 1771; will of Elizabeth Akin, proved by witnesses (ChOB 5.37); 1 Nov 1771;
    inventory of Elizabeth Akin returned (ChOB 5.48)
[Elizabeth Akin; Chesterfield County Wills and Administrations (1754-1800) Inventory - dated
1771 Returned 1 November 1771. (O.B.5, p. 48.) Chesterfield Will Book 2, p. 21; Proved 4 Oct.
1771. (O.B. 5, p. 37.) (LOV)]

11-1 **William Akin**; he may have been the William who d. aft. 30 Aug
    1794; m. ____; a William & James Akin appraised an estate in
    Chesterfield Co. in 1766 (ChOB 3.751); children from William's will:

111-1 **Joseph Akin**
111-2 **James Akin**; m. 12 Mar 1782 Chesterfield Co. **Sally Pleasants**;
    sur. William Aiken (MCC p. 2)
111-3 **Arthur Akin**; d. 1809 Chesterfield Co. (ChWB 7.114); he may have
    married the following in Chesterfield Co. (MCC p. 2): m/1 13 Jul 1785
    Elizabeth Pleasants; m/2 13 Sep 1797 **Mary (Lockett) Cheatham**;
    widow of Henry Cheatham; m/3 15 Dec 1808 **Ann Beasley**, widow of
    Thomas Beasley; Arthur wit. the will of Francis Lockett 4 Mar 1800
    which names dau. Polly Akin among his children (ChWB 5.381); Polly
    might be the same person as Mary Lockett who m. William Akin
111-4 **Elizabeth (Betty) Akin**; m. 11 Nov 1782 Chesterfield Co.
    William Ellis; consent of William Akin, her father; sur. Joseph Aiken
    (MCC p.45)
111-5 **Sally Akin**; m. ____ **Landrum**
111-6 **Mary Akin**; m. ____ **Beasbitch**

12 Apr 1762; from William Akin of Chesterfield Co. to William Northcut of same; for
£15; 149 ac. part of 298 ac. bounded by *Turkey Branch*, Cumberland Co. line, etc.;
James Akin one of the witnesses (ChDB 4.560)

Dec 1764; Mar 1765; from Bartley Baugh to William Akin, both of Chesterfield Co.;
for £60; 99 ac. on n. side of *Swift Creek* (ChDB 5.307)

18 Aug 1766; Nov 1766; from John Russell to William Akin, both of Dale Parish,
Chesterfield Co.; for £140; 150 ac. on s. side of *Swift Creek* to mouth of *Dry Creek*
(ChDB 5.441)

Will of William Akin of Manchester Parish; Chesterfield Co.; 30 Aug 1794
To wife items & 1 negro for life, then to my son Joseph
To daus. Betty Ellis, Sally Landrum, Mary Beasbitch
To son Joseph, land he lives on and ½ land mortgaged to me by Francis Lockett, Sr.
To son James, ½ of above land

Remainder of estate divided between sons Joseph, James & Arthur, they to be exs. Wit: Joel Chetham, Thomas Beasley, John Ecols (ChWB 4.408)

11-2 **James Akin**, b. aft. 1717; he inherited 80 ac. on s. side of *Swift Creek* from his father's will; he may have been the following James:

5 Jul 1765; 5 Jul 1765; from James Akin to Allison Clark, both of Chesterfield Co.; for £50; land on s. side of *Spring Run* including mill place; Akin's wife released dower (ChDB 5.321)

11-3 **Peter Akin**; m. by 1747 **Martha Hill**; d/o James Hill whose 11 Jan 1750 will calls her Martha Akin (ChWB 1.23); Peter is said to have m/2 **Mary** ___ who ack. a deed he made 30 Nov 1777 in Granville, NC; he was tithable in St. James Parish, Lunenburg Co. 1764; child:

113-1 Ann Akin

5 Feb 1744/5; 1st Mon Mar 1745; from Henry Walthall, Jr. to Peter Akin, both of Dale Parish, Henrico Co.; for £12; ½ of 400 ac. (HCVD-3 p. 10)

10 Aug 1747; 1st Mon Oct 1747; from Peter Akin of Henrico Co. to William Riggin of Goochland Co.; for £60; eastern part of 200 ac. divided between Akin and Wm. Walthall on *Sapponey Creek*; Martha, w/o Peter Akin, relinquished dower rights (HCVD-3 p. 46)

31 Dec 1765; 6 Feb 1767; agreement between Peter Akin of Mecklenburg Co. and Edmund Logwood of Chesterfield Co. regarding estate of James Hill, dec'd; Logwood to pay £12.17.6 and deliver up estate to Ann Akin, d/o Peter Akin, and to Thomas Logwood, s/o Edmund; and to give sd. Ann and Thomas a negro boy and £37 at their marriage (ChDB 5.306)

113-1 **Ann Akin**; m. ca 1767 **Thomas Logwood**; s/o Edmund Logwood of Chesterfield Co.

31 Dec 1765; 6 Feb 1767; We, Peter Akin of Mecklenburg Co. and Edmond Logwood of Chesterfield Co. have agreed that sd. Akin is to deliver all of the estate of James Hill, dec'd, to Logwood, whether due by gift, legacy or dower; Logwood is to pay £12.17.6 by 10 Jan next half in goods at Mr. Esdale's store and half in cash; Logwood is to diver up all of the estate to Ann Akin, d/o Peter Akin, and to Thomas Logwood, s/o sd. Edmund, and to give sd. Ann & Thomas a negro boy and £37 on their marriage; /s/ Peter Akin, Edmond Logwood (ChDB 5.308)

11-4 **Joseph Akin**; he may have m. **Ann Lockett**; d/o William Lockett whose will written 3 Nov 1794 names the 4 children of Joseph and Ann (ChWB 4.591):

114-1 **William Akin**
114-2 **Ann Akin**
114-3 **Joseph** Akin
114-4 **James Akin**

11-5 **Isham Akin**

5 Feb 1762; 6 Aug 1762; from Thomas Watkins of Henrico Co. to Isham Akin of Cumberland Co.; for £185; 350 ac. bounded by *Horsepen Branch*, Cumberland Co. line, etc. (ChDB 5.234)

14 Apr 1765; 6 Jun 1765; from Isham Akin to Josiah Turpin, both of Chesterfield Co.; for £15; 25 ac on s. side of *Horsepen Branch* (ChDB 5.319)

3 Jun 1767; Sep 1767; Isham Akin of Chesterfield Co. sold land on s. side of *Swift Creek* at mouth of *Horsepen Branch* to Josiah Turpin for £100 (ChDB 5.63)

    11-6 **Jean Akin**; m. ____ **Farmer**
    11-7 **Mary Akin**; m. ____ **Pleasants**
    11-8 **Elizabeth Akin**; m. **Stephen Cheatham**; d. after 12 May 1783 when
       he wrote his will naming his 5 sons & 5 daughters (ChWB 3.404); s/o
       Benjamin Cheatam; she inherited a negro and items from her father's will

1-2 **Thomas Akin**, b. est. ca 1686; m. ____; Thomas wit. deed 7 Aug 1732
    (HCVD-2 p. 139); he inherited all land in his possession, land in Dale Parish
    from the will of his father as well as mulattoes for life, they to then go to his
    3 sons Joseph, Thomas & James; he also inherited remainder of his father's
    estate; 1st 5 children from the 1744 will of their grandfather Akin:

          12-1 Joseph Akin, b. est. ca 1730's
          12-2 Thomas Akin, b. est. ca 1730's
          12-3 James Akin, b. est. ca 1730's
          12-4 Frances Akin, b. est. ca 1730's
          12-5 Isham Akin, b. est. ca 1730's

    12-1 **Joseph Akin**, b. est. ca 1730's; a deed dated 26 Aug 1766 shows
       Joseph owned a tract in Henrico Co. adj. William & Susannah Childers
       (HCVD-4 p. 988; TVF 11.42); he is said to have died in NC

7 Apr 1758; 7 Apr 1758; Joseph Akin, s/o.Thomas Akin of Chesterfield Co., with consent of his father, apprentices himself to James DeSear (ChDB 3.269)

    12-2 **Thomas Akin**, b. est. ca 1730's; ?d. aft 1783; he is said to have d.
       Wilkes Co., GA
    12-3 **James Akin**, b. est. ca 1730's; said to have m. **Francis** ____

7 Apr 1758; 7 Apr 1758; James Akin, s/o Thomas Akin of Chesterfield Co., with consent of his father, apprentices himself to James DeSear for 7 years to learn trade of carpenter (ChDB 3.270)

    12-4 **Frances Akin**, b. est. ca 1730's
    12-5 **Isham Akin**, b. est. ca 1730's; although he is not called s/o Thomas in
       the will of his grandfather Akin, he is tentatively placed here; he is said to
       have died in NC

1-3 **James Akin**, b. est. ca 1688; m. by 1724 **Mary** ____; James was named
    in his father's will

15 Jan 1706; 1 Jun 1708; survey Henrico Parish, Henrico Co.; James Akin, minor, held 450 ac. (HCVD-2 p. 12)

2 Sep 1720; from James Akin, Jr. to John Worley, both of Henrico Co. & Parish; for £15; 56 ac. on n. side of *Swift Creek*; part of greater tract granted James Aken, Sr. & Richard Ligon (HCVD-2 p. 81)

Sep Ct. 1724; from James Akin, Jr. to John Farlee, Jr.; deed; Nov Ct. 1724; Mary, wife of Akin, relinquished dower (HCVD-2 p. 201, 202)

1 Dec 1729; 1st Mon Dec 1729; Apr 1764; from James Akin, Jr. to Thomas Tanner, both of Henrico Co.; land where Tanner now seated and Akin formerly lived near head of *Proctors Creek* (HCVD-2 p. 121)

1-4 **John Akin**, b. est. ca 1690 Henrico Co.; d. bef. 8 Dec 1763 Chesterfield Co.; m. bef. 1739 **Kathrine** ____; in 1739 he wit. a deed in Goochland made by Thomas Lockett (GCWD-2 p. 33); John's land was on the s. side of the James River near *Butterwood Creek* (HCVD-2 p. 33); John was named in his father's will; child:

   14-1 Lewis Akin

Jul Ct. 1739; from John Aken to Robert Hancock, deed; Kathrine, w/o John, relinquished dower (HCVD-3 p. 82)

   14-1 **Lewis Akin**; d. 16 Jul 1791 Laurens, SC; he is said to have married **Elizabeth** ____; he was tithable for 1 in St. James Parish, Lunenburg Co. in 1764

8 Dec 1764; Apr 1764; from Lewis Akin of Lunenburg Co. to James Akin of Chesterfield Co.; for £25; 80 ac. formerly belonging to John Akin, dec'd, father of sd. Lewis, bounded by sd. Lewis, *Swift Creek*, etc. (ChDB 5.323)

1-5 **Elizabeth Akin**, b. est. ca 1692; m. bef. 4 Oct 1717 **John Baugh, Jr.**, b. est. ca 1687; s/o John Baugh and Margaret ____; Elizabeth's father gave them 50 ac. in Bristol Parish in 1717 next to James Baugh and *Cobbs Slash*

1-6 **Ann Akin**; est. ca 1694; d. by 7 Aug 1728 Henrico Co.; said to have m. **William Moore**; child:

   16-1 **Thomas Moore**; inherited 200 ac. *Butterwood*, Goochland Co. from the 1744 will of his grandfather Akin

7 Aug 1728; 2 Sep 1728; inventory of Anne Moore presented in court by James Akin (HCVW-1 p. 168)

2. **Mary Akin**, b. est. ca 1664; m. **John Womack**, b. ca 1653, age 35 on 12 Oct 1688 (HCVD-1 p. 152); d. by 8 Feb 1725 Prince George Co.

10 Feb 1680; 1 Jun 1681; from Richard Womeck to bro. John Womeck, both of Bristol Parish; 100 ac. of land I live on next to *Holmes Spring*, etc. (HCVD-1 p. 12)

20 Oct 1692; 1 Feb 1692; from John Womack to John Farley, Sr., both of Bristol Parish, Henrico Co.; exchange of land; for 25 ac. at *Blackwater* in Charles City Co., I

sell my plantation I live in, 100 ac. given me by my brother Richard Womeck, dec'd; bounded by *Holmes Spring, Reecy* (sic) *Branch*, etc.; Mary, w/o John, relinquished dower right (HCVD-1 p. 75)

[John Womack, Sr.; Prince George Co. Wills and Admns. (1713-1800); p. 856-857, will pro. 8 Feb 1725; p. 884-885, inv. & appr. rec. 10 May 1726; p. 1034, inv. & appr. rec. 12 Sep 1727; Deeds, etc. 1713-1728, Pt. 3 (Reel 2) (LOV)]

3. **Elizabeth Akin**, b. est. ca 1666; m. **John Farley**; d. aft. 6 Apr 1754; Elizabeth's father and brother sold 80 ac. of their land to John Farley, Jr. in 1696; his name is spelled Farlow in the wills of her father and mother; children from John's will:

    3-1 **John Farley**
    3-2 **Peter Farley**
    3-3 **Mary Farley**; m. ____ **Womack**
    3-4 **Francis Farley** (m)
    3-5 **William Farley**
    3-6 **Sarah Farley**; m. ____ **Thompson**
    3-7 **James Farley**
    3-8 **Joseph Farley**
    3-9 **Matthew Farley**
    3-10 **Henry Farley**

Will of John Farley, Dale Parish; 6 Apr 1754 [dated]
To wife Elizabeth, plantation and all of estate for life; at her death sd. 300 ac.
   plantation to son John and his wife for life, then to son Peter
To dau. Mary Womack, negro for life, then to son Francis Farley
To sons John & William Farley & dau. Sarah Thompson, each a negro
To sons James, Joseph, Matthew, Francis and Henry, each a negro & 2 negros to son
   Peter; remainder of estate to be sold and money divided among children
Ex: son John Farley
Wit: Jno. Archer, James Clay, Richard Nunnally (ChWB 1.200)
[John Farley; Chesterfield Co. Wills & Admns. (1754-1800); will dated 1754; proved 5 Dec 1755 (O.B. 2 p. 150); W.B. 1 p. 200-201; inv. & appr. dated 1756, returned 2 Jul 1756 (O.B. 2 p. 200) (LOV)]

4. **Sarah Akin**, b. est. ca 1668; m. **Richard Nunnaly**; d. by 3 Jul 1727; he was probably a descendant of the Nunnally/Nunnelly family of Charles City Co.; children:

                    4-1 Richard Nunnaly
                    4-2 Daniel Nunnaly
                    4-3 Joseph Nunnaly
                    4-4 John Nunnaly
                    4-5 Walter Nunnaly
                    4-6 William Nunnaly

17 Aug 1725; Richard Nunnely granted 350 ac. Henrico Co. on s. side of James River and s. side of *Coldwater Road* (LOP 12.314)

Will of Richard Nunaley; 29 Mar 1722; 3 Jul 1727

To son Richard, tract where he now lives

To son William, 10s when of age

To son Daniel, the plantation he hath cleared and builded; to give his bro. Joseph the plantation 3 years rent free and 100# tobacco

To son John, all land on n. side of the swamp; if he dies to my grandson James Nunaley, s/o Richard

John to give his bro. Joseph 10s

To son Walter, rest of my lands; to give his bro. William 200# of tobacco when William of age

To wife Sarah, extx., to have this plantation for life; at her death to son Walter

Wit: John Worley, John Blankenship (HCVW-1 p. 161)

28 Aug 1727; 4 Sep 1727; inventory of estate of Richard Nunneley; value £16.2.7; presented in court by Sarah Nunneley (HCVW-1 p. 163)

[Richard Nunaley; Henrico County Wills and Administrations (1662-1800) p. 118-119. Will pro. 3 July 1727. p. 130. Inv. & appr. rec. 4 Sept. 1727. Deeds & Wills, 1726-1737 (Reel 7a); p. 2367-2368. Will incomplete. Misc. Court Records, Vol. 7, [1770-1807] (Reel 3) (LOV)]

4-1 Richard Nunnalyy; m. Mary ____; child:

41-1 James Nunnaly

3 Dec 1737; 1st Mon Dec 1737; from Richard Nunnally to his brother John Nunnally, both of Henrico Co.; for £10.6.4; 88 ac. being land given Richard by will of his father Richard Nunnally, dec'd; Mary, w/o Richard, relinquished dower right (HCVD-2 p. 187; HCVD-3 p. 76)

2 Mar 1770; from Richard Nunnally to John Bolling, both of Dale Parish; for £5; 83 ac. Chesterfield Co. on *Flintons Slash*; being land where Richard Nunnally, dec'd, father of sd. Richard formerly lived (ChDB 1749-1756, p. 189)

4-2 Daniel Nunnaly; he witnessed a deed Henrico Co. 7 Apr 1746 (HCVD-3 p. 23)

15 Jul 1732; 1st Mon in Jul 1732; from William Pride to Daniel Nunnally, both of Bristol Parish, Henrico Co.; for £30; 300 ac. Henrico Parish on s. side of *Ashen Swamp*; being all of the land given sd. William by will of his father (HCVD-2 p. 139)

4-3 Joseph Nunnaly
4-4 John Nunnaly
4-5 Walter Nunnaly

Jul Ct. 1740; from Thomas Chetham to Walter Nunnally, deed (HCVD-3 p. 86)

4-6 William Nunnaly

Unplaced:

Elizabeth Akin; d/o Joseph Goode whose will left dau. Elizabeth Akin a negro in 1761, then to go to her children (ChWB 1.371)

Frances Akin & John Akin grandchildren. of Frances Baugh, Manchester Parish; will dated 19 Jul 1793 (ChWB 4.469)

Francis Akin; grandchild of John Baugh of Manchester Parish; will dated 29 Sep 1784 (ChWB 3.528)

James Akin; d. by 22 Feb 1753 Amelia Co.; m. Ann ____; orphans James and Charles of Raleigh Parish (AmOB 5.172)

[James Akin; Amelia Co. Wills & Admns. (1734-1800); 22 Feb 1753 inv. & appr. rec., p. 84a; 23 May 1752 adms. bond rec. p. 51a (2nd pagination) Will Book 1, 1734-1761 (reel 28) [James Akin; 1774; Henrico Co. Miscellaneous Records, Vol. 4 p. 1287 (Torrence) (LOV)]

Sarah Akin; d/o John Baugh; named in will of Jane Baugh in 1802 (ChWB 5.567)

Thomas Akin; m. Elizabeth ____; possibly d/o Joseph Baugh & Jane Clarke; their children said to have been Margaret Akin who m. William Pleasants and Sarah Akin who m. Nicholas Formby, one of the wit. to the will of John Baugh of Dale Parish written 23 Oct 1772 (ChWB 3.253)

6 Jan 1758; 6 Jan 1758; from Thomas Akin to Nicholas Formbe, both of Chesterfield Co.; for £20; 60 ac. in Dale Parish; mentions *Flintons Slash*; Elizabeth, w/o Akin, relinquishes dower (ChWB 3.213)

William Akin; d. aft. 6 Feb 1767; m. Mary Lockett; d/o Benjamin Lockett

13 Oct 1748; 1st Mon May 1749; from John Russell, Jr. of Henrico Co. to William Akin, Jr. of Goochland Co.; for £3; 3 ac. on s. side of *Swift Creek* adj. sd. Russell and William Akin, Sr.; Isham Akin was one of the witnesses (HCVD-3 p. 68)

26 Jun 1760; 5 Sep 1760; from John Pride of Amelia Co. to William Akin, Jr. of Chesterfield Co.; for £112.10; ancient bounds of 322 ac. on s. side of great swamp of *Swift Creek* (ChDB 5.164)

5 Dec 1766; 5 Dec 1766; from Benjamin Locket, Sr. of Chesterfield Co. gives to his dau. Mary Akin; negro to be in her possession at death of sd. Benjamin and his wife (ChDB 5.399)

Will of William Akin, Jr. of Dale Parish; Chesterfield Co.; 18 Jan 1767; 6 Feb 1767
To wife Mary, one negro and items
Wit: Jacob Ashurst, William Lockett, James Hill (ChWB 1.325)
6 Feb 1767; will of William Akin, Jr. presented by Mary Akin, his widow (ChOB 3.802)

GEORGE ARCHER

George Archer of Bristol Parish; d. by 16 Mar 1675/6 Henrico Co.; m. **Mary** ____; she m/2 by 1681 **Joseph Royall**; George lived on n. side of the Appomattox in Bristol Parish in area of *Old Town* and a branch of *Swift Creek*; George was transported by Capt. Francis Eppes who claimed land 26 Aug 1635 & 29 May 1638 for his transport (PB 1.1.280; 1.2.537); known children:

1. George Archer, Jr., b. ca 1654
2. John Archer
3. Margery Archer
4. Elizabeth Archer
5. Ann Archer

26 Aug 1635; Capt. Francis Eppes was granted land in Henrico Co. for transport of George Archer & others (PB 1.1.280); 29 May 1638; same ac., same transportees; Charles City Co. (PB 1.537)

[undated] 2,827 ac. of land in Henrico Co. was granted to George Archer, Richard Kennon, Francis Eppes and Joseph Royall (LOP 8.153)

30 Dec 1663; 250 ac. Henrico Co. granted to George Archer according to ancient bounds formerly granted Tunstall & lately found escheat (PB 5.441 [527]; LOP 5.527)

2 Jun 1665; George Archer granted 550 ac. Henrico Co.; n. side of Appomattox in Bristoll Parish; near *Old Town*, neck called *Tunstalls*; bounding Wm. Harris; 250 ac. purchased of Edward Tunstall, found to escheat to His Majesty who confirmed to Archer; 300 ac for transport of 6 persons (PB 5.180 [69]; LOP 5.69)

25 September 1671; George Archer; Henrico Co.; granted 784 acres in Bristol Parish, on the north side of Appamattock River, next above the *Old Town* land (LOP 6.260).

31 October 1673; George Archer; Henrico County; granted 1,395 ac. 3r. 2po. in Bristol Parish on the North side of Appamattock River, next above the *Old Town* land (LOP 6.487)

1. **George Archer**, b. est. ca 1654, age 26 on 10 Feb 1680 (HCVD-1 p. 148); d. by Dec 1731 Henrico Co.; ?m/1 _____ **Clerk**; d/o Richard Clerk; m/2 by 19 Apr 1690 **Elizabeth Harris**; d. aft. 1702; she was the only sister of whole blood and next of kin of William Harris, dec'd (HCVW-1 p. 39); George was charged with 2 taxables in Henrico Co. in 1678 and held 1,738 ac. in the 1705 rent roll of Henrico Co.; children from his will:

> 1-1 Judith Archer
> 1-2 Blanche Archer
> 1-3 George Archer
> 1-4 William Archer
> 1-5 Elizabeth Archer
> 1-6 Margery Archer
> 1-7 Mary Archer

This George Archer is believed to have been married twice. The 16 Mar 1675 will of Richard Clerke of Henrico Co. calls him "son" and appoints him executor (HCVW-1 p.2) which suggests his 1st wife was the daughter of Richard Clerke. By deed in 1702 George gave dau. Judith and her husband and their heirs a tract of land on *Fleets Run* and in his will he gave the husband of Blanche 100 ac. next to *Old Town Creek*. Although the other daughters were married at the time his will was written, they only rec'd 10s each. This suggests that Judith and Blanche and possibly his son George were children of his 1st wife to whom he was conveying property or an equivalent value of what had come to him through their mother. His son George named a daughter Judith which could have been honoring his older sister, or it could suggest he was also a child of the 1st wife whose name might have been Judith. Also note his father left George's land to him for life, then to George's sons, meaning it could not revert back to the estate.

George Archer of Henrico Co., by his will dated 24 Nov 1675 bequeathed a tract to his son John Archer; for brotherly love, I, George Archer, confirm sd. tract to John Archer; recorded 1 Oct 1694 (HCVD-1 p. 85)
[George Archer, Sr.; Henrico County Wills & Administrations (1662-1800) Note p. 35. Exors. bond rec. 16 Mar. 1675/76. Records, 1677-1692 (Reel 4) (LOV]

16 Mar 1675; George Archer, Jr. called son & appt. ex. of Richard Clerke of Henrico Co. (HCVW-1 p. 2)

21 Apr 1695; George Archer granted 1,536 ac. on n. side of Appomattox in Bristol Parish; adj. Thos. Batts (LOP 8.416)

30 May 17__; 2 Jun 1701; from George Archer of Bristol Parish to Joseph Pattison; 500 ac. patented to George in 1695; Elizabeth, wife of George, relinquished dower rights (HCVD-1 p. 117)

1 Dec 1702; from George Archer of Bristol Parish, Henrico Co. to James Thweat, Jr. of Bristol Parish, Charles City Co.; to son in law William Traylor and Judith his wife, d/o sd. George; in trust for use of sd. William & Judith and their heirs; land on n. side of Appomattox River on s. w. side of *Fleets Run*; Elizabeth, wife of George, relinquished her dower rights (HCVD-1 p. 124)

24 Apr 1703; George Archer, Capt. Francis, Isham and Francis Epes, Jr., George Robinson [minister], Elizabeth Kennon, Phillip Jones, Martha Stratton and James Hill; granted 4,000 ac. in Henrico Co.; on *Wintopock* main creek (LOP 9.540)

1 Oct 1707; 1 Nov 1707; from George Archer of Bristoll Parish, Henrico Co. to son in law Charles Cousins and my dau. Margery his wife; 157 ac. bounded by Timothy Harris (HCVD-2 p. 9)

22 Jan 1717; George Archer & Godfrey Fouler granted 500 ac. Henrico Co. (LOP 10.347)

21 Dec 1723; George Archer of Henrico Co. granted 900 ac on s. side of Appamattocks River (LOP 11.303)

<u>Will of George Archer, Sr. of Bristol Parish; 15 Oct 1729; Dec 1731</u>
To son in law Lewis Epes, 100 ac. next to *Old Town Creek*
To son George, land I live on for life, then to his sons George & Peter
To son William, land adj. above land
To son William and son George's 2 sons, lower side of *Stony Creek*
To abv. grandsons, equally, *Wintopock*
To dau. Blanche Epes, Negro & items
To daus. Blanche Epes, Judith Traylor, Elizabeth Granger, Margery Cousins & Mary
   Worsham, each 10s and to William Worsham, 120s
Remainder to 2 sons George and William
Wit: Henry Royall, John Bevill, Peter Ragsdale (HCVW-1 p. 178-179)
[George Archer, Sr.; Henrico County Wills & Administrations (1662-1800) Note p. 320-322. Will pro. 6 Dec. 1731. Deeds & Wills, 1725-1737 (Reel 7a) (LOV)]

1-1 **Judith Archer**; m. by 5 Dec 1695 **William Traylor**; sur. Peter Jones
(MHC p. 85); Judith inherited 10s from the 1729 will of her father; William
was called son in law [stepson] and named ex. of the will of John Porter of
Bristol Parish written 27 Feb 1721/2 (HCVW-1 p. 232) and he inherited the
entire estate of his mother, Martha Porter, from her will written 15 Apr
1725 (HCVW-1 p. 150); a 1748 deed mentions a patent being bounded by
Edward Traylor, being a patent granted William Traylor which he sold to
John Porter who gave the land to George Traylor and George Ford (HCVD-3
p. 69); Judith and her husband rec'd land in trust from her father 1 Dec 1702;
she rec'd 10s from 1731 will of her father

> 11-1 William Traylor, Jr.
> 11-2 Humphrey Traylor

24 Oct 1701; William Traylor granted 700 ac. in Bristol Parish Henrico Co. on n. side
of Appomattox River above land of George Archer (LOP 9.407)

1 Dec 1702; from William Traylor of Bristol Parish, Henrico Co. to Edward Traylor;
for £5; 100 ac. in Bristol Parish on n. side Appomattox River above George Archer;
patented William 14 Oct 1701; Judith, wife of William, relinquished dower rights
(HCVD-1 p. 125)

17 Aug 1720; William Traylor granted 500 ac. on n. side of Appomattox in Bristol
Parish a little below *Nooning Creek* (LOP 11.47)

17 Aug 1725; William Traylor granted 200 ac. on n. side of Appomattox River in
branch of *Traylors Branch* (LOP 12.285)

24 Aug 1724; 3 May 1725; from William Traylor of Bristol Parish, Henrico Co., to
William Dunifunt; for £50; 150 ac. on n. side of Appomattox River in Bristol Parish
near *Cattail Meadow*; part of patent to Traylor 17 Aug 1720 (HCVD-2 p. 84)

13 Oct 1727; William Trayler granted 1,635 ac. on n. side of Appomattox River; adj.
George Worsham and e. side of *Buckshorn Branch* (LOP 13.226)

14 May 1745; from William Traylor, planter, to Edward Traylor, both of Henrico Co.;
for £30; 317 ac. bounded by 1st branch of *Wintopock* (HCVD-3 p. 17)

27 Jul 1745; 1st Mon Aug 1745; from William Trayler of Henrico Co. to son
Humphrey Traylor; 400 ac. lower end part of 700 ac. tract; the other 300 ac. being
disposed of to Edward Traylor; Joseph Traylor on the of the witnesses (HCVD-3 p. 16)

27 Oct 1746; from William Traylor to Joel Traylor, s/o William Traylor, Jr., all of Dale
Parish, Henrico Co.; for £5; 317 ac. granted William Traylor by patent 13 Oct 1737;
bounded by Edward Traylor [and others] (HCVD-3 p. 40)

> 11-1 **William Traylor, Jr.**; d. by 2 Feb 1762 Lunenburg, Co.; m. **Mary**
> ____; he was tithable in Lunenburg Co. in the 1750's; children from his
> will signed 18 Sep 1761, probated 2 Feb 1762 (LuWB 1.345):

111-1 **Joel Traylor**; he was in Lunenburg Co. when he purchased 100 ac. on the *Mehearen River* from John Weatherford in 1760 and tithable in 1764

111-2 **William Traylor**

111-3 **Mary Traylor**; m. ____ **Hood**

111-4 **Ann Traylor**; m. ____ **Moore**

111-5 **Elizabeth Traylor**

111-6 **Isabelle Traylor**

111-6 **Agnes Traylor**

11-2 **Humphrey Traylor**; m. **Elizabeth Cousins**; d/o Charles Cousins and Margery Archer

1-2 **Blanche Archer**; m. **Lewis Epes**; d. by Feb 1745 Henrico Co.; s/o Edward Epes; Blanche rec'd negroes, items, 10s and her husband rec'd 100 ac. next to *Old Town Creek* from the 1731 will of her father; two of their children:

12-1 **Anne Epes**; orphan of Lewis Eppes, dec'd; chose William Gates guardian; Feb Ct. 1745 (HCVW-2 p. 43)

12-2 **George Epes**

[Eppes, Lewis. Henrico County Wills and Administrations (1662-1800) Note p. 1361. Guardian bond for Anne Eppes rec. Feb. 1745. p. 1405-1406. Guardian bond for George Eppes rec. 2 Mar. 1746. Misc. Court Records, Vol. 4, [1738-1746] (Reel 2) (LOV)]

1-3 **George Archer, Jr.**; d. by Sep Ct. 1738; m. **Mary Bevill**; d/o John Bevill whose will dated 11 Feb 1767 leaves dau. Mary Archer 2 negroes (ChWB 1.531); m/2 by Jun 1741 as 2nd w/o **Henry Royall**; d. by Oct 1747 (HCVW-2 p. 37); s/o Joseph Royall (HCVD-2 p. 45); George inherited his father's plantation for life, then to his sons George and Peter, from 1731 will of his father plus remainder of estate; children:

        13-1 George Archer

        13-2 Peter Archer

        13-3 John Archer

        13-4 Frances Archer, b. 8 May 1721

        13-5 Judith Archer, b. 23 Apr 1723

        13-6 Sarah Archer, b. 13 Dec 1730

        13-7 Jean Archer, b. 12 Jul 1732

22 Jan 1717; George Archer & Godfrey Fouler granted 500 ac in Henrico Co. (LOP 10.3437)

21 Dec 1723; George Archer of Henrico Co. granted 900 ac. on n. side of Appomattox; adj. Capt. William Kennon (LOP 11.456)

Sep Ct. 1738; Mary Archer presented will of George Archer; security William Archer (HCVW-2 p. 3)

Jul Ct. 1739; inv. of George Archer presented by Christopher Martin (HCVW-2 p. 5)

Nov Ct. 1739; petition of William Archer; to summon Mary Archer, admx. of George Archer to next court (HCVW-2 p. 5); Jun Ct. 1741; motion of William Archer, security of admn. of estate of George Archer, dec'd; ordered that Henry Royall and Mary his wife, the adms., be summoned to court (HCVW-2 p. 12)

3 Aug 1747; from Mary Royal of Henrico Parish to William Kennon, Jr.; for 5s; my right of dower in 50 ac. called *Harrises Neck* on n. side of Appomattox River, lately belonging to my husband George Archer, dec'd (HCVD-3 p. 45)

13-1 **George Archer**; m. **Rachel** ____; the will of his grandfather Archer recorded in 1731 left him ½ *Wintopok* and part of *Stony Creek*; a deed mentions George was the heir of his bro. Peter, dec'd (ChDB 5.90); children:

        131-1 William Archer
        131-2 John Archer
        131-4 Mary Archer
        131-5 Bevill Archer

5 Dec 1751; 7 Feb 1752; George Archer son of George Archer of Dale Parish to George (sic) Archer, Jr. son of William Archer of same land .... Rachel, wife of George Archer son of George relinquished her dower right on 25 Mar 1752 (ChDB 1.320)

131-1 **William Archer**

131-2 **John Archer**; d. by 13 Oct 1794 Chesterfield Co.; m. **Mary** ____; children from their father's will:

        1312-1 Stephen Archer
        1312-2 George Archer
        1312-3 Rebecca Archer
        1312-4 Mary Archer
        1312-5 Bevill Archer

20 Jun 1763; 3 Aug 1764; from George Archer to David Holt, both of Chesterfield Co.; tract in *Town of Pocahontas* seized in fee simple under will of his grandfather (ChDB 4.612)

Will of John Archer of *Wintipock*; Chesterfield Co.; 22 Oct 1794; 13 Oct 1794
Lend to wife Mary, use of negroes, etc. for life, then 4 negroes to my son Bevill & 3 to my dau. Mary
To son Stephen, my land and plantation after death of my wife
To son George, negro, feather bed
To grandson Peter, s/o Rebecca, items
Son Bevill to be bound to Daniel Ferguson or other carpenter
Remainder to children Stephen, Bevill & Mary
Exs: George Markham, Thomas Watkins
Wit: Egbert Woodfin, John Markham, Jr., George Markham (ChWB 4.400)
Ct. 13 Oct 1794; will of John Archer proved (ChOB 7. 571); Ct. of Feb 1796; Stephen Archer granted admn. on estate of John Archer, with will annexed; the executors named refused to act (ChOB 11.338)

1312-1 **Stephen Archer**; m. 28 Dec 1795 **Fanney Patrum** (MCC p. 6)

1312-2 **George Archer**
1312-3 **Rebecca Archer**; m. ____; child:

    13123-1 **Peter** ____

1312-4 **Mary Archer**
1312-5 **Bevill Archer**; mb. 21 Dec 1805 Chesterfield Co. **Nancy Perdue**, age 21, d/o Ezekiel Perdue, dec'd; surety John Perdue (MCC p. 5); the Ct. of 14 Sep 1795 lists Bevill as one of the poor orphans bound by the Overseers of the Poor, Dist. 3 (ChOB 11.215); Ct. of 8 Feb 335 Bevill chose John Graves as guardian (ChOB 11.335)

13-2 **Peter Archer**; d. ca 1753 (ChDB 5.90); he inherited ½ of *Wintopok* plantation from the 1731 will of his grandfather after death of his father

Feb Ct 1738; Peter Archer chose William Archer as guardian (HCVW-2 p. 3); Sep Ct. 1740; acct. produced by William Archer, guardian for Peter Archer (HCVW-2 p. 9)

13-3 **John Archer**; mb/1 8 Feb 1760 Amelia Co. to **Elizabeth Townes** of Amelia Co. (she may have been Elizabeth Burk who m. 23 Jan 1753 Middlesex Co. Richard Townes; he d. by 11 Dec 1758 (AmWB 2x.202); 16 Feb 1764 John was one of the trustees of *Bermuda Town* (ChDB 4.557)
13-4 **Frances Archer**, b. 8 May 1721 Bristol Parish
13-5 **Judith Archer**, b. 23 Apr 1723 Bristol Parish
13-6 **Sarah Archer**, b. 13 Dec 1730 Bristol Parish
13-7 **Jean Archer**, b. 12 Jul 1732 Bristol Parish

1-4 **William Archer**; d. by 2 Mar 1750 when his will was presented to the Chesterfield Co. Court (ChOB 2.93); m. **Ann** ____; he rec'd land adj. home plantation in Henrico Co. plus part of *Stony Creek* plus remainder of estate from the 1731 will of his father; more records in Chesterfield Co. courts; known children:

    14-1 George Archer, b. 31 Jul 1720
    14-2 Martha Archer, b. 1727
    14-3 Frances Archer, b. 1730
    14-4 Phebe Archer, b. 1733
    14-5 Mary Archer
    14-6 Ann Archer
    14-7 William Archer
    14-8 John Archer, b. ca 1742

Jun Ct. 1742; from William Archer to William Gates, deed; Ann, w/o Archer, relinquished her dower rights (HCVD-3 p. 95)

Will of William Archer of Dale Parish; 13 Jul 1750 [dated]
To wife Ann, land I live on until death or marriage, negroes, items
To son George, land & plantation where he lives at *Winterpock* , negroes after death of my wife
To son William, 200 ac. on *Old Town Creek*, negro after death of my wife
To son John, after death of my wife, plantation & part of land I live on, negro

To daus. Martha Dudley, Frances Archer, Phebe Archer & Ann Archer, each a negro
To dau. Mary Bevil, £20 to buy a negro
Remainder of estate divided between my wife and all children, equally
Exs: wife and son George
Wit: George West, Obadiah Howerton, William Herringham (ChWB 1.27, 61)

9 Jul 1764; James Bevill & Mary his wife, James Archer (infant s/o William Archer, dec'd, by sd. James, his next friend), Thomas Dudley & Martha his wife, Thomas Neal & Frances his wife, and Phebe Archer, spinster; vs.; Martha Archer (infant d/o George Archer, dec'd), William Rowlet & Sarah his wife, late widow & relict of George Archer, dec'd; opinion of court that negro in question and her increase shd. be divided according to residuary clause in will of William Archer among the complainants Mary, John, Martha, Frances & Phebe and the defendant Martha in equal parts (ChOB 4.79)

14-1 **George Archer**, b. 31 Jul 1720 Bristol Parish; d. bef. 3 Dec 1756 Chesterfield Co.; his estate was appraised 5 May 1758 and inventory returned 6 Oct 1758 (ChOB 2.401, 462); m. **Sarah Neal**; d. aft 1785; d/o Thomas Neal whose will left dau. Sarah Rowlett 1s dated 23 Mar 1764 (ChWB 1.428); she m/2 by 1764 **William Rowlett**; d. aft. 12 Apr 1785 ChWB 3.53); children:

> 141-1 Martha (Patty) Archer
> 141-2 William Rowlett
> 141-3 Thomas Rowlett
> 141-4 Mary Rowlett

5 May 1758; estate of George Archer ordered; 6 Oct 1758 inventory returned (ChOB 2.405, 462); [undated]; inventory of George Archer; value £188.13.8 (ChWB 1.II.283)

Will of William Rowlett; Chesterfield Co.; 12 Apr 1785
Lend to wife Sarah, use of plantation & 5 negroes for widowhood, and items
To son William, plantation I live on after death of my wife, island in the river, 435 ac. tract in Amelia Co., 300 ac. Mecklenburg Co. adj. 200 ac. my sd. son purchased of John Archer; also 5 negroes
To son Thomas, remainder of land in Mecklenburg Co., 5 negroes, lot in *Town of Gatesville* (commonly called *Osbornes*)
To dau. Mary, 4 negroes, items
Tract on *Cattail Creek*, Chesterfield Co. to be sold and money divided among my 3 above children and remainder of estate divided among same
Exs: sons William and Thomas
Wit: Parker Hare, Susanna Burton, George Robertson, Rich'd Booker (ChWB 3.517)

141-1 **Martha (Patty) Archer**, b. 19 Jan 1727 Bristol Parish; 3 Dec 1756; Sarah Archer appointed guardian to Martha Archer, orphan of George Archer, dec'd (ChOB 2.242); William Rowlet presented accts. as guardian of Patty Archer 3 Aug 1764 (ChOB 3.573; LOV); acct. 7 Aug 1767 of Martha Archer in hands of guardian William Rowlet (ChOB 4.79); on 3 May 1772 Patty Archer choose William Green as guardian (ChOB 4.513)

141-2 **William Rowlett**

     141-3 **Thomas Rowlett**
     141-4 **Mary Rowlett**

   14-2 **Martha Archer**, b. 19 Jan 1727/8 Bristol Parish; d. by 6 Mar 1778
     Chesterfield Co.; m/1 **Thomas Dudley**; d. by 1768; mb/2 3 Jun 1774
     Chesterfield Co. **John Elam**; surety George Markham (MCC p. 43); Martha
     also held property in Mecklenburg Co.; no descendants

5 Dec 1768; inventory of Capt. Thomas Dudley; 4 May 1770; inventory returned
(ChWB 2.84; ChOB 4.409)

6 Jul 1768; 7 Sep Ct. 1768; Martha Dudley, widow of Thomas Dudley, to prove his
nonocupative will; John Dudley, heir at law, summoned to next court; Amos Lipford
swore he heard Thomas Dudley in his last illness say he intended every for his wife,
for life; William Rowlett swears he heard same; Francis Osborne swears the same
(ChWB 2.272; ChOB 4.272)

2 Dec 1768; Martha Dudley, relict of Thomas Dudley, granted administration of his
estate (ChOB4.248)

Will of Martha Elam; Chesterfield Co.; 10 Apr 1776; 6 Mar 1778
To bro. John Archer, negro
To nephews, John & William Archer (both under 21), negroes
Exs: bro. John Archer, friend William Green
Wit: Geo. Markham, John Hill (ChWB 3.148)
Ct. 6 Mar 1778; will of Martha Elam proved (ChOB 6.162)

     14-3 **Frances Archer**, b. 14 Aug 1730 Bristol Parish; m/1 **Thomas Neal**
       (ChOB 3.570); mb/2 4 Sep 1758 Amelia Co. **Daniel Allen**; security John
       Hodgison
     14-4 **Phebe Archer**, b. 3 Sep 1733 Bristol Parish; mb. 17 Nov 1767
       Amelia Co. **James Chappell**; sec. John Archer
     14-5 **Mary Archer**, b. ca 1730's; m. **James Bevill**; named in the will of his
       grandfather John Bevill of Bristol Parish which left him land on *Old
       Town Creek* probated 7 Jul 1735 (HCVW-1 p. 205) which he and Mary sol 1
       Feb 174/6 (HCVD-3 p. 241)
     14-6 **Ann Archer**
     14-7 **William Archer**; d. by 1764; Jun 7 Ct. 1754; William Archer, orphan
       of William, chooses bro. George Archer his guardian, who is also
       guardian to John Archer, his other brother (ChOB 1.489); 4 Aug 1756 & 3
       Aug 1759 accts. were presented by his guardian (ChOB 3.446; 4.12)
     14-8 **John Archer**; m. ____; 1 Oct 1756; as orphan of William, he chose
       James Bevill guardian (ChOB 2.224); he and his sons were legatees in 1778
       will of his sister Martha Elam:

         148-1 **John Archer**; mb. Dec 1768 Amelia Co. **Ann Hall**; sec. Thos.
         Hall
         148-2 **William Archer**

  1-5 **Elizabeth Archer**; she rec'd 10s from the 1731 will of her father

1-6 **Margery Archer**; m. **Charles Cousins**; d. aft. 21 Dec 1752; Margery rec'd 10s from the 1731 will of her father (HCVW-1 p. 178); children from their father's will:

    16-1 **Robert Cousins**; will probated 27 Apr 1769 Amelia Co. (AmWB 2x.277)

    16-2 **Charles Cousins**; b. Henrico Co.; d. 10 Nov 1759 Amelia Co.; will probated 22 Nov 1759 (AmWB 1.154); 28 May 1760 (AmWB 1. p. 167a); Inv. & Appr. d. m. **Rosamond Webster**

    16-3 **George Cousins**

    16-4 **William Cousins**

    16-4 **John Cousins**

    16-6 **Judith Cousins**; m. ____ **Webster**

    16-7 **Rose Cousins**; m. ____ **Grant**

    16-8 **Ann Cousins**; m. ____ **Overby**

    16-9 **Amy Cousins**; m. ____ **Vaughn**

    16-10 **Elizabeth Cousins**; m. ____ **Traylor**

    16-11 **Mary Cousins**; m. ____ **Willson**

Will of Charles Cousens of Dale Parish, Chesterfield Co.; 21 Dec 1752
To son Charles, 175 ac. lower side of *Middle Creek*, Amelia Co., negro
To son George, 150 ac. on n. side *Yowles Branch*, Chesterfield Co., negro, items
To son William, 280 ac. on *Middle Creek*, Amelia Co., negro, items
To son John, Plantation where I live, negro; my still to remain and sons John and George to profit from it
To son Robert, negro
To daus. Judith Webster, Rose Grant, Ann Overby, Amy Vaughn, Elizabeth Traylor, Mary Willson
Remainder to be divided between youngest sons George, William & John
Exs: sons Robert and Charles
Wit: Richard Stiles, Wm. Herringham, Thomas D. (ChWB 1.78)
6 Mar 1754; inventory of Charles Cousins by Charles Cousins; no value given (ChWB 1.72)

1-7 **Mary Archer**; m. **William Worsham**; d. by 1788 Amelia Co.; she rec'd 10s from the 1731 will of her father and he may have been the William Worsham who inherited 120s from the will

2. **John Archer**; d. by 4 Nov 1718; of Bristol Parish; m/1by Jan Jan 1695 **Frances Shippey**; surety James Royall (MCC p. 3); m/2 **Martha Field**; d/o Peter Field & Judith Soane, widow of Henry Randolph; by his will dated 24 Nov 1675, George Archer bequeathed a tract to his son John and on 1 Oct 1694, his brother George, confirmed the gift (HCVD-1 p. 85); he held 335 ac. Henrico Co. in the 1705 rent roll; children:

        2-1 John Archer

        2-2 Field Archer

        2-3 William Archer

2-4　Frances Archer
2-5　Judith Archer
2-6　Mary Archer
2-7　Martha Archer
2-8　Elizabeth Archer

28 Feb 1708; 1 Mar 1708/9; from Richard Kendall & Frances his wife to John Archer of Henrico Co.; for £150; 400 ac. in Bermuda Hundred (HCVD 2.18) [Bond of John Archer says it was originally patented by Thomas Shippy]

1 Aug 1711; 1ˢᵗ Mon Aug 1711; from John Archer and Martha his wife to William Randolph, both of Henrico Co.; for £20; 961 ac. 6 tracts in Bristol Parish devised to Martha by will of Peter Field; 3 Aug 1711 John Archer purchased from William Randolph; for £20; 960 ac. as in previous deed (HCVD-2 p. 30, 31)

Will of John Archer of Henrico Parish; 14 Mar 1717; 4 Nov 1718
To son John land at Bermuda Hundred, except 100 ac. to son Field; to son John, 188
　　ac. deeded me by my bro. George 1 Oct 1694; John 46 ac. in *Roxdale* and 80 ac.
　　called *Learwoods*
To son Field 2 tracts of 370 ac. on s. side of *Swift Creek* called *Youls* and *Loftis's*
To son William, 108 ac. called *The Saw Mill Dividend* & 300 ac. at *Cross Swamp*
My ¼ part of 1,600 ac. at *Pine Creek* to 3 sons, equally
To daus. Frances, Judith, Mary, Martha, Elizabeth, and 3 sons, Negroes
Guardianship of children to bro. Joseph Royall
Wit: William Randolph, George Archer, Abraham Womack, Thomas Buckner,
　　Thomas Morris (HCVW-1 p. 225-226)
[John Archer; Henrico County Wills & Administrations (1662-1800) p. 393-396. Will pro. 4
Nov. 1718. Misc. Court Records, Vol. 1, [1718-1726] (Reel 1) (LOV)]

2-1　**John Archer**; of *Archer's Hall* in Dale Parish; d. by 3 Dec 1773 when his will was presented to the Chesterfield Co. Court (ChOB 5.378); m. **Sarah Randolph**, b. 10 Mar 1715; d. aft. 29 Mar 1774 Chesterfield Co.; d/o Capt. Henry Randolph & Elizabeth Eppes; John was in Henrico Parish in 1745; he inherited land in Bermuda Hundred, 188 ac. his father got from his bro. George, 46 ac. in *Roxdale* and 80 ac. *Learwoods* from 1718 will of his father; children from John's will:

21-1　John Archer
21-2　Henry Archer
21-3　Sarah Archer
21-4　Judith Archer
21-5　Ann Archer
21-6　Martha Archer

13 Apr 1737; from John Archer, son & heir of John Archer, dec'd, of Dale Parish, to Field Archer; for £150; 188 ac. in Dale Parish deeded to John Archer by George Archer 1 Oct 1694 (HCVD-2 p. 182)

May Ct. 1744; John Archer, s/o John Archer dec'd, vs. Joseph Royall, ex. of will; plaintiff granted court costs (HCVW-2 p. 22)

5 Sep 1761; from John Archer to John Archer, Jr., both of Chesterfield Co.; for £25; 120 ac. (ChDB p. 405)

6 May 1763; Aug 1763; from John Archer of Raleigh Parish, Amelia Co. to Thomas Daves of Dale Parish, Chesterfield Co.; for £150 ac.; 150 ac. at head of *Youls Branch*; being part of 313 ac. surveyed by John Bevill on 18 Nov 1708 (ChDB 4.468); appears to be a land swap for 150 ac. from Daves (ChDB 4.478)

5 Apr 1764; 6 Apr 1764; from Thomas Eanes to John Archer, both of Dale Parish, Chesterfield Co.; 175 ac.; Thomas' wife released dower (ChDB 4.685)

Will of John Archer, Sr., Dale Parish, Chesterfield Co.; 5 Sep 1773 [dated]
To son John, plantation where I live in Bermuda Hundred, *Clarkes* of 120 ac., negroes, 400 ac. on s. branch of *Willises Creek*, Cumberland Co.
To son Henry, plantation on *Pine Creek*, Cumberland Co., my estate at *Ashen Swamp*, items
To wife, negroes, to live on plantation during her widowhood
To dau. Sarah Archer, negroes in her possession, items
To dau. Judith Archer, £500, negroes, items
To dau. Ann Robertson, £50, negroes, items
To 2 grandsons, Christopher & Archer Branch, £160, divided
Rest of money due me from mortgage of Elizabeth & Grief Randolph's estate to be used to raise legacy to daus. and grandsons
Rest of goods and lot in *Bermuda Hundred Town*, to son John, remainder between sons John & Henry, my exs.
Wit: Amey Turnbull, Mary Isham (ChWB 2.28)

Will of Sarah Archer, Dale Parish, Chesterfield Co.; 29 Mar 1774; 7 Oct 1774
To son Henry Archer, land called *Ashen Swamp* in Chesterfield Co.
Remainder to be sold and money to my 3 daus.: Sarah, Judith & Ann
Exs: sons John & Henry Archer
Wit: Thomas Stratton, John Burton, William Ray (ChWB 2.221)
7 Oct 1774; will of Sarah Archer presented by John & Henry Archer; inv. presented 1777 (ChOB 6.59; ChWB 3.166)

21-1 **John Archer**; d. by 7 May 1784 Chesterfield Co.; mb. 8 Feb 1760 Amelia Co. **Elizabeth Trent**; John was one of the legatees of his grandmother Elizabeth Randolph of Dale Parish written 1775 (ChWB 3.209); John's undated will names his children, his sister Judith Archer, his bro. Henry Archer and his cousin John Archer, s/o William; children from their father's will:

    211-1 Peter Field Archer, b. aft 1763
    211-2 Mary Archer
    211-3 Elizabeth Archer
    211-4 Martha Field Archer
    211-5 Ann Archer

Will of John Archer of Bermuda Hundred, Chesterfield Co.; 22 Feb 1784; 7 May 1784
To son Peter Field Archer, land in Amelia Co. at age 21, negroes, cattle, livestock, furniture, items, he to pay £200 of my debts

To each of my daus. at age 18 or when married, 1/5 of my negroes not already willed, 1/5 of livestock, items

My 400 ac. in Cumberland Co. to be sold to discharge my sister, Judith Archer, attached bond

To my wife, use of all the estate until each of my children have their share

If my wife should now be with child and it shd. be a son, to him the plantation in Bermuda Hundred, also lands adjacent in Chesterfield Co.; if it be a dau. to share equally with daus.

Daus: Elizabeth, Martha Field, Ann & Mary

Exs: wife, bro. Henry Archer, bro. James Robertson, cousin John Archer (s/o William), son Peterfield Archer

Wit: Samuel Shearwin, Blackman Moseley, Thomas Poullan (ChWB 3.423)

Spring 1784; inventory of John Archer (ChWB 4.82)

Ct. 7 May 1784; will of John Archer proved (ChOB 6. 523)

211-1 **Peter Field Archer**, b. aft. 1763; mb/1 23 Jan 1787 Amelia Co. **Elizabeth Walthall**; d. ca 1797; mb/2 8 Sep 1812 **Ann Jones**

211-2 **Mary Archer**

211-3 **Elizabeth Archer**; mb. 8 Jul 1790 Chesterfield Co. **Dougald Ferguson**; sur. Henry Archer (MCC p. 48)

211-4 **Martha Field Archer**; m/c. 18 Aug 1788 Chesterfield Co. **James Robertson**; John Archer, admn. consents for Martha (MCC p. 102)

211-5 **Ann Archer**

21-2 **Henry Archer**; mb. 22 Feb 1776 **Mary Randolph**, b. est. ca 1761; d/o Henry Randolph and Tabitha Poythress; Henry called brother in the will of John Archer dated 22 Feb 1784

21-3 **Sarah Archer**

21-4 **Judith Archer**; called sister in the will of John Archer dated 22 Feb 1784

21-5 **Ann Archer**; m. **James Robertson** who was called bro. in will of his brother in law John Archer

21-6 **Martha Archer**; d. bef. 5 Sep 1773 when her father's will was written which names the 2 Branch grandsons; m. **Christopher Branch**; d. by 17 Mar 1772 Chesterfield Co.; his will names wife Mary and their 3 children:

216-1 **Archer Branch**

216-2 **Christopher Branch**

216-3 **Elizabeth Branch**

2-2 **Field Archer**; d. bef. 5 Mar 1785 Dale Parish, Chesterfield Co.; m. **Elizabeth** ____; d. aft. 3 Jul 1785 when she wrote her will in Chesterfield Co.; they were in Dale Parish, Henrico Co. in May 1748 (HCVD-3 p. 68); he is called son in 1718 will of his father; children and the daughters' spouses from his will:

22-1 John Archer
22-2 Edward Archer
22-3 Agnes Archer
22-4 Martha Field Archer
22-5 Michal Archer
22-6 Elizabeth Archer
22-7 Mary Archer

5 Jul 1765; 5 Jul 1765; agreement between Field Archer of Chesterfield Co. and Neil Buchanan, Jr. of Dinwiddie Co.; for £425 to convey the plantation on Appomatox River which Archer claims by will of John Archer his father, as by the ancient known bounds (ChDB 5.328)

Will of Field Archer of Dale Parish, Chesterfield Co.; 22 Oct 1784; 5 Mar 1785
To wife Elizabeth, negroes, furniture, silver spoons, china and cash & bonds in her
 possession, also lend to her to her during life or widowhood negroes, plantation
 where I live, livestock, etc.
To son John Archer, negroes
To son Edward Archer, negroes, lot in *Petersburg* held in common with George
 Robertson
To dau. Agnes Downman, £80 besides what has already been given her or her husband
 William Downman
To dau. Marthafield Walthall, £250 besides what has already been given her
To dau. Michal Robertson, negroes, £110, besides what has already been given her
 and her husband George Robertson
To dau. Elizabeth Moseley, negroes, £60, besides what she and her husband, Blackman
 Moseley have already received
To dau. Mary Archer, negroes, silver spoons, £600; shd. she die without heirs of her
 body, to be equally divided between my 6 other children
Remainder of estate to be divided equally between sons John & Edward; John's part
 to be held during his natural life then to his 5 children John, Polly, Field, Sally &
 Billey Eppes
Exs: son Edward Archer, sons in law George Robertson, William Downman,
 Blackman Moseley and George Markham of Chesterfield Co.
Wit: George Markham, James Gill, Edward Gill (ChWB 3.514)
Ct. 5 Mar 1785; will of Field Archer proved (ChOB 7.98)

Will of Elizabeth Archer; Chesterfield Co.; 3 Jul 1785; 9 Mar 1786
To daus. Agnes Downman & Martha Field Walthall, 1 negro each
To dau. Mary Archer, negro, furniture
I lend to Edward Archer, William Downman and George Robertson for my dau.
 Elizabeth Moseley during life, negro, then to her children
Grandchildren: James Robertson, Elizabeth Osborne Downman, Elizabeth Osborne
 Moseley, Martha Moseley, Martha Field Robertson, Martha Field Walthall, Martha
 Field Downman
To my 5 daus. Agnes, Martha Field, Michal, Elizabeth & Mary, residue of estate
Exs: Edward Archer, William Downman, George Robertson
Wit: Edward Archer, Benjamin Osborne, George Robertson, William Downman
 (ChWB 4.1)
Ct. 9 Mar 1786; will of Elizabeth Archer proved (ChOB 7.299)

22-1 **John Archer**; of *Second Branch*; d. ca 1798; m. **Mary** ____; a Mary Archer of Chesterfield Co., widow of John Archer, appointed Alexander Snellings her attorney to transact plantation business on 13 Jul 1795; children from will of their grandfather Archer:

221-1 **John Archer**
221-2 **Polly Archer**
221-3 **Field Archer**
221-4 **Sarah (Sally) Archer**
221-5 **William (Billey) Epes Archer**

20 Oct 1766; Nov 1766; from Daniel Vaden of Dale Parish, Chesterfield Co. to John Archer, s/o Field Archer; for £50; 60 ac. in Dale Parish; Vaden's wife releases dower (ChDB 5.471)

22-2 **Edward Archer**; wrote his will 30 Dec 1789 Chesterfield Co.; d. bef. 21 Jul 1795; m. **Mary Walthall**; d. by 14 Oct 1790; d/o William Walthall of Chesterfield Co. who made a deed to all his grandchildren 8 Dec 1888 naming the following children who were also to receive 1/6 of the estate of their aunt Mary Archer:

222-1 **William Archer**; he was one of the legatees of John Walthall (ChWB 4.456); he may have been the William who m/c. 8 Feb 1796; m. 25 Feb 1796 Dale Parish **Unity Claiborne Jones** who signed her own consent
222-2 **Field Archer**; m/c. 10 Feb 1794 Dale Parish, Chesterfield Co. **Martha Bolling**; consent of John Bolling, her father (MCC p. 5); Field & his bro. Edward chose Archibald Walthall as guardian Ct. 14 Oct 1790 (ChOB 7. 497)
222-3 **Edward Archer**; m/c. 10 Apr; m. 27 May 1797 Dale Parish, Chesterfield Co. **Mary Jefferson Bolling**; d/o John Bolling who consents; sur. Robert Bolling
222-4 **Mary (Polly) Archer**; m/c 13 Aug 1798; m. 14 Aug Dale Parish, Chesterfield Co. **John Royal Bradley** (MCC p. 18); consent William Archer; Mary was a legatee in will of her mother; Ct. of 8 Jun 1795 appointed William Archer her guardian (ChWB 6. 137)
222-5 **Elizabeth Archer**; inherited land & lots in *Gatesville* from the 1780 will of grandfather William Walthall of Dale Parish (ChWB 4.196)

Will of Edward Archer of Chesterfield Co.; 30 Dec 1789; 11 Feb 1790

To wife Mary Archer, negro, chairs, use of plantation and my estate during her natural life to be in lieu of her dower in my estate
To son William Archer, 300 ac. on n. side of *Swift Creek*, tract on the Appomattox River, 1/3 of lots and vacant land in *Petersburg* held in common with George Robertson
To son Edward Archer, land and plantation left to my wife during her life or widowhood, also part of the tract where my father lived on *Second Branch Road*,

after her death or widowhood, also 1/3 of the lots in *Petersburg* held in common
with George Robertson
To sons at age 21 and daus. at age 18 or marriage, reminder of slaves, furniture, stock,
money
To my 3 sons, William, Field & Edward, lands in Nelson Co., KY on *Beaverdam
Creek*, a branch of the *Green River*
Tracts in Dinwiddie and Halifax Cos. to be sold
Exs: sons Wiliam, Field & Edward
Wit: George Robertson, C. Hornlove, William Downman, John Archer (ChWB 4.244)
Ct. 11 Feb 1790; will of Edward Archer proved (ChOB 8. 373)

Will of Mary Archer of Dale Parish, Chesterfield Co.; 27 Jul 1790; 14 Oct 1790
To my 3 sons William, Field & Edward Archer, 1 horse
To dau. Mary Archer, 1 negro and my riding chair
Ex: son William
Wit: Nath'l Friend, Benjamin Osborne, John Moseley (ChWB 4.255)
Ct. 14 Oct 1790; will of Mary Archer proved (ChOB 7.495)

22-3 **Agnes Archer**; d. aft. 3 Jul 1785 & bef. 21 Jul 1795; m. **William
Downman**; the following children to receive 1/6 of the estate of their
aunt Mary Archer:

223-1 **Robert Downman**
223-2 **William Downman**
223-3 **Martha Field Downman**; called granddau. in will of her
grandmother Elizabeth Archer written 1785
223-4 **Agnes Archer Downman**
223-5 **Elizabeth Osborne Downman**

22-4 **Martha Field Archer**; d. by 9 Dec 1805 Chesterfield Co. (ChWB
6.279); m/1 **William Walthall**; d. by 3 Aug 1781 when Edward Archer
and Archibald Walthall granted adms. of his estate (ChOB 6.321); m/2 23
Jul 1789 Dale Parish **Francis Osborne** (MCC p. 92); d. Chesterfield Co.;
will names Benjamin among his children (ChWB 4.350); Martha to receive
1/6 of the estate of her sister Mary Archer; one of the Walthall children:

224-1 **Mary Walthall**; m. 13 Feb 1783 Chesterfield Co. **Benjamin
Osborne**; William Downman, guardian of Mary (MCC p. 92); Benjamin
was the s/o Francis Osborne , 2nd husband of his mother in law

22-5 **Michal Archer**; m. **George Robertson**; d. aft. his will was written in
1795 which lists his vast land holdings in VA & KY and appears to say
all children except James were minors (ChWB 5.122); Michal to receive 1/6
of estate of her sister Mary Archer; children from will of their
grandmother Archer & the will of their father :

225-1 **James Robertson**; m/c. **Martha Field Archer**; John Archer,
executor, consents for marriage (MCC p. 102)
225-2 **Archer Robertson**

225-3 **George Robertson**
225-4 **Martha Field Robertson**; m. 19 Mar 1791 Dale Parish, Chesterfield Co. **John Brander** (MCC p. 20)
225-5 **Ann Robertson**

22-6 **Elizabeth Archer**; m. **Blackman Moseley**; she to receive 1/6 of estate of her sister Mary Archer; children from will of their grandmother Archer:

226-1 **Elizabeth Osborne Moseley**
226-2 **Martha Moseley**

22-7 **Mary Archer**; d. aft. 21 Jul 1795 Chesterfield Co.

21 Jul 1795; Indenture between Mary Archer of Chesterfield Co., spinster, of the 1st part and William, Field, Edward & Polly Archer [children of Edward, dec'd]; John Archer of *Second Branch*; George Roberson & wife Michal; Blackman Moseley & wife Elizabeth; Martha Field Osborne; Robert, William, Martha Field & Agnes Archer Downman [children of Agnes Archer Downman, dec'd]; said Edward Archer (dec'd), John Archer, Michal Robertson, Elizabeth Moseley, Martha Field Osborne & Agnes Downman were and are brothers and sisters of the whole blood to sd. Mary Archer & were sons and daughters of Field Archer, dec'd, of the other part; [long complicated document regarding distribution of her estate; not abstracted; failed to record reference)

2-3 **William Archer**; d. ca 1782 Amelia Co.; m. **Elizabeth** ____; children from family histories:

23-1 **Elizabeth Archer**; mb. 24 Nov 1767 Amelia Co. **James Powell Cocke**
23-2 **Martha Field Archer**; mb. 11 Apr 1767 (or 1769) Amelia Co. **Christian (Chastain) Cocke**
23-3 **Joseph Archer**
23-4 **John Archer**
23-5 **Peter Field Archer**; mb/1 22 Oct 1782 Amelia Co. **Frances Tanner**; d/o Branch Tanner of Amelia Co.; mb/2 Jul 17; m. 24 Jun 1799 **Judith E. Cocke**; 3 of their children:

235-1 **William Archer**; identified in will of Branch Tanner
235-2 **Mary Page Finney Archer**; identified in will of Branch Tanner
235-3 **Branch Tanner Archer**, b. 13 Dec 1790 Fauquier Co., VA according to his biography in Texas documents

23-6 **Judith Archer**; mb. 14 May 1782 Amelia Co. **William Bentley**
23-7 **Richard Archer**; mb. 19 Jun 1794 Amelia Co. **Mary Magdalene Chastain Cocke**; sec. Stephen Cocke; d/o Stephen Cocke

12 Feb 1736; 1st Mon Jun 1737; from William Archer, Jr. of Henrico Co. to William Pride; for £60; 108 ac. called *Saw Mill Dividend* devised by John Archer to sd. William (HCVD-2 p. 180)

6 May 1745; from William Archer of Henrico Co. to William Pride; £20; 2 tracts of 50 ac. by s. side of main road from Appomattox River to Amelia (HCVD-3 p. 19)

2-4 Frances Archer

2-5 Judith Archer; m. **Daniel Worsham**; d. by 14 Aug 1727; s/o John Worsham of Henrico Parish whose will mentions "my son Daniel's widow Judith to live on my plantation until she can provide for herself a house on her plantation at *Coldwater Run*" and leaves a negro to Daniel's daus. (HCVW-1 p.172):

25-1 **Phebe Worsham**
25-2 **Martha Worsham**
25-3 **Elizabeth Worsham**

14 Aug 1727; 1 Jul 1728; inventory of Daniel Worsham; value £135.18.9; presented in court by Judith Worsham (HCVW-1 p. 168)

2-6 Mary Archer

2-7 Martha Archer

2-8 Elizabeth Archer

3. **Margery Archer**; d. by 1 Feb 1691/2 Henrico Co.; m. **Nicholas Bullington, Jr.**; d. by 1 Feb 1691 Henrico Co.; son:

3-1 **John Bullington**, b. aft. 1675

21 Apr 1690; patent granted James Blair, Jeremiah Brown and Nicholas Bullington (HCVD-1 p. 101, 102)

Will of Nicholas Bullington; 2 Nov 1691; 1 Feb 1691
To wife Margery; son to be of age at 16
Wit: John Worsham, Joseph Royall, John Harwood (HCVW-1 p. 44-45)
[Nicholas Bullington; Henrico County Wills and Administrations (1662-1800) p. 287-288. Will pro. 1 Feb. 1691. p. Adms. bond rec. 29 Apr. 1691. p. 305-306. Inv. & appr. rec. 1 June 1691. p. 306. Accounts rec. 1 June 1692. Deeds, Wills, Etc., 1688-1697 (Reel 5) (LOV)]

Will of Margery Bullington, widow; 20 Jan 1691/2; 1 Feb 1691/2
Land in Appomattox to son; if he dies to bro. John Archer
Bros. John Archer and Henry Royall
I leave my son to my father in law Joseph Royall, ex.
Wit: John Worsham, Martin Elam (HCVW-1 p. 45)
Inv. of estate of Margery Bullington; court order 16 May 1692; recorded 1 Jun 1692 by
    Capt. Joseph Royall, ex.; [son John Bullington named in inventory] (HCVW-1 p. 46)
[Margery Bullington; Henrico County Wills and Administrations (1662-1800) p. 288. Will pro. 1 Feb. 1691. p. 290-291. Exors. bond rec. 29 Apr. 1692. p. 305. Inv. & appr. rec. 1 June 1692. p. 306. Accounts rec. 1 June 1692. Deeds, Wills, Etc., 1688-1691 (Reel 5) (LOV)

4. **Elizabeth Archer**; orphan of George Archer; m. by 1 Oct 1689 Henrico Co. **Thomas Branch, Jr.** (MHC p. 11), b. ca 1654; d. by Dec 1728

5. **Ann Archer**; d. by 1 Dec 1701 Henrico Co.; m/1 **William Walthall**; d. by
Sep 1672 Henrico Co.; m/2 **Rev. Richard Morris**, rector of Bristol Parish; d.
by 1685; children:

    5-1 **William Walthall**
    5-2 **Richard Walthall**
    5-3 **Henry Walthall**
    5-4 **Elizabeth Walthall**; m. **Hugh Ligon**
    5-5 **Ann Morris**; d. by 1685; unmarried

1 Feb 1685; Anne Morris, late of Henrico, d. intestate; Samuel Morris, next of kin
appointed administrator (HCVW-1 p. 18)

28 Jan 1685; 1 Feb 1685; Mrs. Anne Morris, relict of Mr. Richard Morris, dec'd of
Henrico Co.; relieved of responsibility of estate of Richard by Samuel Morris of James
City, cousin & admn. of estate of Anne Morris, d/o Richard & Anne (HCVW-1 p. 20)

4 Feb 1685; Samuel Morris petitions for admn. of estate of his cousen Anne Morris,
d/o Richard Morris, formerly of Henrico & minister of Bristol Parish, but afterwards to
his death a resident of Isle of Wight Co.; Mrs. Anne Morris, mother & guardian to sd.
Anne Morris agrees (HCVW-1 p. 29)

23 Jan 1689/90; 1 Oct 1690; William, Richard & Henry Walthall, sons of William
Walthall, and Henry (?Hugh) Ligon in right of wife Elizabeth, d/o sd. dec'd have rec'd
of our mother Anne Morris, widow, relict and extx. of dec'd all our portion due from
dec'd (HCVW-1 p. 41)

1 Dec 1701; Henry Walthall granted admn. of estate of his mother, Mrs. Ann Morris
(HCVW-1 p. 80); 24 Dec 1701; 1 Feb 1701; inventory of estate of Ann Morris;
presented by Henry Walthall (HCVW-1 p. 78)

PETER ASHBROOK

    Peter Ashbrook, b. ca 1643-9, age 30 on 2 Jun 1679; age 45 on 12 Oct
1688, age 48 on 1 Dec 1694 (HCVD-1 p. 152, 155); d. by 7 Feb 1714 Bristol Parish;
m. **Jennett** ____; d. by 7 Apr 1718; widow of ____ **Farguson**; Peter was
charges with 3 taxables in the list of 1678 Henrico Co. and as Peter Ashbrook,
Sr., he held 200 ac. in the 1705 rent roll of Henrico Co.; known children:

        1. Elizabeth Ashbrook
        2. Peter Ashbrook, Jr., b. ca 1673

Jane Ashbrook, b. ca 1640, age 48 on 12 Oct 1688 (HCVD-1 p. 152) [This may be the same
person as Jennett or an earlier wife]

1 Jan 1707; 2 Feb 1707; from Richard Holmes to Peter Ashbrooke, Sr., both of Bristol
Parish, Henrico Co.; for 2,500# tobacco; 252 acres on *Swift Creek* on s. side of James
River (HCVD-2 p. 10)

7 Feb 1714; inventory of Peter Ashbrooke by James Baugh (and others); presented in court by Jennett Ashbrooke, widow & relict (HCVW-1 p. 129)
[Peter Ashbrook; Henrico County Wills and Administrations (1662-1800) p. 7. Inv. & appr. rec. 7 Feb. 1714. Deeds, Wills, Etc., 1714-1718 (Reel 7) (LOV)]

Will of Jennet Ashbrook; 3 Aug 1717; 7 Apr 1718
To son Robert Fargason, Sr.; dau. Ann Hopkins
To grandson John Fargason, Sr.; eldest great-grandson John Farguson, Jr.
To son Peter Ashbrook, granddau. Elizabeth Ashbrook
Wit: Peter Hudson, William Baugh, Mary Baugh (HCVW-1 p. 145)
[Jennet Ashbrook; Henrico County Wills and Administrations (1662-1800) Note p. 251. Will pro. 7 Apr. 1718. Deeds, Wills, Etc., 1714-1718 (Reel 7) (LOV)]

1. **Elizabeth Ashbrook**; m. **James Baugh, Jr.**, b. ca 1655; d. bef. Jul 1723 according to Baugh family histories; they are said to have had several children including a son named Peter Baugh; marriage not confirmed

2. **Peter Ashbrook**, b. ca 1673, age 19 on 1 Aug 1692 (HCVD-1 p. 154); d. aft. 22 Oct 1756; m. Jul 1696, Moses Wood, surety; m. Sep 1696 St. John's Parish, Henrico Co., **Mary Forest** (QRH p. 92); d/o James & Allice Forest (HCVW-1 p. 133; HCVD-2 p. 2); children from their father's will:

    2-1 Peter Ashbrook, b. est. ca 1696
    2-2 Isabell Ashbrook, b. est. ca 1698
    2-3 Elizabeth Ashbrook, b. est. ca 1700

13 Dec 1742; Dec Ct. 1742; 1st Mon Jan 1742; from Alexander Womack to Peter Ashbrook, both of Dale Parish, Henrico Co.; for £204; 200 ac. (HCVD-3 p. 6, 97)

Will of Peter Ashbrook of Dale Parish "very ancient & weak"; 22 Oct 1756 [dated]
To wife Mary, 2 slaves, at her death to my grandson Peter Ashbrook; also items
To dau. Elizabeth Akin, items
To dau. Isabell Edwards' children, 20s each
Livestock to be divided between wife, grandson Peter & children of Elizabeth & Isabell; remainder of estate to grandson Peter Ashbrook, ex.
Wit: Edward Wilkinson, James Baugh, Elizabeth Baugh (ChWB 1.228)
3 Dec 1756; will of Peter Ashbrook presented by Peter Ashbrook, ex. (ChOB 2.243)
3 & 4 May 1759; inventory of Peter Ashbrook, Sr. (ChWB 1.291; ChOB 2.516)

2-1 **Peter Ashbrook**, b. est. ca 1696; d. by 1 Oct 1756 Chesterfield Co.; m. **Martha Edwards**; d. by 13 Feb 1792 Chesterfield Co.; d/o Thomas Edwards of Dale Parish, Chesterfield Co. whose will written 26 Jun 1772 left her a negro (ChWB 3.300); children:

    21-1 Peter Ashbrook
    21-2 Sarah Ashbrook
    21-3 Joseph Ashbrook
    21-4 Mary Ashbrook
    21-5 William Ashbrook

Will of Peter Ashbrook; Chesterfield Co.; 6 Sep 1756; 1 Oct 1756
To dau. Sarah Baugh, to niece Martha Edwards

To son Joseph, one pistole; to dau. Mary Farguson, 20s
To son William, mulatto
Ex: son Peter, he to have remainder of estate (ChWB 1.222)
1 Oct 1756; will of Peter Ashbrook presented by Peter Ashbrook, Jr., ex. (ChOB 2.226)
3 & 4 May 1759; inventory of Peter Ashbrook, Jr. (ChWB 1.292; ChOB 2.516)

Ct. 13 Feb 1792; Thomas Ashbrook granted administration on estate of Martha Ashbrook (ChOB 9.268)

21-1 **Peter Ashbrook**; of Chesterfield Co.; d. by 4 Aug 1780; m. ____; on 5 Dec 1760 he bought a ½ ac. lot #117 in the town laid off on Glebe land for £7.10 (CHDB 4.aft. 56); children:

> 211-1　Peter Ashbrook
> 211-2　Thomas Ashbrook
> 211-3　Leonard Ashbrook
> 211-4　Sarah Ashbrook
> 211-5　Martha Ashbrook
> 211-6　Jeremiah Ashbrook
> 211-7　William Ashbrook

3 Dec 1756; from Peter Ashbrook to William Ashbrook of Dale Parish, Chesterfield Co.; for £50; 252 ac. in Dale Parish (ChDB 3.95)

4 Aug 1780; Edward Featherston granted administration of estate of Peter Ashbrook (ChOB 6.297)

Ct. 1 Mar 1782; Martha Ashbrook appointed guardian to Jeremiah & William Ashbrook, orphans of Peter Ashbrook; Thomas Ashbrook and Martha Ashbrook choose Martha Ashbrook as their guardian (ChOB 6.339)

Ct. May 1782; Division of estate of Peter Ashbrooke by court order of Nov 1781; to Mrs. Martha Ashbrooke, Peter Ashbrooke, Thomas Ashbrooke, Leonard Ashbrooke, Sarah Featherstone, Martha Ashbrook (ChOB 6.___) [between page 345 & 350]

211-1 **Thomas Ashbrook**
211-2 **Martha Ashbrook**

2112-1 **Polly** ____; she inherited a negro from her uncle William

211-3 **Jeremiah Ashbrook**
211-4 **William Ashbrook**; Martha Ashbrook appointed guardian in 1782 and William chose Archud Bass as guardian 20 Sep 1792 (ChOB 9.495); unmarried

Will of William Ashbrook; Chesterfield Co.; 7 Mar 1796 [dated]
To Jeremiah Ashbrook, 1 negro
To my sister Martha's child named Polly, negro
Wit: James Milne, Thomas Baugh (ChWB 5.121)
Ct. 12 Sep 1796; will of William Ashbrooke proved (ChOB 12.2)
Ct. 12 Dec 1796; ordered that sheriff admn. estate of William Ashbrooke (ChOB 12.76)

21-2 **Sarah Ashbrook**; m. ____ **Baugh**

21-3 **Joseph Ashbrook**; m. **Susanna Lockett**; d/o William Lockett of Dale Parish (ChWB 1.253); Joseph was ex. of the will of his sister in law Jane Lockett in 1759 (ChWB 1.II.284); children:

        213-1 Mary Ashbrook
        213-2 Susanna Ashbrook
        213-3 Elizabeth Ashbrook
        213-4 James Ashbrook
        214-5 ____ Ashbrook (f)

Will of Joseph Ashbrook; Chesterfield Co.; 18 Sep 1801 [dated]
To daus. Mary Lockett, Susannah Lockett, Elizabeth Baugh, 1 negro each & items
To dau. Sarah Gates, 3 negroes, items
To granddau. Nancy Bailey, 1 negro, items
To grandsons Henry Bailey, John Bailey, 1 negro
To son in law Joseph Baugh, 1 negro, bed
To son James, 5 negroes; also land I am possessed of for life, then to his lawfully
    begotten heirs; if none, land to be sold & money to all my children
Wit: John Smith, And'w Laprade, Peter Franklin (ChWB 5.565)
Ct. 13 Sep 1802; will of Joseph Ashbrooke proved (ChOB 13.351)

    213-1 **Mary Ashbrook**; m. ____ **Lockett**
    213-2 **Susanna Ashbrook**; m. ____ **Lockett**
    213-3 **Elizabeth Ashbrook**; m. **Joseph Baugh**
    213-4 **James Ashbrook**
    213-5 ____ **Ashbrook** (f); m. **Benjamin Bailey**; d. by 8 Oct 1798;
    children:

        2145-1 **Benjamin Bailey**

Ct. 8 Oct 1798; Benjamin Bailey, adm'r; vs. Benjamin Bailey, dec'd; Henry, John & Nancy Bailey, by Joseph Ashbrooke, their next friend; children and heirs at law of Benjamin Bailey, dec'd; court orders estate divided (ChOB 12.584)

        2135-1 **Nancy Bailey**; Ct. 10 Apr 1797; Nancy chose Jos. Ashbrooke
        as her guardian (ChOB 11.156)
        2135-2 **Henry Bailey**
        2135-3 **John Bailey**

21-4 **Mary Ashbrook**; m. ____ **Farguson**
21-5 **William Ashbrook**; of Dale Parish, Chesterfield Co.

5 May 1754; May 1764; from William Ashbrook to John Forgueran, both of Dale Parish, Chesterfield Co.; for £78; 100 ac. on n. side of *Swift Creek*; part of a tract granted Peter Ashbrook (ChDB 4.556)

3 Oct 1766; Oct 1766; from John Cobbs to William Ashbrook, both of Dale Parish, Chesterfield Co.; 200 ac. at head of *Licking Creek* (ChDB 5.352)

2-2 **Isabell Ashbrook**, b. est. ca 1698; m. ____ **Edwards**

2-3   **Elizabeth Ashbrook**, b. est. ca 1700; m. aft. 3 Aug 1717 **William Akin, Sr.**, b. est. ca 1686; d. aft. 26 Aug 1757; Elizabeth called granddaughter in the 1715 will of Alice Forrest and the 1717 will of Jennett Ashbrook

Unplaced:
     Daniel Ashbrook; m. by 14 Nov 1791 **Phebe Gates** (MCC p. 6)
     Martha Ashbrook; m. 29 Jun 1788 Dale Parish **James Hodge** (MCC p. 68)

BABBICOM - PARKER - MILNER

Will Parker; d. bef. 1 Oct 1684; m. **Katherine** ____; d. by 30 May 1721; she m/2 **John Milner**, b. ca 1638-41, age 38 or 39 on 2 Jun 1679, age 43 or 44 on 1 Jun 1683 (HCVD-1 p. 21, 147, 149); d. by 13 Aug 1684; she m/3 by 29 Nov 1690 **James Babbicom**; d. by 1 Dec 1692; known children:

     1. William Parker
     2. Mary Parker
     3. ____ Parker
     4. Elizabeth Milner
     5. Martha Milner
     6. Mary Milner

[Will Parker; Henrico County Wills and Administrations (1662-1800) p. 286. Gdn. accounts rec. 1 Oct. 1684. Records, 1677-1692 (Reel 4) (LOV)]

13 Aug 1684; 10 Oct 1684; inventory of John Milner; value 9,380# tobacco; sworn in court by Mrs. Katherine Milner; certain items belonging to orphans of Will Parker, dec'd, not to be charged to the estate; items belong to Will Parker, Mary Parker, and one of the orphans, now w/o Robert Easly (HCVW-1 p. 15, 16)
[John Milner; Henrico County Wills and Administrations (1662-1800) p. 286. Inv. & appr. rec. 1 Oct. 1684. p. 288-289. Adms. bond rec. 9 Oct. 1684. Records, 1677-1692 (Reel 4) (LOV)]

Will of James Babbicom; 23 May 1692; 1 Dec 1692
To daughters in law Elizabeth, Martha and Mary Milner, items
To son in law William Parker, cow; to Joseph Allen, a cow calf
To wife, extx., remainder of estate
Wit: James Morris, Will Peirce, Fra. Peirce (HCVW-1 p. 49)
[James Babbicom; Henrico County Wills and Administrations (1662-1800) Note p. 374-375. Will pro. 1 Dec. 1692. Deeds, Wills, Etc., 1688-1697 (Reel 5) (LOV)]

Will of Katherine Babbicom; 30 May 1721 [dated]
To daus. Martha Redford and Mary Childers, 1s each
To William Burton, Sr., 1s
To William Perce, livestock
To granddau. (sic) Matthew Parker, items [? Martha Parker]
Ex.: son William Parker
Wit: William Frogmorton, Henry Woodcock, Judah Allen (HCVW-1 p. 232)

Aug Ct. 1720; will of Catherine Babbicum presented by William Parker (HCVW-2 p. 155)

[Katherine Babbicom; wills not listed in Virginia Wills and Administrations, 1632-1800 (Torrence). Will - 1721 Henrico Co. Miscellaneous Records. Vol. 2, p. 521 (LOV)]

1. **William Parker**; m. ____ **Hatcher**; d/o William Hatcher and Ann Burton; child from will of her grandmother Babbicom:

   1-1 **Martha Parker**

2. **Mary Parker**; m. bet. 1688-1689 Henrico Co. **William Burton** (MHC p. 14); d. by Sep 1751 (HCVW-2 p. 54, 55)

3. ____ **Parker**; m. **Robert Easly**

4. **Elizabeth Milner**; m. **William Peirce**

5. **Martha Milner**; m. by 20 May 1698 Henrico Co. **John Redford** (MHC p. 71), b. ca 1674; d. by Oct 1752 (HCVW-2 p. 58)

6. **Mary Milner**; m. ____ **Childers**

BATTE

Early records mention settlers named Batt, Battie, Batty, Batts, Bate, Bott, Botte. No connection was found between the Michaell Batt and his wife, found in the Living & Dead in Virginia in 1623, and the family of John Batte who arrived with his sons in the same period.

16 Feb 1623/24 Muster of Warwick Squeake, VA; John Batt; [this area called County of Warraskoyak in early patents and from 1639 became Isle of Wight Co.]

7 Nov 1643; John Batt granted 526 ac. James City Co. at head of easternmost branch of *Back River* called *Drinking Swamp* or *Otter Dam Swamp*; Dorothy Batt included in the list of 11 transportees (LOP 1.944; PB 1.2.944)

JOHN BATTE

John Batte, Capt., of Yorkshire, England; d. ca 1650's VA; said to have m. **Martha Mallory**; d/o Thomas Mallory, Dean of Chester (Torrence); John is said to have been a Royalist Officer who came to Virginia in 1646 with the following four sons:

> 1. William Batte
> 2. Thomas Batte
> 3. Henry Batte, b. 13 Aug 1628
> 4. John Batte, b. 22 Jul 1630

1. **William Batte**, b. England; in 1654 William, who had returned to England where he is said to have died, made a deed which was filed in Charles City Co. in 1657 giving his under age brothers, Thomas and Henry, who stayed in Virginia, equal right in his Charles City Co. plantation called *Spring Gardens* along with cattle, servants, etc.; the document stated the Isle of Wight Co. plantation could be sold for their benefit. He had apparently returned to England to handle his father's estate there.

8 Jun 1639; Thomas Symons claimed 800 ac. in James City Co.; 300 ac. by assignment from William Batt due him for his adventure and bro. Henry Batts and 4 persons (PB 1.2.678)

5 Sep 1643; William Batt granted 250 ac. on west side of North River in *Mockjack Bay*; county unnamed (LOP 1.901)

11 Apr 1649; William Batt claimed 128 ac. James City Co. on lower *Chipokes Creek* called by the native the *Indian Pacotacke* (LOP 2.161)

2. **Thomas Batte, Sr.**, b. est. ca 1634 England; d. aft. 28 May 1690 Henrico Co. (HCVW-1 p. 42); m/1 by 1684 **Mary** ____; m/2 **Amy** ____; Thomas was co-discoverer of New River in 1671; he left many descendants through the Jones & Evans families (Torrence); 1st 4 children from the John Farrar will:

> 2-1 Thomas Batte, Jr.
> 2-2 Mary Batte
> 2-3 Amy Batte
> 2-4 Sarah Batte
> 2-5 Martha Batte

23 Apr 1683; 2 Jun 1684; Thomas Batte appointed a Justice of the Peace (HCVD-1 p. 20, 26)

13 Sep 1684; 1 Oct 1684; from Thomas Batte, Sr., Gent., and Mary his wife, to Gabriel Arther of Appomattox, planter; for 2.500# tobacco; 100 ac. on n. side of Appomattox above *Old Indian Town* granted Batte 8 Apr 1674 (HCVD-1 p. 27)

1 Dec 1686; 1 Dec 1686; from Thomas Batte, Sr. to Thomas Batte, Jr. to William Byrd, Esq.; Thomas, Sr. granted 1,862 ac. on n. side Appomattox 8 Apr 1674 to Thomas, Sr. with 903 ac. bounded by his land above the falls and *Appamattock Indian Town* and *Old Town Creek*; he conveyed 200 ac. 1 Jun 1678 to Col. John Farrar who, by his will dated 4 Mar 1684 gave Thomas Batte, Jr. the 200 ac.; Mary, w/o Thomas Batte, Sr., relinquished dower (HCVD-1 p. 37)

1 Jun 1689; 1 Jun 1689; from Thomas Batte the elder to John Banister, Clerk; mortgage on servants (HCVD-1 p. 52)

23 Oct 1690; Thomas Batt granted 400 ac. Henrico Co. on Appomattox River; bounded by a creek and toward *Conjurer's Field* (LOP 8.122)

2-1 Thomas Batte, Jr., b. ca 1661, age 19 on 10 Feb 1680 (QRH p. 148); d. by 29 Apr 1691 Henrico Co.; m. bef. 2 Apr 1688 Henrico Co. **Temperance Brown** (MHC p. 6); d. by 5 Feb 1721 Henrico Co. (HCVW-2 p. 161); d/o John

Brown and Sarah [Sarah m/2 John Woodson; her will written 4 Feb 1701/2 names dau. Temperance & her husband Farrar, granddau. Martha Batte, d/o Thomas (dec'd) as well as grandchildren John & Mary Farrar (HCVW-1 p. 90, 92)]; as Temperance Batte, she was a legatee in the estate of her brother Jeremiah Brown; Temperance m1/2 11 Nov 1691 Henrico Co. **John Farrar**; surety Richard Jones and Jos. Pattison or Pleasants (MCH p. 31; ORH p. 90), this John Farrar was said to have been the "cousin" named in the estate of his uncle John Farrar whose will written 4 Mar 1684/5 left Thomas Batte a horse and 200 ac. on Appomattox River formerly purchased from his father Thomas, Sr. (HCVW-1 p. 16); Batte child:

21-1 Martha Batte

1 Aug 1691; Thomas Batte, Jr.; d. leaving an estate; Temperance Batte, admn. (HCVW-1 p. 42); 10 Apr 1691; 1 Oct 1691; inv. of Thomas Batte, Jr.; value 22,205# tobacco; presented by Temperance Batte, admx. (HCVW-1 p. 43)
[Thomas Batte, Jr.; Henrico County Wills and Administrations (1662-1800); p. 194-195. Adms. bond rec. 28 Apr. 1691. p. 234-235. Inv. & appr. rec. 1 Oct. 1691. Deeds, Wills, Etc., 1688-1697 (Reel 5) (LOV)]

Ct. 5 Feb 1721; John Sutton Farrar granted administration of estate of Temperance Farrar, dec'd (HCVW-2 p. 161)

21-1 **Martha Batte**; one of the legatees of her mother's sister, Sarah (Brown) Knibb, written 1695 (HCVW-1 p. 61); she inherited a negro man and items from the will of her maternal grandmother Sarah (_) Brown Woodson written 1701/2 (HCVW-1 p. 90)

2-2 **Mary Batte**; m. 1688 Henrico Co. **Peter Jones** (MHC p. 49); Mary and her sisters, Amy & Sarah, inherited "remainder of estate" from will of John Farrar in 1685 for their care of him in his last illness (HCVW-1 p. 16); one of their children:

22-1 **Peter Jones**; said to have m. **Dorothy Chamberlayne**; lived Prince George Co.

13 Dec 1736; Henry Batte and Elizabeth his wife & Peter Jones and Dorothy his wife, granted 1,600 ac. Henrico Co. on n. side of Appamattox River; known by name of *Cunneecock* (LOP 17.211)

2 May 1746; 1st Mon Jun 1746; from Peter Jones and Dorothy his wife of Prince George Co. to Henry Batte of Henrico Co.; for 500; 1,600 ac. Henrico Co. n. side of Appomattox River as in patent to Peter & Dorothy Jones and Henry & Elizabeth Batte on 13 Dec 1736 (HCVD-3 p. 26)

2-3 **Amy Batte**; m. **Richard Jones, Jr.**; s/o Rev. Richard Jones & Martha Llewellyn (TVF 11.74)

2-4 **Sarah Batte**; m. 27 Jan 1696 Henrico Co. **John Evans, Jr.**; surety Peter Jones and Stephen Cocke (QRH p. 92; MHC p. 30)

2-5 **Martha Batte**; m/1 **Abraham Wood Jones**; d. bef. 3 Dec 1689 Charles City Co.; m/2 **Rev. John Banister**; d. by 3 Jun 1682 ; ml/3 26 May 1694 Henrico Co. **Stephen Cocke**, b. ca 1666-8; d. by 14 Aug 1711

3. **Henry Batte, Capt.**, b. 13 Aug 1628 Yorkshire, England; d. ca 1702 Prince George Co.; m. bef. 1678 **Mary Lound** (HCVD-1 p. 139); Mary inherited 258 ac. "½ of patent" from her father, Henry Lound, in 1708 (HCVW-1 p. 102); in Oct 1748 the fee was set by the 1st session of the Legislature for service from land of Henry Batte to Varina and to Alexander Bolling's in Prince George Co. (Henning); he was in the part of Charles City Co. which became Prince George Co. in 1702; he served in the House of Burgesses for Charles City Co. 1685-1686, 1692-1693 and was a Justice of Charles City Co. in 1693; children (LF&C p. 366):

> 3-1 Elizabeth Batte
> 3-2 Mary Batte
> 3-3 Ann Batte
> 3-4 Rachel Batte
> 3-5 Sarah Batte
> 3-6 Henry Batte
> 3-7 William Batte

29 Apr 1668; Thomas & Henry Batte granted 5,878 ac. 2r. 8po. Charles City Co. at head of Charles City Creek; for transport of 118 persons including William Bate, Jr. (2 times), Martha Bate, Jno Bate, Sr., Jno. Batte, Jr., Henry Batte, Thomas Batte (LOP 6.126); [names also given as Thomas & Henry Batts, sons of John Batts, dec'd]

28 Oct 1673; Hen. Batts and John Sturdivant granted 3,528 ac. Charles City Co. on s. side of Appomatock River on 2nd branch of the *Blackwater* (LOP 6.480)

20 Apr 1682; Henry Batts and James Thweate granted 673 ac. 2r. 32 po. "recorded twice" Charles City Co. in the parish of *Jordans* (LOP 7.156); also recorded as Hen. Bates & James Thweat (LOP 7.150)

24 Apr 1695; Capt. Henry Batt granted 700 ac. Charles City Co. on s. side of head of *Baylys Creek* (LOP 8.411)

24 Apr 1695; Capt. Henry Batt granted 270 ac. Charles City Co. on s. side of Appomattox River on the river adj. lands called *Baylys* (LOP 8.411)

1 Nov 1708; probate granted Mary Batte (widow) on will of her father Henry Lound (HCVW-1 p. 105)

4 Jun 1715; 6 Jun 1715; Mary Batts and William Lygon agree to division of *Neck of Land* formerly owned by Henry Lound (HCVD-2 p. 48)

3-1 **Elizabeth Batte**; m. bef. 1704 **William Ligon**, b. est. ca 1682 (LF&C); d. 1764 Amelia Co.; s/o William Ligon & Mary Tanner; living in Prince George Co. in 1715

3-2 **Mary Batte**; m. ca 1690 **John Poythress**

3-3 **Ann Batte**; m. **Edward Stratton**; s/o Edward Stratton & Martha
Sheppey
3-4 **Rachel Batte**; m. **James Parham** of Isle of Wight
3-5 **Sarah Batte**; m. cousin **Abraham Jones**; s/o
3-6 **Henry Batte**; d. by 2 Oct 1727 Prince George Co., VA; unmarried

Will of Henry Batte; Prince George Co.; 5 Jul 1727; 10 Oct 1727
Mother: Mary Batte
Sisters: Mary Poythress, Elizabeth Ligon, Ann Stratton, Rachel Parham, Sarah Jones
Brother: William Batte
Wit: Abraham Cocke, Samuel Jordan, John Cureton, Robert Poythress (PGWB 1713-28
p.140)
[Henry Batte; Prince George County Wills and Administrations (1713-1800); p. 1042-1043. Will
pro. Oct. 10, 1727. Deeds, Etc., 1713-1728, Pt. 3 (Reel 2) (LOV)]

3-7 **William Batte**, b. ca 1678; d. by 1754 Prince George Co.; m. by May
1704 Henrico Co. **Mary Stratton** (MHC p. 6); d/o Martha ____ & her m/2
Edward Stratton, Sr. & [Martha m/1 Thomas Sheppy & m/3 John Brown];
William presented the will of Martha Brown on 7 Aug Ct. 1721 (HCVW-1 p.
231) and the inventory on 4 Sep 1721 (HCVW-2 p. 159); on 5 Aug Ct. 1723
Elizabeth Chamberlain chose William as guardian (HCVW-2 127, 167);
possible children from family histories:

> 37-1   William Batte, Jr.
> 37-2   Thomas Batte, b. 31 May 1721
> 37-3   Robert Batte, b. 16 Oct 1727
> 37-4   Henry Batte.
> 37-5   John Batte

[William Batte; wills not listed in Virginia Wills and Administrations, 1632-1800 (Torrence).
Will dated 9 December 1754; proved 11. January 1755 Virginia Genealogical Society Quarterly,
vol. 4, p. 71, from copy in private possession, Another copy is in the Virginia Historical Society,
Formerly of record in Prince George County Will Book 1750-1755, p. 545 [lost], printed from
this in the National Genealogical Society Quarterly, vol. 60, pp. 209-210 (LOV)]

37-1 **William Batte, Jr.**; d. aft. 9 Apr 1762 Prince George Co.; m. **Agnes
Birchett**; children from family histories:

371-1 **William Batte**, said to have m. **Sarah Parham**
371-2 **John Batte**
371-3 **Martha Batte**; m. 26 Dec 1769 Brunswick Co. **Judkins Hunt**

[William Batte; wills not listed in Virginia Wills and Administrations, 1632-1800 (Torrence).
Will dated 9 Apr. 1762 Will proved Nat'l Gen. Soc. Quarterly. v. 60. p. 209, from a copy made
from [lost] Prince George Co. Will Book 1758-1762. p. 511; as "William Batte, Jr."; also in
"Virginia Genealogical Society Bulletin," v. IV (1966), p. 71; also the National Genealogical
Society Quarterly, vol. 60, pp. 209. (LOV)]

37-2 **Thomas Batte**, b. 31 May 1721 Prince George Co.

37-3 **Robert Batte**, b. 16 Oct 1727 Prince George Co.; m. **Martha Peterson**; d/o John Peterson & Martha Thweatt of Prince George Co.; child from his will:

37-3 **Robert Batte, Jr.**

Will of Robert Batte of Prince George Co.; 13 Jul 1790; [recorded]
To son Robert Batte, Jr., 150 ac. bounded by Theodorick Bland, Edmund Epes & John
   Batte; also slaves
Wit: Richard Bland, William Ragsdale, Jr., William Scott (PGWB 1787-1792, p. 396)

37-4 **Henry Batte**; d. bef. 1 Nov 1770 Chesterfield Co.; m. **Elizabeth Chamberlayne**; d/o Thomas Chamberlayne & Elizabeth Stratton; he was probably the Henry who wit. deeds in 1729/30 in Henrico Co.(HCVD-2 p. 124, 80); children:

           374-1 Henry Batte
           374-2 Thomas Batte
           374-3 Mary Batte
           374-4 Elizabeth Batte
           374-5 Richard Batte
           374-6 William Batte
           374-7 Chamberlayne Batte

Will of Henry Batte, Chesterfield Co.; 24 Sep 1770; 1 Nov 1771
To son Henry, all my lands in Prince George Co.; also 4 negroes
To son Thomas, land in Chesterfield Co. bought of Maj. Peter Jones & Dorothy his
   wife; also 15 negroes
To son Richard, 3 tracts in Chesterfield Co. called *Packers, Strattons, Dawsons*; also
   remainder of estate
To dau. Mary Cox, 19 negroes
To dau. Elizabeth Jones, riding chair & harness
Exs: sons Thomas, Henry & Richard
Wit: Josiah Daly, John Elam, Richard Baugh (ChWB 2.46)
1 Nov 1771; Will of Henry Batte presented by Henry & Thomas Batte, exs. (ChOB
   5.48)

374-1 **Henry Batte**; he inherited the Prince George Co. lands of his
   brother William
374-2 **Thomas Batte**; d. by 11 Oct 1787; mb. 5 Jun 1778 Henrico Co.
   Dorothy Baugh; surety Richard Baugh (MCC p. 9); d/o Richard Baugh
   whose 1777 will leaves her a negro; children:

   3742-1 **Richard Baugh Batte**
   3742-2 **Elizabeth Chamberlayne Batte**; mb. 1 Jun 1808 Chesterfield
     Co. **John Archer**; surety John Stratton (MCC p. 5)

Ct. 11 Oct 1787; will of Thomas Batte proved (ChOB 7.577); Ct. 13 Dec 1787; Stephen
Clarke appointed guardian to Elizabeth Chambelaine Batte & Richard Baugh Batte
(ChOB 8.29); 2 Feb 1791; Elizabeth Batte, orphan of Thomas Batte, to Stephen Cocke,
her guardian (ChWB 2.305); 2 Feb 1791; Stephen Cocke, executor of estate of Thomas

Batte (ChWB 2.307); Ct. 8 Apr 1793; Archibald Baugh appointed guardian to Richard
B. Batte & Elizabeth C. Batte, orphans of Thomas Batte (Ch OB 10.73)

374-3 **Mary Batte**; m. **George Cox**; d. by Apr 1780 Henrico Co.
374-4 **Elizabeth Batte**; m. aft. 10 Jun 1760 ____ **Jones**; she inherited the
   remainder of the estate of her brother William
374-5 **Richard Batte**; d. aft. 10 Nov 1782 Chesterfield Co.; unmarried

Will of Richard Batte of Dale Parish, Chesterfield Co.; 10 Nov 1781; 7 Feb 1783
To bro. Thomas Batte, all land my father gave me by his will
To Mary Adderson, I lend *Eliams* for life, 6 negroes, then to Henry Cox
To Henry Batte, remainder of estate
Wit: Alex. Childers, Meredith Childers (ChWB 3.359)
Ct. of 7 Feb 1783; will of Richard Batte proved (ChOB 6.393)

374-6 **William Batte** d. by 3 Oct 1766 Chesterfield Co.

Will of William Batte; 10 Jun 1760; 3 Oct 1766
To bro. Henry Batte, all my lands in Prince George Co. called *Mitchels*
To sister Elizabeth Batte, 11 negroes and remainder of my estate
Ex: father Henry Batte
Wit: Walter Hebble, Robert Elam, Thomas Clarke (ChWB 1.532)
3 Oct 1766; will of William Bate presented by Henry Batte, ex. (ChOB 3.771)
Oct 1766; Nov 1766; inventory of William Batte; value £900.16.4 ½ and £40.13
   (ChWB 1.538); 3 Apr 1767; inventory returned (ChOB 4.29)

374-7 **Chamberlayne Batte**; d. by 1 Apr 1757; m. 22 Aug 1754 Amelia
   Co. **Margaret Jones**; child:

3747-1 Thomas Batte

1 Apr 1757; Margaret Batte, widow and relict of Chamberlayne Batte, granted
administration of her husband's estate (ChOB 2.287); 1 Jul 1757; inventory of
Chamberlayne Batte returned (ChOB 2.324); [undated] inventory of Chamberlain
Batte; value £512.4.3 (ChWB 1.248); 6 Oct 1757; inventory of Cham'br Batte; by
Margaret Batte (ChWB1.II.274); 5 May 1758; inventory returned (ChOB 2.405)

3747-1 **Thomas Batte**; d. aft. 4 May 1800; m. ____;1 Apr 1757,
   Henry Batte to be guardian to Thomas Batte, orphan of Chamberlain
   Batte (ChOB288); 1 Nov 1771; orphan of Chamberlayne, chose
   Thomas Batte guardian (ChOB 5.49); children from their father's will:

37471-1 **Chamberlain Batte**; mb. 6 Nov 1802 **Sarah Akin**; d/o
   Thomas Akin who consents (MCC p. 9)
37471-2 **Thomas Batte**; Ct. Dec 1800 he chose John Stratton
   guardian (ChOB 14.7)
37471-3 **Margaret Jones (Peggy Jones) Batte**; mb. 12 Feb; m. 20
   Feb 1796 Dale Parish Episcopal Church **Marley Walthall**; consent
   of Thomas Jones, her father; surety Henry Walthall & Chambling
   Bate

37471-4 **Elizabeth Batte**; she chose Benjamin Graves as guardian (ChOB 14.7)

Will of Thomas Batte; Chesterfield Co.; 4 May 1800; 9 Sep 1800
To son Chamberlain, all my land in Prince George Co. except *Robertsons*, featherbed
To son Thomas, land I live on called *Bull Hill*, featherbed, mare
Shd. Chamberland lose his land in current law suit with Cox, then my land to be divided between Chamberlain & Thomas
Lend to dau. Margaret Walthall, my estate for life, then to her children
To dau. Eliz'a Batte, $100, feather bed saddle & bridle
Robertsons in Prince George Co. to be sold for debts
Dau. Elizabeth to keep her negroes at *Bull Hill* until her bro. Thomas is of age or she marries
Exs: John Stratton, George Cox, Benjamin Graves
Wit: Alexander Marshall, John Varnier, Wm. Moore (ChWB 5.426)
Ct. 9 Sep 1800; will of Thomas Batte proved (ChOB 13.311)

37-5 **John Batte**; d. 8 Oct 1729 Prince George Co.

3. **John Batte**, b. 22 Jul 1630; said to have drowned in the Irish Sea returning to England with his father in 1652

Note: There was a **Thomas Botte**, b. ca 1656, age 30 on 2 Aug 1686 (HCVD-1 p. 34, 151); m. **Amy** ____; widow of **Essex Bevill** and **Thomas Daulby**. Thomas Botte witnessed documents and appraised estates in Henrico Co. from the 1680s to ca 1750 and, it appears he held land in the same locale as Thomas Batte.

Last day Feb 1689; 2 Jun 1690; there was an escheat grant to Thomas Botte and Amy, his wife, and Thomas Batte, Sr., of 400 ac. in *The Old Town* in Appomattox River; Thomas Botte, for valuable consideration, makes over his part to John Bevill; /s/ Tho. Bott (HCVD-1 p. 56)

Since the name Amy was not all that common in this era in the Virginia Colony, it is odd that Thomas Batte had a daughter named Amy while Thomas Botte had a wife named Amy. Although the Batte names was frequently misspelled, there appears to be no doubt that these were two different individuals with no relationship found between the two families.

CHRISTOPHER BRANCH

Christopher Branch, Gent., b. ca 1598 Kent, England; d. by 20 Feb 1681/2; according to Torrence, he was s/o Lionel Branch of London, Gent.; said to have m. in England **Mary Addie (Addy)**; they came to Virginia aboard the *London Merchant*. The 16 Feb 1623 List of the Living and Dead in Virginia shows Christopher Branch among the living at College Land. The Muster of 1624 includes Christopher, Mary and their son Thomas, age 9 mos.; children:

1. Thomas Branch, b. 1619
2. Christopher Branch, b. aft. 1624
3. William Branch, b. ca 1625

20 Oct 1634; Christopher Branch, Planter of *Arrowhattocks* in Henrico Co., 21 year lease of 100 ac. granted Thomas Sheffeild (PB 1.1.155; LOP 1.155)

8 Dec 1635; Christopher Branch granted 250 ac. at *Kingsland* "over against *Arrowhattocks*" east on the main river; 50 ac. for his own transport plus 3 others (PB 1.1.326; LOP 1.326)

14 Sep 1636; Christopher Branch granted 100 ac. Henrico Co. on the river against *Harrow Attocks* westly upon head of *Proctors Creek* due by exchange from James Place for transport of 2 servants; renewed and 350 ac. added (LOP 1.281)

8 [or 28] Feb 1638; Christopher Branch granted 450 ac. Henrico Co. on the great river and *Proctors Creek*; 100 ac. due James Place assigned. and 350 ac. for transport of 7 persons (PB 1.2.634; LOP 1.634)

12 Mar 1638; Christopher Branch granted 250 ac. Henrico Co. at *Kingsland* over against *Long Fields*; for his own personal adventure and the same 4 persons in the patents of 8 Dec 1635 and 12 Mar 1638 (PB 1.2.608; LOP 1.608)

8 May 1638; Christopher Branch granted 250 ac. Henrico Co. at *Kingsland* against *Arro Attacks*; for his own personal adventure and that of the same 4 persons in the 8 Dec 1635 patent (PB 1.2.553; LOP 1.553)

20 Oct 1665; Christopher Branch, Sr. granted 1,380 ac. Henrico Co. on s. side of James River called *Kingsland*; adj. William Baugh; for 250 ac. by patent 12 Feb 1638; 450 ac. by patent 28 Feb 1638: 50 ac. escheate land and 630 ac. for transport of 13 persons (PB 5.450; LOP 5.590)

1 Dec 1681; from Christopher Branch, Sr. of *Kingsland* of Henrico Co. to son Thomas Branch of same; to clarify previous give of 300 ac. next to John Branch's 100 ac.; to Thomas' heirs after his decease; and if no heirs to James Branch, if no heirs to Elizabeth Branch, if no heirs to Martha Branch; my grandson Christopher Branch my attorney (HCVD-1 p. 14)

Will of Christopher Branch of *Kingsland*; 20 Jun 1678; 20 Feb 1681/2
To son Thomas Branch, 240 ac. already given him, items
To grandson Christopher Branch, land between river to line of my son Thomas and *Proctors* provided he help build his bro. Samuel a house
To grandson Samuel Branch, *Jacks Bottom* at *Proctor's Creek*, provided he help build his bro. Benjamin a house

To grandson Benjamin Branch, land between *Jacks Bottom* and *Proctors Creek*
William and John Branch to have permission to hunt and fish in creek and swamp
Remainder of estate to grandsons Christopher, ex., Benjamin and Samuel; Sarah and
  Mary Branch, the wife of Thomas Jefferson, equally
Wit: Abell Gower, Richard Ward (HCVW-1 p. 11)
13 Apr 1682; inventory of Mr. Christopher Branch, Sr.; value £38.7.10 (HCVW-1 p. 11)
13 Apr 1682; division of estate of Christopher Branch to: Christopher Branch, Samuel
  Branch, Thomas Jefferson, Sarah Branch, Benjamin Branch (HCVW-1 p. 12)
[Christopher Branch, Sr.; Henrico County Wills and Administrations (1662-1800); p. 209-210.
Will pro. 20 Feb. 1681/82. p. 217-218. Inv., appr., & division dated 13 Apr. 1682. Records, 1677-
1692 (Reel 4) (LOV)]

1. **Thomas Branch, Sr.**; b. ca 1624, age 9 mos. in the muster of 1624/5; d. by 1
    Feb 1694 Henrico Co.; m. **Elizabeth** ____ ; d. by 20 Aug 1697 Henrico Co.;
    he is said to have m. Elizabeth Gough, d/o Matthew, yet the land Matthew
    Gough claimed 25 Jul 1639 in Henrico Co., for his own transport and that 6
    others (PB 1.II.111), is said by and undocumented source to have reverted back
    to the colony for lack of heirs; as Mr. Thos. Branch, Sr., he was responsible
    for 2 taxables in the Henrico Co. list of 1678; children:

                1-1 Thomas Branch
                1-2 Matthew Branch
                1-3 James Branch
                1-4 Elizabeth Branch
                1-5 Martha Branch

1 Aug 1691; 1 Aug 1691; Thomas Branch, Sr. makes wife Elizabeth Branch his atty. in
case between him and Christopher Branch, defendant (HCVD-1 p. 64)

Will of Thomas Branch, Sr.; [undated]; 1 Feb 1694
To sons Thomas, Matthew and James Branch, 3s each
To wife Elizabeth, ex., remainder of estate
To daus. Elizabeth Richardson and Martha Ward, 5s each to buy a ring (HCVW-1 p. 54)
[Thomas Branch, Sr.; Henrico County Wills and Administrations (1662-1800) p. 99-100. Exors.
bond rec. 21 Feb. 1695. Misc. Court Records, Vol. 1, [1650-1717] (Reel 1); Henrico County
Wills and Administrations (1662-1800) Note p. 543. Will pro. 1 Feb. 1694. p. 549. Exors. bond
rec. 21 Apr. 1695. Deeds, Wills, Etc., 1688-1697 (Reel 5) (LOV)]

Will of Elizabeth Branch of Varina Parish; 2 Aug 1697; 20 Aug 1697
To sons Thomas, Mathew and James Branch, household items
To dau. Elizabeth Richardson, clothes
To son in law Melchizadek Richardson, ½ crown to buy gloves
To grandson Mathew Branch, clothes
Remainder to 3 sons
Exs: sons Thomas and James
Wit: Joseph Tanner, John Cooke (HCVW-1 p. 67, 68)
[Elizabeth Branch; Henrico County Wills and Administrations (1662-1800) p. 10-11. Will pro. 20
Aug. 1697. Deeds, Wills, Etc., 1697-1704 (Reel 6) (LOV)]

1-1 Thomas Branch, Jr., b. ca 1654, age ca 54 on 3 Mar 1710/1 (HCVD-2 p. 26); d. by Dec 1728; m. by 1 Oct 1689 **Elizabeth Archer**; orphan d/o George Archer (MHC p. 11); children:

> 11-1 Thomas Branch
> 11-2 William Branch
> 11-3 James Branch
> 11-4 Tabitha Branch
> 11-5 Agnes Branch
> 11-6 Elizabeth Branch
> 11-7 Frances Branch
> 11-8 Mary Branch
> 11-9 Amy Branch
> 11-10 Martha Branch
> 11-11 Margery Branch

1 Feb 1686; 1 Feb 1686; from Thomas Branch, Jr. of Henrico Co.; for 2,000# tobacco to bro. Matthew Branch; 288 ac. on s. side of James River next to Abel Gower; Elizabeth, w/o Thomas, relinquished dower (HCVD-1 p. 37)

1 Feb 1686; 1 Feb 1686; from Thomas Branch, Jr. of Henrico Co.; deed of gift to bro. James Branch; 200 ac. on s. side of James River next to Matthew Branch; Elizabeth, w/o Thomas, relinquished dower (HCVD-1 p. 37)

18 Oct 1688; 1 Jun 1689; will of Edward Deely gives "to each of Thomas Branch, Jr.'s daughters one cow at their marriage (HCVW-1 p. 35)

Will of Thomas Branch; 3 Dec 1727; Dec 1728
To sons Thomas and William, negroes, items
To son James, tract on *Deep Bottom* of *Proctors Creek*
To dau. Tabitha Mitchell, 4s credit in a London store
To dau. Amey Branch, 10s credit in a London store
To dau. Martha, items; to dau. Margery, £8
To sons William and James, 2 old guns
To wife Elizabeth, extx., during widowhood, use of labor of 3 negroes; after her death, estate to be divided between 3 sons and 2 unmarried daus.
Wit: Richard Ward, Jr., Higginson King, Charles Griffith (HCVW-1 p. 170)
Apr 1731; [recorded]; inventory of Thomas Branch; value £66.15.10 (HCVW-1 p. 177)
[Thomas Branch; Henrico County Wills and Administrations (1662-1800) p. 221. Will pro. Dec. 1728. p. 298-299. Inv. & appr. rec. Apr. 1731. Deeds & Wills, 1725-1737 (Reel 7a) (LOV)]

11-1 Thomas Branch; d. by 6 Jun 1766 Chesterfield Co.; unmarried

27 Sep 1728; Thomas Branch granted 390 ac. in the fork of *Beaverpond Branch* of *Deep Creek* (LOP 13.403)

29 Jul 1737; 1st Mon Sep 1737; from Joseph Ward and Henry Branch, trustees of Henry Vanderhood to Thomas Branch; all of Henrico Co.; for £50; 100 ac. of *Kings Land* conveyed by Christopher Branch to his grandsons William & John Branch on 17 Oct 1659; and by John's will dated 17 Jan 1687, the survivor, to his dau. Obedience, late wife of Thomas Turpin, to James Branch by deed 2 Apr 1716 and by James to

Vanderhood 2 Nov 1726; also 101 ac. bounded by *Sheffeild Swamp* (HCVD-2 p. 183, 184)

5 Nov 1762; Nov 1762; from Thomas Branch to Henry Branch, both of Chesterfield Co.; for love and affection, 600 ac. conveyed by John & Betty Quarles to sd. Thomas (ChWB 4.524)

Will of Thomas Branch; Chesterfield Co.; 30 Oct 1765; 1 Aug 1766
To William Branch, land on Appomattox River where my bro. William Branch
   formerly lived
Remainder of estate to Henry Mitchel, Edward Osborn, Robert Goode (s/o Robert
   Goode, dec'd), Josiah Tatem, Branch Tanner, Christopher Branch, Thomas Branch
   Wilson and John Goode, equally; they all to be exs.
Wit: Ben Watkins, Ben Cellion, Charles Burton (ChWB 1.535)
6 Jun 1766; will of Thomas Branch presented by Edward Osborne, Robert Goode,
   Thomas Branch Wilson and Branch Tanner; 4 of the exs. (CHOB 3.735)
1 Aug 1766; will of Thomas Branch further proved & recorded (ChOB 3.744)

5 Sep 1766; 3 Oct 1766; the above named legatees who inherited the remainder of the Thomas Branch estate sold 133 ac. of Thomas's land to Thomas Franklyn (ChDB 5.370)

22 Oct 1766; Nov 1766; from Christopher Branch (& Martha his wife), Edward Osborne (& Elizabeth his wife), Josiah Tatum (& Sarah his wife), and Robert Goode of Chesterfield Co.; Branch Tanner (& Mary Page his wife), Thomas Branch Wilson (& Elizabeth his wife) of Amelia Co.; Henry Mitchell (& Priscilla his wife) of Sussex Co. to Leonard Ward; 146 ac. where Thomas Branch, dec'd, lived (ChDB 5.333)

3 Jan 1767; 3 Apr 1767; the above legatees sold 219 ac. adj. *Kingsland* where Thomas Branch, dec'd, lived to Seth Ward, Jr. (ChDB 5.499)

4 Sep 1767; 4 Sep 1767; from above legatees sold to another of the legatees, Josiah Tatum of Chesterfield Co.; 102 ac. of the above land left by Thomas Branch (ChDB 5.523)

6 Apr 1767; 4 Sep 1767; from above named legatees to another of the legatees, Christopher Branch of Chesterfield Co.; 133 ac. of the land of Thomas Branch (ChDB 5.525)

4 Sep 1767; 4 Sep 1767; from above legatees to another of the legatees Thomas Branch Wilson of Amelia Co.; 102 ac. of above named land of Thomas Branch (ChDB 5.526)

   11-2 William Branch of Henrico Co.; d. ca 1741 Chesterfield Co.; on Henrico Co. jury of Jun 1741 (HCVD-3 p. 91)

Will of William Branch of Henrico Co.; 4 Oct 1741; 5 Mar 1762
To bro. Thomas Branch, all my estate and he to be ex.
Wit: William Osborne, Henry Ward (ChWB 1.336)
5 Mar 1762; will of William Branch presented by Thomas Branch; proved by William
   Osborne, wit. (ChOB 3.209)

   11-3 James Branch; d. by Oct 1737; he made a land swap in 1689 with his
   bro. Matthew; he held 555 ac. in 1705 rent roll Henrico Co.

Will of James Branch; Henrico Co.; 5 Aug 1736; Oct 1737
To sisters Martha and Margery Branch, a negro each
To bro. Thomas, £10
Remainder to 2 bros. Thomas and William
Wit: John Worsham, Jr., Edward Osborn, Jr., Josiah Tatum (HCVW-1 p. 217)
Oct Ct. 1737; will of James Branch presented by Thomas and William Branch, exs. &
   proved (HCVW-2 p. 1)
[James Branch; Henrico County Wills and Administrations (1662-1800) p. 662. Will pro. Oct.
1737. Deeds & Wills, 1725-1737 (Reel 7a) (LOV)]

   11-4 **Tabitha Branch**; d. 15 Jan 1752 Albemarle Co.; m. **Henry Mitchell**;
      d. 27 Mar 1754 Albemarle Co.; their eldest son, Henry, was one of the
      legatees of his uncle Thomas Branch
   11-5 **Agnes Branch**; d. bef. 11 Oct 1744; m/1 **Edward Osborne**; d. by 5
      Oct 1724; m/2 by 1726 **John Worsham, Jr.** of Dale Parish; d. by Nov
      1745 when his will was recorded in Henrico Co. (HCVW-1 p. 27); Agnes'
      eldest son, Edward Osborne, was a legatees of his uncle Thomas Branch

Ct. 5 Oct 1724; Agnes Osborn granted administration of estate of Edward Osborn,
dec'd (HCVW-2 p. 171)

11 Oct 1726; 7 Nov 1726; from John Worsham, Jr. and Agnes his wife pursuant to a
premarital agreement give to William and Joseph Osborne, sons of Agnes, 2 negro
girls (HCVD-2 p. 94)

   11-6 **Elizabeth Branch**; d. aft 1727; m/1 **Robert Goode**; d. by 7 Jul 1718
      Henrico Co.; m/2 **Page Punch**; d. by 6 Nov 1727 Henrico Co.; children:

      116-1 **Robert Goode**; he was one of the legatees of his step-father, Page
         Punch, in 1727 and his uncle Thomas in 1766
      uncle Thomas Branch in & in 1727 his step-father Page Punch
      116-2 **Francis Goode**
      116-3 **Mary Punch**

Will of Robert Goode; Henrico Co.; 25 May 1718; 7 Jul 1718
To son Robert, 100 ac. *Whitby* plantation where I live; if he die before age so son
   Francis
To son Francis, negro
To my sister Anne Goode, heifer at age 18 or marriage
To sons Robert & Francis, my livestock when they are of age
To John Green, 10s
Ex: wife Elizabeth, she to have remainder of estate
Wit: John Willie, Mary Willie, John Green (HCVW-1 p. 146)

Will of Page Punch; Henrico Co.; 31 Aug 1726; 6 Nov 1727
To dau. Mary Punch, negroes, items, money; if she d. bef. 21 or marriage then all to
   wife
To son in law Robert Good, items
Ex: wife, she to have remainder of estate
Wit: none (HCVW-1 p. 164)

11-7 **Frances Branch**; d. bef. 4 May 1764; m. **Lodowick Tanner**; d. aft.
10 Aug 1773 Amelia Co.; he mb/24 May 1764 Amelia Co. **Ann Johnson**,
widow, sec. Richard Hayes; children from his will (AmWB 1.106, 107):

117-1 **Branch Tanner**; he was one of the legatees of his uncle Thomas
Branch; his dau. Frances mb. 22 Oct 1782 Amelia Co. to Field Archer
117-2 **Elizabeth Tanner**

11-8 **Mary Branch**; said to have m. **Henry Tatum**; as Josiah, probably
their eldest son, was one of the legatees of Mary's bro. Thomas Branch
11-9 **Amy Branch**; m. cousin **Henry Branch**; s/o Christopher Branch &
Ann Sherman; their eldest son was one of the legatees of Amy's brother,
Thomas Branch
11-10 **Martha Branch**; m. **Daniel Wilson**; their eldest son, Thomas
Branch Wilson, was one of the legatees of his uncle Thomas Branch
11-11 **Margery Branch**; m. **John Goode**; d. by Sep Ct. 1743 Henrico Co.
when Margery, extx., presented his will (HCVW-2 p. 20); John inherited 100
ac. *Whitby* from the 1718 will of his brother Thomas Goode (HCVD-1 p.
147); their eldest son, John Goode, was one of the legatees of his uncle
Thomas Branch

1-2 **Matthew Branch**, b. ca 1661, age 30 on 1 Sep 1691 (HCVD-1 p. 153); d. by
4 Jul 1726 Chesterfield Co.; m. ____; in 1686 his bro. Thomas sold him 288
ac. Henrico Co.; he inherited the land, plantation & more as "cozen" in the
will of Edward Deely written 18 Oct 1688; he was ex. and heir of William
Burroughs whose will was written 14 Jan 1710; and he or his son Matthew
inherited books and wearing apparel from Thomas Taylor, mariner, in 1725;
known children:

     12-1 Matthew Branch
     12-2 John Branch
     12-3 Olive Branch
     12-4 Daniel Branch
     12-5 Thomas Branch
     12-6 Phebe Branch
     12-7 Elizabeth Branch

27 Sep 1689; Oct 1689; from James Branch, 280 ac. on s. side of James River, 200 ac.
of which formerly given bros. Thomas Jr. and Matthew plus 80 ac. part of land
Thomas Branch sold sd. Matthew to Matthew Branch, both of Henrico Co. & Parish;
for 200 ac. on s. side of James River next to Abell Gower (HCVD-1 p. 54)

29 Oct 1696; Mathew Branch granted 50 ac. Henrico Co. escheated land of Wm. Jones
(LOP 9.70)

24 Apr 1703; Matthew and James Branch granted 710 ac. Henrico Co. (LOP 9.527)
[They divided the land in 1711, with each taking 355 ac. (HCVD-2 p. 31)]

20 Sep 1704; Matthew Branch, Tho. Jefferson, Thomas Harris & Thomas Turpin
granted 628 ac. Henrico Co. (LOP 9.627)

Apr 1705; Henrico Co. rent roll; Matthew Branch held 947 ac.

1 Mar 1710; from John Tullit, Gent. to Matthew Branch, Gent.; both of Henrico Co.; for £27; 450 ac. part of 7,650 ac. on *Reedy Creek*, s. side of *Powhite Creek* and Col. Byrd (HCVD-2 p. 28)

Will of Matthew Branch, Sr.; 15 Dec 1722; 4 Jul 1726
To son Matthew, plantation I dwell on; other lands adj. my bro. Thomas, my bro. James' plantation *Barbadoes*, etc.
To wife, lower half of dwelling house for life; to have privilege of son Matthew's land to get timber
To son John, land between my bro. James and myself
To sons Olive [next to *Poewhite*] and Daniel [next to *Reedy Creek*]
To son Thomas, land
To son Olive, colt; to daus. Phebe & Elizabeth Branch, a bay mare each
To wife, ex., remainder of estate
Wit: Thomas Harris, Jr., Ralph Burgis, Charles Griffith (HCVW-1 p. 152)
[Matthew Branch, Sr.; Henrico County Wills and Administrations (1662-1800) p. 31-32. Will pro. 4 July 1726. Deeds & Wills, 1725-1737 (Reel 7a) (LOV)]

12-1 Matthew Branch; of *Hannah Spring*; d. ca 1766 Chesterfield Co.; he inherited 10s from 1733 will of Daniel Mecarter (HCVW-1 p. 190); both Matthew, Sr. & Jr. were legatees of the 1740 will of Caleb Ware (ChWB 1.19); m. ____; children from Matthew's will:

> 121-1 Matthew Branch
> 121-2 Samuel Branch
> 121-3 Edward Branch
> 121-4 Thomas Branch

2 Jun 1735; from Henry Cary to Matthew Branch, both of Henrico Co.; for £39.12; 660 ac. part of 17,653 ac. granted John Tillett (HCVD-2 p. 161)

Will of Matthew Branch; Chesterfield Co.; 7 Jul 1766; 5 Jun 1767
To son Matthew, land at *Warwick*, and land adj. my bro. John on n. side *Grindol's Run*, negroes
To son Samuel, 280 ac. called *Barbadoes* back of *Kingsland*; also £100
To son Edward, 300 ac. part of land I live on joining *Beaver Pond Branch*, 2 negroes
To son Thomas, ex., *Hannah Spring*, plantation I live on; also land bought of John Wood; 7 negroes and remainder of estate
Wit: Thomas Branch, Judith Fowler, Mary Branch (ChWB 1.527)
5 Jun 1767; will of Matt. Branch presented by Thomas Branch; proved by Thomas Branch and Judith Fowler, witnesses (ChOB 4.45)

121-1 Matthew Branch;of *Warwick*; d. aft. 1 Jun 1772; ?mb. Feb 1749 Amelia Co. **Ridley Jones**; [d/o] Peter Jones, sec.; Matthew inherited *Warwick* from his father; children:

> 1211-1 Matthew Branch
> 1211-2 Peter Branch
> 1211-3 Elizabeth Branch
> 1211-4 Mary Branch

Will of Matthew Branch; Chesterfield Co.; 1 Jun 1772; 11 Sep 1772
To son Matthew, land I live on, 3 negroes
To son Peter, land back of *Rock Ridge Road*, between *Stoney Creek* and *Grindels*,
  negro
To dau. Elizabeth Branch, £250, negro
To dau. Mary Branch, £20, negro
If either dau. die under age, the other to get her share
To wife Ridley, rest of estate
Exs: Capt. Robert Goode, Francis Goode, Thomas Branch, Edward Branch
Wit: Thos. Cheatham, Thos. Clayton, Matthias Chitwood, Jr. (ChWB 2.32)
11 Sep 1772; will of Matthew Branch presented by Thomas & Edward Branch &
  Robert Goode, exs. (ChOB 5.150)
20 Mar 1773; inventory of Matthew Branch at *Warwick* by Edward and Thomas
  Branch; no value given (ChWB 3.214)

> 1211-1 **Matthew Branch**
> 1211-2 **Peter Branch**; d. Amelia Co.; m/1 21 Mar 1785 Amelia Co.
>   **Judith Jones**; d/o John Jones
> 1211-3 **Elizabeth Branch**; d. by 1 Aug 1766 Chesterfield Co.;
>   unmarried

Will of Betty Branch of Dale Parish, Chesterfield Co.; dated 5 Oct 1765
To brother Matthew Branch, my whole estate and he to be my executor
Wit: Samuel Branch, William Markham (ChWB 1.535)
1 Aug 1766; will of Betty Branch presented by Matthew Branch, ex. (ChOB 3.744)

> 1211-4 **Mary Branch**; mb. 3 Nov 1783 Chesterfield Co. **Benjamin
>   Moseley**; sur. Peter Branch (MCC p. 88)

121-2 **Samuel Branch**; he inherited *Barbadoes* from his father; said to
  have m. **Winifred ____** and lived in Goochland Co.
121-3 **Edward Branch**; d. by Aug 1804 Chesterfield Co. when his will
  was probated; said to have m/1 **Margaret ____**; m/2 **Mary Ann
  Pankey**; d/o Stephen Pankey (ChWB 4.185); children from family
  history:

> 1213-1 **Stephen Branch**
> 1213-2 **Edward Branch**
> 1213-3 **Matthew Branch**
> 1213-4 **Mary Ann Branch**; m/c 13 May 1793 Chesterfield Co.
>   **Robert Cary**; consent of her father Edward Branch (MCC p. 26)
> 1213-5 **Judith Branch**, b. ca 1784, age 21 in 1805; mb. 28 Feb 1805
>   Chesterfield Co. **Joseph Warren Robertson**; sur. Charles Burton
>   (MCC p. 102)
> 1213-6 **Elizabeth Branch**; m/c 7 Feb 1801 Chesterfield Co. **Charles
>   Burton**; consent of her father Edward Branch, Sr.; m. 26 Feb 1801
>   (MCC p. 24)

121-4 **Thomas Branch**; of *Hannah Spring* which he inherited from his father; said to have m. bef. 1786 **Mary** ____; children from family history:

    1214-1 **Bolling Branch**; mb. 19 Feb 1800 Chesterfield Co. **Rebecca Graves**; s/o Arthur Graves who gave consent (MCC p. 19); they lived Buckingham Co.

    1214-2 **Matthew Branch**

12-2 **John Branch**; b. aft. 1684; not yet 17 when William Burroughs willed him a Negro man (HCVW-1 p. 141); d. by 1 Feb 1750 Chesterfield Co.; m. **Johan Hancock**, b. ca 1723 Chesterfield Co.; d. by 5 Jul 1771; d/o Samuel Hancock whose will, written 1 Sep 1760, leaves her a negro (ChWB 1.377); children:

         122-1   John Branch
         122-2   Samuel Branch
         122-3   Matthew Branch
         122-4   Johanna Branch
         122-5   Frances Branch
         122-6   Betty Branch

1 Feb 1750; Johanna Branch granted administration of estate of her husband John Branch; Matthew Branch and David Bell, security (ChOB 1.80); 2 Aug 1751; appraisers appt. for estate of John Branch (ChOB 1.136); 16 Aug 1751; inventory of John Branch appraised; value £278.16.9 (ChWB 1.59); Dec Ct. 1751; inventory returned (ChOB 1.159)

2 Aug 1754; Matthew & Frances Branch, orphans of John Branch, chose Samuel Branch as guardian; he was assigned guardian to Betty Branch, another orphan of John (ChOB 1.524)

Will of Johan Branch of Dale Parish; Chesterfield Co.; 11 Jan 1769; 5 Jul 1771
To dau. Johannah Sandefur, feather bed & furniture
To son Samuel Branch, 1 negro, a bed
To son Matthew Branch, remainder of estate
Ex: son Samuel Branch
Wit: Simon Hancock, Mary Cobbs, John Cobbs (ChWB 2.44)
5 Jul 1771; will of Joana Branch proved (ChOB 5.12)

    122-1 **John Branch**; d. ca 1768 Chesterfield Co.; m. ____;

11 Sep 1761; Jun 1762; from Charles Stewart of Norfolk Co., merchant, to Matthew Branch, s/o John of Chesterfield Co.; for £110; 600 ac sold by late dec'd John Branch 2 Feb 1735 to Henry Cary who sold to sd. Steward by a suit in chancery 6 Apr 1759 of Stewart vs John Branch, son and heir of John Branch, dec'd (ChDB 1.448)

12 Sep 1761; Sep 1763; from John Branch, Sr. to John Markham, both of Chesterfield Co.; for £20.18; 38 ac. part of 333 ac. in Dale Parish adj. sd. Markham; Branch's wife released dower (ChDB 3.511)

4 Jun 1762; 6 Aug 1762; from John Branch to Samuel Branch; for £760; 109 ac. bounded by sd. Samuel Branch; John's will released dower (ChDB 3.598)

Jul 1766; from John Branch, Sr. to Daniel Weiseger, both of Dale Parish, Chesterfield Co.; for £110; 183 ac. next to Mathew & Samuel Branch, *Herring Creek, Shampoke Creek*, John Markham and Brett Randolph (ChDB 5.311)

Will of John Branch of Dale Parish; Chesterfield Co.; 27 Nov 1768; 6 Jan 1769
To bro. Matthew Branch, my whole estate; he to be executor
Wit: Edward Branch, Henry Winfree, Archibald ____ (ChWB 1.528)
6 Jan 1769; will of John Branch presented by Mat Branch and proved by Edward Branch (ChOB 4.250)

> 122-2 **Samuel Branch**; d. aft. 11 Dec 1789; m. ____; Samuel purchased 204 ac. for £40 bounding John Branch, the Amelia Road and *Shampoker Bridge* from Archibald Cary 6 Jun 1760 (ChDB 4.640) and 109 ac. on *Shampoker Creek* from John Branch 4 Jun 1762 (ChDB 4.598); children:

> > 1222-1 **Samuel Branch**; d. by 9 Apr 1790; m. 9 Sep 1764 **Jane (Jeane) Martin**, b. 9 Sep 1764; d/o Anthony Martin & Sarah Holman; she m/c/2 19 Feb 1791 Chesterfield Co. **Thomas Whitworth**; wit. Walter & Samuel Ford (MCC p. 128); inv. of Samuel Branch, Jr. 9 Apr 1790; value £24.6.6 (ChWB 4. 241)
> > 1222-2 **Arthur Branch**; d. by 20 Jan 1802 Powhatan Co.; m. 16 Sep 1779 **Katherine Moseley**
> > 1222-3 **William Branch**; d. by 14 Apr 1817 Chesterfield Co.; m. 6 Dec 1766 **Sarah Martin**
> > 1222-4 **Charles Branch**, b. aft 1768; d. by 5 Oct 1835 Powhatan Co.
> > 1222-5 **Thomas Branch**, b. aft. 1768; Ct. 9 Dec 1793; he chose Archer Branch as guardian (ChOB 10.294)
> > 1222-6 **Elizabeth Branch**; mb. 16 Feb 1779 Chesterfield Co. **John Harris**; consent of her father Samuel Harris (MCC p. 64)
> > 1222-7 **Hannah Branch**; m/c 3 Dec 1784 Chesterfield Co. **William Hopkins**; she is called "Hamey" d/o Samuel Branch (MCC p. 60)
> > 1222-8 **Mary Branch**; m. 27 Jun 1788 Powhatan **Samuel Marshall**

Will of Samuel Branch of Dale Parish, Chesterfield Co.; 11 Dec 1789; 4 Apr 1790
To son Arther, all estate I have given him
Estate given my son Samuel, dec'd, in his lifetime to his next of kin
To daus. Elizabeth Harris, Hannah Hopkins and Mary Marshall, all estate given them
To sons William, Charles & Thomas, tract I live on, equally divided; (Charles and Thomas under 21)
To Elizabeth Jackson for life, 2 negroes, then equally to her children John, Rachel, Chandler & Lucy Jackson; also to Elizabeth £30, items
Remainder to 3 sons, William, Charles & Thomas
Exs: Isaac Salle and my sons Charles and Thomas
Wit: Thomas Bridgewater, John Salle (ChWB 4.329)
Ct. 8 Apr 1790; S. Anthony Martin given admn. of estate of Samuel Branch (ChOB 8.394)

122-3 Matthew Branch; d. ca 1786 Chesterfield Co.; m. **Ann Walthall**; d/o Henry Walthall; Ann inherited negroes from the will of her father dated 28 Dec 1766 (ChWB 2.352); children from his will:

1223-1 **Matthew Branch**; according to his father's will, he was mentally incompetent
1223-2 **Archibald Branch**
1223-3 **Thomas Spencer Branch**
1223-4 **John Branch**
1223-5 **Francis Branch**
1223-6 **Mary Branch**
1223-7 **Elizabeth Branch**
1223-8 **Nancy Spencer Branch**

11 Sep 1761; Jun 1762; from Charles Stewart of Norfolk Co., merchant, to Matthew Branch, s/o John, of Chesterfield Co.; for £110; 600 ac. which the late John Branch sold Henry Cary on 2 Feb 1735 and devised to sd. Stewart by the Chancery Court 6 Apr 1759 of Stewart vs. John Branch, son and heir of John Branch, dec'd (ChDB 4.448)

Will of Matthew Branch of Manchester Parish, Chesterfield Co.; [undated]; Apr 1786
To wife Ann, use of land I live on till son John is 21, then to him 200 ac.
To wife Ann, 183 ac. incl. house, gardens, orchards where I live, at her death to son Francis
To sons Archibald and Thomas Spencer (both under 21), remainder of lands
To daus. Mary, Elizabeth & Nancy Spencer, each, 1 negro at age 16
Wife to maintain my son Matthew for life; then my estate to maintain him
Remainder of estate to children (except Matthew)
Exs: wife Ann, friend Archibald Walthall, and David Pattison
Wit: J. Trabue, Jr., Thos. Bridgwater, John Morgan (ChWB 4.6)
Ct. Apr 1786; will of Matthew Branch proved (ChOB 7.311)

122-4 Johanna Branch; m. **Abram Sandifer**; d. ca 1784 Cumberland Co.; two of their children:

1224-1 **Susannah Sandifer**, b. 5 Aug 1764 (DR)
1224-2 **Diana Sandifer**, b. 30 Nov 1766 (DR)

122-5 Frances Branch
122-6 Betty Branch

12-3 Olive Branch; d. by 5 Apr 1782; m. cousin **Verlinshe Branch**; d/o James Branch; Olive wit. a conveyance of William Byrd on 5 Jun 1751 Charles City Co. (HCVD-4 p. 357; TVF 9.186); Olive mortgaged his home plantation 8 Jul 1766 to Thomas Branch for £74.11.1 (ChDB 3.19); children:

123-1 **James Branch**; living in Chesterfield Co. in 1790
123-2 **Olive Branch, Jr.**; held land in Lunenburg Co.

123-3 Judith Branch; mb. 7 Sep 1772 Chesterfield Co. **Matthew Anderson**; consent of her father Olive Branch (MCC p. 3)

8 Jul 1755; 5 Mar 1756; mortgage; from Olive Branch to Thomas Branch, both of Chesterfield Co.; for £74.11.1; 450 ac. plantation where he now lives; unless he repays money by 8 Jul 1756 (ChDB 3.19)

6 Apr 1764; 6 Apr 1764; from Olive Branch, Sr. to his son Olive Branch, Jr., both of Chesterfield Co.; for 5s; 100 ac. bounded by John Markham, etc. (ChDB 4.587)

Will of Olive Branch of Manchester Parish, Chesterfield Co.; 16 Oct 1779; 5 Apr 1782
To wife Verlinshe for life, all my estate, then to my son James
Exs: son James and friend Bernard Markham
Wit: Bernard Markham, Charles Clarke, Thomas Howlett, John Mallory (ChWB 3.299)
Ct. 5 Apr 1782; will of Olive Branch proved; James Branch, ex. (ChOB 6.345)

12-4 Daniel Branch; d. by 15 Aug 1782 Powhatan Co.; m. **Elizabeth Porter** (DR); d/o Thomas Porter of Cumberland Co.; Daniel inherited £18 from the 1736 will of Stephen Woodson of Goochland Co. (GCWD-1 p. 90); Daniel wit. several wills in Goochland Co.; children from Daniel's will:

         124-1   Daniel Branch
         124-2   Thomas Branch
         124-3   Dutoy Branch
         124-4   Mary Branch, b. 18 Nov 1761
         124-5   Mathew Branch, b. 30 Mar 1764
         124-6   Elizabeth Barbara Branch, b. 27 Mar 1766
         124-7   Frances Branch, b. 15 Sep 1768

Will of Daniel Branch; Powhatan Co.; 13 Apr 1782; 15 Aug 1782
To son Daniel, 301 ac. where I live in Powhatan, 2 negroes & a mare
To sons Thomas, a colt; Dutoy, a horse; & Matthew, a mare; and to each 2 negroes
To daus. Mary, Elizabeth Barbara & Frances, each 2 negroes
To my 4 sons, 4 other negroes provided they pay £30 to each of my daus.
Exs: my 4 sons (PoWB 1.76)
[Daniel Branch; Powhatan Co. Wills & Adms.; 15 Aug 1782. p. 76-77; inv. & appr. rec. 17 Oct 1782, p. 80 Will Book 1, 1777-1795 (Reel 15) (LOV)]

124-1 Daniel Branch; d. by 8 Oct 1792 Chesterfield Co.; children from Daniel's will:

1241-1 **James Branch**
1241-2 **Olive Branch**; m. 6 July 1799 Chesterfield Co. **Sally Ash**; d/o John Ash who consents; sur. Edward Bennett (MCC p. 20)
1241-3 **Daniel Branch**; d. by 1824 Powhatan Co.; m/1 **Mary Britton**; m/2 **Sally Clarke**
1241-4 **Sarah (Sally) Branch**
1241-5 **Verlinshe Branch**; m. 24 May 1802 Henrico Co. **William Bowles**; sur. John B. Winn (MHC p. 10)
1241-6 **Washington Branch**; he chose James Branch as his guardian at the Ct. of 11 Jan 1802 Chesterfield Co. (ChOB 14.196)

Will of Daniel Branch; Chesterfield Co.; [undated]; 8 Oct 1792
To sons James, Olive & Daniel; daus. Sally & Verlinshe; son Washing, each 1 negro
My land & negroes not given to be divided equally among my 4 sons
[no signature; no witnesses] (ChWB 4.494)
8 Oct 1792; will of Daniel Branch proved; James Branch granted administration (ChOB
    9.509)
10 Jan 1793; inventory of Daniel Branch; value £348.19.0 (ChWB 4.529)

> 124-2 **Thomas Branch**; mb. 26 Dec 1789 Amelia Co. **Nancy Clements**,
> d/o John (family histories report marriage and bonds show Thomas
> B___ m. Nancy Clements)
> 124-3 **Dutoy Branch**
> 124-4 **Mary Branch**, b. 18 Nov 1761; bapt. 10 Jan 1762 (DR); mb. 21
> Oct 1782 Powhatan Co. **John Cocke**
> 124-5 **Mathew Branch**, b. 30 Mar 1764; bapt. 6 May 1764 (DR); d. by
> 20 Nov 1823 Powhatan Co.; no descendants
> 124-6 **Elizabeth Barbara Branch**, b. 27 Mar 1766; bapt. 11 May 1766 (DR);
> mb. 3 Feb 1786 Powhatan Co. **Henry Holman**
> 124-7 **Frances Branch**, b. 15 Sep 1768; bapt. 20 Nov 1768 (DR); mb. 9
> Jul 1788 Powhatan Co. **John Price**

> 12-5 **Thomas Branch** of *Shampoke*; d. by 5 Nov 1773; m. **Mary** ____; he
> held 540 ac. in the Apr 1705 rent roll, Henrico Co.; 2 Feb 1760 Thomas
> bought 250 ac on the west side of *Pocoshock* from Robert Cary
> (ChDB 4.415); Thomas & his wife sold 100 ac. for £50 to John, s/o James
> Branch 7 Jun 1766 (ChDB 5.315); children from Thomas' will:

> > 125-1 Edward Branch
> > 125-2 James Branch
> > 125-3 Garner Branch
> > 125-4 Pheby Branch
> > 125-5 Patty Branch
> > 125-6 Mary Branch
> > 125-7 Elizabeth Branch

7 Mar 1760; 7 Mar 1760; from Thomas Branch of *Shampoco*, s/o Matthew Branch, to
Stephen Pankey, both of Chesterfield Co.; for £100; 150 ac. part of land where sd.
Thomas now dwells; being ¼ of 600 ac. granted by patent 20 Oct 1704 to Thomas
Jefferson, Matthew Branch (father of sd. Thomas), and Thomas Turpin, all since dead;
wife of Thomas Branch released dower (ChWB 4.358)

Will of Thomas Branch of Dale Parish, Chesterfield Co.; 29 Aug 1769; 5 Nov 1773
To wife Mary, plantation I live on for life, at her death to son Edward and grandson
    Edward Branch
To son James Branch, negro
To son Garner Branch, 1s
To 4 daus.: Pheby Locket and Patty Branch, Mary Branch and Elizabeth Branch,
    remainder of estate after my wife's death
Exs: Robert Cary and Matthew Branch, Jr.

Wit: Olive Branch, Thomas Cary, James Hill (ChWB 2.2)
5 Nov 1773; will of Thomas Branch proved; Matthew Branch, ex., granted probate
(ChOB 5.349)

9 Jun 1793; from Edward Branch (s/o Edward Garner Branch) and his wife Judy of
Powhatan Co. and Edward Branch (s/o Thomas Branch, dec'd) and his wife Tabitha, to
William Burton; 25 ac. on s. side of *Pokoshock Creek*, being ½ of the tract where
Thomas Branch, dec'd, formerly lived which, by his will dated 29 Aug 1769
Chesterfield Co. was to be divided between his son Edward Branch and grandson
Edward Branch [from family history, not referenced]

> **125-1 Edward Branch**; d. aft. 24 May 1814 Chesterfield Co. (ChWB
> 8.205); m. Jun 1786-Jun 1787 Chesterfield Co. **Tabitha Horner** by
> Baptist Minister; Edward inherited the home plantation from his father;
> children from family histories:
>
> > 1251-1 **Thomas Branch**
> > 1251-2 **Arthur Branch**
> > 1251-3 **Garner Branch**
> > 1251-4 **Polly Branch**
> > 1251-5 **Patsy Branch**
>
> **125-2 James Branch**; he inherited a negro from his father
> **125-3 Garner Branch**; d. by 24 May 1782 Chesterfield Co.; m/1
> **Elizabeth Branch**; m/2 **Frances (Fanny) Hill**; she m/c/2 14 Feb 1792
> Chesterfield Co. **Thomas Brooks**; sur. Olive Hill; m. by Rev. James
> Smith (MCC p. 22); Garner inherited 1s from his father's will; children of
> Garner & Elizabeth:
>
> > 1253-1 **Edward Branch**; m. **Judith** ____
> > 1253-2 **Jonathan Branch**, b. 2 May 1762; bapt. 25 Jul 1762 (DR)
> > Possible dau. of m/2:
> > 1253-3 **Fanny Branch**; mb. 22 Apr 1795 Chesterfield Co. **Reuben
> > Bottom**; sur. Olive Hill; wit: William & Thomas Finney (MCC p. 17)

24 May 1782; inventory of Garner Branch; value £95.5 (ChWB 4.316)
Ct. May 1782; Fanny Branch & Edward Hill granted admn. of estate of Gardner
Branch (ChOB 6.352)

> > 125-4 **Pheby Branch**; m. ____ **Locket**
> > 125-5 **Patty Branch**
> > 125-6 **Mary Branch**
> > 125-7 **Elizabeth Branch**

> 12-6 **Phebe Branch**
> 12-7 **Elizabeth Branch**; m/1 **Stephen Woodson**; d. by 10 Jul 1736; s/o
> John Woodson & Judith Tarleton; m/2 **Charles Bates**; lived Goochland
> Co.

1-3 James Branch, b. ca 1666, age 25 on 1 Sep 1691 (HCVD-1 p. 153); d. ca 1749 Chesterfield Co.; m. **Mary** ____; d. by 1 Apr 1757; James' bro. Thomas gave him 200 ac. Henrico Co. in 1686; one of the legatees of the 1688 will of Edward Deely; he bought 100 ac. at *Kingsland* from Thomas & Obedience Turpin 2 Apr 1716 (HCVD-2 p. 52); Mary inherited a negro from the 1740 will of Caleb Ware (ChWB 1.19); children:

> 13-1 Frances Branch
> 13-2 Elizabeth Branch
> 13-3 Verlintche Branch
> 13-4 Mary Branch
> 13-5 Phebe Branch
> 13-6 John Branch

1 Aug 1711; 1ˢᵗ Mon Nov 1711; James Branch & Matthew Branch, both of Henrico Co. and Parish; dividing the 710 ac. granted them 24 Apr 1703 (HCVD-2 p. 30)

18 Mar 1717; James Branch granted 31 ac. Henrico Co. on s. side of James River adj. Richard Dennis (LOP 10.369)

2 Nov 1726; from James Branch of Henrico Co., planter, to Henry Vanderhood, merchant; for £150; 100 ac. of *Kingsland* on s. side of James River; tract conveyed by Christopher Branch to grandson William and John by deed 17 Oct 1659; John conveyed to dau. Obedience, widow of Thomas Turpin, by will 1687; who sold to James Branch 2 Apr 1716; Mary w/o Branch, relinquished dower (HCVD-2 p. 93)

Will of James Branch, Chesterfield Co.; 19 Aug 1726; 4 Aug 1749
To daus. Frances, Elizabeth, Verlinche, Mary & Phebe Branch, each 1s
To son John Branch, 1s
Remainder to be disposed of as wife sees fit
Wit: Thomas Branch, Jr., William Branch, Matthew Branch (ChWB 1.55)
4 Aug 1749; will of James Branch proved by Thomas Branch, Jr. & Matthew Branch; Mary Branch, extx. (ChOB 1.8)
5 Oct 1749; 6 Oct 1749; inventory of Mr. James Branch; value £107.4.6 (ChWB 1.56)

Will of Mary Branch, Chesterfield Co.; 28 Nov 1750; 1 Apr 1757
To dau. Verlintche, items, spoon marked TBE
To daus. Mary Branch and Phebe Hill, each a spoon, items
To granddau. Elizabeth Wooldridge, items
To son John Branch, ex., remainder of estate
Wit: John Branch, Jr., Samuel Branch, John Hancock (ChWB 1.235)
1 Apr 1757; will of Mary Branch presented by John Branch, ex. (ChOB 2.287)

13-1 Frances Branch
13-2 Elizabeth Branch; m. ____ **Wooldridge**

> **132-1 Elizabeth Wooldridge**

13-3 Verlintche Branch; m. **Olive Branch**; s/o Matthew Branch
13-4 Mary Branch
13-5 Phebe Branch; m. ____ **Hill**

13-6 **John Branch**; m. **Susannah** ____; as John, s/o James, dec'd, he purchased 100 ac. on 7 Jul 1766 from Thomas Branch & his wife of Chesterfield Co. including land John lived on (ChDB 5.315); some of his children:

136-1 **James Branch**; mb/1 9 Oct 1789 Bedford Co. **Frances Terry** (d/o Polly), m. 11 Oct 1789 by Jeremiah Hatcher; mb /2 23 Apr 1792 Bedford Co. **Martha Minor**; Edmund Goode & William Minor, sureties; m. 28 Apr 1792 by Jeremiah Hatcher

136-2 **Sarah (Salley) Branch** (d/o Susannah); mb. 19 Nov 1791 Bedford Co. **Edmund Goode**, m. 25 Nov 1791 by Jeremiah Hatcher

1-4 **Elizabeth Branch**; m. ca 1680 **Melchizadek Richardson**, b. ca 1648, age 38 on 2 Aug 1686; age 43 on 1 Dec 1691 (HCVD-1 37, 151, 154); in 1697 he and Elizabeth are named in the will of her mother, Elizabeth Branch

30 Jul 1686; 2 Aug 1686; from Maj. Thomas Chamberlain and Mary his wife to Melchizadek Richardson and Elizabeth his wife; 50 ac. for 1 bowl of good made punch (HCVD-1 p. 34)

1 Apr 1701; Elizabeth Richardson granted probate on the will of her husband Melchizadek Richardson (HCVW-1 p. 77)

1-5 **Martha Branch**; m. bef. 1694 ____ **Ward** when her father's will calls her Martha Ward; she is not mentioned in her mother's will

2. **Christopher Branch**, b. aft. 1619; d. by Nov 1665; m. ____; children:

2-1 Christopher Branch, b. ca 1658
2-2 Mary Branch
2-3 Sarah Branch
2-4 Samuel Branch, b. ca 1663
2-5 Benjamin Branch, b. ca 1665

24 Nov 1665; inventory of Christopher Branch, Jr.; taken by John Farrar (HCVW-1 p. 220)
[Christopher Branch, Jr.; Henrico County Wills and Administrations (1662-1800); p. 31-32. Inv. & appr. rec. 1665. Misc. Court Records, Vol. 1, [1650-1717] (Reel 1); wills not listed in Virginia Wills and Administrations, 1632-1800 (Torrence). Inv. - 1665 Henrico Co. Miscellaneous Records. Vol. 1, p. 31 (LOV)]

2-1 **Christopher Branch, Jr.** , b. ca 1658, age 24 1 Oct 1653 (HCVD-1 p. 150); d. by 1 Jan 1727; m. by 1 Oct 1695 Henrico Co. **Ann Sherman**; d/o Henry Sherman (MHC p. 11); as Xtopher Branch, Jr., he was charged with 3 tithables 2 Jun 1679 Henrico Co. & held 646 ac. in the Henrico rent roll of Apr 1705; although the marriage record calls her Ann Sherman, she was the widow of **John Crowley** whose will, written 9 Oct 1686, probated 1 Apr 167, calls her "wife Anne" (HCVW-1 p. 23); the will of Henry Sherman, Jr. written 20 Feb 1686 calls her "sister Ann Crowley, widow of John Crowley" and makes a bequest to the eldest child at age 21 that she might have from a future marriage (HCVW-1 p. 24); Ann inherited 20s from her mother in 1703/4

(HCVW-1 p. 86); Ann & her sister Elizabeth were residual legatees of the will of their bro. John Sherman in 1686 (HCVW-1 p. 24); children from wills of their father and grandmother Sherman:

        21-1 Christopher Branch
        21-2 Ann Branch
        21-3 Ciceley Branch
        21-4 Mary Branch
        21-5 Henry Branch
        21-6 Susannah Branch
        21-7 Obedience Branch

1 Jun 1704; 1 Jun 1704; from Christopher Branch and Ann his wife of Varina Parish, Henrico; deed of gift to son Henry, an infant; 125 ac. part of *Garners* willed to Ann by her former husband John Crowley; bounded by *Falling Creek* (HCVD-1 p. 132)

Will of Christopher Branch; Henrico Co.; 11 Aug 1727; 1 Jan 1727
To daus. Mary Walter and Sissanah Bass, items
To dau. Obedience Cheatham, a cow in poss. of William Cheatham
To son Henry, ex., remainder
Wit: Henry Vanderhood, Seth Ward, William Baugh (HCVW-1 p. 165)

   21-1 Christopher Branch.; he rec'd a gift of a negro girl to be delivered to his parents at the death of his grandmother Ciscelia Sherman (HCVD-1 p. 107); he is not mentioned in the will of his father; ?d. young
   21-2 Ann Branch; she inherited a cow from her grandmother Sherman; not mentioned in father's will; ?d. young
   21-3 Ciceley (Cecellia) Branch; m. **William Bass**; d. aft. 27 Feb 1746/7; Ciceley inherited a heifer from her grandmother Sherman; children:

     213-1 William Bass
     213-2 Christopher Bass; d. aft. 8 Nov 1772 Chesterfield Co.; m. **Frances** ____
     213-3 Edward Bass
     213-4 Joseph Bass
     213-5 Mary Bass; m. ____ **Walthall**
     213-6 Ann Bass; m. ____ **Branch**; she chose William Walthall as guardian Jan 1755 (ChOB 2.30)
     213-7 Elizabeth Bass; m. ____ **Wilkinson**; she chose Joseph Bass as her guardian 5 Oct 1759 (ChOB 3.24)
     213-8 Sarah Bass; m. **Thomas Friend**; d. by 7 Apr 1769 Chesterfield Co. (ChWB 2.93)

Jun Ct. 1722; from William Bass to Henry Farmer, deed; Cicely, w/o William, relinquished dower right (HCVD-2 p. 196)

3 Jan 1731; 1st Mon Jun 1732; from William Bass to Arthur Mosely, both of Henrico Co.; for £8; 100 ac. on s. side of James River on *Cattail Branch*; Cicely, w/o William relinquished dower rights (HCVD-2 p. 138)

Will of William Bass of Dale Parish, Chesterfield Co.; 27 Feb 1746/7
To wife Stella (sic), 400 ac. Henrico Co. near *Skin Quarter Creek* for widowhood, then
   to son William
To son Christopher, plantation where he now lives; also 250 ac. Goochland; 2 negroes
To son Edward, 400 ac. Henrico, part of 800 ac., 3 negroes, items
To son Joseph, plantation where I live, 3 negroes, items
To dau. Mary Walthall, 2 negroes, livestock, silver
To daus. Ann Bass, Elizabeth Bass & Sarah Bass, 2 negroes, items
To wife Siselia, ½ of *Redwater Mill*, then to son Joseph
Friends Thomas & Benjamin Branch and Seth Ward to settle any disputes between
   wife & children
Remainder of negroes & personal estate to wife for widowhood, then equally to
   children
Exs: wife and son William
Wit: Jonathan Shackleton, Thomas Bass, Jeffrey Robertson (ChWB 1.134)

Will of Ciceley Bass of Dale Parish; Chesterfield Co.; 11 Nov 1769; 6 Jul 1770
To my 4 daus., Mary Walthall, Anne Branch, Elizabeth Wilkinson & Sarah Friend,
   wearing clothes, equally divided; and to the first three, 20s each
Rest of estate to son Joseph Bass and dau. Sarah Friend, equally divided
Ex: son Joseph
Wit: Samuel Hatcher, Charles Burton, Edward Hatcher (ChWB 2.38)
6 Jul 1770; will of Cecily Bass proved; Joseph Bass, ex., granted probate (ChOB 4.429)

21-4 **Mary Branch**; although some family histories disagree,
   circumstantial evidence suggests she m. bef. 1722 **Richard Walthall**; d.
   by Oct 1744; s/o Richard Walthall; children from his will:

   214-1 **Richard Walthall**
   214-2 **Ann Walthall**
   214-3 **Isabel Walthall**
   214-4 **Mary Walthall**
   214-5 **Elizabeth Walthall**
   214-6 **Christopher Walthall**
   214-7 **Henry Walthall**
   214-8 **William Walthall**

Jun Ct. 1722; from Richard Walthall to William Pride; deed; Mary, w/o Richard,
relinquished dower rights (HCVD-2 p. 195)

Will of Richard Walthall; Henrico Co.; 19 Jun 1744; Oct 1744
To son Richard, plantation I live on
To daus: Ann, Isabel, Mary & Elizabeth Walthall, negroes, items
To son Christopher, 300 ac. in Amelia Co., negroes, items
To son Henry, remainder of land in Amelia Co., negroes, items
To son William, negro
Remainder to wife Mary; she and son Richard to be exs.
Wit: Henry Walthall, Jarrat Walthall, William Walthall (HCVW-2 p. 111)
Oct Ct. 1744; Mary & Richard Walthall, exs., present will of Richard Walthall (HCVW-
   2 p. 23)

2 Sep 1745; Sep 1745; inventory of Richard Walthall taken and recoded by Richard and Mary Walthall (HCVW-2 p. 27)

21-5 **Henry Branch**; infant in 1704; d. by 28 Jul 1748; m. cousin **Amy Branch**; d/o Thomas Branch and Elizabeth Archer; he was given 125 ac. part of *Garners* in 1704 by his parents; children from family histories:

> 215-1 Christopher Branch
> 215-2 Martha Branch
> 215-3 Henry Branch
> 215-4 Elizabeth Branch
> 215-5 William Branch
> 215-6 Ann Branch

7 Oct 1728; 1st Mon Oct 1728; from Henry Branch to Dudley Diggs, Gent., both of Henrico Co.; for £200; 180 ac. called *Gardners* on s. side of James River; Amy, w/o Henry, relinquished dower rights (HCVD-2 p. 114)

28 Jul 1748; Aug 1748; inventory of Henry Branch appraised; value £407.3.9 (HCVW-2 p. 46)
[Henry Branch; Henrico County Wills and Administrations (1662-1800) p. 23-24. Inv. & appr. rec. Aug. 1748. Deeds, Etc., 1748-1750 (Reel 8) (LOV)]

6 May 1751; Christopher Branch, orphan of Henry, dec'd, chooses Amey Branch as guardian (ChOV 1.110); Aug 8 Ct. 1752 Amy Branch guardian to Christopher Branch (ChOB 1.257) ; 1 Apr Ct. 1754; Henry, orphan of Henry bound out by the churchwardens of Dale Parish (ChOB 1.436); 5 Aug 1757; Amy was ordered to return accounts as guardian of Christopher and Elizabeth Branch (ChOB 2.335); 2 Jun 1758; William Branch, orphan of Henry bound by churchwardens (ChOB 2.422)

215-1 **Christopher Branch**; d. 1772 Chesterfield; m. **Mary** ____; 5 Jun 1767 Christopher bought 468 ac in Chesterfield Co. from Archibald Cary and 140 ac. from Charles Burton, Jr. (ChDB 5.518, 519); children from wills:

> 2151-1 Archer Branch
> 2151-2 Christopher Branch
> 2151-3 Elizabeth Branch

6 May 1763; May 1763; whereas my father, Henry Branch, dying intestate, and I being under guardianship, about 1752 William Giles who m. my sister Mary, brought suit in Chancery for division of my father's estate; division was made and he had from it a negro girl who has since had 2 children who have since been in his possession; I give up any possible right to these negroes to sd. Giles for love for my sister Mary and him; /s/ Christopher Branch (ChDB 4.475)

Will of Christopher Branch of Dale Parish; Chesterfield Co.; 17 Mar 1772; 7 Aug 1772
To wife Mary, I lend my plantation, *The Grove*, for life, negroes, items
To my sister Martha, 1 negro
To son Christopher, all my lands in this county
To son Archer, all my lands in Henrico County
To my dau. Elizabeth Branch, £1,000 at marriage or 21, 1 negro
Remainder of negroes to be divided between my 2 sons when Christopher is 21

Exs: Friend John Archer, brother Henry Branch
Wit: E. Osborne, Benj. Horner, Nathan Horner (ChWB 2.31)
7 Aug 1772; will of Christopher Branch presented by John Archer & Henry Branch,
exs. (ChOB 5.132)

> 2151-1 **Archer Branch**; minor in 1773; d. by 13 Oct 1794; m. 28 Jun
> 1786 Manchester Parish, Episcopal Church **Mary Bernard**; d/o
> William Bernard who gave consent 20 Apr 1789; on 8 Jun 1786
> William Fleming also gave consent for her to marry (MCC p. 19);
> Archer mentioned in deed of 7 Dec 1772 as "infant son of
> Christopher Branch" (HCVD-5 p. 498; TVF 12.122); he inherited from the
> 1773 will of his grandfather, John Archer, Sr. (ChWB 2.28) and the
> 1773 will of his aunt Martha Branch

Ct. 13 Oct 1794; Joseph Branch granted administration of estate of Archer
Branch (ChOB 10.507); Ct. 11 Jun 1798; Mary Branch, widow of Archer Branch,
dec'd, granted administration of his estate (ChOB 12.482)

> 2151-2 **Christopher Branch**; minor in 1773; ?d. by ca Ct. 8 Jan 1798
> when administration of the estate of a Christopher Branch was
> granted William Ball by the Chesterfield Co. Court (ChOB 12.373); he
> inherited from the 1773 will of his grandfather, John Archer, Sr., and
> the 1773 will of his aunt Martha Branch
>
> 2151-3 **Elizabeth Branch**, orphan of Christopher chooses Henry
> Archer, Gent., as her guardian Ct. 6 Jun 1782 (ChOB 6.356)

> 215-2 **Martha Branch**; d. by 1 Apr 1774 Chesterfield Co.; unmarried

Will of Martha Branch of Dale Parish, Chesterfield Co.; 31 Oct 1773; 1 Apr 1774
To nephews Christopher & Archer, sons of Christopher, dec'd, 1 negro when Archer is
21
To niece Amy Giles, my wearing apparel
Exs: bro. Henry Branch, John Archer, Jr.
Wit: John Archer, Jr., Henry Branch (ChWB 2.232)
Ct. 1 Apr 1774; will of Martha Branch proved by John Archer & Henry Branch (ChOB
6.3)

> 215-3 **Henry Branch**; d. by 8 Jan 1798 Chesterfield Co.; m. **Tabitha**
> ____ Chesterfield Co.; children:

> > 2153-1 **Joseph Branch**; d. aft. 15 Oct 1801; m. **Susanna** ____;
> > Joseph's will written 15 Oct 1801 Chesterfield Co. left £5 to his
> > unnamed son by his wife Susanna and remainder of estate to his bro.
> > Henry; proved 14 Dec 1801, ex, Henry Branch; inventory 19 Dec
> > 1801, value £372.9.6 (ChWB 5.461, 554; ChOB 14.185)
> >
> > 2153-2 **William Branch**
> > 2153-3 **Judith Branch**
> > 2153-4 **John Branch**

2153-5 **Pollina Fowler Branch**; mb. 5 Sep 1805 Chesterfield Co.
Thomas Fore (MCC p. 50)

2153-6 **Henry Branch**; m. by 1800 ____ **Markham**; d/o George
Markham (ChWB 5.344)

2153-7 **Matthew Hobson Branch**

2153-8 **Robert F. Branch**; mb. 19 Dec 1711 **Mary Tatum**; d/o Henry
Tatum; sur. Parke Poindexter (MCC p. 20)

2153-9 **Lucy** or **Leroy Branch**

Ct. 8 Jan 1798; Tabitha Branch granted administration of estate of Henry Branch
(ChOB 12.373)

Ct. 14 Jan 1799; William, Judith, John, Palina, Henry, Matt. Hobson, Robert and Lucy
Branch, infants under 21, by William Branch their next friend, also Joseph Branch and
Susanna his wife; vs.; Tabitha Branch, widow and adm'x of Henry Branch, dec'd;
court orders division of estate into 9 equal parts after widow has taken her dower
(ChOB 12.652)

Ct. 9 Dec 1799; Tabitha Branch appointed guardian to Judith, John, Pollina Fowler,
Henry, Matt Hopson, Robert and Leroy Branch, orphans of Henry Branch, dec'd
(ChOB 13.164)

215-4 **Elizabeth Branch**; m. ____ **Worsham**; as orphan of Henry
Branch, she chose Thomas Branch as guardian 7 Feb 1752 (ChOB 1.170)

215-5 **William Branch**; d. by 10 Apr 1797 Chesterfield Co.; mb. 20 Sep
1764 Amelia Co. **Judith Scott**; children from William's will:

2155-1 **William Branch**

2155-2 **Joseph Branch**

2155-3 **Henry Branch**

2155-4 **Thomas Branch**

2155-5 **Francis Branch**

2155-6 **Judith Branch**

2155-7 **Martha Branch**

Will of William Branch, Sr.; Chesterfield Co.; 14 Nov 1796; 10 Apr 1797
To son William, 344 ac. where he lives, all slaves he has, items
To son Joseph, 400 ac. called [illegible]
To son Henry, 700 ac. my land in Georgia on *Upton Creek*
To son Thomas, 250 ac. and 900 ac. on *Crump Creek* in Georgia
To son Francis, land I live on after death of his mother
To 2 daus. Judith and Martha, 260 ac. Botetourt Co. on w. fork of *Little River*
To wife Judith; land we live on for life, when a child separates from the family he or
she may receive their lot
Wit: George Evans, Richard Watkins (ChWB 5.132)
Ct. 10 Apr 1797; will of William Branch proved by abv. witnesses (ChOB 12.153)
Ct. 9 Oct 1797; Judith Branch, extx. of William Branch, granted probate (ChOB 12.318)

215-6 **Ann Branch**; m. **William Giles**; d. by 25 Sep 1794 Amelia Co.

[William Giles; Amelia County Wills and Administrations (1734 - 1800) p. 107-109. Will pro. 25 Sept. 1794. Will Book No. 5, 1793-1799 (Reel 30) (LOV)]

21-6 Susannah Branch
21-7 Obedience Branch; d. aft. 12 Feb 1771 Chesterfield Co.; m. bef. Aug 1727 William Cheatham; d. aft. 25 Apr 1751; children from their wills:

    217-1 **William Cheatham**
    217-2 **Thomas Cheatham**
    217-3 **Christopher Cheatham**
    217-4 **Obedience Cheatham**
    217-5 **Ann Cheatham**
    217-6 **Mary Cheatham**

1733; 1st Mon Jul 1733; from William Cheatham of Henrico Co. & Parish to William Pride of Bristol Parish; for £35; 370 ac. in Bristol Parish on n. side of *Swift Creek*; bounded by *Hatcher's Run, Cross Swamp*, etc.; Obedience, w/o William, relinquished dower (HCVD-2 p. 147)

3 Dec 1733; from William Cheatham to his bro. Thomas Cheatham, both of Henrico Co. & Parish; for £20; 75 ac. taken up by Mr. Robert Hancock; Obedience, w/o William, relinquished dower (HCVD-2 p. 153)

Will of William Cheatham of Dale Parish, Chesterfield Co.; 27 Apr 1751
To son Thomas, my plantation at *Dry Creek*, also negro & livestock
To son Christopher, plantation where I live, negro, livestock, to be in his possession at age 18
To daus. Obedience Cheatham & Ann Hill, each a negro
To dau. Mary Cheatham, 3 negroes, items
To wife Obedience, use of labor of 4 negroes during widowhood; then to my 3 sons, William, Thomas & Christopher; sons to also have money and rest of negroes equally
Exs: sons William and Thomas
Wit: William Bass, Jr., Mary Bass, Stephen Beasley, Jr. (ChWB 1.90)

Will of Obedience Cheatham of Dale Parish, Chesterfield Co.; 12 Feb 1771
To grandson William, orphan of my son Christopher, negro & 40s
To other orphans of sd. Christopher: Christopher, Thomas, Lucy & Polly Cheatham, 40s
1/3 of remainder to son William; 1/3 to son Thomas; 1/3 to children of Christopher
Exs: sons William & Thomas
Wit: Jo. Bass, Samuel Moody, William Beasley (ChWB 2.250)
13 Oct 1774; inventory of Obedience Cheatham; value £109.0.6 (ChWB 2.240)

2-2 Mary Branch; m/1 Thomas Jefferson; d. by 1 Apr 1701 Henrico Co. & Parish; she m/2 1 Apr 1701/2 Joseph Mattox of Charles City Co. (QRH p. 93)

16 Nov 1700; 1 Apr 1701; marriage contract agreement between Joseph Mattocks of Charles City Co. and Mary Jefferson, relict of Thomas Jefferson, dec'd of Henrico Co. & Parish; trustees Seth Ward, Christopher Branch, Thomas Jefferson, all of Henrico

Co.; Mary to retain all the estate she is possessed of and to have ½ of his estate after Mattocks decease; [16 Dec 1700; list of Mary Jeffersons' possession (HCVD-1 p. 115, 116)

2-3 Sarah Branch
2-4 Samuel Branch, b. ca 1663, age 28 on 8 Jun 1691 (HCVD-1 p. 64, 153); d. by 1 Aug 1700; m. **Ursula** ____; she m/2 bef. 15 Sep 1708 **Walter Scott** (MHC p. 75), b. ca 1667, age 43 on 5 Mar 1710 (VP p. 1519); d. by Feb 1746; in the 1691 deposition Samuel described where the road ran through the old field from the road through the thicket from the trees now standing a little about Xpher Branch's house the year his grandfather died; p in 1723 Walter and Ursula brought suit against Christopher Branch "action of Dower" (VP p. 1520); known children:

> 24-1 Samuel Branch
> 24-2 Martha Branch
> 24-3 Ursula Branch

Will of Samuel Branch of Varina Parish; 3 May 1700; 1 Aug 1700
To son Samuel, items, exs. to build house for him
To dau. Martha Branch, slave, items
To dau. Ursula Branch, Indian child
To wife Ursula, ex., all the plantation
Wit: John Woodson, Christopher Branch, Judith Franklin, John Goode (HCVW-1 p. 74)
1 Aug 1700; probate granted Ursula Branch on will of husband Samuel Branch (HCVW-1 p. 76)
[Samuell Branch; Henrico County Wills and Administrations (1662-1800) p. 100. Gdn. accounts rec. 1 Oct. 1711. Records, 1710-1714 (Reel 6); Henrico County Wills and Administrations (1662-1800) Note p. 191. Will pro. 1 Aug. 1700. Deeds, Wills, Etc., 1697-1704 (Reel 6) (LOV)]

20 Aug 1708; Walter Scott who m. the relict of Samuel Branch, dec'd, to give security to the orphans for what estate he has under his care (HCOB 1677-92 p. 50; VP p. 1518)

26 Feb 1729; 6 Apr 1730; from Walter Scott or Varina Parish, Henrico Co. to Thomas Green of James City Co. & Parish; for £28; 400 ac. in Varina Parish; Ursula, w/o Walter, relinquished dower right (HCVD-2 p. 123)

Will of Walter Scott of Henrico Co.; 29 Mar 1743; Feb 1746
To wife Usseley, 2 negroes and personal estate for life; then to my son William
To son Walter, 1 negro, £6
To dau. Mary Fore, 1s
To dau. Elizabeth Mullens, 1s
Ex: son William
Wit: Robert Goode, Warham Easly, Robert Easly (HCVW-2 p. 32)
[Walter Scott; Henrico County Wills and Administrations (1662-1800) p. 230-231. Will pro. Feb. 1746. Deed Book, 1744-1748 (Reel 8) (LOV)]

24-1 **Samuel Branch**; on 10 Jul 1714 he gave power of atty. to "Trusty & well beloved father Walter Scott" of Henrico Co. (VP p. 1519)
24-2 Martha Branch

24-3 **Ursula Branch**; she d. bef. 1768; m. **William Trent**; d. aft. 17 Oct
1768 Chesterfield Co.

2-5 **Benjamin Branch**, b. ca 1665; age 24 on 2 Dec 1689, age 25 on 8 Jun
1691 (HCVD-1 p. 64, 152, 153); d. by 20 Dec 1706; m. **Tabitha Osborne**; d/o
Edward Osborne; she m/2 2 Feb 1707/8 **Thomas Cheatham, Jr.**; Benjamin
held 550 ac. Henrico Co. rent roll of Apr 1705; child:

25-1 Benjamin Branch

1 Feb 1686; petition of Benjamin Branch, orphan in tuition of Christopher Branch, that
he is of lawful age to receive his estate (HCVW-1 p. 30)

6 Jun 1696; Benjamin Branch, son in law of Edward Osborne of Varina Parish (HCVW-
1 p. 64)

1 Feb 1706; inventory of Benjamin Branch; value 32,740# tobacco; Tabitha Branch,
relict and admn. presented in court (HCVW-1 p. 95)
Dec 1706; Tabitha Branch granted admn. on estate of her husband Benjamin Branch
(HCVW-1 p. 97)
10 Jul 1711; inventory of negroes on estate of Benjamin Branch; value £105.0.0;
present and recorded Aug Ct. 1711 by Thomas Chetham, Jr. who m. widow of
Benjamin Branch (HCVW-1 p. 116)
Aug 1711; accounts of estate of Benjamin Branch presented & recorded in Orphan's
Ct. by Thomas Chetham (HCVW-1 p. 116)
[Benjamin Branch; Henrico County Wills and Administrations (1662-1800) p. 16-17. Inv. & appr.
rec. 1 Feb. 1706. Records, 1706-1709 (Reel 6); Henrico County Wills and Administrations
(1662-1800) p. 167-168. Inv. & appr. rec. 1 Feb. 1706. Misc. Court Records, Vol. 1, [1650-1717]
(Reel 1); Henrico County Wills and Administrations (1662-1800) p. 95. Inv. & appr. rec. Aug.
1711: p. 96. Accounts rec. 20 Aug. 1711. Records, 1710-1714 (Reel 6) (LOV)]

25-1 **Benjamin Branch**; d. aft. 31 Dec 1760; m/1 **Mary Osborne**; d/o
Thomas Osborne whose will left his dau. Mary Branch a negro with her
issue to Mary's daus., Mary and Martha Branch (HCVW-1 p. 186); m/2
Obedience Turpin; d. aft. 31 Dec 1760 children from wills:

251-1 Mary Branch
251-2 Martha Branch
251-3 Benjamin Branch, Jr.
251-4 Thomas Branch
251-5 Edward Branch
251-6 Obedience Branch
251-7 Prudence Branch

Will of Benjamin Branch of Dale Parish, Chesterfield Co.; 31 Dec 1760; 5 Nov 1762
To son Benjamin, negro
To son Thomas, 1,023 ac. on upper *Sapony Creek* in Chesterfield and 200 ac on little
fork of *Nibs Creek* in Amelia Co., negroes
To son Edward, 427 ac. on upper *Sapony Creek* and my part of *Redwater Mill*, negroes
To daus. Obedience Bass & Prudence Thweatt, each £3; to dau. Mary Branch, £3, 8
negroes, items

To sons Thomas & Edward, all household goods not given; they to be exs. with Robert Goode

Wit: Samuel Hatcher, Jr., Charles Hatcher, Edward Hatcher (ChWB 1.II.335)

5 Nov 1762; will of Benjamin Branch presented by Thomas & Edward Branch (ChOB 3.271)

Aug 1763; inventory returned (ChOB 3.444); [undated]; accounts of Benjamin Branch (ChWB 2.52)

251-1 **Mary Branch**; she inherited from her grandfather Osborne and from her father she inherited £3, 8 negroes & items; as orphan of Benjamin, she chose Robert Goode as guardian (ChOB 3.272)

251-2 **Martha Branch**; she was a legatee of her grandfather Osborne

251-3 **Benjamin Branch, Jr.**; d. by 13 Jul 1786; m. **Mary** ____; children:

2513-1 **Benjamin Branch**; mb. 1 Dec 1780 **Betty Eppes Osborne**; d/o Edward Osborne; 5 Dec 1750 Benjamin Branch, Jr. of Amelia Co. is listed as the owner of lot #18 sold by the Vestry of Dale Parish (ChDB 4.187); Betty's father's will dated 21 Apr 1781 left her 7 negroes and use of 9 negroes for life, to be divided among her children at her death (ChWB 3.260); Betty was a legatee of the will of her brother, Edward Osborne, dated 7 Mar 1783 which also left Benjamin a stud horse (ChWB 3.380; ChOB 6.426); he inherited the plantation of his uncle Thomas of 600 ac. in Chesterfield Co.

2513-2 **Edward Branch**

2513-3 **Anne Branch**; m. ____ **Jones**

2513-4 **Thomas Branch**; he inherited 2 negroes from his uncle Thomas

2513-5 **Obedience Branch**; mb. 28 Feb 1788 Amelia Co. **Joseph Wilderson**

Will of Benjamin Branch of Dale Parish; [undated]; 13 Jul 1786

To wife Mary, 6 negroes got by her when I married her

To son Benjamin, 3 negroes, items

To son Edward, plantation & land I live on; ½ of *Red Water Mill*, 3 negroes

To dau. Anne Jones, 3 negroes, items

To son Thomas, land & plantation in Amelia Co., 3 negroes

To dau. Obedience Branch, 3 negroes

Rest to sons Edward & Thomas equally

Exs: 3 friends & kinsmen, Edward Bass, Edward Branch, Thos. Augt's Taylor (ChWB 4.119)

Ct. 13 Jul 1786; will of Benjamin Branch proved; Thomas Augustus Taylor, wit. (ChOB 7.344)

251-4 **Thomas Branch**; d. aft 22 Apr 1778; unmarried

Will of Thomas Branch of Manchester Parish; 22 Apr 1778; 5 Jun 1778

To nephew Benjamin Branch, s/o Benjamin, my home plantation of 600 ac. in Chesterfield Co.; bounded by Henry Branch & John Rudd, also 6 negroes

To nephew Thomas Branch, s/o Benjamin, 2 negroes
To nephew Thomas Branch, s/o Edward, 2 negroes
To nephew Benjamin Thweatt, 2 negroes
To niece Molly Branch, d/o Edward, 1 negro
Rest of my Chesterfield lands to be divided equally between Benjamin Thweatt and
   Thomas Branch, s/o Edward; tract where William Thweatt lives to Benjamin after
   death of my sister Prudence Thweatt
I lend to my sister Prudence Thweatt the plantation she lives on for life and 14 negroes
   to be divided among her children
Rest of estate to be divided among 4 above named nephews
Exs: brothers Benjamin and Edward Branch
Wit: John Robertson, John Rudd, Mary Pilkinton (ChWB 3.150)
Ct. 5 Jun 1778; will of Thomas Branch proved; Benjamin & Edward Branch, exs.;
   above 3 witnesses (ChOB 6.173)

   251-5 **Edward Branch**; d. by Apr 1786 Manchester Parish; mb. 6 Jul
   1764 Amelia Co. **Lucy Finney**; 3 Jun 1763 he conveyed ½ part of *Red
   Water Mill* and lands belonging thereto to Benjamin Branch, recorded 4
   Jun 1765 (ChWB 4.586); children from Edward's will and guardian bond:

      2515-1 **Edward Branch**, b. ca 1765; of age when his father died; mb.
      5 Nov 1787 Amelia Co. **Martha Bott**; d/o Miles Bott
      2515-2 **Thomas Branch**; mb. Dec 1792 Amelia Co. **Mary Walker**;
      he inherited 2 negroes & ½ the remainder of the Chesterfield lands of
      his uncle Thomas Branch
      2515-3 **William Branch**
      2515-4 **Benjamin Branch**; m. Jan 1801 Amelia Co. **Sarah Botts**;
      Benjamin not named in guardian bond; as orphan of Edward Branch,
      he chose Thomas Branch as his guardian Ct. 12 Oct 1795 (ChOB
      11.228)
      2515-5 **Mary (Molly) Branch**; m. 18 Oct 1781 Chesterfield Co.
      William Parham; surety Edward Branch (MCC p. 93); Molly inherited
      a negro from her uncle Thomas Branch
      2515-6 **Lucy Branch**; m. **James Botte**
      2515-7 **Obedience Turpin Branch**; m. 28 Apr 1789 Chesterfield Co.;
      William Williamson Hall; Obedience m. with consent of her mother
      Lucy Branch; sur. William Bottoms (MCC p. 62)
      2515-8 **Judith Finney Branch**; mc. 14 Dec 1793 **George Walker**;
      consent of Judith's mother Lucy Branch; wit. Edward Branch, D.
      Coleman (MCC p. 124)
      2515-9 **Elizabeth Branch**; m. 3 Jun 1794 Chesterfield Co. **William
      Mann**; Elizabeth m. with consent of her mother Lucy Branch; sur.
      Edward Branch (MCC p. 83)
      2515-10 **Prudence Branch**
      2515-11 **Page Branch**, b. after father's will was written
      2515-12 **Sally Branch**, b. after father's will was written

3 Jun 1763; 4 Jun 1765; from Edward Branch of Chesterfield Co. to Benjamin Branch of Amelia Co.; for 5s; ½ part of *Red Water Mill* (ChDB 3.586)

Will of Edward Branch of Manchester Parish; Chesterfield Co.; 5 Jan 1781; Apr 1786
To wife Lucy, plantation I live on for life, 4 negroes, etc.
To son Edward, 400 ac. Charlotte Co., 2 negroes
To son Thomas, 2 negroes, 10,000# tobacco
To son William, 624 ac. Lunenburg Co., 2 negroes
To son Benjamin, aft. my wife's death, plantation I live on, 2 negroes
To my 6 daus. Molly, Lucy, Obedience Turpin, Juday Finney, Elizabeth & Prudence Branch, equally 6 negroes
To my daus. Lucy Branch, Obedience Turpin Branch, Juday Finney Branch, Elizabeth Branch & Prudence Branch, each a bed, etc.
Remainder of personal estate to my 4 sons Edward, Thomas, William & Benjamin
Exs: brother Benjamin Branch and William Finney
Wit: William Thweatt, Jr., Benjamin Thweatt (ChWB 4.104)
Ct. Apr 1786; will of Edward Branch proved; William Finney, one of the exs. (ChOB 7.335)
Ct. 11 Oct 1787; administration with will annexed of estate of Edward Branch granted to Lucy Branch (ChOB 7.576)

Ct. 11 Oct 1787; Francis Goode appointed guardian to Juddy, Elizabeth, Prudence, Obedience, Page and Sally Branch and was chosen guardian by Thomas and William Branch, orphans of Edward Branch (ChOB 7.577)

Ct. 12 May 1786; James Botte & Lucy his wife, William Parham & Molly his wife, William Mann & Elizabeth his wife, William Hall & Obedience his wife, George Walker and Lucy (sic) his wife, and Prudence Branch; vs.; Lucy Branch, adm'x, de bonis non of Edward Branch, dec'd; estate to be divided by court order (ChOB 11.466)

    251-6 Obedience Branch; m. ____ **Bass**
    251-7 Prudence Branch; m. ____ **Thweatt**; she inherited the land she lived on for life, also 14 negroes to be divided among her children after her death; known child:

        2517-1 Benjamin Thweatt; he inherited 2 negroes from his uncle Thomas Branch & the land where William Thweatt lived after his mother's death

3. **William Branch**; d. bef. 1678; m. **Jane** ____, b. ca 1640; d. by Jan Ct. 1710 (HCVD-1 p. 152); she m/2 **William Baugh**; m/3 **Abel Gower** (d. by 1 Jun 1689); known children:
        3-1 William Branch
        3-2 John Branch

3-1 **William Branch**; unmarried

17 Aug 1725; William Branch granted 400 ac. Henrico Co. on n. side of Appomattox between Branch and Joseph Irby (LOP 12.312)

3-2　**John Branch** of *Kingsland*; d. by 2 Apr 1688; m. **Martha ?Grigg**; she
m/2 **Thomas Osborne, Sr.**; d. by 1 Aug 1692; m/3　26 Oct 1693 Henrico
Co. **Thomas Edwards**; known children:

32-1　Obedience Branch
32-2　Priscilla Branch

2 Apr 1688; [recorded]; Martha Branch, relict and extx. granted probate on will of
John Branch (HCVW-1 p. 31)

1 Jun 1700 [recorded]; John Cocke of Varina Parish and Obedience his wife, d/o John
Branch, release Thomas Edwards for all debts as ex. of John Branch or his dau.
Obedience in right of Martha, our mother, w/o sd. Edwards; Prisilla Branch one of the
witnesses (HCVD-1 p. 112)

32-1　**Obedience Branch**; d. aft. 1724; m/1 24 Nov 1696 Henrico Co.
John Cocke; sur. Richard Cocke, Thomas Edwards (MHC p. 20); John d.
by 1699; m/2 **Alexander Trent**, d. by 1703; m/3 by 1710 **Thomas
Turpin**, d. by 1724; Obedience and Priscilla were contingent legatees in
will of Abel Gower written 1688 (HCVW-1 p. 34)

32-2　**Priscilla Branch**; ml/1 16 Jul 1699 **Edward Skerme** (MHC p. 77); she
m/2 7 Jul 1700 St. John's Church to **Joseph Wilkinson**

31 Mar 1711; Thomas Turpin & wife Obedience and Joseph Wilkinson & wife
Priscilla, all of Henrico Co., deeded to Richard Dennis the 101 ac. tract (HCVD-1 p.
27) near a *Great Stone* granted Abel Gower in 1673; Abel's 1689 will names
Obedience & Priscilla Branch contingent legatees should his dau. Tabitha d. before age
21; Jane Gower lived on the tract until 1710 when she died leaving a will conveying
the tract to her granddaus. Obedience and Priscilla.

Unplaced:
____ Branch; m. Jemima Brittain, d/o William Brittain of Chesterfield Co.;
William's will written 22 Jul 1764 leaves dau. Jemima Branch a negro for life
and at her death to his granddau. Lucy Branch, with the increase to her
brothers & sisters (ChWB 2.48)

BURTON

Family histories of the Burton family suggest that John Burton and Thomas
Burton were brothers and that there were at least two sisters:
Jane; who married William Branch, William Baugh and Abel Gower
Mary; who married Edward Hatcher

JOHN BURTON

John Burton; of *Longfield*; d. by 1 Apr 1690 Henrico Co.; possibly m.
____ **Hutchins** as that appears as a given name in male descendants; children
from wills:

1. John Burton, Jr.
2. Robert Burton
3. Benjamin Burton
4. Anne Burton
5. William Burton
6. Rachel Burton
7. Mary Burton

22 March 1665/1666; John Burton patented in Henrico Co. 700 acres part of the land
being northerly on a great swamp; Southly towards the land of Alice Edlowe, widow.
The residue of the land lying at the head of the *Long Field* (LOP 5.585)

27 Feb 1683/4; 1 Oct 1684; from John Burton of Henrico Co. & Parish to sons William
and Benjamin Burton; 100 ac. called *The Leavill* between *Longfield* and *Roundabout*;
part next to *Longfield* goes to John (sic) and that next to *Roundabout* to Benjamin
(HCVD-1 p. 27)

Will of John Burton; 12 Feb 1689; 1 Apr 1690
To son Robert, ex., plantation where I lived
To son William, plantation where he lives
To dau. Rachel, items
Grandchildren: Mary, William and Elizabeth Davis, items
Mentions dau. Mary Glover and her dau. Elizabeth
Wit: William Glover, James Morris, Richard Perrin (HCVW-1 p. 39)
[John Burton; Henrico County Wills and Administrations (1662-1800) p. 115. Will pro. 1 Apr.
1690. p. Exors. bond rec. 19 Apr. 1690. Deeds, Wills, Etc., 1688-1697 (Reel 5) (LOV)]

1. **John Burton, Jr.**, b. est. ca 1650's; d. by 2 Feb 1679/80; m. **Mary Hatcher**;
    d/o Edward Hatcher & Mary; she m/2 **Gilbert Elam, Jr.**; d. by 5 Dec 1697;
    Gilbert's will mentions his father in law Edward Hatcher (HCVW-1 p. 68); ml/3
    3 Jan 1697 Henrico Co. **James Fale (Fall)**; d. by 2 Mar 1712 (HCVW-1 p. 122);
    John Burton & his dau. were both dec'd before his father; John identified by
    the plantation name and siblings mentioned in his will; child:

    1-1 Elizabeth Burton

1679; Henrico Co. list of tithable; John Burton, Jr., 5

Will of John Burton of *Longfield* Henrico Co.; 30 Dec 1679; 2 Feb 1679/80
To bros. Robert, Benjamin and Will, items
To sister Anne Burton, livestock; to sister Rachel's 3 children
To wife, extx., and young dau., remainder; bro. Robert to assist
Wit: George Cogbill, Edmund Blesher, Leon Ballowe (HCVW-1 p. 7)
1 Apr 1682; inv. of John Burton, Jr. (HCVW-1 p. 11)
[John Burton, Jr.; Henrico County Wills and Administrations (1662-1800) p. 118. Will pro. 2 Feb.
1679. p. 145. Exors. bond rec. 1 Oct. 1679. p. 215. Inv. rec. 1 June 1682. Records, 1677-1692
(Reel 4) (LOV)]

1-1 **Elizabeth Burton**, b. est. ca 1679-80; d. by 1687

1 Oct 1687; Elizabeth Burton; d. intestate; her mother, Mary, w/o Gilbert Elam, Jr., to admn. estate "after some debate" (HCVW-1 p. 25, 30)
[Elizabeth Burton; Henrico County Wills & Administrations (1662-1800) p. 468. Adms. bond rec. 21 Oct. 1687. Records, 1677-1692 (Reel 4) (LOV)}

2. **Robert Burton**; of *Longfield*; b. est. ca 1650's; m. **Mary** _____; some family histories say he m. ca 1686 Charles City Co. **Mary Nowell**; d/o John Nowell and Lydia Perkins; while others say he m. **Mary Knowles**, relation of a Capt. John Knowles; Robert held 1,350 ac. in Henrico Co. according to the 1705 rent rolls; [sons are speculative; use with caution]:

> 2-1 Robert Burton
> 2-2 John Burton
> 2-3 Benjamin Burton
> 2-4 Hutchins Burton
> 2-5 Nowell Burton

1 Dec 1686; 300 ac. due Robert Burton for importation of 6 persons (HCVD-1 p. 140)

2 Oct 1693; John Iremonger announces he is bound home for England and is living at Robert Burton's at *Longfield* (HCVD-1 p. 80)

6 Jun 1699; Robert Burton patented 1,300 ac. in Henrico Co.; next to *Lilly Valley* (LOP 9.187)

1 Apr 1700; 1 May 1700; from Robert Burton to William Hobson; for 291# tobacco; 150 ac. part of 1,300 ac. on n. side of James River near *Cornelius Creek*; part of 1,300 ac. granted me and lapsed; Mary, w/o Robert, relinquished dower (HCVD-1 p. 112)

25 Apr 1701; Robert Burton, Sr. patented 300 ac. in Varina Parish of Henrico Co. on e. side of *Corneleses Creek* (LOP 9.307)

1 Apr 1711; 1st Mon Apr 1711; from Robert Burton, Sr. of Henrico Co. & Parish, to William Cox, Sr.; for 20s; 50 ac. in same parish; n. side of James River; Mary, w/o Robert, relinquished dower (HCVD-2 p. 27)

15 Jul 1717; Robert Burton patented 17 ac. 3 rood in Varina Parish Henrico Co. on n. side of James River bounding on head of *Longfield* patent (LOP 10.324)

2-1 **Robert Burton, Jr.**; d. by 18 Oct 1748 Goochland Co.; said to have m. **Priscilla Farrar**; b. est. ca 1698 Henrico Co.; d. aft. 18 Oct 1748 Goochland Co.; children from their father's will:

> 21-1 Robert Burton
> 21-2 Noel Burton
> 21-3 Anne Burton, b. 24 Sep 1725
> 21-4 Judith Burton
> 21-5 Priscilla Burton
> 21-6 William Burton
> 21-7 Elizabeth Burton, b. 24 Sep 1738

5 May 1746; 1ˢᵗ Mon May 1746; from Robert Burton of Henrico Co. to William Hopkins; for £40; lots # 85, 86, 99, 100, 101 in *Town of Richmond*; Priscillah, w/o Robert, relinquished dower rights (HCVD-3 p. 25)

Will of Robert Burton of Goochland Co.; "sick & weak" 30 Mar 1748; 18 Oct 1748
To my wife, mare, slaves, if she does not want negro Jane, then to dau. Anne
To son Noel, negro at wife's death, my desk, mare & land where I dwell
To grandson Charles Burton, s/o Robert, negro
To daus. Judah and Presilah, negro now with each of them
To son Robert, negro
To grandson Robert Sanders, items
To son William, large table
To dau. Anne, cows & calves
Rest of estate to wife and after her death to Noel
Exs: my wife, son Robert and William Miller
Wit: Will'm Miller, Richard Farrar, Gideon Hogg (GCWD-1 p. 28)
18 Apr 1749; inventory of Robert Burton, dec'd; value not totaled (GCWD-1 p. 29)
[Robert Burton; Goochland County Wills and Administrations (1728 - 1800) p. 487-489. Will pro. 18 Oct. 1748. p. 538-539. Inv. & Appr. rec. 18 Apr 1749. Deed Book No. 5, 1745-1749 (Reel 2) (LOV)]

21-1 **Robert Burton, Capt.**, b. est. ca 1718; said to have d. Orange Co., NC; m/1 ____; mb/2 17 Mar 1752 Henrico Co. **Sarah Jordan**; mb/3 1 Oct 1757 Goochland Co.; m/3 13 Oct 1757 St. James Northam Parish **Judith LaForce**, both of this parish, mb. certificate giving her age upwards of 21, wit. William Stamps and William Burton; Robert was a member of the Vestry of St. James Northam Parish Oct 1756; children from the Douglas Register:

211-1 **Charles Burton**, b. Jan 1740; d. Pittsylvania Co.; mb. 2 Nov 1763 Goochland Co.; m. 3 Nov 1763 **Mary Holland** (DR); letter of consent from Robert Burton, father of Charles who was b. Jan 1740; he inherited a negro from the will of his grandfather Burton; children:

2111-1 **George Burton**, b. 3 Jul 1764; bapt. 9 Sep 1764 (DR); d. ca 1815 Pittsylvania Co.
2111-2 **Edmund Burton**, b. 22 Sep 1765; bapt. 28 Sep 1765 (DR)

211-2 **Ann Burton**; mb. 20 Jul 1762 Goochland Co.; m. 22 Jul **Robert Payne, Jr.**, both of this parish (DR); Robert d. ca 1785 Pittsylvania Co.; 3 of their children:

2112-1 **Elizabeth Payne**, b. 31 Mar 1763; bapt. 1763 (DR)
2112-2 **Kiturah Payne**, b. 2 Jan 1765; bapt. 17 Feb 1765 (DR)
2112-3 **Ann Payne**, b. 13 Nov 1766; bapt. 14 Dec 1766 (DR)

Children of Judith Laforce:
211-3 **Sarah Burton**, b. 16 Jul 1758; bapt. 29 Jul 1758 (DR)
211-4 **Elizabeth Burton**, b. 11 Nov 1759; from family histories

211-5 **Priscilla Burton**, b. 29 May 1761; bapt. 12 Jul 1761 (DR)
211-6 **Jean Burton**, b. 29 Mar 1765; bapt. 27 Apr 1765 (DR)
211-7 **Lucy Burton**, b. 13 May 1767; bapt. 5 Jul 1767 (DR)

21-2 **Noel Burton, Capt.**; d. May 1769; funeral 31 May 1769 St. James
Northam; m. **Lucy Barrett**; only d/o James Barrett of Goochland whose
1740 will left her 2 negroes (GCWD-2 p. 46) and Sarah _____ his wife; Noel
was a warden of St. James Northam Parish in 1761; he bought 317 ac. in
Goochland Co. in 1757 (GCDB 7.162, 163); Lucy is said to have gone to NC;
children from Douglas Register:

212-1 **Robert Burton**, b. 9 Apr 1756; bapt. 9 May 1756 (DR)
212-2 **Priscilla Burton**, b. 26 Dec 1757; bapt. 1 Jan 1758 (DR)
212-3 **Elizabeth Burton**, b. 11 Nov 1759; bapt. 25 Dec 1759 (DR)
212-4 **William Barrett Burton**, b. 2 Apr 1765; bapt. 28 Apr 1765 (DR)
212-5 **Anne Burton**, b. 20 Feb 1768; bapt. 3 Apr 1768 (DR) [probably this
d.o.b. belongs to Anne]
212-6 **James Burton**

22 Feb 1780; from Sarah Barrett of Caswell Co., North Carolina, deed of gift to her
grandsons James Burton & William Barrett Burton & granddau. Anne Burton;
household goods and furniture to be distributed after her death (Caswell Co. Deed Book
A.305)

22 Feb 1780; from Sarah Barrett of Caswell Co., North Carolina, deed of gift [after her
death] to her grandson Robert Burton, negroes, articles (Caswell Co. Deed Book A.306)

21-3 **Anne Burton**, b. 12 Aug 1725 (DR)
21-4 **Judith Burton**; m. **George Payne**, b. 21 Nov 1707 (DR); d.
Goochland; he was said to have been a relative of Dolly (Payne)
Madison; part of his children:

214-1 _____ **Payne**; d. by 5 Nov 1774 (funeral) (DR)
214-2 **Robert Burton Payne**; mb. 22 Dec 1773 Goochland Co.
Margaret Sydenham Morton, both of Goochland
214-3 **Joseph Payne**, b. 23 Mar 1758; bapt. 1758 (DR)
214-4 **Elizabeth Payne**, b. 19 Sep 1760; bapt. 6 Dec 1760 (DR)
214-5 **Richard Payne**, b. 29 Apr 1765; bapt. 26 May 1765 (DR)

21-5 **Priscilla Burton**, b. ca 1723; m. ca 1742 **Stephen Sanders**, b. 11 Dec
1714 New Kent Co.; s/o James Sanders and Sarah Scrimshire; 15 Jun
1742 Stephen was conveyed land in Goochland Co. by Robert Sanders
(GCDB 4.24) and he sold Goochland Co. land to William Johns 4 May 1745
(GCDB 4.539); children from family histories:

215-1 **Robert Sanders**; named in will of his grandfather Burton
215-2 **Stephen Sanders**; m. 29 Sep 1768 Bedford Co. **Milly Haynes**
215-3 **Sarah Sanders**; m. Buckingham Co. **Jesse Johns**
215-4 **Daniel Sanders**

215-5 Samuel Sanders

21-6 William Burton, Capt.; d. by Mar 1778 Albemarle Co.; m. bef. 1758 **Rebecca Cobbs**; d/o John Cobbs; she m/2 **Michael Thomas**; William was a churchwarden of St. James Northam Parish in 1756; children from William's will which suggests that the first 2 children listed might have been from an earlier marriage:

> 216-1 Jesse Burton
> 216-2 Rebecca Burton
> 216-3 Robert Burton
> 216-4 John Cobbs Burton
> 216-5 Philip Farrar Burton
> 216-6 William Barrett Burton
> 216-7 Mary (Polly) Burton
> 216-8 Susanna Burton

Will of William Burton, Albemarle Co.; 11 Feb 1776; Mar Ct. 1778
To son Jesse tract where he lately lived, 5 negroes
Land where I now live to be sold and money equally divided between sons Robert, John Cobbs, William & Philip Farrar Burton
I lend to my wife 4 negroes for life, then to sons Robert, John, William, Philip and daus. Polly & Susannah
Remainder of estate to divided between my 4 youngest sons and 2 daus. Polly & Susannah
To dau. Rebecca Thompson, 5s
My estate to be kept together until son William is 21
Pending suit against John Cobb to be renewed and what is recovered to be equally divided between sons Robert, John, William & Philip and 2 daus. Polly & Susannah
Exs: Jesse Burton and Robert Burton
Wit: W. Henry, William Burton, Richard Burton, Richard Perkins, Spencer Norvill (A1WB 2.360)

216-1 Jesse Burton; m. **Anne ____**; lived Albemarle Co.

5 Jul 1774; Jesse Burton granted 245 ac. on e. side of *Dover Mill Creek* Goochland Co. (LOP 42.644)

25 Jan 1775; 17 Apr 1775; from William Burton & Rebecca his wife & Jesse Burton & Anne his wife; all of Albemarle Co. to Matthew Woodson of Goochland Co.; 245 ac. on e. side of *Dover Creek* (GCDB 10.27; VP p. 1902)

216-2 Rebecca Burton; m. **____ Thompson**
216-3 Robert Burton
216-4 John Cobbs Burton, b. 27 Jan 1758; bapt. 27 May 1758 St. James Northam Parish (DR)
216-5 Philip Farrar Burton
216-6 William Barrett Burton
216-7 Mary (Polly) Burton
216-8 Susanna Burton

21-7 **Elizabeth Burton**, b. 24 Sep 1738 (DR)

2-2 **John Burton**; d. by 18 Mar 1778; m/1 **Catherine Cocke**; d. 10 Sep 1725; d/o William Cocke; m/2 ca 1726-7 **Sarah Chappell**; d. by 28 Feb 1782; d/o Robert and Sarah Chappell of Amelia Co.; Catherine is not mentioned when her sisters sold *Worlds End*; known children, partially from family histories:

> 22-1 John Burton, b. 7 Sep 1725
> Children of Sarah Chappell:
> 22-2 Mary Burton, b. 15 Jun 1728
> 22-3 Martha Burton, b. 26 May 1732
> 22-4 Rachel Burton, b. 13 Feb 1734/5
> 22-5 Sarah Burton
> 22-6 Magdalene Burton

1st Mon Sep 1728; 1st Mon Sep 1728; from John Burton to John Anderson; for £240; 317 in Henrico Parish on n. side of James River where father Robert Burton lived and now John lives; part of land granted 16 (sic) Jul 1717 to John (sic) by patent (HCVD-2 p. 113)

5 Jun 1736; John Burton granted 1,560 ac. on upper side of *Flatt Creek*, Amelia Co. (LOP 17.113)

Will of John Burton; Amelia Co.; 12 Aug 1776
To wife Sarah Burton, negroes, beds, furniture; for life: the old survey of land, furniture, etc.
To grandson Samuel Hudson, the new survey land, negroes, furniture, livestock; £100 at my wife's death; shd. he die before age 21, then to grandson Robert Hudson
To grandson Samuel Hudson; £100 to be paid at my wife's death
To granddau. Martha Burton, money to buy a negro
To grandson Robert Hudson, at my wife's death, land, slaves, etc. lent her; shd. he die without lawful heirs, then to his bro. Edward, shd he die without lawful heirs to his bro. William Hudson
To grandson Robert Hudson, remainder of estate lent wife (AmWB 2.1771-1780)
[John Burton; Amelia County Wills and Administrations (1734 - 1800) p. 254-255. Will dated 12. Aug. 1786. p. 293-295. Inv. & Appr. dated 18 Mar. 1778. Will Book No. 2, 1771-1780 (Reel 29) (LOV)]

Will of Sarah Burton; Amelia Co.; 18 Aug 1781
To daus. Martha Ward & Magdalene Walker
To grandsons William Ward, William Walker
To granddau. Mary Walker, d/o Warren Walker
To Martha Burton, granddau. of my dec'd husband, John Burton (AmWB 3.65)
[Sarah Burton; Amelia County Wills and Administrations (1734-1800) p. 54-55. Will dated 18 Aug. 1781. p. 65-66. Inv. & Appr. rec. 28 Feb. 1782. WB No. 3, 1780-1786 (Reel 29) (LOV)]

22-1 **John Burton**, b. 7 Sep 1725 Bristol Parish; s/o Catherine Cocke; m. ____; children from will of her step-grandmother, Sarah Burton and Amelia marriage records:

221-1 **Martha Burton**, b. bef. 18 Aug 1781

221-2 **John Burton**; mb. 3 Dec 1781 Amelia Co. **Martha Cocke Farley**; they went to NC

22-2 **Mary Burton**, 15 Jun 1728 Bristol Parish

22-3 **Martha Burton**, b. 25 May 1732 Bristol Parish; mb. 20 Jan 1748 Amelia Co. **Joseph Ward**; John Burton, sec.; Martha & her son named in the will of her mother:

223-1 **William Ward**, b. bef. 18 Aug 1781

22-4 **Rachel Burton**, b. 13 Feb 1734/5 Bristol Parish

22-5 **Sarah Burton**; m. **Nicholas Hudson**; d. by 28 Sep 1769 Amelia Co. when his will was recorded (AmWB 2X.301); their children from the will of their grandfather Burton:

225-1 **Samuel Hudson**, b. bef. 12 Aug 1776
225-2 **Robert Hudson**, b. bef. 12 Aug 1776
225-3 **Edward Hudson**, b. bef. 12 Aug 1776
225-4 **William Hudson**, b. bef. 12 Aug 1776

22-6 **Magdalene Burton**; d. aft. 14 Sep 1795 Cumberland Co.; m. **Warren Walker**; d. by 26 Apr 1790 Cumberland Co.; the inventory of his slaves and personal estate recorded Cumberland Co. 10 Jun 1790 & certified by Magdalene Walker and Warren Walker (CuWB 2.476); named in her mother's will; children from her mother's will:

226-1 **William Walker**
226-2 **Mary Walker**
226-3 **Warren Walker**
226-4 **Magdalene Walker**

2-3 **Benjamin Burton**; d. by Sep 1758; m/1 _____ **Cox**; d/o Sarah Cox; m/2 bef. 1734/5 **Elizabeth** _____; Benjamin's father gave him ½ of 100 ac. of *The Level* in 1684; he wit. several deeds & appraised several estates 1716-1735 Henrico Co.; Elizabeth inherited from the will of her son John; known children from wills of Benjamin and his son John:

23-1 Benjamin Burton, Jr.
23-2 Magdalene Burton
23-3 John Burton
23-4 Jacob Burton
23-5 Jesse Burton
23-6 James Burton
23-7 Edward Burton
23-8 Richard Burton

6 Jun 1737; from Benjamin Burton of Henrico Co. to Michael Turpin; 100 ac. n. side of James River where Burton formerly lived; Elizabeth, w/o Benjamin, relinquished dower (HCVD-2 p. 181)

30 Jul 1742; Benjamin Burton patented 600 ac. Henrico Co. on both sides of *Deep Run* (LOP 20.362)

5 Jun 1749; 1st Mon Jun 1749; from Benjamin Burton, Sr. of Henrico Co. & Parish, to son Jacob Burton; land now in poss. of sd. Jacob bounds mention *Coles Run* and *Mirery Run* (HCVD-3 p. 70)

Will of Benjamin Burton of Henrico Parish; 4 Sep 1758 [recorded]
To sons John and Jesse, equally, 300 ac. land I live on after death of wife, Elizabeth
To James and Jesse, 300 ac. *White Oak Swamp*, lower part of 400 ac. tract
To son Jacob, 100 ac. remainder of tract
Mentions John Allday and grandson Benjamin Allday
To son Edward, land in Goochland
To son John, 2 negroes; to son Richard
Ex: Jesse Burton (HCVW-2 p. 116)
Sep Ct. 1758; will of Benjamin Burton produced by Jesse Burton, ex. (HCVW-2 p. 75)
Oct Ct. 1758; inv. of Benjamin Burton returned (HCVW-2 p. 76)
[Benjamin Burton; Henrico County Wills and Administrations (1662-1800); p. 1777-1778. Will pro. 4 Sept. 1758. Misc. Court Records, Vol. 6, [1758-1769] (Reel 3) (LOV)]

23-1 **Benjamin Burton, Jr.**; d. by 2 Feb 1770 Chesterfield Co.; m. **Ann**
_____; Benjamin is not mentioned in father's 1758 will but is identified by witnessing deeds with his father in 1735; a Rachal Burton witnessed a deed in Henrico Co. 7 Jul 1735 with Benjamin, Jr. and his father (HCVD-2 p. 162)

1st Mon Jun 1752; [recorded]; from Benjamin Burton, Jr. to John Parker, both of Henrico Co.; for £15; 198 ac. on *Deep Run*, adj. Benjamin Burton, Jr. [and others]; Anne, w/o sd. Burton, relinquished dower (HCVD-4 p. 124; TVF 9.37)

12 May 1759; Benjamin Burton, Jr.; patented 198 ac. Henrico Co. on a branch of *Deep Run* (LOP 34.243)

30 Dec 1762; 1 Aug 1763; from Benjamin Burton of Henrico Co. to James Lyle, merchant, of Chesterfield Co.; for £192.10; ½ ac. Lot #52 in *Town of Richmond*; negro slaves, horses, cattle, furniture, etc. (HCVD-4 p. 849; TVF 10.248)

2 Feb 1770; Ann, widow of Benjamin Burton, to be summoned to say if she will take administration of estate (ChOB 4.375); 6 Apr 1770; James Lyle granted administration (Ch OB 4.388)
9 Apr 1770; inventory of Benjamin Burton; value 226.10.1; 4 Jun 1770; sale of estate; 6 May 1774; sale of estate amount £185.11.5 (ChWB 2.319, 320, 321)
[Benjamin Burton; Chesterfield County Wills and Administrations (1754-1800); Inv. & Appr. - dated 1770 Returned 6 May 1774 (O.B. 6, p. 18); ChWB 2, p. 319 (LOV)]

23-2 **Magdalene Burton**, b. bef. 1726; she may have m. **John Allday**; d. by Oct Ct. 1759 when his will was presented by Josiah Alday and proved by Luzby Turpin and Jacob Burton (HCWB-2 p. 77); Magdalene inherited a bed from her grandmother Sarah Cox in 1726 & furniture from bro. John in 1761; known child from the 1758 will of his grandfather Benjamin Burton:

232-1 Benjamin Allday

  23-3 John Burton; d. by Feb 1761 Henrico Parish; to inherit ½ of home plantation from 1758 will of his father after death of Elizabeth

26 Feb 1706; survey of Henrico Parish; John Burton, 300 ac.; 22 Mar 1707; survey of Henrico Parish; John Burton 500 ac. (HCVD-2 p. 13)

16 Jun 1714; John Burton granted 341 ac. at *Deep Creek* on s. side of James River in Henrico Co. (LOP 10.134)

17 Aug 1720; John Burton granted 500 ac. on n. side of *Swift Creek* Henrico Co. (LOP 11.46)

12 Feb 1742; John Burton granted 400 ac. in Henry Hatcher's line, Henrico Co. (LOP 21.186); John Burton granted 133 ac. on s. side of James River, adj. Henry Hatcher, etc. (LOP 21.189)

Will of John Burton of Henrico Parish; Feb Ct. 1761 [recorded]
To bro. Jesse Burton plantation given me by my father Benjamin Burton adj. plantation where I live; if he die to bro. Jacob
To bro. Jacob, land on *White Oak Swamp* given by my father
To sister Magdalene, furniture
To mother Elizabeth Burton, remainder of estate for life, then to be divided equally between bro. Jesse and Jacob, exs.
Wit: John Redford, Jr., John Stewart Redford and William Cock Redford (HCVW-2 p. 117)
Feb Ct. 1761; will presented by Jesse Burton, ex. (HCVW –2 p. 79)
Aug Ct. 1761; inv. of John Burton recorded (HCVW-2 p. 81)
[John Burton; Henrico County Wills and Administrations (1662-1800) p. 1841-1842. Will pro. Feb. 1761. Misc. Court Records, Vol. 6, [1758-1769] (Reel 3) (LOV)]

  23-4 Jacob Burton; d. by May Ct. 1765; m. **Mary** ____; in 1749 his father gave him the land he was living on and left him 100 ac. of upper part of *White Oak Swamp* in 1758; also one of the legatees of his bro. John in 1761

6 Feb 1764; 2 Apr 1764; from Jacob Burton & Mary his wife and Jesse Burton and Mary his wife to Richard Adams, all of Henrico Co.; for £60; 400 ac. adj. Robert Burton (formerly), *Deep Run*, Robert Burton (formerly), etc.; sd. tract granted Benjamin Burton 30 Jul 1742 (HCVD-4 p. 846; TVF 10.247)

May Ct. 1765; Jacob Burton, dec'd; Mary Burton renounced right of admn.; Jacob was guardian of Mary Alday (HCVW-2 p. 89)

Aug. Ct. 1765; inv. of Jacob Burton recorded (HCVW-2 p. 90)

  23-5 Jesse Burton; d. 1776 Chesterfield Co.; m. **Mary** ____; Jesse to inherit ½ of home plantation from the 1758 will of his father after death of Elizabeth, ½ of 300 ac. of lower part of *White Oak Swamp* from father's will; a legatees of his bro. John in 1761

3 Oct 1763; 3 Oct 1763; from Jesse Burton to John Burton, both of Henrico Co.; for £110; 150 ac. on branch of *Roundabout Swamp*; Mary, w/o Jessee Burton, relinquished dower (HCVD-4 p. 811; TVF 10.241)

17 Mar 1764; 1 Oct 1764; from Jessee Burton & Elizabeth Burton, both of Henrico Co. to James Vaughn; for £122.14; a negro, late property of Benjamin Burton, dec'd (HCVD-4 p. 888; TVF 10.254)

Apr Ct. 1764; sheriff to summon Jesse Burton and Elizabeth Burton to give acct. of estate of Benjamin Burton or deliver up estate; motion of exs. of John Williamson who was security for their admn. (HCVW-2 p. 86)

7 Nov 1768; 7 Nov 1768; from Jesse Burton and James Vaughan to John Burton, all of Henrico Co.; for £14.13.4; 20 ac.; 150 ac. conveyed to John Burton 2 Oct 1763; subsequent mortgage to James Vaughan 2 Oct 1763; 20 Apr 1764 survey found 20 ac. to be overplus (HCVD-5 p. 97; TVF 11.107)

31 Oct 1771; 2 Mar 1772; from Jesse Burton and James Vaughan to Lisbit Turpin, all of Henrico Co.; for £73.9; 130 ac. being remainder of land given sd. Jesse by his father Benjamin Burton; adj. John Burton, Christopher Branch & William Randolph (dec'd) (HCVD-5 p.21; TVF 11.254)

[Jesse Burton; Chesterfield County Wills and Administrations (1754-1800) The Sheriff to administer his estate, 1 March 1776. ChOB 6, p. 100 (LOV)]

> **23-6 James Burton**; may have d. by 4 Aug 1783 Charlotte Co.; inherited ½ of lower part of *White Oak Swamp*

[James Burton; Chesterfield County Wills and Administrations (1765 - 1800) p. 342-343. Inv. & Appr. rec. 4 Aug. 1783. p. 381-381a. Acc'ts rec. 6 Feb. 1786. p. 335. Will pro. 2 June 1783. WB No. 1, 1765-1791 (Reel 16) (LOV)]

> **23-7 Edward Burton**; he inherited land in Goochland from the 1758 will of his father
>
> **23-8 Richard Burton**; m. ____; named in 1758 will of his father
>
> > **238-1 John Pleasant Burton**, b. 8 Jul 1758; m. Ashe Co., NC **Susannah Stamper**, b. 22 Aug 1767

2-4 Hutchins Burton, b. 9 Apr 1694 Henrico Co.; d. by 3 Oct 1763 Henrico Co.; m. 31 Mar 1719 St. Peter's Parish, New Kent Co. **Susannah Watkins Allen**, b. 17 May 1700 New Kent Co., age 67 on 6 Oct 1767; d/o Samuel Allen of New Kent; Hutchins wit. several deeds and wills from 1709 to 1736 in Henrico Co. & was a member of the Curles Church of Henrico Parish which granted him 700# tobacco for the years 1730 to 1732 for keeping Sarah Rawlins; from 1733 to 1735 he was granted the same for keeping Susanna Rawlins plus 364# tobacco for 6 months of 1736 (Vestry Book of Henrico Parish; children from Hutchins' will & family histories:

> > 24-1 Samuel Burton, b. 25 Dec 1719
> > 24-2 Hutchins Burton, b. 25 Sep 1723
> > 24-3 William Allen Burton, b. 25 Jul 1727

24-4   Noel Burton b. 27 Apr 1729
24-5   Charles Burton, b. 4 May 1734
24-6   David Burton, b. 25 Jun 1735; d. 1757
24-7   Robert Burton
24-8   Richard Burton, b. 5 Dec 1740; d. 1775
24-9   Julius Burton
24-10 Ann Burton
24-11 Susannah Burton

5 Sep 1723 & 24 Mar 1725; Hutchins Burton patented 400 ac. Henrico Co. on n. side James River and *Wistham (Westham) Creek*; being Col. Randolph's corners (LOP 11.246; 12.406)

28 Sep 1730; Hutchinson Burton granted 3 tracts of 400 ac. on n. side of Appamattox Goochland Co.; one beginning at mouth of *Letalone Creek* Henrico Co. (LOP 13.537; 14.49; 14.141)

1 Aug 1735; Hutchinson Burton granted 400 ac. on n. side of James River adj. his own land, etc. on n. side of a branch of lower *Westham* Henrico Co. (LOP 16.104)

2 Apr 1733; 1st Mon Apr 1733; from Hutchins Burton of Henrico Co. to Benjamin Burton of same; for £25; 200 ac. given me by my father next to land Benj. purchased of Perkins; next to John Ellis, Col. Francis Eppes, *Gallows Slash* & Richard Cox; Susanna, w/o Hutchins relinquished dower rights (HCVD-2 p. 144, 145)

Apr Ct. 1738; from Hutchins Burton to John Eals, deed; Susanna, w/o Hutchins, relinquished dower rights (HCVD-3 p. 78)

7 Nov 1743; 1st Mon Nov 1743; from Hutchins Burton of Varina Parish, Henrico Co. to Valentine Ball of St. Margaret's Parish; for 5s; land granted sd. Burton 1 Aug 1735 bounded by *Lower Westham* and Wm. Randolph; one of the witnesses was David Burton (HCVD-3 p. 7)

10 Jul 1745; Hutchens Burton granted 390 ac. s. side of *Westham Creek* in Mr. Randolph's line; also 191 ac. adj. Beverley Randolph and his own line (LOP 22.303, 315)

12 May 1759; Hutchins Burton; patented 404 ac. Lunenburg Co.; on *Miles Creek* & adj. Morgan's line (LOP 34.248)

Will of Hutchins Burton; Henrico Co.; 9 May 1763; 3 Oct 1763
To son Samuel, negro [not mentioned in other abstracts of the will]
To son Hutchins, negro and 300 ac. where he lives and ½ interest in the mill
To son William Allen, negro
To son Noel, 90 ac. on upper side *Westham Creek*, negroes
To Ann, d/o my son Noel, negro at Noel's decease
To son in law Anthony Mathews, his wife, dau. Anne, their daus. Elizabeth & Susanna
     Mathews, negroes
To son Charles, 2 negroes and £100
To son Robert, 5s
To son in law William Price and my dau. Susanna his wife & their daus. Barley
     (?Sally), Susanna, Elizabeth

To son Julius, 2 negroes; if he dies to son Richard; Julius to have other part of tract where I live (400 ac.) at death of his mother
To Magdalene Burton, d/o Hutchins Burton, a cow
To wife Susanna Burton, house, plantations, tract of land, negroes, during life
Exs: wife Susannah, sons Hutchings & William (HCVW-2 p. 118, 119)
Apr Ct. 1764; inv. of Hutchens Burton returned (HCVW-2 p. 85)
Aug Ct. 1764; William Allen Burton to make acct. of estate of Hutchins Burton, dec'd (HCVW-2 p. 87)
[Hutchins Barton; Henrico County Wills and Administrations (1662-1800); p. 1887-1888. Will pro. 3 Oct. 1763. Misc. Court Records, Vol. 6, [1758-1769] (Reel 3) (LOV)]

11 Jul 1766; 3 Nov 1766; from Susannah Burton, widow & extx. of Hutchens Burton, dec'd, to William Allen Burton, s/o sd. Hutchens Burton; for £37.0.3; 2 slaves, 6 head of black cattle, 6 head of sheep, 1 black horse (HCVD-4 p. 989; TVF 11.42)

24-1 **Samuel Burton**, b. 25 Dec 1719; lived Prince Edward Co.

24-2 **Hutchins Burton**, b. 25 Sep 1723; d. ca 1763, of *Westham*, Henrico Co.; mb. 16 Mar 1742 Goochland Co. **Judith Allen**; William Allen, sec.; Judith was a sister of William Allen; Hutchins rec'd 300 ac. where his father lived, ½ the mill and 2 negroes from his father's will; known child:

242-1 **Magdalene Burton**; grandfather Burton's will left her livestock

12 May 1759; Hutchins Burton granted 404 ac. on *Miles Creek* Lunenburg Co. (LOP 34.248)

12 Jul 1762; Hutchings Burton granted 624 ac. on n. side of *Roanoak River*, Lunenburg Co. (LOP 34.1039)

8 Nov 1770; 3 Jun 1771; from Hutchings Burton of Mecklenburg Co. to William Burton of Cumberland Co.; for £500; 390 ac. in *Westham Creek*; wit. Charles Burton, Julius Burton & Mark Moor (HCVD-5 p. 188; TVF 11.188)

24-3 **William Allen Burton**, b. 25 Jul 1727; d. 1773 Cumberland Co.; believed to have m. **Mary Walthall**, b. 15 Sep 1730 Bristol Parish; d/o Richard Walthall; William Allen rec'd 2 negroes from his father's will; wit. a will in Chesterfield Co. in 1761 & Henrico Co. in 1772 (ChWB 1.II.543; HCVW-2 p. 147); two of their children:

243-1 **Mary Burton**; d/o William Allen Burton, dec'd, m. 27 Feb 1775 Cumberland Co. **Allen Burton**; s/o Nowell Burton and Judith Allen; d. Caswell Co,. NC
243-2 **Walthall Burton**; said to have m. 13 Feb 1773 **Sally Price**

[William Allen Burton; Cumberland County Wills and Administrations (1749 - 1810) p. 94-95. Will, pro. 28 June 1773. p. 106. Inv. rec. 26 July 1773. Will Book No. 2, 1769-1792 (Reel 17) (LOV)]

24-4 **Nowel (Noel) Burton**, of *Westham*, b. 27 Apr 1729; m. **Mary** ____; he inherited 90 ac. on upper side *Westham Creek* from his father's will, plus items; he sold land in Goochland Co. 1762-1768 (VP p. 1901); children from wills:

244-1 Ann Burton; mentioned in 1763 will of her grandfather Burton

14 Dec 1768; 2 Jan 1769; from Norvel Burton to John Stark, infant son and heir of Thomas Stark, dec'd, both of Henrico Co.; for £45; 90 ac. lying between the two *Westhams* adj. Robert Carter Nicholas, Julius & Hutchens Burton; being tract which Hutchens Burton devised Norvel Burton by will (HCVD-5 p. 110; TVF 11.109)

[Noel Burton; Goochland County Wills and Administrations (1728 - 1800) p. 33-36. Inv. & Appr. rec. 16 Apr 1770. DB No. 10, 1769-1775 (Reel 4) (LOV)]

24-5 Charles Burton, b. 4 May 1734; d. ca 1800 Spartanburg Co., SC; m. ca 1755 **Mary Hunt**; he may have been the Charles who patented 25 ac. in Chesterfield Co. 15 Jun 1773 (LOP 41.305); there are also several later grants in Pittsylvania Co. (LOP); children:

245-1 **Mary Burton**, b. 10 May 1781; bapt. 14 Jan 1785
245-2 **Nancy Burton**, b. 14 Oct 1784; bapt. 14 Jan 1785

24-6 David Burton, b. 25 Jun 1735; d. bef. his father; m. by Jun 1757 **Mary ____** (QRH p. 94); widow of **Gilleygrove (Gilley) Marrin** whose will was recorded by Mary Jul 1747 (HCVW-2 p. 35; TVF 6.222); family histories say David d. by May Ct. 1758 when his bro. William Allen Burton, as ex. of his father's will sued Mary, widow of David; known Marrin children:

246-1 Wiltshire Marrin
246-2 Susannah Marrin
246-3 Mary Marrin

Dec 1748; inv. of Gilley Marrin; value £567.16.6 by Mary Marren (HCVW-2 p. 48)

10 Feb 1757; Jun 1757; David Burton m. Mary ____; widow of Gilley Marrin; deeded slaves to Robert Goode who was security for Mary Marrin's executorship to insure and protect the interest of Gilley Marrin's children (HCVW-2 p. 66)

May Ct. 1758; inv. of David Burton returned and recorded (HCVW-2 p. 73)

Apr Ct. 1764; 29 Apr 1760; Wiltshire and Susannah Marrin, infants and orphans of Gilligrove Marrin, dec'd by Robert Goode vs. Mary Burton; 6 negroes valued £370 to Susannah, w/o Charles Lewis, and 11 negroes valued £740 to Wilshire and Mary Marrin; since David Burton rec'd profits of sd. estate for 9 yrs., Burton's estate to pay £100 in part of sd. legacies; Wiltshire Marrin, of lawful age, appeared and agreed to report (HCVW-2 p. 85, 86)

Feb Ct. 1764; Mary Marrin, orphan of Gillgrew Marrin, chooses Mary Burton as her guardian (HCVW-2 p. 85)

Aug Ct. 1764; acct. of estate of David Burton, dec'd (HCVW-2 p. 87)

Sep Ct. 1764; Mary Burton guardian for estate of Wiltshire and Mary Marrin (HCVW-2 p. 87)

1 May 1764; 5 Nov 1764; lease from Mary Burton, late widow of Gillee Gromarrin of Henrico Co., dec'd, & now widow of David Burton, dec'd, and Wiltshire Marrin, otherwise called Wiltshire Gromarrin, eldest son & heir of sd. Gillee Gromarrin to Samuel Duval; for 15 years; 200 ac on w. side of *Gillead's Creek*; being part of demised land known as *Rocket's Landing*; containing about 20 ac. (HCVD-4 p. 893; IVF 10.255)

Feb Ct. 1768; inventory of Mary Burton returned (HCVW-2 p. 101)

Apr Ct. 1769; accounts of estate of David Burton returned (HCVW-2 p. 105)

246-1 **Wiltshire Marrin**, b. ca 1739; d. by Feb Ct. 1766

Feb Ct. 1766; inventory of Wilshire Marrin returned (HCVW-2 p. 101)
Dec Ct. 1767; administration granted for estate of Wiltshire Marin (HCVW-2 101)

246-2 **Susannah Marrin**; m. **Charles Lewis**

5 Feb 1770; 5 Feb 1770; Charles Lewis, Sr. and Susanna his wife made bond re property Wiltshire Marrin possessed two tract in Henrico Co. & died without lawful heirs; according to the will of Gilly Marrin, the land became property of Susannah Marrin (w/o Charles Lewis) and Mary Marrin (w/o Colwell Pettypool) (HCVD-2 p. 145)

246-3 **Mary Marrin**; m. **Colwell Pettypool**

24-7 **Robert Burton**, b. 5 Dec 1740; d. ca 1775; he rec'd 5s from his father's will

24-8 **Richard Burton**; m. _____; he rec'd 2 negroes and items from his father's will; land patented by Nowell Burton 25 Jan 1735 was conveyed to Richard (CuOB 1749-51 p. 13); he may have moved to Augusta Co.

20 Sep 1748; Richard Burton patented 400 ac. Augusta Co. on branches of *Buffalo Creek*; adj. Benjamin Borden (LOP 28.366)

24-9 **Julius Burton** of Henrico; m. 9 Mar 1763 St. James Northam Parish, Goochland Co. **Rebecca Clayton** (DR); he rec'd 2 negroes and items from his father's will; after death of mother to have 400 ac. of home plantation

24-10 **Ann Burton**, b. ca 1729, age 38 on 6 Oct 1767; m. **Anthony Mathews**, b. ca 1717, age 50 on 6 Oct 1767; they rec'd slaves from her father's will which named their children:

> 24(10)-1 Elizabeth Mathews
> 24(10)-2 Susannah Mathews

5 Aug 1769; 7 Aug 1769; from Anthony Mathews, and Anne his wife, to Anselm Gathright, all of Henrico Co.; for £23; 6 negroes (HCVD-5 p. 163; TVF 11.117)

21 Mar 1781; 1 Oct 1781; will of Anthony Matthews of Henrico Co. leaves 5s to dau. Elizabeth Gathright; sec. Benjamin Gathright, Joseph Gathright & Michael Turpin (HCVD-3 p. 5; TVF 6. 40)

24(10)-1 **Elizabeth Mathews**; m. by Jun 1763 **Anselm Gathright**

Jun Ct. 1763; Case of Anselm Gathright and Elizabeth his wife vs. Anthony Matthews, his wife Ann and dau. Susannah; Hutchen Burton made a gift of a slave to his granddau. Elizabeth, w/o Anselm Gathright, after the death of her mother; deposition 6 Oct 1767; Susannah Burton, age 67, says her husband Hutchens Burton gave the slave to Anthony & Ann Mathews 18 yrs. ago; they had possession and her increase since. Anthony Matthews, age 50, says in Oct 1749 he and his wife called on him on their way to Cumberland Co. and he said they might have the negro on his Cumberland land. Ann Matthews, age 38, says same and that she delivered slave to Elizabeth Gathright (HCVW-2 p. 102)

5 Aug 1769; Deed of Gift from Anselm Gathright to Susanna Mathews, d/o Anthony Mathews; negro girl 6 yrs. old (HCVD-5 p. 163; TVF 11.117)

24(10)-2 Susanna Mathews

24-11 **Susannah Burton**; m. **William Price**; they rec'd slaves from her father's will which mentions their 3 eldest children:

24(11)-1 **Sally Price**; m. 13 Feb 1773 **Walthall Burton**, both in Goochland Co. (DR)

24(11)-2 **Susannah Price**

24(11)-3 **Elizabeth (Betsey) Price**; m. 21 Dec 1775 **Joseph Perkins**, both in this parish (DR)

24(11)-4 **Nansy Price**, b. 7 May 177_; bapt. 28 Mar 1774 (DR)

24(11)-5 **Patsy Price**, b. 21 Jun 1776; bapt. 21 Jul 1776 (DR)

2-5 **Nowell Burton**; d. by 13 Oct 1766 Mecklenburg Co.; m. ca 1720 **Judith Allen**; vestryman of St. James Parish (GCWD-1 p. 10); 1717 & 1728 lived near *Chickahominy Swamp* (HCVD-2 p. 64, 74, 115); children from will & family histories:

> 25-1 Robert Burton
> 25-2 John Burton
> 25-3 Josiah Burton
> 25-4 Benjamin Burton
> 25-5 Noel Burton
> 25-6 Allen Burton
> 25-7 Hutchins Burton
> 25-8 Judith Burton

28 Jan 1733; Noel Burton granted 400 ac. on s. side of *Willis River* below mouth of *Reedy Branch*, Goochland Co. (LOP 15.141)

26 Mar 1739; Nowel Burton granted 400 ac. on s. branches of *Willis River*, Goochland Co. (LOP 18.213)

26 Nov 1739; 19 Feb 1739; from Nowel Buton and Judith his wife of St. James Parish, Goochland Co., planter, to Robert Bernard; for £80; 265 ac. on s. side of *Willis River*; bounded by the river, *Reedy Branch, Soakarse Run*; part of 400 ac. grant 28 Jan 1733 (GCWD-1 p. 35)

Will of Nowel Burton; Mecklenburg Co.; 31 Jun 1766; 13 Oct 1766
To son Hutchins, 800 ac. on *Bannister River*, Halifax Co. now in poss. of John Burton
  of Cumberland Co.; also personal estate, excepting items held by son Allen and
  Judith Young
To sons John, Josiah, Robert and Benjamin, 1s
Ex: Hutchins Burton (MeWB 1.29)

  25-1 **Robert Burton**, the younger; m. ____ **Traylor**; d/o Joseph &
    Elizabeth Traylor; children from family histories:

    251-1 **Archer Burton**; 10 Sep 1777 his grandfather Traylor wrote his
      will leaving him a negro at age 21 and he was not 18 when his
      grandmother Traylor called him grandson in her will 22 Apr 1782
      (ChWB 3.217, 360)

3 Dec 1782; 9 Dec 1782; from Archer Burton to Robert Burton, Jr., both of
Mecklenburg Co.; for £20; livestock, household goods (MeDB 6.213)

    251-2 **Robert Burton, Jr.**; m. 1805 Mecklenburg Co. **Elizabeth**
      Chamberlain
    251-3 **Minnie Burton**; m. 16 Jul 1687 Mecklenburg Co. **Edward Rolfe**
    251-4 **John Burton**
    251-5 **Allen Burton**, b. ca 1764; m. Mecklenburg Co. **Rebecca**
      Hammer; Allen witnessed several documents in Mecklenburg Co

16 Mar 1741; 18 May 1742; from John Scruggs to Robert Burton, the younger, s/o
Nowel Burton of Goochland Co.; for £20; 200 ac. on w. side of *Willis River* being
upper portion of a 400 ac. tract (GCWD-2 p. 71)

1 Aug 1772; Robert Burton granted 375 ac. Mecklenburg Co. (LOP 40.847)

  25-2 **John Burton, Capt.**, b. ca 1730; d. ca 1785 Cumberland Co.; mb. 24
    Aug 1752 Cumberland Co. **Agnes Merryman**; letter of consent from
    John Merryman; John Burton was a Capt. of the Cumberland Co. Militia

8 May 1755; John Burton granted 64 ac. on both sides of *Groomes Quarter Branch* of
Willis River, Cumberland Co. (LOP 32.528)

  25-3 **Josiah Burton**; he & Richard Burton wit. an inventory in Goochland
    Co. 24 Nov 1744 (GCWD-3 p. 13); he later went to NC

20 Aug 1748; Josiah Burton granted 400 ac. at heads of branches of *Soakarse* and
Little Guinea and both side of *Buckingham Road*, Goochland Co. (LOP 26.573)

  25-4 **Benjamin Burton**; mb. 19 Jun 1775 Mecklenburg Co. **Monica**
    Humphries
  25-5 **Noel Burton**; lived Cumberland Co.
  25-6 **Allen Burton**; d. Caswell Co., NC; m. 27 Feb 1775 Cumberland Co.
    Mary Burton; d/o William Allen Burton, dec'd; children from family
    histories:

    256-1 **Allen Burton**, b. ca 1775

256-2 **John Burton**, b. ca 1777

256-3 **Thomas A. Burton**, b. 29 Oct 1779; d. 25 Feb 1855

256-4 **Drury Burton**, b. 11 Mar 1781 Cumberland Co.; d. ca 1835 AL;
m/1 4 Oct 1808 Caswell Co., NC **Jenny Huston**; m/2 3 Dec 1816
Caswell Co., NC **Margaret S. Richmond**

256-5 **David Burton**

256-6 **Susannah Burton**, b. 2 Feb 1785; d. 2 Dec 1862

256-7 **Elizabeth (Betsey) Burton**

256-8 **Hutchins Burton** (twin), b. 19 Nov 1789; d. 10 Aug 1838

256-9 **Francis Howard Burton** (twin), b. 19 Nov 1789; d. 8 May 1857

25-7 **Hutchins Burton**; d. ca 1789 Mecklenburg Co.; m. **Tabitha Minge**;
d/o Robert Minge & Mary Hunt; he inherited land on the *Bannister
River,* Halifax Co., from the will of his father; children from family
histories:

257-1 **John Burton**; mb. 24 Oct 1779 **Mary Gordon**; sur. John B.
Forsee (MCC p. 25)

257-2 **Hutchins Burton**, b. ca 1764, age 68 on 15 Oct 1832 when he
relinquished claim to a pension for his Revolutionary War service; he
was drafted Jun 1780; served in NC

257-3 **Noel Burton**

257-4 **Robert Burton, Col.**, b. 20 Oct 1747 Mecklenburg Co.; he lived
Granville Co., NC

257-5 **James Minge Burton**

257-6 **Martha Burton**

257-7 **Mary Burton**

25-8 **Judith Burton**; m. ____ **Young**

3. **Benjamin Burton**; d. by 1 Feb 1687; called bro. in 1679 will of John Burton;
in 1683/4 his father gave him ½ of 100 ac. of *The Levell*

1 Feb 1687; probate granted Robert Burton, ex., on will of Benjamin Burton (HCVW-1
p. 30)

4. **Anne Burton**; she inherited livestock from the 1679 will of her bro. John;
she may have been the d/o John Burton who m. ca 1682 **William Hatcher**
(QRH p. 90)

5. **William Burton** of *The Level*; d. by Sep 1751; m/1 1688-89 Henrico Co.
Mary Parker (QRH; MHC p. 14); d/o Katherine & Will Parker; m/2 by Apr 1723
Elizabeth (__) Harwood; widow and extx. of Thomas Harwood; d. ca 1718
Henrico Co.; in 1683/4 his father gave him ½ of 100 ac. of *The Levell* and he
inherited the plantation where he was living in 1689 from the will of his
father; her mother left him 1s in her will written 30 May 1731 (HCVW-1 p. 232);
possible children:

5-1 William Burton
5-2 John Burton
5-3 Martha Burton
5-4 ____ Burton (m)
5-5 ____ Burton (f)
5-6 Martin Burton

26 Apr 1698; William Burton patented 144 ac. on n. side of James River in Parish of Varina, Henrico Co.; bounded Capt. Epes and Robert Burton (LOP 9.144)

1705 rent rolls; Henrico Co.; William Burton; 294 ac.

27 Dec 1707; survey of Henrico Parish; William Burton, 400 ac. (HCVD-2 p. 13)

Ct. Apr 1723; Alexander Robinson who m. Mary, d/o Thomas Harwood, dec'd, petitions court that William Burton who m. Elizabeth Harwood, extx. of sd. Harwood, be ordered to deliver to him the part of Harwood's estate that belongs to his wife Mary; court will assign plaintiffs their share (HCVW-2 p. 166)

5 Jul 1751; William Burton granted 410 ac. in Henrico Co. on s. side of *Gilley's Creek* (LOP 30.458)

Will of William Burton of Henrico Parish; 7 May 1751; Sep 1751
To wife Elizabeth use of plantation, slaves, items for life; then to son William
Son John, 1s; dau. Martha Wood, 1s
Grandsons Peter Burton, John Burton, Francis Frankling
Wit. John Redford, John Redford the younger, Francis Redford (HCVW-2 p. 54, 55)
30 Oct 1751; Jun 1752; inventory of William Burton; value £107.3.7 ½ (HCVW-2 p. 55)
[William Burton; Henrico County Wills and Administrations (1662-1800) p. 86. Will pro. Sept. 1751. p. 111-112. Inv. & appr. rec. June 1752. Deeds, Wills, Etc., 1750-1767 (Reel 9) Henrico County Wills and Administrations (1662-1800) p. 1525-1526. Will pro. Sept. [1751]. Misc. Court Records, Vol. 5, [1747-1757] (Reel 3) (LOV)]

5-1 **William Burton**; following land could belong to this William:

5 Jul 1751; William Burton granted 410 ac. on s. side of *Gilleys Creek* Henrico Co. (LOP 30.458)

5-2 **John Burton**; d. by 6 Dec 1784; m. ____ ; known children:

52-1 William T. Burton
52-2 John Burton
52-3 Sarah Burton

Will of John Burton of Henrico Co.; 27 Mar 1784; 6 Dec 1784
Lend to my son William T. Burton, *The Leavel, Reedy Branch & Squire* for life; then
   to his son John Burton
To my son John Burton, plantation on *Gilley's Creek* for life
Son John to raise £200 to be paid the four daus. of William T. Burton
To dau. Sarah Ward & her children, I lend slaves for life
Ex: wife and sons William & John
Wit: Henry Jordan, David Breeding (HCVW-3 p. 158; TVF 6.247)

52-1 **William T. Burton**; m. ____; the land he inherited from his father was for life then to his son John; children were 4 (unnamed) daus. & known son:

521-1 **John Burton**

52-2 **John Burton**; he inherited land on *Gilley's Creek* for life

52-3 **Sarah Burton**; m. ____ **Ward**

5-3 **Martha Burton**; m. ____ **Wood**

5-4 ____ **Burton**

54-1 **Peter Burton**; d. by 19 Jul 1721 Elizabeth City Co.; mentioned in will of grandfather Burton; known child:

541-1 Mary Burton

[Peter Burton; Elizabeth City County Wills and Administrations (1689-1800) p. 2. Inv. & Appr. rec. 16 Aug. 1721 p. 1. Adms. bond rec. 19 July 1721 Record Book No. 10, 1721-1723 (Reel 4); Elizabeth City County Wills and Administrations (1689-1800) Note p. 111-h [322]. Gdn. bond rec. 19 July 1721 Deeds, Wills & Orders, 1724-1730, Pt. 3 (Reel 4) (LOV)]

541-1 **Mary Burton**

19 Jul 1721; John Weymouth, guardian of Mary Burton, orphan of Peter Burton, dec'd (Elizabeth City Co. Court Records, 1720-1721; TVF 12.259)

5-5 ____ **Burton**; m. ____ **Franklin**

55-1 **Francis Franklin**; b. bef. 1751

5-6 **Martin Burton**; d. 1792 Henrico Co.; appears in estate document ca 1760's & 1770's in Henrico Co. (HCVW-2)

30 Mar 1750; from William Smith of Henrico Co. & Parish to Martin Burton; for £45; 100ac bounded by *Horse Swamp* (HCVD-3 p. 74)

6. **Rachel Burton**; m. ____; 3 unidentified children mentioned in will of her bro. John; she could possibly be the following "Accot of Lycenses returned to Town this 25th of 7ber, 1682, viz: Wm. Holden for marryage with ye daughter of John Burton"

7. **Mary Burton**; m/1 1686 Henrico Co. **John Davis**; if this is the John Davis who m. Mary Burton, then she was a 2nd wife of the same name as the 1st wife for whom he claimed transport in 1642 was also named Mary; Mary Burton m/2 bef. 16 Feb 1689 **William Glover**; d. by 16 May 1692; she and her children are identified in the 1689 will of her father and the 1679 will of her brother John; known children:

        7-1 John Davis
        7-2 Mary Davis
        7-3 Elizabeth Davis
        7-4 William Davis

15 Aug 1637; John Davis and Robert Craddock patented 600 ac. in Henrico Co. adj. *Longfield* (PB 1.1.451)

Last of Oct 1642; John Davis patented 200 ac. Henrico Co.; adj. former patent called *Longfield*; due for transport of his wife Mary Davis and 3 servants (PB 1.2.842)

1679; John Davis tithable in Henrico Co.

1682; John Davis in list of debts of inv. of Charles Fetherstone (HCVW-1 p. 12)

11 Aug 1684; inv. of John Davis; value 32,435# tobacco (HCVW-1 p. 15)

9 Oct 1684; Mary, widow and relict of John Davis who d. intestate, granted admn. of estate (HCVW-1 p. 16)

16 May 1692; division of estate of John Davis, dec'd; formerly held by William Glover, dec'd; to Davis orphans: John, Mary, Elizabeth and William (HCVW-1 p. 45)

7-1 **John Davis**; b. est. ca 1670 as he attained his estate in 1691; d. by 1 May 1700; m. **Elizabeth** ____; d. by 2 Oct 1721; she m/2 by 1707 **Charles Russell**; known child:

71-1 John Davis

18 Oct 1688; John Davis & William Glover held tobacco "to go to finish house" of Edward Deely of Henrico Co. & Parish (HCVW-1 p. 35)

1 Feb 1691; John Davis, s/o John Davis, of lawful age; made guardian of bro. William Davis; former guardian William Glover and wife have departed county; Mary, orphan of John Davis, chooses Sarah Woodson, and Elizabeth is put in charge of her uncle, Robert Bu(r)ton (HCVW-1 p. 67)

1 Jun 1694; 1 Jun 1694; I, John Davis, son and heir of John Davis of *Longfield* Henrico Co., dec'd, sell to Nicholas Perkins; for 2,500# tobacco; 100 ac. on n. side of James River; which 100 ac. from Edward Hatcher to my dec'd father 1 Dec 1675 (HCVD-1 p. 83)

30 Mar 1696; 1 Apr 1696; from John Davis of *Longfield* to Francis Epes, Gent., both of Henrico Co. & Parish; for £50; 250 ac. known as *Longfield* where John Davis, dec'd, father of John Davis did lately dwell (HCVD-1 p. 93)

1 Mar 1699/00; 1 Mar 1699; from John Davis, late of *Longfield*, planter, to John Redford; for £10; 254 ac. on n. side of James River; Elizabeth, w/o John, relinquished dower right (HCVD-1 p. 110)

1 May 1700; William Farrar & John Davis to Michael Turpin; all of Henrico Co.; for £34; *Blair's Quarter* sold to Farrar & Davis 26 Oct 1699; Priscilla Farrar & Elizabeth Davis relinquish their dower rights (HCVD-1 p. 111)

· 1 May 1700; deed mentions land sold by Edward Hatcher to John Davis of *Longfield*, dec'd, and by his heir, John Davis of Henrico Co., who sold to Nicholas Perkins 1 Jun 1693 (HCVD-1 p. 112)

1 Apr 1701; Elizabeth Davis granted probate on will of husband John Davis (HCVW-1 p. 77)

22 Jul 1702; 1 Aug 1702; inventory of estate of John Davis, taylor, sold at outcry by court order of June past (HCVW-1 p. 80)

1 Mar 1707; accounts of estate of John Davis presented in Ct. by his admx. now w/o Charles Russell (HCVW-1 p. 100)

Jan Ct. 1720; William Pettipool proves deed from Oct 1720 of Charles Russell to John Boling; he says he knew sd. Russell in VA and that he is the person who m. the widow of John Davis (HCVD-2 p. 191)

Ct. 2 Oct 1721; John Davis granted administration of estate of Elizabeth Russel, dec'd; John Davis comes into court and discharges the persons who were his mother's security for delivery of his estate to him (HCVW-2 p. 160)

Ct. 6 Nov 1721; John Davis presents inventory of Elizabeth Russel (HCVW-2 p. 160)

71-1 John Davis

7-2 Mary Davis; chose Sarah Woodson as guardian in 1691; m. 14 Jan 1692 Henrico Co. **Jacob Colson** (QRH p. 91)

7-3 Elizabeth Davis; made ward of her uncle Robert Burton in 1691

7-4 William Davis; his bro. John was made his guardian in 1691

THOMAS BURTON, Sr.

Thomas Burton, Sr.; of *Cobbs*; d. by 1 Feb 1685/6; m. Henrico Co. **Susannah Hatcher** ; she ml/2 2 Oct 1685 Henrico Co. **John Steuart (Steward, Stewart)** (QRH p. 90; MHC p. 81); known children:

1. Thomas Burton, b. ca 1664
2. John Burton, b. ca 1666
3. Abraham Burton, b. ca 1669
4. Isaac Burton
5. Ann Burton

10 Jul 1680; Thomas Burton patented 350 ac. Henrico Co. on Appomattox River; adj. John Baugh (LOP 7.44)

1 Jan 1685; 1 Feb 1685; deed from Thomas Burton, Sr. to his 4 sons at his decease; Thomas (eldest), 100 ac. adj. my plantation; 100 ac. to John; 100 ac. to Abraham where I now live; 100 ac. to Abraham (sic); probate of deed and land given sons Thomas, John, Abraham and Isaac (HCVW-1 p. 19; HCVD-1 p. 32)

1 Feb 1685; Thomas Burton, Sr. d. intestate; Susanna Burton, widow, appointed admx. (HCVW-1 p. 18)

1 Apr 1686; estate of Thomas Burton; value 7,380# tobacco; presented in court by Susannah Burton (HCVW-1 p. 20)

4 Oct 1686; list of debts of Thomas Burton, Sr.; 1,750# tobacco paid since his death; presented in court by Susanna Burton, admx. (HCVW-1 p. 23)

[Thomas Burton, Sr.; Henrico County Wills and Administrations (1662-1800) p. 342. Adms. bond rec. 1 Feb. 1685. p. 358-359. Inv. & appr. rec. 1 Apr. 1686. p. 401. Accounts rec. 1 Dec. 1686. Records, 1677-1692 (Reel 4) (LOV)]

1 Dec 1699; 1 Dec 1699; from John Stewart of Henrico Co., glover, to Michael Turpin; for tract conveyed to me by Turpin, sell *Cobbs* in Bristol Parish on n. side Appomattox River which I purchased of my son in law Abraham Burton (HCVD-1 p. 109)

1. **Thomas Burton**, b. ca 1664, age 16 on 1 Apr 1680 (HCVD-1 p. 148); d. aft. 1685; m. **Elizabeth** ____; she m/2 **John Bucanan** of Boston; as Thomas Burton, Jr., he inherited 226 ac. of land from the will of William Hatcher of Henrico Co. written 20 Feb 1676 (HCVW-1 p. 7); son:

   1-1 **Thomas Burton**; d. by 16 May 1692 Boston

   16 May 1692; letter presented to court: to "Honored Mother" Mrs. Susannah Burton from Elizabeth Bucanan, wife of John Bucanan of Boston; mentions Elizabeth's late husband, Thomas Burton, s/o Susannah, and the recent death of Elizabeth's son, Thomas Burton (HCVW-1 p. 45)

2. **John Burton, Sr.**, b. ca 1666, age 22 on 12 Oct 1688 (HCVD-1 p. 152); d. by 5 Jun 1756 Chesterfield Co.; m. **Elizabeth** ____; d. by 1 Jun 1759 Chesterfield Co.; widow of ____ **Sheppard** & mother of William Sheppard; in 1699 John bought *Cobbs* of 100 ac. from John Archer which his father left his bro. Abraham who sold the tract to their stepfather John Stewart who sold it to Michael Turpin, who, in turn, sold it to John Archer (HCVD-1 p. 108, 109, 110); a deed in 1759 mentions land recently purchased of William Sheppard and his mother, Elizabeth Burton, both of Dale Parish (ChDB 3,339); children:

   2-1   John Burton, Jr.
   2-2   Isaiah Burton
   2-3   Thomas Burton
   2-4   Samuel Burton
   2-5   James Burton
   2-6   Sarah Burton
   2-7   Elizabeth Burton
   2-8   Susannah Burton
   2-9   Phebe Burton
   2-10 Ann Burton
   2-11 Ezar Burton

13 Dec 1681; 1 Feb 1683; deed of gift from Thomas Burton, Sr. to son John Burton, 1 yearling, calf (HCVD-1 p. 24)

17 May 1694; John Burton owed 58s to William Hatcher, Jr. (HCVW-1 p. 54)

30 Nov 1704; 1 Dec 1704; from John Burton, planter of Henrico Co., to John Bolling; for £60; 300 ac. *Cobbs* on s. side of James River bounded by Appomattox River, James Baugh, Isaac Burton; 103 ac. given by will of my father Thomas Burton; 100 ac. fell to me as heir of my bro. Thomas Burton; 100 ac. I purchased of John Archer (HCVD-1 p. 136)

16 Jun 1714; John Burton patented 341 ac. on *Deep Creek* on s. side of James River in Henrico Co. (LOP 10.134)

5 Jan 1729; 1ˢᵗ Mon Jan 1729; from John Burton, Sr. to son Isaiah Burton, both of Henrico Co. & Parish; for 5s; 85 ac on s. side of *Falling Creek* (HCDB-2 p. 122)

3 Mar 1734/5; 3 Mar 1734; from John Burton of Henrico Co. to son James Burton; land on s. side of *Falling Creek* (HCVD-2 p. 158)

4 Mar 1736/7; 1ˢᵗ Mon Jun 1736; from John Burton of Henrico Co. to son Thomas Burton; 85 ac. next to James Burton on s. side of *Falling Creek* (HCVD-2 p. 180)

Jun Ct. 1738; from John Burton to Edward Logwood proved by Thomas Burton and Thomas Burton, Jr. (HCVD-3 p. 82)

Will of John Borten; Dale Parish, Chesterfield Co.; 23 Feb 1754; Ct. Jun 1756; [says Burton in margin]
To wife Elizabeth, land and plantation I live on for life, and moveable estate
After her death sd. plantation to William Shapperd, Jr.
To son John Borten's heir, 5s
To children Thomas, Samuel and James Borton, Sarah Jackson, Elizabeth Tirpin, Susannah Tanner, Febue Johnson, Ann Borton, Ezar Borton; granddaughter Arrobello Borton, each 1s
Ex: wife
Wit: John Baker, Robert Cayce, Sarah Baker (ChWB 1.208)
4 Jun 1756; will of John Borten presented by Elizabeth, the relict; estate appraised (ChOB 2.195, 220)
Ct. Jun 1756; inventory of Mr. John Burton; value £28.12 (ChWB 1.210)
[John Burton; Chesterfield County Wills and Administrations (1754-1800) Will - dated 1754 Proved 5 June 1756. (O.B. 2, p. 195) Chesterfield County Wills and Administrations 1, p. 208-210; Chesterfield County Wills and Administrations (1754-1800) Note Inv. & Appr. - dated 1756 Returned 3 Sept. 1756. (O.B. 2, p. 220) Chesterfield County Wills and Administrations 1, p. 210 (LOV)]

Will of Elizabeth Burton; Chesterfield Co.; 24 Sep 1757; 1 Jun 1759
To grandson William Shepord, items
To granddau. Ann Pain, items
To Elizabeth Gresel, Judith Burton, Isack Shepord, 1s each
To grandson Charles Pain, 5s
To Arrobello Burton, 1 bed
To Jane Turpin, a work horse
Ex: William Shepord
Wit: Gearrard Ellyson, Aquilar Snelling, Ann Snelling (ChWB 1.314)
[undated]; inventory of Elizabeth Burton; no value give (ChWB 1.315)
1 Jun 1759; will of Elizabeth Burton presented by William Shepard (ChOB 3.3)
[Elizabeth Burton; Chesterfield County Wills and Administrations (1754-1800) Inventory - undated Returned 6 July 1759. (Order Book 3, p. 11) Chesterfield County Will Book 1, p. 315; Chesterfield County Wills and Administrations (1754-1800) Will - undated Proved 1 June 1759. (Order Book 3, p. 3) Chesterfield County Will Book 1, p. 314 (LOV)]

2-1 **John Burton, Jr.**; d. by Oct 1747; m. **Elizabeth Ware**; d. by 1 Jul 1759; d/o of Caleb & Susannah Ware of Henrico Parish; she inherited a chest of drawers from the 1734/5 will of her mother (HCVW-1 p. 202; VP p. 2) and named a son for her father; children:

21-1 John Burton
21-2 Caleb Burton
21-3 Joseph Burton
21-4 Elizabeth Burton
21-5 Sarah Burton
21-6 Joannah Burton
21-7 Mary Burton
21-8 Robert Burton
21-9 Agnes Burton

17 Aug 1720; John Burton patented 500 ac. on n. side of *Swift Creek* in Henrico Co.; adj. Michel Michel (LOP 11.46)

6 Mar 1735; from Robert Hudson of Henrico Co. to John Burton; for £50; ¼ of mill & 2 ac.; [John Burton, Jr., Henry Hatcher, Jr., Henry Hatcher & Robert Hudson formerly created *Beaver Ponds* of *Swift Creek*] (HCVD-2 p. 167)

23 Jun 1740; the will of Caleb Ware makes no mention of his dau., but leaves "young John Burton," s/o John Burton, Sr., negro, clothes, cow & calf and "my plantation I now live on" (ChWB 1.19)

12 Dec 1740; 1st Mon Jan 1741; John Burton, Henry Hatcher, Sr. & Jr., Robert Hudson; of Dale Parish, Henrico Co.; to Henry Hudson; for £50; a mill with 2 ac. on s. side of James River on *Beaver Ponds* of *Swift Creek*; Elizabeth Burton [among other wives] relinquished dower (HCVD-3 p. 4)

4 Apr 1746; John Burton, Jr. of Henrico Co. and Parish, to Robert Burton of same; for £5; 100 ac. part of 130 ac. granted sd. John by patent 12 Feb 1710; on upper side of *Nison's Branch* (HCVD-3 p. 28)

4 Apr 1746; 1st Mon Jun 1746; from John Burton, Jr. of Henrico Co., Dale Parish, to John Burton the younger of same; for £5; 100 ac. now in poss. of sd. John the younger, being part of 400 ac. granted John Burton, Jr. 12 Feb 1742; adj. Henry and Josiah Hatcher (HCVD-3 p. 26)

Will of John Burton of Dale Parish, Henrico Co.; 5 Sep 1746; Oct 1747
Wife Elizabeth; personal estate for life then divided between 2 sons & 4 daus.: Caleb, Joseph, Elizabeth, Sarah, Joannah and Mary
To Caleb land at fork of *Nisoms Branch* & 50 ac. on s. side; 130 ac. total
To son Joseph, plantation where I live
If sons die before age 21 to dau. Elizabeth; if she dies to son John
Dau. Agnes Farmer
Wit: Henry Hatcher, Josiah Hatcher, John Popham (HCVW-2 p. 37)
26 Jan 1747; May 1748; inventory of John Burton (HCVW-2 p. 42)
[John Burton; Henrico County Wills and Administrations (1662-1800) p. 1445-1446. Inv. & appr. rec. May 1748. Misc. Court Records, Vol. 5, [1747-1757] (Reel 3); p. 303-303a. Will pro. Oct. 1747. p. 379-380. Inv. & appr. rec. May 1748. DB, 1744-1748 (Reel 8) (LOV)]

1 Jun 1759; Will of Elizabeth Burton presented by William Shepard, ex. (ChOB 3.3); inventory returned (ChOB 3.11)

21-1 **John Burton**; the younger; d. ca 1799 Chesterfield Co.; his father gave him 100 ac. in 1746 and he was a contingent legatee of land from his father's will; children & grandchildren from John's will:

    211-1 Joseph Burton
    211-2 Thomas Burton
    211-3 John Burton
    211-4 Mary Burton
    211-5 ____ Burton
    211-6 Sarah Burton
    211-7 Edith Burton
    211-8 ____ Burton

Will of John Burton; Chesterfield Co.; 2 Jun 1799; 14 Oct 1799
To wife for life, negroes, items
To sons in law Miles Gibson, Charles Duberl & Littlebury Sublet, each 2 negroes
To son in law Abraham Sublet for life, 1 negro, & another for life of his wife Edith
To son Joseph, negroes
To granddau. Phebe Forsee, negro
To dau Mary Crumpton, estate to raise £200 to purchase a negro for her for life; then to her children excluding Laban Gibson
To son Thomas, tract I live on
To son John, confirmation of all I have previously given him
To Josiah Hatcher, confirmation of land sold him by my son Joseph in Buckingham Co.
Exs: sons Joseph & Thomas
Wit: Isaac Salle, Sam'l Pankey, Martha Pankey (ChWB 5.244)
14 Oct 1799; will of John Burton proved by Joseph Burton & wit. Isaac Salle & Samuel Pankey (ChOB 13.115)

211-1 **Joseph Burton**; lived Buckingham Co.

211-2 **Thomas Burton**

211-3 **John Burton**

211-4 **Mary (Nancy) Burton**; it appears she m/1 **Thomas Gibson**; d. by Mar 1775; m/2 **Miles Gibson**; s/o Miles Gibson; m/3 **John Compton** or **Crumpton**, late of Halifax Co.; d. drunk 1 Apr 1786; on 3 Apr an inquisition was held by justices of Chesterfield Co. regarding his death (ChWB 3.67); children from the will of Mary's father, John Burton, & 1788 will of grandfather Miles Gibson (ChWB 4.163) & 1791 will of grandmother Hannah Gibson (ChWB 4.450):

    2114-1 Laban Gibson
    2114-2 Elizabeth Gibson
    2114-3 Nancy Gibson
    2114-4 Hannah Gibson

Ct. 3 Mar 1775; appraisal ordered of estate of Thomas Gibson (ChOB 6.75); recorded Oct 1779; estate of Thomas Gipson, John Burton, adm'r (ChWB 4.29); 1784 estate of Thomas Gipson in account with John Burton (ChWB 4.37)

2114-1 **Laban Gibson**; the will of his grandfather Burton mentions he is not to inherit from the estate; Ct. 7 May 1779; John Compton appointed guardian to Laban Gibson, orphan of Thomas Gibson (ChOB 6.225); Ct. 2 Aug 1782; John Burton, Sr. was appointed guardian to Laban Gibson, orphan of Thomas Gibson (ChOB 6.361)

2114-2 **Elizabeth Gibson**; legatee of her uncle William Burton

2114-3 **Nancy Gibson**; Ct. of 8 Jul 1783 she choose William Finney as her guardian and Philip Turpin is appointed guardian for her sister Hannah (ChOB 10.159); her grandfather Gibson left her a negro in 1788

2114-4 **Hannah Gibson**; in 1794 Aaron Haskins was appointed her guardian (ChOB 10.509) and in 1796 she chose William Flounoy as her guardian (ChOB 12.7); her grandfather Gibson's will states she is to have the home plantation after the death of his wife, also 1 negro

211-5 **William Burton**; d. by 11 Sep 1791 Manchester Parish; m. **Mary** ____; d. before his father's will was written

Will of William Burton of Manchester Parish; 23 Nov ____; Ct. 11 Sep 1791
To wife, use of all estate for life, but John, s/o my bro. John, to have land where I live
To John Dubrel, s/o Charles Dubrel, negro
To my sister Nancy Gibson's dau. Elizabeth Gibson, rest of my estate
To wife Mary, 1 negro
Wit: Edward Farley, Joseph Burton, Mary Farley (ChWB 4.423)
Ct. 11 Sep 1791; will of William Burton proved; Joseph Burton, wit.; Mary Burton, widow, refused to qualify (ChOB 9.194)
25 Oct 1791; inventory of William Burton in Mecklenburg Co.; value £20.13.0; value in Chesterfield Co. £14.15 (ChWB 4.537)

211-6 ____ **Burton**; m. **Charles Duberl**; known child:

2116-1 **John Duberl**; legatee of William Burton of Manchester Parish

211-7 **Sarah Burton**; m. **Littlebury Sublet**

211-8 **Edith Burton**; m. **Abraham Sublet**

211-9 ____ **Burton**; m. ____ **Forsee**; child:

2119-1 **Phebe Forsee**

21-2 **Caleb Burton**; inherited 130 ac from his father; lived Augusta Co.

4 Jun 1757; 7 Oct 1757; from Calep (sic) Burton of Augusta Co. to John Burton of Chesterfield Co.; for £26; 150 ac. on n. side of *Nisons Branch* (ChDB 3.184)

21-3 **Joseph Burton**; inherited family plantation from his father's will

21-4 **Elizabeth Burton**

21-5 **Sarah Burton**

21-6 **Joannah Burton**

21-7 **Mary Burton**

21-8 **Robert Burton**; went to SC

21-9 Agnes Burton; m. ____ **Farmer**

2-2 Isaiah Burton; m. **Obedience** ____; he was not mentioned in his father's will, but identified by the 1729 deed of gift of land on *Falling Creek*; he was living in Albemarle Co. 4 Mar 1757 when he made land deals in Chesterfield Co. (ChDB 3.120, 122, 129); 20 Oct 1763 as Isaiah Burton, Sr., if Buckingham Co., he sold 200 ac. at upper end of Thomas Burton's tract in Chesterfield Co. to John Burton of Dale Parish (ChDB 3.456)

1 May 1736; 1st Mon Jun 1736; from Henry Cary of Henrico Co. to Isaiah Burton; for £36; 600 ac. in Dale Parish on s. side of James River (HCVD-2 p. 170)

3 Oct 1751; 4 Oct 1751; from Isaiah Burton and Obediance his wife to John Fowler of Henrico Co.; for £207.16; 600 ac. bound by *Pockashock*, etc. (ChOB 1.282)

2-3 Thomas Burton, Sr.; d. ca 1773 Chesterfield Co.; m. **Joanna** ____; d. bef. 1771; children:

> 23-1 Thomas Burton, Jr.
> 23-2 William Burton
> 23-3 John Burton

2 Dec 1745; 1st Mon Dec 1745; from Thomas Burton, Sr. of Henrico Co., planter, to Ware Rockett, carpenter; for £40; 85 ac. in Dale Parish on s. side of *Falling Creek*; given him by his father John Burton; bounded by John Burton and Col. Wm. Bird; Joanna, w/o Thomas, relinquished dower (HCVD-3 p. 21)

Will of Thomas Burton; Chesterfield Co.; 8 Dec 1771; 5 Nov 1773
To son Thomas, great Bible and one dollar
To grandson Thomas, my plantation and all my land, 4 negroes
To granddau. Martha, d/o son John, 1 negro
Remainder to be equally divided between son John & grandson Thomas; they to be exs.
Wit: Robert Cary, John Wood, John Wood (ChWB 2.1)
5 Nov 1773; will of Thomas Burton presented (ChOB 5.349)
16 Dec 1773; inventory of Thomas Burton, Sr.; value £587.14.0 (ChWB 1.2)
7 Jan 1774; inventory of Thomas Burton, returned (ChOB 5.387)
[Thomas Burton; Chesterfield County Wills and Administrations (1754-1800) Will - dated 1771 Proved 5 November 1773. (O.B. 5, p. 349) Chesterfield County Will Book 2, p. 1; Thomas Burton, Sr.; Chesterfield County Wills and Administrations (1754-1800) Inv. & Appr. - dated 1773. Returned 7 January 1774. (O.B. 5, p. 387.) Chesterfield County Will Book 2, p. 2-3 (LOV)]

23-1 Thomas Burton, Jr.; he inherited the Great Bible and $1 from his father; he m. ____; children from wills:

> 231-1 Thomas Burton
> 231-2 Sarah Burton

6 __ 1763; May 1763; from Thomas Burton, Jr. for good causes to son in law George Hancock, both of Chesterfield Co. and Sarah his wife, my daughter; 200 ac. on *Beaver Pond Branch* of *Falling Creek* (ChDB 4.480)

Will of Thomas Burton; Chesterfield Co.; 28 Apr 1790
To grandson George Hancock, s/o George Hancock, Sr., my whole estate and he to be ex.
Wit: Morris Roberts, Olive Roberts, Charles Burton, Sarah Hatcher (ChWB 4.370)

    231-1 **Thomas Burton**; he was a legatee of his grandfather Burton
    231-2 **Sarah Burton**; m. **George Hancock**; child:

        2312-1 **George Hancock**

    23-2 **William Burton**; he was bound out by the Churchwardens of Manchester Parish, Chesterfield Co., 7 May 1773 (ChOB 5.274)
    23-3 **John Burton**; d. by 12 Feb 1801; m. ____; children from wills:

        233-1 Thomas Burton
        233-2 Martha Burton
        233-3 William Burton
        233-4 Mary Burton
        233-5 Hannah Burton
        233-6 Sally Burton
        233-7 Hardin Burton
        233-8 John Burton
        233-9 Charles Burton

Will of John Burton; Chesterfield Co.; 10 Jan 1801; 12 Feb 1801
To son Thomas, 20 ac between the old road and *Pokershock Creek*
To dau., Martha Pankey, 1 cow
To grandson Sam'l Pankey, s/o Martha, 1 negro
To son William, 2 negroes
To dau. Mary Gibson, widow of William Gibson, £20
To dau. Hannah, w/o William Cary, 2 negroes
To granddau. Nancy Gibson, d/o Mary, 2 negroes
To dau. Sally Burton, 4 negroes
To grandson William Burton, s/o John, 1 negro
To granddau. Frances Burton, d/o W. Burton, 1 negro
To son Charles, tract I live on, 7 negroes, rest of person estate
Ex: son Charles
Wit: Thos. Branch, Dan'l Hudson (ChWB 5.351)
Ct. 12 Feb 1801; Will of John Burton proved; probate granted to Charles Burton (ChOB 14.32)

Ct. 9 Sep 1800; Samuel Pankey & Polly his wife, Eliza. Burton, Frankey Burton, and infants William, Sally & Benjamin Burton by said Pankey, their next friend; vs. Charles Burton admn. of John Burton, dec'd, and Sarah Burton, widow of sd. John; court orders estate divided among heirs (ChOB 12.315)

    233-1 **Thomas Burton**; he inherited 20 ac. from the will of his father and was named in 1801 will of his sister Sally
    233-2 **Martha Burton**; m. **Samuel Pankey**; she is named in the will of her father & grandfather Burton

2332-2 **Samuel Hardin Pankey**; named in wills of his Uncle Hardin & Aunt Sally and grandfather John Burton

233-3 **William Burton**; m. _____; 13 Apr 1801 a William Burton chose Miles Cary as his guardian (ChOB 14.82); named in wills of his bro. Hardin & his father; children from wills:

2333-1 **John Burton**; named in will of his Aunt Sally
2333-2 **Frances Burton**; named in will of her grandfather Burton

243-4 **Mary Burton**; m. **William Gibson**; d. bef. 1801 Bedford Co.; Mary called widow in will of her sister Sally and the will of her father

2334-1 **John Gibson**; named in will of his Uncle Hardin
2334-2 **Nancy Gibson**; named in will of her Aunt Sally & her grandfather Burton

233-5 **Hannah Burton**; m. **William Cary**, b. 14 Apr 1756 Chesterfield Co.; d. bef. 10 Jan 1801

2335-1 **Elizabeth Cary**; named in will of her Aunt Sally

233-6 **Sally Burton**; d. aft. 1 Oct 1801; named in wills of her bro. Hardin & her father

Will of Salley Burton; 1 Oct 1801; 11 Jan 1802
To my sister Mary Gibson, widow of William Gibson in Bedford Co., money from sale of negro
To bro. Charles Burton, 2 negroes
To nephew John Burton, s/o my bro. William, negro
To niece Elizabeth Cary, d/o William Cary, 1 negro
To bro. Thomas Burton, 2 head of cattle
To nephew Samuel Pankey, 2 head of cattle
To niece Elizabeth Burton, d/o my bro. John Burton, feather bed
To niece Nancy Gibson, d/o William Gibson, items
Ex: bro. Charles Burton
Wit: Matthew Branch, Dan'l Hudson (ChWB 5.490)
11 Jan 1802; will of Salley Burton, probate granted Charles Hudson (ChOB 14.192)

233-7 **Hardin Burton**; d. aft. 8 Jan 1788; he and Stephen Pankey made oath at an inquisition taken at Manchester on 30 Oct 1786 (ChWB 4.195)

Will of Hardin Burton; Chesterfield Co.; 8 Jan 1788; 10 Apr 1788
To bros. John and William Burton, all my land
To nephew John Gibson, s/o William Gibson, negro
To sister Sally Burton, if she dies with heirs of her body to my bro. Charles
To nephew Samuel Hardin Pankey, my gun and case
Exs: my father John Burton, friend Stephen Pankey, Jr.
Wit: Edw'd Branch, Thomas Baker, Edward Branch (ChWB 4.151)
Ct. 10 Apr 1788; will of Hardin Burton proved (ChOB 8.83)

233-8 **John Burton**; d. by ca 1797; mb. 6 Aug 1775 Chesterfield Co. **Sarah Horner**; surety William Walthall (MCC p. 24); John was named in will of his bro. Hardin; children from wills:

2338-1 **Elizabeth Burton**; named in will of her Aunt Sally
2338-2 **William Burton**; named in will of his grandfather Burton

Ct. 14 Feb 1797; Sarah Burton & Charles Burton granted administration of estate of John Burton, dec'd (ChOB 12.89); estate of John Burton to Charles Burton (ChWB 5.552); 8 May 1797; inventory of John Burton produced by Charles Burton, adm'r, and Sarah Burton, admx. (ChOB 10.100); 1797; estate of John Burton to Charles Burton, admn. (ChWB 5.552); will of John Burton proved by Thomas Burton

233-9 **Charles Burton**; named in will of his bro. Hardin & ex. of estate of his father, his sister Sally and his bro. John

2-4 **Samuel Burton**
2-5 **James Burton**; m. **Judith** ____; James made deeds in Henrico Co. in May 1738 & Dec 1744 (HCVD-3 p. 78, 106)

1 May 1761; May 1761; from James Burton of Lunenburg Co. and Judith his wife to John Baker of Dale Parish, Chesterfield Co.; for £15; 85 ac. on s. side of *Falling Creek* being land given sd. Burton by his father, John Burton (ChDB 4.374)

2-6 **Sarah Burton**; m. ____ **Jackson**
2-7 **Elizabeth Burton**; m. ____ **Turpin**
2-8 **Susannah Burton**; m. ____ **Tanner**
2-9 **Phebe Burton**; m. ____ **Johnson**
2-10 **Ann Burton**
2-11 **Ezar Burton**

3. **Abraham Burton**, b. ca 1669, age 23 on 1 Oct 1692; d. ca 1736 Amelia Co.; m. Feb 1692 Henrico Co. **Anne Featherstone**; d. 12 Dec 1745 Amelia Co.; d/o Charles Featherstone; children from family histories:

3-1 Abraham Burton, Jr., b. ca 1691
3-2 Susannah Burton, b. ca 1695
3-3 Charles Burton, Sr., b. ca 1696
3-4 Thomas Burton
3-5 Phebe Burton
3-6 Stephen Burton

13 Dec 1681; 1 Feb 1683; deed of gift from Thomas Burton to son Abraham Burton; cow calf and young sow (HCVD-1 p. 24)

1 Feb 1691; [recorded]; Abraham Burton, who m. Anne, one of the orphans of Charles Featherstone dec'd, ack. receipt of Anne's share of her father's estate (HCVW-1 p. 67)

20 Dec 1692; 17 Apr 1693; from Abraham Burton, s/o Thomas Burton, dec'd, who gave me 100 ac. in Bristol Parish in his lifetime, sell to John Steward, glover; Anne, w/o Abraham, relinquished dower (HCVD-1 p. 77)

28 Sep 1730; Abraham Burton patented 400 ac. on upper side of *Flatt Creek* in Prince George Co. (LOP 13.527)

28 Sep 1730; Abraham Burton patented 200 ac. on upper side of *Deep Creek* on Appomattox River in Prince George Co. (LOP 13.532)

20 May 1735; Abraham Burton patented 150 on lower side of *Beaverpond Branch* of *Deep Creek* in Prince George Co. (LOP 15.508)

3-1 **Abraham Burton, Jr.**, b. ca 1691; d. ca 1758 Amelia Co.; m. by 1729 **Mary Bevill**; d/o Essex Bevill and Elizabeth Webster (HCVW-1 172, 180); Mary and her dau. Elizabeth inherited from the will of Elizabeth Bevill, Mary's mother, written 14 Apr 1732 (HCVW-1 p. 180); in 1729 Abraham was living in Prince George Co. (HCVW-1 p. 172); children:

  31-1 **Elizabeth Burton**, b. Apr 1726 Bristol Parish; she inherited items from will of her grandmother Bevill
  31-2 **Abraham Burton**, b. 24 Jan 1727/8 Bristol Parish; m. **Ann Neal**; d/o Thomas Neal from whose will she inherited 1s in 1764 (ChWB 1.428)
  31-3 **Phoebe Burton**, b. 11 Sep 1730 Bristol Parish
  31-4 **Robert Burton**, b. 24 Aug 1732 Bristol Parish
  31-5 **Abel Burton**, b. ca 1734 *Deep Creek*, Amelia Co.; m. **Anne Cousins**

3-2 **Susannah Featherstone Burton**, b. ca 1695; d. Sep 1751 Amelia Co.; m. ca 1717 **John Garrett**, b. ca 1690 Amelia Co.; d. by 18 May 1743 when his will was recorded in Amelia Co.; children from family histories:

  32-1 **Isaac Garrett**, b. 9 Dec 1720 Bristol Parish; d. by 2 Jun 1775 Chesterfield Co. when his will was proved; 5 Aug 1775 George Markham was granted probate (ChOB 6.84, 88)
  32-2 **Anne Garrett**, b. 22 Sep 1721 Bristol Parish
  32-3 **Susannah Garrett**, b. 1 Sep 1723 Bristol Parish
  32-4 **John Garrett**, b. 10 Jul 1726 Bristol Parish
  32-5 **Abraham Garrett**, b. 3 Jul 1729 Bristol Parish
  32-6 **Thomas Garrett**, b. 6 Dec 1730 Bristol Parish; d. Mecklenburg Co.
  32-7 **Stephen Garrett**, b. 9 Apr 1733 Amelia Co.; d. Buckingham Co.
  32-8 **Charles Garrett**, b. ca 1735 Amelia Co.; d. Buckingham Co.
  32-9 **Nanney Garrett**, b. ca 1737 Amelia Co.

3-3 **Charles Burton, Sr.**, b. ca 1696; m. **Loveday Franklin**; d/o James Franklin; she is named in the 26 Jul 1746 will of her father, which also mentions Charles & Thomas Burton (HCVW-2 p. 35); Charles rec'd 2 negroes and £100 from his father's will; he was living in Dale Parish, Henrico Co. in 1746 & 1748 (HCVD-3 p. 37, 63); he lived *Swift Creek*, Chesterfield Co.; children from family histories:

                33-1 Thomas Burton
                33-2 Henry Burton
                33-3 Abraham Burton

33-4   Charles Burton, Jr.
33-5   Robert Burton

9 Jul 1736; 9 Dec 1736; from James Franklin of Dale Parish, Henrico Co. to dau. Lovesday Burton, w/o Charles Burton of same; 150 ac. bounded by sd. Charles Burton, Thomas Burton & James Franklin, Jr. (HCVD-2 p. 183)

33-1   **Thomas Burton**; he may have been Thomas who d. by 6 Sep 1765

[Thomas Burton; Chesterfield County Wills and Administrations (1754-1800) His suit against Henry Burton to abate due to death of Thomas Burton, 6 Sept. 1765. ChOB 3, p. 685 (LOV)]

33-2   **Henry Burton**
33-3   **Abraham Burton**; her inherited £10 from the 1786 will of Frances Turpin (ChWB 4.362); in 1783 an Abraham Burton was living in Mecklenburg Co. (MeDB 6.269); as Abraham, s/o Charles, he inherited £10 from will of Ann Cousins of Dale Parish written 27 Jun1786 (ChWB 4.362)
33-4   **Charles Burton, Jr.**
33-5   **Robert Burton**.

3-4   **Thomas Burton**
3-5   **Phebe Burton**
3-6   **Stephen Burton**

4.   **Isaac Burton**; he held 100 ac. in Henrico Co. according to the 1705 rent rolls

2 Sep 1735; from Isaac Burton to John Bolling, both of Henrico Co.; for £12.10; 100 ac. on n. side of Appomattox River; by tract called *Cobbs* (HCVD-2 p. 164)

5.   **Ann Burton**; ml. 8 Aug 1693 Henrico Co. **Bar. Stovall**; surety John Steward (QRH p. 91; MHC p. 81)

COCKE

The Cocke family was prominent among the early settlers of Henrico County. Before 1640 Richard Cocke, the progenitor of the family, had established his home at *Bremo*. He was a member of the House of Burgesses, a Lt. Col. in the militia and very active in the political life of Henrico Co. His descendants served as officers in the militia, patented thousands more acres of land in Henrico and adjoining counties and served in appointed positions.

RICHARD COCKE

Richard Cocke, Lt. Col.; of *Bremo*; d. by 1665; said to have m/1
Temperance Bayly; d/o Thomas Bayly and Cecily Reynolds; he m/2 by 1666
Mary Aston; d/o Walter Aston (d. 6 Apr 1656) & sister of Lt. Col. Walter
Aston of *Cawsey's Care*, Shirley Hundred (d. 29 Jan 1666); Mary m/2 ____
Clarke; Richard patented 100 ac. in Elizabeth City Co. in 1628 and in 1632 was
a member of the House of Burgesses from Weyanoke, Charles City Co.;
children from wills:

1. Thomas Cocke
2. Richard Cocke, the elder
3. Elizabeth Cocke, b. aft. 1646
4. William Cocke
Sons of Mary Aston:
5. John Cocke
6. Richard Cocke, the younger
7. Edward Cocke

6 Mar 1636; Richard Cocke granted 3,000 ac. Henrico Co. on the main river; due for
transport of 3 score persons (LOP 1.413) (PB 1.1.54)

10 Mar 1638; Richard Cocke, Gent., granted 2,000 ac. Henrico Co. on the river; 300
ac. of that at *Bremo*; 1,700 ac. at head of *Turkie Island Creek* called *Mamburne Hills*;
1,000 ac. of original 3,000 ac. grant surrendered to Ann, widow of Robert Hallum; sd.
2,000 ac. in right of transport of 40 persons (LOP 1.707) (PB 1.2.707)

10 Oct 1652; Richard Cocke granted 2,482 ac. Henrico Co.; 1,860 ac. near head of
Turkey Island Creek & 622 ac. called *Bremo*; bounded by *Curles*, etc.; 100 ac. due
Temp. Bayley 20 Sep 1620; 2,000 ac. by patent; residue for transport of several
persons (PB 3.133)

21 Jun 1664; Mr. Richard Cocke and Mr. John Beachamp granted 2,993 ac. 1r. 35per.
Henrico Co.; 2093 ac. s. side of *Chickahomeny Swamp* & 901 ac. 1 rod on n. side of
James River in fork of *Cattaile Run* adj. land formerly surveyed for Mr. Cocke; for
transport of 60 persons (LOP 5.399) (PB 5.367 [399])

Will of Richard Cocke, Sr., Henrico Co.; 4 Oct 1665 [dated]; 1665
Body to be interred in orchard near my first wife; Church of England ceremony
To Mary, 1/3 of my estate, goods & land for life; she to make no claim to lands I have
   given sons Thomas & Richard by deeds of gift
To sons Wm. and John equally; residue of a dividient of land not disposed of by deed of
   gift & the mill to be divided between them at age, excepting gift of 640 ac. of *Bremo*
   to my eldest son Richard Cock and male heirs of his body lawfully begotten; for
   want of heirs to son Thomas, then to son Wm., then to son John, then to youngest
   son Richard
Richard or successive heir to pay dau. Elizabeth £100 at age 17 or marriage
To Richard, the younger, 1,750 ac. from patent taken up jointly with John Beauchamp;
   residue has been given to Thomas & Richard the older
To Richard, the older, items from his mother; not part of my estate
Rest of estate to be divided between my children by present wife Mary Cocke

To cozen Daniel Jordan, land for life to be shared with my son

To son Thomas, the mill, also for the use of other children; also 3,000# tobacco

Sons: Richard [the elder], Thomas, Will, John, Richard [the younger]

Exs: wife Mary, sons Richard and Thomas; with the Justices of the county as overseers

Wit: Henry Randolph, Joseph Tanner, Henry Isham (HCVW-1 p. 219; VP p. 640, Package 12)

[undated; with ca 1679 records]; debts rec'd by estate of Lt. Col. Cocke, dec'd; valued 30,126# tobacco (HCVW-1 p. 6)

[Richard Cocke, Senior; Henrico Co.Wills and Admns. (1662-1800) p. 27-28. Will dated 4 Oct. 1665. Misc. Court Records, Vol. 1, [1650-1717] (Reel 1); wills not listed in Virginia Wills and Admns., 1632-1800 (Torrence). Will - 1665 Henrico Co. Misc. Records. Vol. 1, p. 27; Henrico Co. Wills and Admns. (1662-1800) p. 33. Inv. & appr. rec. [Jan. 1677/78]. p. 108-109. Accts. rec. 3 Oct. 1679. Records, 1677-1692 (Reel 4) (LOV)]

Will of Walter Aston, of *Cawsey's Care*; Shirley Hundred; 21 Dec 1666; 4 Feb 1666-7

To Hannah Hill, his mother, he gives that parcell of land called *The Level*

To godson John Cocke, the son of Richard Cocke, deceased, 4,000# of tobacco to be paid in 1668

To godson Edward Cocke, son of the abovesaid Cocke, 6,000 pds. of tobacco, to be paid in 1669 survivor to have the whole 10,000, and in case both die, to the rest of the children

To sisters Mary Cocke and Elizabeth Binns 20 shillings apiece for a ring (Charles City Co. Wills)

[Walter Aston (Walter of *Cawsey's Care*) wills not listed in Virginia Wills and Administrations, 1632-1800 (Torrence). Will dated 21 Dec. 1666 Will proved 4 Feb. 1666 [William Byrd Title Book in 50V259 (LOV)]

1. **Thomas Cocke, Sr., Capt.**, of *Pickthorn Farm*; b. ca 1639, age 46 on 1 Aug 1685 (QRH p. 150); d. by 1697; m/1 ____; m/2 by 1687 **Margaret Powell** (TVF 6.6); d. by 4 Aug 1719; said to have been the widow of **Peter Jones**; the descendants named in Margaret's will have not been researched, but it appears she was not the mother of any of the Cocke children; the abstract of Thomas' will does not mention the Wynn grandson of Margaret which her will states was in his will; Thomas of *Turkey Island* was charged with 8 taxable in the list of 1678 and he was a Justice of Henrico Co.; children of m/1:

> 1-1 Thomas Cocke, Jr.
> 1-2 Stephen Cocke
> 1-3 James Cocke
> 1-4 William Cocke
> 1-5 Agnes Cocke
> 1-6 Temperance Cocke

25 Nov 1662; Mrs. Smith, w/o John I near *Turkey Island*, said Mr. Thomas Cocke's wife was shewd and misfed servants (TVF 7.229)

4 Oct 1675; Thomas Cock granted 3,087 ac. 3r. 24po. Henrico Co. on n. side of James River and s. side of *Chickehominy Swamp* (LOP 6.564)

4 Oct 1675; Thomas Cock granted 1,983 ac. 3r. Charles City Co. on n. side of James River near mouth of *Mongoies* (LOP 6.563)

20 Aug 1680; ordered that Mr. Tho. Cocke have a license granted him for an ordinary in the town intended to be built at Varina provided he give security according to law (CRHC 4.6)

30 Aug 1681; 1 Oct 1681; from Thomas Cocke, Sr. to Richard Cocke, Sr., both of Varina Parish, Henrico Co.; 1,000 ac. on *Chickahominey Swamp*; taken up by Richard Cocke, Sr., dec'd, and John Beauchamp; Richard Cocke, Sr. appoints atty. in deed of land between me and my bro. Thomas Cocke (HCVD-1 p. 13)

30 Aug 1681; 1 Oct 1681; agreement between Thomas Cocke, Sr. and Richard Cocke, Sr., both of Varina Parish, Henrico Co., regarding division of the profits from an ordinary licensed to Thomas and in keeping the ferry; Thomas to run the ordinary and the ferry and to have the ground for his own use for one year (HCVD-1 p. 13)

14 Feb 1681/2; 1 Aug 1682; survey for Thomas Cocke; 84 ac. bought of his bros. William and John on n. side of James River and *Mill Creek* in Varina Parish (HCVD-1 p. 18)

23 Apr 1683; 1 Jun 1683; Capt. Thomas Cocke and Mr. Richard Cocke appointed Justices of Henrico Co. (HCVD-1 p. 20) ; 25 Mar 1684; Thomas Cocke, Gent., appointed Sheriff of Henrico Co.; 1 Apr 1684; Thomas Cocke sworn as Sheriff and Stephen Cocke sworn as Undersheriff (HCVD-1 p. 25) ; 10 May 1684; 7 Dec 1685; 26 Apr 1686; Capt. Thomas Cocke & Mr. Richard Cocke appointed Justices (HCVD-1 p. 26, 30, 33); 1 Apr 1687; Capt. Thomas Cocke appointed High Sheriff of Henrico Co. (HCVD-1 p. 41)

20 Apr 1687; Thomas Cock granted 296 ac. 3r. 19po. Henrico Co. on n. side of James River near *Cedar Branch* & *Watson's* (LOP 7.557)

1 Jun 1687; 1 Jun 1687; from Thomas Cocke, Sr., to Thomas Cocke, Jr., both of Henrico Co. & Parish; deed of gift of 200 ac. part of dividént at *Malvern Hills*; next to the shallop landing on *Turkey Island Creek*, land of Thomas, Jr. and Stephen (2nd s/o Thomas, Sr.); Margaret, w/o Thomas, Sr., relinquished dower (HCVD-1 p. 42)

1 Aug 1687; 1 Aug 1687; from Thomas Cocke, Sr. of Henrico Co. & Parish to son Stephen Cocke; 200 ac. in *Malvern Hills*, part of land I bought of my bros. William and John Cocke (HCVD-1 p. 42)

20 Oct 1688; Thomas Cock, Sr. granted 1,650 ac. in Varina Parish, Henrico Co. on n. side of James River (LOP 7.556)

1 Jun 1689; 1 Jun 1689; from Thomas Cocke, Sr. to son James Cocke, both of Henrico Co. & Parish; deed of gift; 559 ac. on n. side of James River (293 ac. part of 901 ac. granted Lt. Col. Richard Cocke, father of sd. Thomas, and John Beauchamp on 21 Jun 1664; after death of Lt. Col. Cocke, the land was confirmed by Beauchamp to Cocke's 3 sons, Thomas Cocke being vested in 263 ac.; the other 296 ac. was granted sd. Thomas, Sr. 20 Apr 1687 (HCVD-1 p. 50)

22 Sep 1688; 1 Oct 1691; from Thomas Cocke of *Pick-Thorn Farm*, Henrico Co. "lets to" Thomas East part of tract patented by my father and John Beauchamp and given by

the will of our father to me and my brothers; East may elect to have it forever by paying what it is worth (HCVD-1 p. 67)

1 Oct 1689; 1 Oct 1689; Mr. Richard Cocke, Sr. of *Bremo* and Mr. John Beauchamp, both of Henrico Co.; on behalf of the 3 sons of Cocke (Thomas, Sr.; Richard, Sr., Richard, Jr.) take up 2 tracts of 2994 ac.; 2,093 ac. on s. side of *Chickahominy Swamp* by patent 21 Jun 1664; the other 901 ac. call *Fork of Cattle Run* on n. side of James River bounded by a tract formerly granted Richard Cocke the elder; Cocke died before division of the land and Beauchamp left the county and has since died [John Pleasants atty. for the estate]; the Cocke sons now being of age, they all agree to divide the land into 4 parts (HCVD-1 p. 54); 3 deeds were made 1 Oct 1690 relating to this land; the first states a tract Lt. Col. Richard Cocke, dec'd gave to his 2 sons Thomas and Richard, Sr. was divided 1 Aug 1667 unequally; the other two deeds between Thomas, Sr. and Richard, Sr. clarify the division (HCVD-1 p. 60)

1 Jun 1692; Capt. Thomas Cocke sworn Sheriff of Henrico Co.; [next page] Thomas Cocke, Sr. among the Justices present (HCVD-1 p. 45, 46)

5 Oct 1693; at Court at Varina both Mr. Thomas Cocke and Capt. Thomas Cocke, Jr. were among the Justices present (HCVD-1 p. 81)

2 Oct 1693; Thomas Cocke, Sr. advertises in Court record that he has land to lease and/or sell in Henrico and Charles City Co.; also seeking Overseer (HCVD-1 p. 83)

1689-1695; [undated]; Thomas Cock, Sr. granted 816 ac. in Varina Parish, Henrico Co. on s. side of *Chicahominy Swamp* adj. *Oposum* (LOP 8.1)

6 Dec 1696; Thomas Cocke, Sr., Thomas Cocke, Jr. and Richard Cocke, Sr. among Justices present at Henrico Court (HCVD-1 p. 97)

Will of Thomas Cocke; Henrico Co.; 10 Dec 1691; 1 Apr 1697
To wife Margaret, plantation I live on for life, negroes
To son Stephen, inherited clothes, a servant, tools, mills and 400 ac. of that patent & land left north of *White Oak Swamp*; to his dau. Agnes, items
To son James, 625 ac. part of a divident where my son Thomas was seated, negroes, hides, etc.; to his dau. Elizabeth, Indian girl
To Henrico Parish Church, 1,000# tobacco to buy a bell
To son William, 1,200 ac. land; livestock; also livestock to his dau. at age 18 or marriage
After death of dau. Agnes Harwood, mullato girl to grandson Thomas Harwood & a mare; other grandsons Joseph and Samuel Harwood, a mare
To granddaus. Agnes & Joyce Harwood, items
To grandson Thomas Cooke, plantation I live on, all land s. side of *White Oak Swamp Run*; division made between my bros. Richard Cocke and John Pleasants
To grandson James, s/o Thomas Cocke, land on s. side of western branch of *Herrin Creek*
To grandson Henry Cocke, all residue of *Moniquies* patent after Davis (sic), Stephen and James Cocke have their parts
To grandson ____ Cocke, calves
Exs. wife and son James; they to divide residue of estate
Wit: Jacob Ware, Thomas Smythe, Thomas Topping (HCVW-1 p. 62, 63, 64)

1 Apr 1697; probate granted James Cocke and Margaret Cocke on estate of Thomas Cocke (HCVW-1 p. 65)
[Thomas Cocke; Part of index to Henrico County Wills and Admns. (1662-1800) Note p. 684-689. Will pro. 1 Apr. 1697. Deeds, Wills, Etc., 1688-1697 (Reel 5) (LOV)]

Will of Margaret Cocke, widow, of Henrico Parish; 12 Aug 1718; 14 Aug 1719
Granddaus. Margaret, wife of Edward Goodrich; granddau. Mary, wife of John
    Worsham; Margaret Jones
Grandsons: Peter Wynn, Joshua Wynn, Robert Wynn, William Wynn and Francis
    Wynn & Peter Jones (s/o my son Abraham Jones)
"To grandson Peter Wynn, a mulatto, willed him by my dec'd husband Thomas
    Cocke"
Exs: son Peter Jones, William Randolph
Wit: Will Jones, Thomas Buckner, Thos. Morris (HCVW-1 p. 229)
[Margaret Cocke; Part of index to Henrico Co. Wills and Admns. (1662-1800) Note p. 433-436.
Will pro. 4 May 1719. Misc. Court Records, Vol. 2, [1718-1726] (Reel 1); Part of index to wills
not listed in Virginia Wills and Admns., 1632-1800 (Torrence). Note Will - 1719 Henrico Co.
Miscellaneous Records. Vol. 2, p. 433 (LOV)]

1-1 **Thomas Cocke, Jr.**, b. ca 1664-1670, age 17 on 22 May 1681 & 10 Oct
1681; age 21 on 1 Dec 1691 (QRH p. 149, 154); d. by 1 Apr 1707; m/1 by 1687
Mary Brasseur; d/o John Brasseur & Mary Pitt; m/2 by 1706 **Frances
Anderson**; d. by 14 Mar 1726 Prince George Co.; d/o Reynard Anderson &
Elizabeth Skiffen; Frances was said to have been the widow of the wealthy
John Herbert of *Puddledock*, Bristol Parish, Prince George Co.; Frances
m/3 **Capt. Joshua Wynne**; d. by 8 Nov 1715 Prince George Co. whose
marriage contract made 10 Feb 1711 allowed Mary to retain control of her
large estate; Thomas' father gave him 200 ac. *Malvern Hills* in 1687 and the
will of his father left him 301 ac. on n. side of *White Oak Swamp* and 250
ac. in Charles City Co. in 1707; children from family histories:

        11-1 Thomas Cocke
        11-2 Brassure Cocke, b. by 1690
        11-3 James Powell Cocke, b. aft. 1690
        11-4 Henry Cocke, b. ca 1695
        11-5 Mary Cocke, b. aft. 1690
        11-6 Elizabeth Cocke, b. aft. 1690
        11-7 Martha Cocke

20 Apr 1687; Thomas Cock, Jr. granted 671 ac. in Varina Parish Henrico Co. on n.
side of James River (LOP 7.556)

1 Oct 1687 [recorded]; from Thomas Cocke, Jr. to Robert Burton, both of Henrico Co.
& Parish; for tobacco; 300 ac on n. side of James River pat of patent 20 Apr 1687;
mentions *Gravelly Hill* and branch of *Roundabout*; Mary, w/o Thomas, Jr.,
relinquished dower (HCVD-1 p. 44)

29 Apr 1693; 29 Apr 1693; Mr. Thomas Cocke, Jr. granted 528 ac. in Varina Parish on
n. side of James River, the head of *Barrow, Sampsons Slash*, etc.; for importation of
11 persons (HVD-1 p. 79) (LOP 8.260); 1 Aug 1693; Thomas Cocke, Jr. sold same to
Giles Webb (HCVD-1 p. 79)

26 Apr 1698; Capt. Thos. Cock granted 49 ac. on n. side of James River in Henrico Co. (LOP 9.139)

6 Jun 1699; Capt. Thomas Cock granted 943 ac. being part of 1,983 ac. 3r. called *Mongyes* on n. side of James River formerly granted his father, Thomas Cock, on 4 Oct 1675 (LOP 9.198)

24 Oct 1701; Thomas Cock granted 1,170 ac. in Westover Parish, Charles City Co., adj. his own land (LOP 9.403)

24 Oct 1701; Thomas Cock granted 628 ac. Henrico Co. on n. side of James River; being added part of a pat. for 1,228 ac. 1r. 26po. (LOP 9.373)

Will of Thomas Cocke; Henrico Co.; 16 Jan 1706; 1 Apr 1707
To son Thomas, 301 ac. on n. side of *White Oak Swamp*; 250 ac. in Charles City Co. granted by patent 24 Oct 1701; negroes, items
To son James Powell Cocke, plantation I live on and adj. 200 ac. I purchased from bro. Stephen; 940 ac. remainder of Charles City Co. land; negroes
To son Henry, 200 ac. remainder of tract purchased from bro. Stephen; 49 ac. on *White Oak Swamp* granted me in 1698; 943 ac. part in Charles City, part in Henrico granted me 6 Jun 1698, negroes, items
To son Brassuir, 628 ac. Henrico Co. granted 24 Oct 1701; 1,150 ac. adj. excepting 100 ac.; negroes, items
To daus. Mary and Elizabeth Cocke, at age 16 or marriage; negroes, items, tobacco; 371 ac. part of 671 ac. granted 20 Apr 1687 (other part sold)
To 4 sons, livestock to be divided when James Powell reaches 16, Brassuir is 16; remainder of estate
Marriage agreement with wife Frances to be honored; none of her property to be infringed on
Ex: son Thomas; overseers friends Thomas Farrar, Littlebury Epes, Samuel Harwood, Sr.
Wit: James Cocke, James Delop, Charles Birk
14 Feb 1706; codicil gives daus. 1/10 of debts due (HVCW-1 p. 95-96)
[Thomas Cocke; Henrico Co. Wills and Admns. (1662-1800) p. 24-28. Will pro. 1 Apr. 1707. p. 28. Codicil rec. 1 Apr. 1707. Records, 1706-1709 (Reel 6) (LOV)]

[Joshua Wynee; Prince George Co. Wills & Admns. (1713-1800); Deeds, Etc., 1713-1728, Pt. 1, p. 81. Accts. rec. 8 Nov 1715 (Reel 1) (LOV)]

Will of Frances Wynne; Prince George Co.; 10/16/1725; 3/14/1726
To daughter Martha Cocke, slaves and items
To son Richard Herbert, slaves and items.
To daughter-in-law Mary Herbert, slaves
To son Buller Herbert, rest of estate and to be executor
Wit: Robert Munford, John Ingles, Miles Thweat (PGWB 1713-1728 p. 973)
[Francis Wynn; Prince George Co. Wills & Admns. (1713-1800); Deeds, Etc., 1713-1728, Pt. 3, p. 973-1974, will pro. 14 Mar 1726 (Reel 2) (LOV)]

11-1 **Thomas Cocke**; d. by 3 Mar 1711 Henrico Co.; he inherited the home plantation & land on *White Oak Swamp Run* from the 1697 will of his grandfather Cocke; from his father's 1707 will he inherited 301 ac. on n. side of *White Oak Swamp* and 250 ac. in Charles City Co.; unmarried

12 Jan 1711; 3 Mar 1711; inventory of Mr. Thomas Cocke; value £247.8.2 ½ (HCVW-1 p. 117); 7 Jun 1714; [recorded]; acc'ts of estate of Mr. Thomas Cocke (HCVW-1 p. 127) [Thomas Cocke, Jr.; Henrico County Wills and Admns. (1662-1800) p. 102-103. Will pro. 5 Nov. 1711. p. 113-115. Inv. & appr. rec. 3 Mar. 1711. p. 265-266. Accounts rec. 7 June 1714. Records, 1710-1714 (Reel 6) (LOV)]

 11-2 **Brassure Cocke**, b. by 1690; d. Brunswick Co.; said to have m. **Frances____**; in 1714/5 he inherited the 500 ac. on *White Oak Swamp* from his bro. Henry who had inherited it from their bro. Thomas; from his father he inherited 628 ac. Henrico Co. granted 1701 and 1,050 ac. of 1,150 ac. tract; possible children [use with caution]:

   112-1 Martha Cocke
   112-2 William Cocke
   112-3 Thomas Cocke
   112-4 Mary Cocke
   112-5 Susan Cocke
   112-6 Anne Cocke
   112-7 James Cocke
   112-8 Elizabeth Cocke

3 Mar 1717; from Breashure Cocke to Thomas Pleasants, both of Henrico Co. & Parish; for £23; 425 ac. on n. side of James River; adj. James Cocke (bro. of Brashure), Richard Cocke, Sr. and others (HCVD-2 p. 71)

5 Jan 1729; 1st Mon Jan 1729; from Brashure Cocke of Henrico Co. & Parish to James Powell Cocke of same; for £216; 270 ac. *Malborn Hills* given Brashure by his late bro. Thomas; adj. James Powell Cock, John Cocke and others (HCVD-2 p. 123)

1 Mar 1743; Brazure Cocke granted 400 ac. Goochland Co. on both sides of *Green Creek* of Appomattox River (LOP 22.50)

 112-1 **Martha Cocke**
 112-2 **William Cocke**; d. by Nov 1796 when his will was probated in Granville Co., NC (Granville Co. NC Will Book 4.50); mb. 23 Jul 1754 Brunswick Co. **Rebecca Edwards**

27 Jul 1761; 27 Jul 1761; from John Jones merchant of Prince George Co. to William Cocke; for £50; 400 ac. on *Reedy Creek* (BrDB 6.722)

 112-3 **Thomas Cocke**; d. bef. 1766; may have m. **Keziah Anderson**; of Surry Co. wit. deed in Brunswick Co. 13 Aug 1743

3 May 1759; 22 May 1759; from Thomas Cocke of Cumberland Co. to John Gunther, Jr.; for 5s; 162 ac. on *Rocky Run* and *Nottaway River*; wit. William Cocke among others (BrDB 6.353)

 112-4 **Mary Cocke**; mb. 5 Feb 1758 Cumberland Co. **Parson Anderson**; Thomas Cocke, sec.; Charles Anderson letter of consent for Parson to marry
 112-5 **Susanna Cocke**; m. ____ **Coleman**
 112-6 **Anne Cocke**; unmarried 1761

112-7 **James Cocke**; d. by 1 Dec 1761; said to have m. **Catherine Richards**

Will of James Cocke, Lunenburg Co.; 1 Jul 1761; 1 Dec 1761
Sisters: Susannah Coleman, Mary Anderson, Anne Cocke, Martha Cocke
Ex: bro. William Cocke
Wit: Richard Hall, Thos. Bracey, John Lynch (LuWB 1.336)

112-8 **Elizabeth Cocke**; m. 20 Sep 1766 Brunswick Co. **Thomas Holt**

11-3 **James Powell Cocke** of *Malvern Hills* & later *Edgemont*, b. aft. 1690; d. by Sep 1747; m. ca 1718 **Martha Herbert**; d. by Aug Ct. 1757; d/o John Herbert & Frances Anderson; sister of Richard Herbert; & niece of James Anderson; James Powell Cocke inherited land on *Herrin Creek* from his grandfather Cocke & 940 ac. on *White Oak Swamp* from his bro. Henry; he inherited 200 ac. his father bought from his uncle Stephen and 940 ac. in Charles City Co. in 1707; 1725 will of James Anderson of Prince George Co. leaves ½ his land on s. side of *Nottoway River* at *Stony Hill Run* to "nephew" Martha Cocke, w/o James Powell Cocke (PGWB 1713-1728 p. 837); he is called "my brother" in the 1730 will of Richard Herbert (HCVW-1 p. 176); known children:

        113-1   James Powell Cocke
        113-2 ____ Cocke (f)
        113-3   Thomas Cocke

7 Nov 1715; 7 Nov 1715; from James Powell Cocke of Henrico Co. & Parish to William Sewell; for 4,000# tobacco; 97 on *White Oak Swamp*; next to Richard Cock (HCVD-2 p. 50)

11 Oct 1727; James Powell Cocke granted 1,581 ac. in Prince George Co. in the main forks of *Knibs Creek* (LOP 13.315)

28 Sep 1732; James Powell Cocke granted 1,050 ac. Prince George Co. in the main fork of *Knibbs Creek* adj. Henry Anderson (LOP 14.490)

10 Sep 1735; James Powel Cocke granted 254 ac. Prince George Co. on s. side of *Appomattox River* below *Saylors Creek* (LOP 16.249)

1 Aug 1737; 1st Mon Oct 1737; from James Powell Cocke of Varina Parish, Henrico Co. to Samuel Wortham of Christ Church Parish, Middlesex Co.; for £100; 792 ac. bounded by *Deep Run*; part of a grant to Capt. Thomas Cocke 21 Oct 1698 (HCVD-2 p. 185); 1st Mon Dec 1737; for deeds drawn 31 Jul and 1 Aug; for £100; 792 ac. (HCVD-2 p. 186)

Nov Ct. 1739; James Powell Cocke took oath as Militia Officer (HCVD-3 p. 84)

Will of James Powell Cocke; 19 Aug 1747; Sep 1747
To wife, estate for life, except what is given to my daughter & her husband in bond
To granddau. Martha Cocke, 4 negroes
To grandson Chasteen Cocke, *Malborne Hills* plantation and the one at *Four Mile Creek* after death of this father

To son James, ex., and Chasteen Cocke; remainder to be divided when he is 21
Wit: John Povall, Elizabeth Povall, Charles Floyd, Stephen Woodson (HCVW-2 p. 36)
Dec 1751; inventory of James Powell Cocke; value £840.4.11; presented by James
Povall (HCVW-2 p. 55)
[James Powel Cocke; Henrico Co. Wills and Admns. (1662-1800) p. 296. Will pro. Sept. 1747.
Deed Book, 1744-1748 (Reel 8); p. 93. Inv. & appr. rec. Dec. 1751. Deeds, Wills, Etc., 1750-
1767 (Reel 9) (LOV)]

26 Oct 1748; 1ˢᵗ Mon Jun 1749; from Martha Cocke, widow of James Powell Cocke,
of Henrico Co., dec'd, deed of gift to son James Cocke *Malborn Hills* and all other
estate left me by my said husband (HCVD-3 p. 70)

Aug Ct. 1757; John James Dupuy granted administration of estate of Martha Cocke,
dec'd (HCVW-2 p. 72)
Nov Ct. 1757; inventory of Martha Cocke, recorded (HCVD-2 p. 72)
[Martha Cocke; Henrico County Wills and Administrations (1662-1800) p. 1609-1610. Adms.
bond rec. 1, 1757. Misc. Court Records, Vol. 5, [1747-1757] (Reel 3) (LOV)]

113-1 **James Powell Cocke**, b. 18 Aug 1718 Henrico Co.; d. 26 May
1753 Lunenburg Co.; mb. 19 Apr 1742 Goochland Co.; m. 22 Oct 1742
Amelia Co. **Mary Magdalene Chastain**; sec., Henry Wood; wit.,
Joseph Dabbs and Isaac Bates; she was b. 23 Aug 1727 d/o Stephen
Chastain & Martha Dupuy; Mary m/2 **Peter Farrar**; children from
family histories:

> 1131-1 Chastain Cocke, b. 13ᵗʰ 9ber 1743
> 1131-2 Martha Cocke, b. 24 Jul 1745
> 1131-3 James Powell Cocke, b. 11 Apr 1747
> 1131-4 James Powell Cocke, b. 20 Jul 1748
> 1131-5 Chastain Cocke, b. 11 Nov 1749
> 1131-6 Elizabeth Chastain Cocke, b. 22 Jan 1753
> 1131-7 Stephen Cocke, b. 5 Jan 1754

12 Oct 1745; from James & Mary Magdalen Cocke to William Kemp, deed (GCWD-3
p. 49, 62)

26 Oct 1748; Bond of James Cocke of Henrico Co. to Martha Cocke; for £1,000; re her
unmolested use of slaves, goods and chattels left her by the will of his father, the late
James Powell Cocke (HCVD-4 p. 410; TVF 9.249)

5 Feb 1749; 1ˢᵗ Mon Feb 1749; from James Cocke of Henrico Co., s/o James Powell
Cocke, late of Henrico Co., to Samuel Garthright, Jr.; for £50; 600 ac. on eastern run of
Four Mile Creek (HCVD-3 p. 73)

Will of James Cocke, Cumberland Parish; Lunenburg Co.; 30 Apr 1753; 3 Jul 1753
To dau. Martha, £500 at age 18 or marriage, provided she acquits her right to legacy
    left her by her grandfather James Powell Cocke
To dau. Elizabeth, £500 at age 18 or marriage
To son James Cocke, 670 ac. Henrico Co. called *Malvern Hills*; also 750 ac.
    Cumberland Co.; negroes, stock, household goods on said plantation, etc.
To son Chastain Cocke, 2,560 ac. on *Staunton River*, Halifax Co., negroes, etc. on sd.
    plantation

To son Stephen Cocke, 300 ac. where I now dwell, negroes, stock, etc. on sd. plantation

To wife, I lend 2,771 ac. in Amelia Co., negroes, stock, etc. on sd. plantation; at her death to my son Stephen & his heirs; if none survive her then to son Chastain; then to my daus.

If all my children and their heirs should die, my estate, except that left to my wife, to be divided between Brazure Cocke's 3 sons

Exs: nephew John James Duprey and his son Bartholomew Duprey, and his son in law John Trabeu

Wit: Hannah Austin, Jas. Scott, Henry May, William Chassels (LuWB 1.96)

> **1131-1 Chastain Cocke**, b. 13th 9ber 1743 King William Parish Register, s/o James and Marie (sic) at Church of Huguenot Refugees Mannikin-town
>
> **1131-2 Martha Cocke**, b. 24 Jul 1745; mb. & m. 24 Jan 1760 Amelia Co. **Henry Anderson**, sec. Benj. Ward; Martha inherited 4 negroes from her grandfather Cocke in 1747; Henry b. 4 Jan 1733/4 Prince George Co.; d. 1766 Albemarle Co.; Henry was s/o Henry Anderson; children from family histories; the number of children suggests Martha may not have been the mother of all of them:
>
> > 11312-1 **Ralph Anderson**
> > 11312-2 **James Powell Anderson**
> > 11312-3 **William Anderson**
> > 11312-4 **Martha Anderson**
> > 11312-5 **Elizabeth Anderson**
> > 11312-6 **Henry T. Anderson**
>
> **1131-3 James Powell Cocke**, b. 11 Apr 1747; d. 20 Apr 1747
>
> **1131-4 James Powell Cocke**, b. 20 Jul 1748 Powhatan Co.; d. 13 Jan 1829; mb/1 25 Nov 1767 Amelia Co. **Elizabeth Archer**; d/o & consent of Wm. Archer; sur. Henry Anderson; m/2 2 Oct 1777 Chesterfield Co. **Lucy Smith** (MCC p. 33), sur. Obadia Smith; Lucy was b. 8 Dec 1756 *Tuckahoe*; d. 27 Feb 1816; he inherited land in Cumberland Co. from his father's will; children from family histories:

5 Aug 1771; 5 Aug 1771; from James Powell Cocke & Elizabeth his wife to Ryland Randolph; all of Henrico Co.; for 5s; 21 ac. on the *Brook*; adj. sd. Randolph & Cocke; on n. side of the great road leading from *Williamburg* to *Richmond* (HCVD-5 p. 288; TVF 11.190); Elizabeth, w/o Cocke, relinquished dower (HCVD-5 p. 439; TVF 12.53, 54)

> **1131-5 Chastain** or **Christian Cocke**, b. 11 Nov 1749; d. 19 Mar 1795; mb. 11 Apr 1767 or 1769 Amelia Co. **Martha Field Archer**; consent of Wm. Archer; he was to inherit *Malvern Hills* and remainder of estate of his grandfather Cocke at age 21 and from his father land in Halifax Co.; children from family histories:

11315-1 **James Powell Cocke**, b. 12 Jan 1770; mb. 4 Jun 1794
Mary Lewis; d/o Eliza; he was a member of the Virginia House of
Delegates
11315-2 **William Archer Cocke**, b. 22 Dec 1771
11315-3 **Chastain Cocke, Jr.**, b. 30 Jan 1775; d. at sea 1797
11315-4 **Bowler Cocke**, b. 15 Aug 1777; d. young
11315-5 **Elizabeth Royall Cocke**, b. 14 Apr 1778
11315-6 **John Field Cocke, Capt.**, b. 9 Apr 1784
11315-7 **Mary Magdalene Chastain Cocke**, b. 29 Oct 1786
11315-8 **Richard Herbert Cocke**, b. 31 Aug 1788
11315-9 **Joseph Archer Cocke**, b. 15 Oct 1790
11315-10 **Stephen Cannon Cocke**, b. 3 Mar 1794

1131-6 **Elizabeth Chastain Cocke**, b. 22 Jan 1753; m. 24 Jun 1790
Amelia Co. 2nd w/o **William Cannon**
1131-7 **Stephen Cocke**, b. 5 Jan 1751/2 or 1754; d. 13 Nov 1794
Amelia Co.; some daughters from marriage records:

11317-1 **Mary Magdalene Chastain Cocke**; mb. 19 Jun 1794
Amelia Co. **Richard Archer**; sec. Stephen Cocke
11317-2 **Judith E. Cocke**; mb. Jul 1799 Amelia Co.; m. 24 Jun
1799 **Peter F. Archer**
11317-3 **Martha Cocke**; mb. Dec 1800 Amelia Co. **William F.
Eggleston**; sec. Jas. Cocke

113-2 **?____ Cocke**; ?d. bef. 1753; she may have m. ____ **Duprey** who
admn. estate of Martha Cocke in 1757; the will of her brother James
calls John James Duprey his nephew
113-3 **Thomas Cocke**; may have been the following Thomas:

Jan 1737; [recorded]; accounts of estate of Thomas Cocke presented by John Archer,
Gent (HCVW-1 p. 218)
[Thomas Cocke; Henrico County Wills and Administrations (1662-1800) p. 678-679. Accounts
rec. Jan. 1737. Deeds & Wills, 1725-1737 (Reel 7a) (LOV)]

113-4 **Ann Cocke**; said to have m. **James Mitchell**; d. 1772 Amelia Co.

11-4 **Henry Cocke**, mariner, b. ca 1695; d. by 4 Apr 1714/5 at sea; he
inherited residue of *Moniquies* patent from his grandfather Cocke and 200
ac. of land his father purchased from his uncle Stephen, 49 ac. on *White
Oak Swamp* and 943 ac. part in Henrico and part in Charles City Co. from
the will of his father

21 Jul 1711; 1 Mar 1711; affidavit of Henry Cocke, s/o Thomas, now age 16 and has
power to receive his portion of his father's estate (HCVW-1 p. 116)

Will of Henry Cocke of Henrico Parish; 1 Feb 1714/5; 4 Apr 1714/5
To bro. James Powell Cocke, 940 ac. on *White Oak Swamp*
To bro. Brassure Cocke, 500 ac. left me by my bro. Thomas next to *White Oak Swamp*

To sis. Elizabeth Cocke, my plantation on *Haulburn Hill,* negroes
To sis. Mary Finny, negroes
Remainder between bros. James Powell Cocke & Brassure Cocke
Exs: bros. William Finney and James Powell Cocke
Signed on board the ship *Harrison,* bound for VA on 1 Feb 1714/5
Wit: Thomas Posford, Will Livingston, William Dun (HCVW-1 p. 131)
6 Jun 1715; inv. of Henry Cock presented in court by William Finney (HCVW-1 p. 132)
[Henry Cocke (Cock); Henrico Co. Wills and Admns. (1662-1800) p. 251. Will dated 1 Feb.
1714/15. p. 254-255. Exors. bond rec. 30 Apr. 1715. p. 279-280. Inv. rec. 6 June 1715. Misc.
Court Records, Vol. 1, [1650-1717] (Reel 1); p. 17. Will pro. 4 Apr. 1715. p. 34. Inv. & appr. rec.
6 June 1715. Deeds, Wills, Etc., 1714-1718 (Reel 7) (LOV)]

> 11-5 **Mary Cocke,** b. aft. 1690; d. by 1747; m. Henrico Co. **William
> Finney**; Mary inherited negroes from her bro. Henry; from her father, she
> inherited ½ of 371 ac. (part of 671 ac. granted 20 Apr 1687) plus negroes,
> items; children:

> > 115-1 William Finney
> > 115-2 Mary Finney

Sep Ct. 1724; from Thomas Farrar and Katherine his wife to William Finney, deed
(HCVD-2 p. 201)

Will of William Finney of University of Glasgow, Master of Arts and Minister of
    Henrico Parish; Henrico Co.; 3 Feb 1726; 5 Jun 1727
To son William, *Worlesend* and e. half of my plantation in St. James Parish, negroes
To dau. Mary, other half of St. James Parish plantation
If either die before 21 or marriage, then all to go to wife Mary; remainder to be divided
    between my wife & 2 children
Extx: wife
Wit: Tarlton Woodson, Henry Wood (HCVW-1 p. 160)

4 Jan 1730; 1st Mon Jan 1730; from James Powell Cocke and Mary Finney jointly
grant to William Finney; 371 ac. left me and my sister Eliza. Cocke by will of my
father; also I, Mary Finney, give my son William Finney, negro; if he dies under 21
then to dau. Mary Finney; also to Mary one negro (HCVD-2 p. 129)

> 115-1 **William Finney,** b. aft. 1709; m. **Mary** _____

26 Sep 1747; 1st Mon Oct 1747; from William Finney, Gent. to William Randolph; for
£960; 240 sc. purchased of Thomas and Katharine Farrar by my father William on 10
May 1723; also 400 ac. *Worlds End* on n. side of James River; also 371 ac. part of a
patent to Thomas Cocke 20 Apr 1687 and by him devised to my late mother, Mary
Finney, dec'd; Mary, w/o William, relinquished dower rights (HCVD-3 p. 47)

> 115-2 **Mary Finney**

> 11-6 **Elizabeth Cocke,** b. aft. 1690; d. bef. Jan 1730; she inherited
> *Haulbum Hill* plantation from her bro. Henry; from her father, she
> inherited ½ of 371 ac. (part of 671 ac. granted 20 Apr 1687) plus negroes,
> items

[undated; recorded with 1712 documents]; rec'd from Samuel Harwood & Littlebury Epes, exs. of will of Thomas Cocke, negroes and items for use of Elizabeth Cocke; /s/ Webb (Giles) (HCVW-1 p. 121)

11-7 **Martha Cocke**

1-2 **Stephen Cocke**, b. ca 1666-8, age 22 on 1 Dec 1688 & age 24 on 16 May 1692 (QRH p. 152, 154); d. by 14 Aug 1711; m/1 ca 1689 Henrico Co. **Sarah (__) Marston**; m/2 26 May 1694 **Martha Batte**; d. Prince George Co.; d/o Thomas Batte, Jr. & Temperance Brown and widow of **Abraham Wood Jones** and **John Bannister**; Stephen rec'd deed of gift from his father of 200 ac. *Malvern Hills* in 1687 and the mills with 400 ac. and land on *White Oak Swamp* from his father's will in 1697; children from family histories:

> 12-1 Agnes Cocke
> 12-2 Batte Cocke
> 12-3 Abraham Cocke
> 12-4 Charles Cocke

29 Apr 1693; Stephen Cock of Henrico Co. granted 1,040 ac. in James and Charles City Cos. on s. w. side of the head of *Chickahominy River* (LOP 8.300)

1 Feb 1697; 1 Feb 1697; from Stephen Cocke of Henrico Co. to Peter Jones of Bristol Parish; land swap; for 240 ac. part of *Old Town* which Thomas Batte granted Peter Jones, Cocke exchanges 200 ac. in Bristol Parish, Charles City Co. on s. side of Appomattox River near *Fort Henry*; Martha, w/o Stephen Cocke, appoints her brother in law James Cocke to relinquish her dower rights in Charles City Co. (HCVD-1 p. 103)

30 Mar 1698; 1 Apr 1698; from Stephen Cocke, Gent. to eldest bro. Thomas Cocke, Gent., both of Henrico Co. & Parish; for 179# tobacco; least of 350 ac. called *White Oak Swamp* on n. side of James River willed me by my dec'd father; bounded by Richard Cocke of Charles City Co. (HCVD-1 p. 103, 104)

17 Jan 1701; 2 Feb 1701; from Stephen Cocke to John Pleasants, both of Henrico Co. & Parish; for 10,000# tobacco and £45; 56 ac. and an old mill on n. side James River which Thomas Cocke gave his son Stephen; adj. his bro. Thomas and William, dec'd; Martha, w/o Stephen, relinquished dower rights by her atty. brother James Cocke (HCVD-1 p. 119)

Aug 1701; deed of gift from Stephen Cocke to Martha Jones; 1 mulatto girl about 8 mos. old (HCVD-1 p. 117)

2 Mar 1703; 1 Apr 1704; from Stephen Cocke, Gent., and Martha his wife, to Thomas Cocke, Gent., both of Henrico Co. & Parish; for £30; 200 ac. where Stephen and Martha live in *Malborn Hills*; bounded by land that Thomas Cooke, father of Stephen, bought of his bros. John and William Cocke; /s/ Stephen and Martha Cocke (HCVD-1 p. 130)

14 Aug 1711; Inventory of Stephen Cocke, dec'd; Martha Cocke returned account (PGWD 1.53); 9 Jul 1717; Martha Cocke, relict of Stephen Cock, dec'd, additional account (PGWD 2.177)

12-1 **Agnes Cocke**; m. **Richard Smith**; d. by 5 Feb 1760 Lunenburg Co.; his will names his wife and children; she was to receive items at age 18 from her grandfather Cocke's will written 10 Dec 1691

12-2 **Batte Cocke**

12-3 **Abraham Cocke**; m. ____; children from his will and marriage records:

    123-1 **Peter Cocke**; mb. 1 May 1769 Brunswick Co. **Mary Whitehead**; d/o Richard Whitehead

    123-2 **Abraham Cocke**; mb. 11 Apr 1767 Lunenburg Co. **Agnes May**; letter of consent from Robert Chappell, Jr.; wit. David and Richard May

    123-3 **Stephen Cocke**; mb. 24 Dec 1764 Amelia Co. **Amey Jones**; d/o Richard Jones

    123-4 **Thomas Cocke**; mb. 3 Feb 1759 Amelia Co. **Margaret Jones**; sec. Stith Hardaway

    123-5 **John Cocke**

    123-6 **William Cocke**

    123-7 **Mary Cocke**; mb. 9 Feb 1754 Amelia Co. **Richard Ellis**; sec. William Watkins

    123-8 **Agnes Cocke**; mb. Dec 1757 Amelia Co. **Charles Hamlin, Jr.**

    123-9 **Martha Cocke**; mb. 28 Nov 1759 Amelia Co. **Theopilus Lacy** of Halifax Co.

    123-10 **Elizabeth Cocke**

Will of Abraham Cocke; Amelia Co.; 23 Sep 1759; 22 May 1760
To son Peter, plantation he now lives on, negroes
To son Abraham, tract on *NottowayRiver*; also 390 ac. with mills, negroes
To son Stephen, tract in Lunenburg Co., adj. land of my sons Peter and Abra; also tract in Amelia Co., negroes
To son Thomas, tract in Lunenburg adj. my son Peter; also tract in Amelia Co. adj. my son Stephen, negroes
To son John, tract in Amelia Co. on *Little Nottoway*
To son William, tract in Amelia adj. my son Abraham, negroes
To dau. Mary Elliss, Martha Cocke, Elizabeth Cocke, each a negro
To dau. Agness Hamlin, 400 ac. tract
To wife, negroes and the plantation I live on and my mill on *Little Nottoway*, etc.; at her death to be divided between my sons, Thomas, John & William
Personal estate to be divided between my 5 sons, Abra, Stephen, Thomas, John, William
Exs: friend Richard Elliss, sons Abra Cocke, Stephen Cocke
Wit: Edm'd Ballad, Benja. Smith, Abra. Shelton (AmWB 1.169)

12-4 **Charles Cocke**

1-3 **James Cocke**; of *Curles*, b. ca 1667, age 30 in Aug 1697 (QRH p. 155); d. by 6 Nov 1721; m. 11 Jan 1691 Henrico Co. **Elizabeth Pleasants**; surety

Capt. Thomas Cocke, Jr. & Will Cocke, Jr. (MDC p. 20); Elizabeth d. by Jul 1752; d/o John & Jane Pleasants, Quaker; Capt. Thomas Cocke, Jr., & William Cocke, Jr., sureties (QRH p. 91); in 1689 his father gave him 559 ac. on n. side of James River; in May 1692 Elizabeth's father made deed of gift for life to James of 2 tracts of 70 ac. and 400 ac. (HCVD-1 p. 69); he inherited 625 ac. plus other items from his father's will in 1697; children:

> 13-1 James Cocke, b. est. ca 1692-4
> 13-2 Elizabeth Cocke, b. est. ca 1692-4

22 Jul 1690 & Mar 1692/3; James Cocke appointed Deputy Clerk of Court of Henrico Co. (HCVD-1 p. 58, 78)

19 Apr 1692; James Cocke, Henry Randolph, John Golightly & Solomon Crook granted 647 ac. Charles City Co. (LOP 8.60)

28 Oct 1697; James Cock granted 311 ac. Henrico Co. along *Old Town Runn* (LOP 9.86)

16 Jan 1698; 1 Feb 1698; William Watts to serve James Cocke for 7 years (HCVD-1 p. 108)

1 May 1700; I have rec'd of mother in law Jane Pleasants items left in will of John Pleasants by right of my wife (HCVW-1 p. 73)

28 Oct 1702 James Cock granted 570 ac. Varina Parish, Henrico Co. on n. side of James River (LOP 9.491)

4 Jan 1713; [land swap]; from James Cocke, Gent. to Jno. Price, both of Henrco Co. & Parish; 50 ac. near *Chickahominy Swamp* where James Cocke lately built a house on the 50 ac.; swapped to Price for 50 ac. on n. side of James land originally descended from Henry Pew (HCVD-2 p. 40)

4 Jul 1715; 4 Jul 1715; from James Cocke the elder of *Curles*, Henrico Co. & Parish, to my son James Cocke; 200 ac. on n. side of James River (HCVD-2 p. 49)

Ct. 6 Nov 1721; will of James Cocke presented by Elizabeth Cocke, extx. (HCVW-2 p. 160)

Aug Ct. 1724; from Elizabeth Cocke to Richard Randolph; Bowler Cocke among witnesses (HCVD-2 p. 201)

Aug Ct. 1724; from Elizabeth and James Cocke [? her son], deed to Richard Randolph; Bowler Cocke among wit. (HCVD-2 p. 201)

<u>Will of Elizabeth Cocke of Henrico Parish; 9 Aug 1751; Jul 1752</u>
To dau. Elizabeth Portriss; negroes, items
To grandson (sic) William Fleming Cocke, negro, items, £10
To granddaus, Rebecca, Anne & Tabitha Cocke, each a slave
Ex: son James Cocke, 4 negroes and remainder of estate
Wit: Joseph Lewis, Daniel Price, William Price (HCVW-2 p. 57)
[Elizabeth Cocke; Henrico County Wills and Administrations (1662-1800) p. 158. Will pro. July 1752. Deeds, Wills, Etc., 1750-1767 (Reel 9) (LOV)]

13-1 James Cocke, Sr., b. est. ca 1692-4; d. by 10 Feb 1775; m. **Sarah _____**; he and his sister each inherited £5 from the will of their grandmother Jane Pleasants in 1709; in 1715 his father gave him 200 ac. on n. side of James River; he inherited 4 negroes and remainder of his mother's estate in 1752; known children from James' will:

> 131-1 James Cocke
> 131-2 Pleasant Cocke
> 131-3 Thomas Cocke
> 131-4 Benjamin Cocke
> 131-5 Tabitha Cocke
> 131-6 Rebecca Cocke
> 131-7 Ann Cocke

May 1692; 16 May 1692; deed of gift from John Pleasants to James Cocke, s/o Thomas Cocke, Sr. of Henrico Co., and wife Jane; 70 ac. plantation on *Curles Swamp* and 400 ac. I bought of Rowen and Woodson (HCVD-1 p. 69)

1 Aug 1735; James Cock granted 88 ac. Henrico Co. on n. side of James River on *Shocco Creek* and e. side of *Cannons Branch* (LOP 16.99)

5 Jun 1736; James Cocke granted 378 ac. Henrico Co. on n. side of James River and n. side of *Reedy Branch* (LOP 17.103)

30 Jan 1741; James Cocke granted 246 ac. Henrico Co. on main run of *Chickahominy Swamp* (LOP 20.103)

Oct Ct. 1742; from James Cocke to his son Pleasant Cocke, deed (HCVD-3 p. 97)

20 Aug 1745; James Cocke granted 400 ac. Goochland Co. on n. side of *Hardware River* adj. Rich'd Damril (LOP 22.388)

20 Sep 1748; from James Cocke to son Thomas Cocke, deed (GCWD-3 p. 60)

19 Feb 1751; 1st Mon Nov 1751; from James Cocke, Gent., of Henrico Co. to William Randolph; being in the Commission of the Peace for Henrico Co.; for £5; Lot #22 in Richmond to build a courthouse; Sarah, w/o James, relinquished dower (HCVD-4 p. 90; TVF 8.238)

2 Dec 1754; 3 Feb 1755; from James Cocke to Richard Randolph, Gent., both of Henrico Co.; for £190; 150 ac. of *Curles*; sold to John Pleasants, grandfather to James Cocke (HCVD-4 p. 441; TVF 9.246)

4 Jan 1755; 5 Aug 1755; from Capt. James Cocke to Samuel DuVal, Gent., both of Henrico Co.; for £110; 110 ac. on branches of *Shark's Creek* (commonly called *Bacon's Quarter Branch*) on e. side of *Cannon's Branch* and west side of *Johnson's Branch*; Sarah, w/o James, relinquished dower (HCVD-4 p. 424; TVF 9.251)

. 6 Jun 1763; 6 Jun 1763; from James Cocke, Sr. to James Cock, Jr.; for better securing the payment of money owed John Pleasants by James Cocke, Sr.; 3 tracts of 863 ac.; 2 containing 485 ac. on *Chickahoiny Swamp* and *Deep Run*; another containing 378 ac.; sum being £138.17.10 paid by James Cocke, Jr. to discharge mortgage (HCVD-4 p. 792; TVF 10.238)

24 Feb 1764; 2 Jul 1764; James Cocke, Gent., and William Fleming Cocke, grandson and heir at law to the said James Cocke, conveyed to Joseph Hobson, planter, all of Henry Co., for £110, 400 a. known as *Hell Garden*, which land was formerly purchased by John Pleasants the Elder, of Robert Woodson, Sr., and Henry Rowen and was conveyed by the said John Pleasants unto James Cocke and Elizabeth (Pleasants Cocke) his dau., the wife of the said James Cocke, by deed dated 16 May 1692 and afterward by the said Elizabeth and her son, the said James, the party to these presents, conveyed to the said Joseph Hobson, by deed of exchange dated 1 Sep 1740 (HCVD-4 p. 864; TVF 10.250)

11 Apr 1765; 6 May 1765; deed of gift from James Cocke of Henrico Co. to his grandson William Fleming Cocke; 287 ac. on *Chichominy Swamp* (HCVD-4 p. 919; TVF 11.29)

Will of James Cocke; 18 Dec 1772; 6 Feb 1775
Wife Sarah to enjoy estate for life
To son Thomas, negro at death of his mother
To grandchild. Sarah Lewis, Ann and Susannah Cocke; Ann, Sarah, William Bobby
   and John Geddes Winston
Exs: wife, Turner Southall, Samuel Price, Robert Price
Wit: Daniel Price, Jacob Childress, William Cocke (HCVW-2 p. 126)
10 Feb 1775; inv. of James Cocke; value £174.18.4 (HCVD-2 p. 126)
[James Cocke, Sr.; wills not listed in Virginia Wills and Admns., 1632-1800 (Torrence). Will -
1775 Henrico Co. Misc.s Records. Vol. 7, p. 2249; p. 2249-2250. Will pro. 6 Feb. 1775. p. 2251-
2252. Inv. & appr. rec. Mar. 1775. Misc. Court Records, Vol. 7, [1770-1807] (Reel 3) (LOV)]

131-1 **James Cocke, Jr.**; d. by 25 Apr 1772; predeceased his father; m.
Mary Lewis (DR); children from his will:

> 1311-1 Elizabeth Pleasants Cocke
> 1311-2 James Cocke
> 1311-3 John Cocke, b. 9 Nov 1757
> 1311-4 Sarah Lewis Cocke, b. 5 Feb 1760
> 1311-5 Anne Cocke
> 1311-6 Susanna Cocke, b. 5 Aug 1764
> 1311-7 William Cocke
> 1311-8 Lucy Cocke

6 Jun 1763; 6 Jun 1763; from James Cocke, Jr. to Daniel Price, Jr., both of Henrico Co.; for £100; 378 ac. on *Reedy Branch* adj. sd. Cocke (HCVD-4 p. 793; TVF 10.239)

Will of James Cocke, Jr.; 25 Apr 1772 [dated]; refiled 1774-1782
To dau. Susanna Cocke, negro, and £30 at age 21 or marriage
To daus. Anne, Sarah Lewis & Elizabeth Pleasants Cock, each a negro
To son James, 273 ac. in Goochland Co.
To son William, upper part of Henrico Co. land on path from meeting house and
   Chickahominy Swamp; if he dies before age 21 to my sons James and John, equally
To son John, remainder of plantation I live on, equally
Rest of estate between all my children equally
Exs: son James, William Lewis of Goochland and Samuel Price
Wit: Daniel Price, Jacob Childress, Charles Watkins (HCVW-2 p. 132)

[James Cocke, Junior; Henrico Co. Wills and Admns. (1662-1800) p. 27-29. Will dated 25 Apr. 1772 & rec. 14 Apr. 1783. Records [Deeds, Wills, Etc.,] 1774-1782 (Reel 10); wills not listed in Virginia Wills and Admns., 1632-1800 (Torrence); Will - 1772 [1783] Henrico Co. Proceedings of Commissioners. . . 1774-1782, p. 27; Henrico Co. Wills and Admns. (1662-1800) p. 2165-2166. Guardian bond for William & John rec. 2 Nov. 1772. p. 2211-2212. Guardian bond for Lucy Cocke 1 Feb. 1773. Misc. Court Records, Vol. 7, [1770-1807] (Reel 3); p. 2165-2166. Guardian bond for William & John rec. 2 Nov. 1772. p. 2211-2212. Guardian bond for Lucy Cocke 1 Feb. 1773. Misc. Court Records, Vol. 7, [1770-1807] (Reel 3) (LOV)]

1311-1 **Elizabeth Pleasants Cocke**; m. 3 Jan 1774 St. James Northam Parish **Will Roberts** (DR); she was named in will of father

1311-2 **James Cocke**; m. 23 Nov 1774 Goochland Co. **Martha Holland Parish**, b. 26 Dec 1758; bapt. 21 Feb 1759; d/o David Parish & Judith Holland (DR); he inherited land in Goochland from his father; part of their children:

13112-1 **David Cocke**, b. 23 Apr 1776; bapt. 23 May 1776; the Douglas Register says "daughter named David"

13112-2 **William Cocke**, b. 1 Aug 1777; bapt. 13 Oct 1777 (DR)

13112-3 **Jack Fleming Cocke**, b. 4 Jan 1782; bapt. 17 Mar 1782 (DR)

13112-4 **Mary Lewis Cocke**, b. 11 Aug 1783; bapt. 18 Apr 1784 (DR)

13112-5 **Judith H. Cocke**; m. Goochland **William Woodson**

13112-6 **Elizabeth Pleasants Cocke**; m. Goochland **Arthur Bowles**

1311-3 **John Cocke**, b. 9 Nov 1757; bapt. 5 Jan 1758 (DR); inherited remainder of home plantation from his father; named in Guardian Bond of 1772

1311-4 **Sarah Lewis Cocke**, b. 5 Feb 1760; bapt. 5 Jun 1760 (DR); named in will of grandfather and father

1311-5 **Anne Cocke**; named in will of grandfather and father

1311-6 **Susanna Cocke**, b. 5 Aug 1764; bapt. 21 Mar 1765 (DR); mb. 15 Mar 1784 Goochland **William Price**; Susanna was named in will of her grandfather and father

1311-7 **William Cocke**; inherited upper part of Henrico Co. land from his father; to go to James and John if he dies before age 21; named in Guardian Bond of 1772

1311-8 **Lucy Cocke**

131-2 **Pleasant Cocke**; d. by Feb Ct. 1743; m. **Mary Fleming**; she is said to have m/2 **Thomas Wild**; Pleasants's father gave him land in 1742; known children:

1312-1 William Fleming Cocke
1312-2 Mary Fleming Cocke

Jun Ct. 1738; from Pleasant Cocke to Humphry Smith; Mary, w/o Pleasant, relinquished dower (HCVD-3 p. 78)

30 Jan 1741; Pleasant Cocke granted 238 ac. Henrico Co. on the main run of
Chickahominy Swamp and *Reedy Branch* (LOP 20.127)

[filed with 1742-1743]; from Pleasant Cocke to Duncan Graham; lots #31 and #46 in
Town of *Richmond*; Mary, w/o Pleasant, relinquished dower (HCVD-3 p. 6)

Feb Ct. 1743; will of Pleasant Cocke presented by James Cocke his ex. (HCVW-2 p. 21)
16 Apr 1744; Jul 1749; inventory of Pleasant Cocke; value £444.18.3; presented by
James Cocke (HCVW-2 p. 49)
[Pleasants Cocke; Henrico County Wills and Admns. (1662-1800) p. 115-115b. Inv. & appr. rec.
July 1749. Deeds, Etc., 1748-1750 (Reel 8) (LOV)]

Jun Ct. 1744; Mary Cocke, widow of Pleasant Cocke, dec'd, relinquishes dower right
in 2 lots and house in *Richmond* Town conveyed by her late husband to Dunkin
Grayham at Oct Ct. (HCVD-3 p. 103)

> ### 1312-1 **William Fleming Cocke**; d. by Aug 1767; m. **Theodosia
> Cowley**; d/o Abraham Cowley (HCVW-2 p. 59); William called
> grandson in 1751will of his great-grandmother Elizabeth Cocke;
> children:
>
> > 13121-1 **Martha Fleming Cocke**
> > 13121-2 **Pleasant Cocke**
> > 13121-3 **William Cocke**
> > 13121-4 **Cowley Cocke**
> > 13121-5 **Theodosia Cocke**

Dec Ct. 1754; Theodosia Cowley, orphan of Abraham Cowley, chooses Abraham
Cowley her guardian (HCVW-2 p. 69)

7 Jun 1762; 5 Jul 1762; from William Fleming Cocke and Theodosia his wife and
Thomas Wild and Mary his wife, the widow of Pleasant Cocke, dec'd, and the mother
of sd. William Fleming Cocke to Miles Selden; for £555.15; 443 ac. on s. side of
Chickahominy Swamp and main rain of sd. swamp and on *Spring Branch* (HCVD-4 p.
735; TVF 10.183)

5 Jul 1762; 7 Feb 1763; Indemnity Bond of William Fleming Cocke as Deputy Sheriff
(HCVD-4 p. 766; TVF 10.187)

15 May 1764; 4 Jun 1764; from William Fleming Cocke & Theodosia his wife, of
Cornwall Parish, Lunenburg Co., to Samuel Mitchell, blacksmith of *Richmond Town*;
for £36; 2 half lots (32, 46) in sd. town; Theodosia Cocke relinquished dower (HCVD-4
p. 860; TVF 10.250)

April Ct. 1767; Theodosia Cocke granted administration of estate of her husband
William Fleming Cocke (HCVW-2 p. 96)
Apr 1767; Abraham Cowley appointed guardian to orphans of William Fleming
Cocke: Martha Fleming, Pleasant, William, Cowley & Theodosia Cocke (HCVW-2 p.
96)
Apr Ct. 1767; appraisers appointed to value estate of William Fleming Cocke (HCVW-2
p. 97); Sep Ct. 1767; Richard Adams, Gent., appointed co-administrator with
Theodosia Cocke of estate of William Fleming Cocke (HCVW-2 p. 99)
Oct Ct. 1767; inventory of William Fleming Cocke returned (HCVW-2 p. 100)

5 Oct 1767; inventory of William Fleming Cock by court order Aug 1767; value £32.10.5 (HCVW-2 p. 119)

[William Fleming Cocke; Henrico Co. Wills and Admns. (1662-1800) p. 1985-1986. Inv. & appr. rec. 5 Oct. 1767. Misc. Court Records, Vol. 6, [1758-1769] (Reel 3); wills not listed in Virginia Wills and Admns., 1632-1800 (Torrence). Inventory - 1767 Henrico Co. Misc.Records. Vol. 6, p. 1985 (LOV)]

131-3 **Thomas Cocke**; m. **Ann Johnson** (DR); Thomas was the only son named in will of his father; he may have been the Thomas Cocke of Goochland who sold land in 1762 (HCVD-4 p. 768; TVF 10.188); part of their children:

> 1313-1 William Cocke
> 1313-2 Pleasant Cocke
> 1313-3 Benjamin Cocke
> 1313-4 James Cocke
> 1313-5 Elizabeth Cocke
> 1313-6 Sarah Cocke
> 1313-7 Samuel Cocke, b. 21 Jan 1754
> 1313-8 John Cocke, b. 27 Jul 1756
> 1313-9 Mary Cocke, b. 24 Oct 1758
> 1313-10 Nansie Cocke, b. 1 Oct 1760
> 1313-11 Agnes Cocke, b. 29 Mar 1765

1313-1 **William Cocke**

1313-2 **Pleasant Cocke**; m. 1 Jul 1762 Goochland to **Elizabeth Fowler** or **Flower**; children from St. James Northam Parish, Goochland Co.:

13132-1 **William Cocke**, b. 21 Dec 1766; bapt. 22 Feb 1767 (DR); m. ____; one of his children:

131321-1 **Thomas W. Cocke**; m. 18 Mar 1793 Henrico Co. **Sally Williamson**; d/o Allen Williamson who consents; wit. Susannah and Elizabeth Williamson (MHC p. 20)

13132-2 **Robert Cocke**, b. 14 Feb 1769; bapt. 19 Mar 1769 (DR); he may have been the Robert who m. 18 Apr 1791 Henrico Co. **Lucy Allen**; sur. Drury Allen (MHC p. 20)

13132-3 **Elizabeth Cocke**; mb. 18 Apr 1794 Henrico Co. **George Pyle**; P. Cocke certifies Elizabeth is his dau. of lawful age; sur. Daniel Hopper (MHC p. 70)

1313-3 **Benjamin Cocke**; m. 23 Jun 1768 (DR); 28 Jun 1768 St. James Northam Parish, Goochland, **Mary Johnson**; one of their children:

13133-1 **Ann Cocke**, b. 24 May 1769 St. James Northam Parish

20 Aug 1744; Benjamin Cocke granted 370 ac. Goochland Co. on both sides of *Buffalo Branch* of *Beverdam Creek* (LOP 23.840)

1313-4 **James Cocke**; m. 20 Oct 1773 **Jean (Jane) Johnson**, both in Goochland (DR); one of their children:

13134-1 **Elizabeth Cocke**, Feb. 3, 1775

1313-5 **Elizabeth Cocke**; mb. 2 Jun 1774 **William Hodges**, both in this parish (DR)

1313-6 **Sarah Cocke**; mb. 28 Oct 1773 **Charles Clarke**, both of Goochland (DR)

1313-7 **Samuel Cocke**, b. 21 Jan 1754; bapt. 28 Aug 1756 (DR)

1313-8 **John Cocke**, b. 27 Jul 1756; bapt. 28 Aug 1756 (DR)

1313-9 **Mary Cocke**, b. 24 Oct 1758; bapt. 14 Feb 1759 (DR)

1313-10 **Nansie Cocke**, b. 1 Oct 1760; bapt. 6 Jan 1761 (DR)

1313-11 **Agnes Cocke**, b. 29 Mar 1765; bapt. 15 Sep 1765 (DR); of lawful age m. 21 Jul 1787 Henrico Co. **John Bryan**; William Cocke, surety (MHC p. 13)

131-4 **Benjamin Cocke**; m. 23 or 28 Jun 1768 St. James Northam Parish, Goochland Co. **Mary Johnson**; both of this parish; daughter::

1314-1 **Ann Cocke**, b. 24 May 1769 St. James Northam Parish

131-5 **Tabitha Cocke**; m/1 **Booth Woodson**; d. bef. Jun Ct. 1757; m/2 **John Winston**; she inherited a slave in 1752 from her grandmother Elizabeth Cocke; no known Woodson children (GCRB 7.179; VP p. 1857); Winston children from the 1775 will of their grandfather James Cocke:

1315-1 **Sarah Winston**, b. 14 Nat 1761; bapt. 8 Jun 1761 (DR)

1315-2 **Ann Winston**, b. 12 Apr 1763; bapt. 23 May 1763 (DR)

1315-3 **William Bobby Winston**

1315-4 **John Geddes Winston**

131-6 **Rebecca Cocke**; m. by 4 Dec 1757 Goochland Co. **Benjamin Woodson, Jr.** of Goochland Co.; she inherited a slave in 1752 from her grandmother Elizabeth Cocke; one of their children:

1316-1 **Booth Woodson**, b. 4 Dec 1757 St. James Northam Parish

131-7 **Ann Cocke**; she inherited a slave in 1752 from her grandmother Elizabeth Cocke

13-2 **Elizabeth Cocke**, b. est. ca 1692-4; m. ____ **Poythress**; she inherited negroes & items from the will of her mother

1-4 **William Cocke**; d. by 3 Feb 1717; ml. 2 Nov 1695 Henrico Co. **Sarah Perrin**; surety Thomas Cocke, Sr. (MHC p. 20); d/o Richard Perrin & Katherine Royall; he inherited 1,200 ac. from his father, plus livestock; known children:

14-1 William Cocke
14-2 Temperance Cocke
14-3 Catherine Cocke
14-4 Mary Cocke
14-5 Sarah Cocke

26 Apr 1698; William Cock granted 256 ac. 1r. 24po. Henrico Co. over a small branch of *Cornelius' Run* (LOP 9.139)

1 Mar 1708; 1 Mar 1708; from William Cocke of Henrico Co., planter; for 2,480# tobacco to Theodorick Carter; 124 ac. on s. side of *Chickahominy Swamp, The Round Hills* & land taken up by Richard Cocke, Sr. and John Beauchamp; Sarah, w/o William, relinquished dower rights by her atty. James Cocke (HCVD-2 p. 18)

1 Mar 1708; 1 Mar 1708; from William Cocke of Henrico Co., planter, to John Webb; for 2,800# tobacco; 130 ac. Henrico Parish on s. side *Chickahominy Swamp*, mentions *Round Hills*; Sarah, w/o William, relinquished dower by her atty. James Cocke (HCVD-2 p. 18)

Will of William Cocke of Henrico Parish; 5 Nov 1717; 3 Feb 1717
To son William Cocke, negro, livestock, items; all my lands
To daus. Temperance, Catherine and Mary Cocke, each, negro, livestock, items
To dau. Sarah Cox, all my sheep
Ex: wife, rest of estate, negro
Wit: John Farrar, Charles Ballow, Leonard Ballow (HCVW-1 p. 144)
[William Cocke; Henrico Co. Wills and Admns. (1662-1800) p. 225-226. Will pro. 3 Feb. 1717. Deeds, Wills, Etc., 1714-1718 (Reel 7) (LOV)]

3 Jan 1725; 7 Feb 1725; from Sarah Cocke, widow of Henrico Co. & Parish, to son William Cocke; easternmost ½ of plantation where I live and eastern half of my dwelling plantation (HCVD-2 p. 86)

14-1 **William Cocke**; d. by 14 Mar 1734/5; m. **Judith Anderson**; the 1733 will of her bro. John and 1734 will of her father Henry Anderson call her Judith Cocke; she m/2 by 1739 **Francis Redford**; d. by 1756; William inherited all his father's lands; known child:

141-1 Judith Cocke

14 Mar 1734/5; Feb 1736; inventory of Capt. William Cocke; presented by Francis Redford (HCVW-1 p. 213); Jun Ct. 1739; securities for Judith Cocke admn. of estate of William Cocke asked to be relieved as they had cause to believe the estate would be embezzled; Francis Redford, who hath m. sd. Judith, brings in new securities (HCVW-2 p. 5); Aug Ct. 1743; Francis Redford presents accts. of estate of William Cocke (HCVW-2 p. 20)
[William Cocke; Henrico Co. Wills and Admns. (1662-1800) p. 1037-1040. Inv. & appr. rec. Feb. 1736. Misc. Court Records, Vol. 2, [1727-1737] (Reel 2); p. 601. Inv. & appr. rec. Feb. 1736. Deeds & Wills, 1725-1737 (Reel 7a) (LOV)]

5 Aug 1747; 1st Mon Sep 1747; from Francis Redford and Judith his wife, relict of William Cocke, dec'd, to William Randolph, Gent., of Goochland Co.; for 60; all the dower rights of sd. Judith in *World's End* and other land held by sd. William Cocke at time of death (HCVD-3 p. 45)

141-1 **Judith Cocke**

Jan Ct. 1742; administration of estate of Mrs. Judith Cocke granted administrators (HCVW-2 p. 17); Aug Ct. 1743; John Redford, Jr., admn. of estate of Judith Cocke, dec'd, to render accts. (HCVW-2 p. 20)

14-2 **Temperance Cocke**; said to have m. **Abraham Bailey**

14-3 **Catherine Cocke**; d. 10 Sep 1725; m. **John Burton**; s/o John Burton of *Longfield*

14-4 **Mary Cocke**; m. **John Redford**; d. aft. 1 Apr 1778

14-5 **Sarah Cocke**; d. by 20 Jan 1747 Goochland Co. (GCWD-3 p. 24); m. **William Cox**; d. by 2 Jun 1712 Henrico Co. (HCWB-1 p. 119); both left wills naming children: son Stephen, daus. Martha, Mary, Prudence, Judith, Edith & Elizabeth Cox; Sarah's will also names granddau. Magdalene Burton

1-5 **Agnes Cocke**; m. ca 1681 **Capt. Joseph Harwood**; Agnes was one of the legatees of Hugh Mackmyell 7 Nov 1678 (HCVW-1 p. 4); she was to inherit items from the will of her grandfather written in 1691; known children from will of Thomas Cocke:

15-1 **Thomas Harwood**; inherited a servant & a mare from grandfather Cocke after death of his mother

15-2 **Joseph Harwood**; inherited a mare from grandfather Cocke

15-3 **Agnes Harwood**; inherited items from grandfather Cocke

15-3 **Joyce Harwood**; inherited items from grandfather Cocke

1-6 **Temperance Cocke**; m. 14 Jun 1694 Henrico Co. **Samuel Harwood** (QRH p. 91); Temperance was one of the legatees of Hugh Mackmyell, 7 Nov 1678 and of Griffin Evans, 15 May 1681 (HCVW-1 p. 4, 10)

2. **Richard Cocke**, the elder, Gent., of *Bremo*, b. 10 Dec 1739; d. 20 Nov 1706, age 66; said to have m. **Elizabeth** _____; he inherited the 650 ac. home plantation of *Bremo* from the 1663 will of his father; in 1678 Mr. Richard Cocke of *Turkey Island* was charged with 5 taxables in Henrico Co.; he was appointed High Sheriff of Henrico 30 Apr 1691 & 9 Apr 1693 (HCVD-1 p. 71, 78); children from his will:

> 2-1 Richard Cocke
> 2-2 Elizabeth Cocke
> 2-3 Martha Cocke
> 2-4 John Cocke, Jr.
> 2-5 Anne Cocke

28 Apr 1691; Richard Cock granted 270 ac. of swamp & marsh below patent of *Curles* in Varina Parish, Henrico Co. (LOP 8. 157)

Will of Richard Cocke, Gent.; Henrico Co.; 18 Nov 1706; 2 Dec 1706
To son Richard, 300 ac. on *White Oak* and *Chickahominy Swamps*

To grandson John Cocke, remainder of land at *White Oak Swamp, Western Run* and *Chickahominy Swamp*, negroes, items, when of age
To granddau. Martha Cocke, negroes, £10, when of age
To grandsons: Richard Cary £20, Thomas Cary £10, Miles Cary £10, Nathaniel Cary £10; at age or when married
To dau. Elizabeth Cary, £20; to her youngest child £10 when of age or married
To dau. Martha Pleasants, £20; to her dau. Elizabeth £10 & her son Joseph when of age or married
To grandson Bowler Cocke, £10; to grandau. Tabitha Cocke, £10 and negro
Ex: son Richard Cocke, remainder of estate
Wit: William Randolph, William Randolph, Jr. (HCVW-1 p. 93, 94)
Dec 1706; 8 Apr 1707; probate granted Richard Cocke, Jr., Gent., on will of his father Richard Cocke, Sr. (HCVW-1 p. 97)
[Richard Cocke; Henrico County Wills and Administrations (1662-1800) p. 9. Will pro. 2 Dec. 1706. Records, 1706-1709 (Reel 6) (LOV)]

Here lyes Interr'd the Body of Richard Cocke Son of Richard Cocke of B-- He was Born the 10th day - -ecember 1639 and departed --- - ife on the 20th November * * (Tombstone at *Bremo*)

2-1 **Richard Cocke, Jr.**, b. ca 1672-3, age 17 on 1 Apr 1689 & age 21 on 1 Oct 1694 (QRH p. 152, 155); d. by Oct 1720; m/1 **Anne Bowler**, b. 23 Jan 1675; d. 24 Apr 1705 (tombstone); d/o Thomas Bowler & Tabitha Underwood; m/2 by Dec 1705 **Rebecca** ____; d. by 21 Jan 1722; he inherited 300 ac. on *White Oak* and *Chickahominy Swamp* and remainder of estate from the will of this father which also named his known children:

> 21-1 Martha Cocke, b. aft. 1685
> 21-2 Bowler Cocke, b. aft. 1685
> 21-3 Tabitha Cocke
> 21-4 Richard Cocke
> 21-5 Benjamin Cocke
> 21-6 Anne Cocke

Here lyeth Interred the Body of Anne, the wife of Richard Cocke, the younger of *Bremo* in this county, and Daughter of Thomas Bowler late of the County of Rappahannock. She was born the 23d day of Jan: 1675 and departed this life the 24th day of April 1705 Aged 30 - - 3 months 1 Day. (Tombstone at *Bremo*)

1 May 1706; Richard Cock, Jr. granted 570 ac. Henrico Co., Varina Parish, on n. side of James River in the fork of *White Oak Swamp* (LOP 9.722)

6 Oct 1712; 6 Oct 1712; from Richard Cocke to Joseph Pleasants, both of Henrico Co. & Parish; for 6,000# tobacco; 130 ac. on n. side of James River purchased by me of Edward Matthews 11 Dec 1705; Rebecca, w/o Richard, relinquished dower rights (HCVD-2 p. 35)

Ct. 3 Oct 1720; will of Richard Cocke presented by Ebenezer Adams, one of the exs.; wit. Henry Wood, Martha Cox, John Toms (HCVW-2 p. 156)
Ct. 6 Feb 1720; exs. of will of Richard Cocke, dec'd; Hon. Nathaniel Harrison, Esq. & Capt. Henry Harrison; Ebenezer Adams, ex. (HCVW-2 p. 157)

Ct. 21 Jan 1722; will of Rebecca Cocke presented by Nathaniel Harrison (HCVW-2 p. 165)

21-1 **Martha Cocke**, b. aft. 1685; d. Surry Co.; said to have m. **Thomas Adams**

21-2 **Bowler Cocke, Col.**, b. aft 1685; of *Bremo* (HCVW-2 p. 158); d. 22 Aug 1769 at his seat at *Shirley* (Virginia Gazette); said to have m/1 **Sarah Fleming**; d/o Charles Fleming of New Kent Co.; m/2 **Elizabeth Hill** of Charles City Co.; said to have been d/o Edward Hill of *Shirley* and widow of John Carter of Lancaster Co.; Bowler was a Justice and Clerk of Henrico Co., a Vestryman of Henrico Parish and a member of the House of Burgess; 1 May 1728 he was appointed Clerk of Henrico Co. (HCVD-2 p. 112); in 1753 he was a churchwarden of Henrico Parish (HCVD-4 p. 269); children from St. John's Vestry Book (QRH p. 101):

> 212-1 Ann Cocke, b. 18 Jun 1720
> 212-2 Susanna Cocke, b. 6 Nov. 1722
> 212-3 Tabitha Cocke, b. 25 Sep 1724
> 212-4 Bowler Cocke, b. 11 Mar 1726
> 212-5 Sarah Cocke, b. 6 Feb 1728
> 212-6 Elizabeth Cocke, b. 15 May 1731
> 212-7 Richard Cocke, b. 7 Mar 1733
> 212-8 Charles Cocke, b. 9 Sep 1735

5 Apr 1718; 7 Apr 1718; from Thomas Williamson to Bowler Cocke, both Gent. of Henrico Co. & Parish; for 20s; 570 ac. on n. side of James River in fort of *White Oak Swamp* bounded by patent dated 1 May 1706 (HCVD-2 p. 74)

4 Apr 1720; from Aaron Leister of Henrico Co. to Bowler Cocke of Essex Co.; 2 negroes, and 91 ac. west of William Cocke on *Curles Swamp*; wit. by John and Richard Cocke, Jr. among others (HCVD-2 p. 80)

16 Jun 1727; Bowler Cocke granted 800 ac. Henrico Co. on s. side of James River on east side of George Stovalls *Horse-pen-branch* (LOP 13.77)

13 Oct 1727; Bowler Cocke granted 400 ac. Henrico Co. on s. side of James River on *Muddy Creek* (LOP 13.194)

26 Jun 1731; Bowler Cocke granted 2,400 ac. Goochland Co. on s. side of James River on *Muddy Creek* (LOP 14.187)

9 Sep 1733; from Bowler Cocke, Gent., to Benjamin Hobson, both of Henrico Co.; for £30; 570 ac. bounded by *White Oak Swamp* granted James Cocke 28 Oct 1702; deserted and then granted to Richard Cocke 1 May 1706 and given by him to his son Bowler (HCVD-2 p. 149)

Sep Ct. 1739; Bowler & James Cocke took oath as officers of the militia for Henrico Co. (HCVD-3 p. 83)

5 Jul 1748; 1st Mon Jul 1748; from Bowler Cocke the elder to Bowler Cocke the younger; for 5s; 90 ac. in Henrico Parish bounded by *Curls Swamp* and by *Bremo*, etc. (HCVD-3 p. 56)

7 Jul 1765; 1 Jul 1765; deed of gift from Bowler Cocke the elder of Charles City Co. to son Bowler Cocke the younger of Amelia Co.; 100 ac. part of 900 ac. formerly belonging to John Cocke, dec'd (HCVD-4 p. 942; TVF 11.33)

31 Mar 1769; 3 Apr 1769; from Bowler Cocke the Elder of *Shirley* to son Bowler Cocke, Jr. of *Bremo*; for love and affection & 10s; 37 slaves (named) (HCVD-5 p. 134; TVF 11.112)

> 212-1 **Ann Cocke**, b. 18 Jun 1720 at *Bowler's Farm* on Rappahannock River; d. ca 1784 Surry Co.; said to have m. **Thomas Adams**
> 212-2 **Susanna Cocke**, b. 6 Nov. 1722 at *Bremo*; d. Oct following
> 212-3 **Tabitha Cocke**, b. 25 Sep 1724
> 212-4 **Bowler Cocke**, b. 11 Mar 1726; the following are probably grandchildren of this Bowler
>
>> **Elizabeth F. Cocke**; m. 8 Nov 1797 Henrico Co. **Walter Coles**; Elizabeth was d/o Bowler Cocke who consents and is surety to her marriage (MHC p. 21)
>> **Bowler F. Cocke**; m. 4 Jan 1808 Henrico Co. **Eliza Agness Pleasants Heth**; surety Charles L. Wingfield (MHC p. 20)

31 Oct 1749; 1st Mon Oct 1749; Bowler Cocke, the younger, appointed Clerk of Henrico Co. (HCVD-3 p. 72)

18 Jan 1753; 5 Mar 1753; from John Monrow of Prince William Co. to Bowler Cocke, Jr. of *Bremo*; for £100; negro (HCVD-4 p. 207; TVF 9.109)

24 Feb 1771; will of Bowler Cocke, Jr. of *Bremo*, Henrico Co.; wit. by Sarah (Cocke) Happer, and others; handwritten copy of original in the Virginia Historical Society, Richmond; copy in the personal papers collection, the Library of Virginia (Accession 28350)

> 212-5 **Sarah Cocke**, b. 6 Feb 1728; m. ____ **Happer**
> 212-6 **Elizabeth Cocke**, b. 15 May 1731
> 212-7 **Richard Cocke**, b. 7 Mar 1733; lived 25 days
> 212-8 **Charles Cocke**, b. 9 Sep 1735; d. 4 Aug 1739

> 21-3 **Tabitha Cocke**; tentatively placed here as the granddau. Tabitha who inherited £10 and a negro from the will of Richard Cocke in 1706; she is said to have m. **Ebenezer Adams**; d. ca 1735; in the court of Dec 1719 Ebenezer sold a tract of land and wife Tabitha relinquished dower (HCDB-2 p. 188)
> 21-4 **Richard Cocke**; d. aft. 1771 Surry Co.; said to have m/1 Surry Co. **Elizabeth Hartwell**; d/o John Hartwell; m/2 **Elizabeth Ruffin**; d/o Robert Ruffin, Jr.
> 21-5 **Benjamin Cocke**; d. aft. 13 Mar 1763 Surry Co.; m. **Catherine Allen**; d/o Arthur Allen & Elizabeth Bray
> 21-6 **Anne Cocke**; d. Charles City Co.; m. **William Acrill**

2-2 **Elizabeth Cocke**; ml. 22 Aug 1695 Henrico Co. **Miles Cary, Jr.** (QRH p. 91; MHC p. 16); s/o Thomas Cary & Anne; Elizabeth inherited £20 from her father; known children from the will of their grandfather Cocke:

   22-1 **Richard Cary**; minor in 1706, inherited £20 from his grandfather
   22-2 **Thomas Cary**; inherited £10 from his grandfather
   22-3 **Miles Cary**; inherited £10 from his grandfather
   22-4 **Nathaniel Cary**; inherited £10 from his grandfather

2-3 **Martha Cocke**; ml/1 15 May 1699 Henrico Co. **Joseph Pleasants** (QRH p. 92); b. est. ca 1670's; d. by 7 Feb 1725; she inherited £20 from the will of her father; m/2 intention 3/10/1726 m. 5d 12m 1726 **Edward Bennett**; d. by May 1742 Henrico Co.; as Martha Bennett, she presented the will of Joseph Pleasants to the court on 11 May 1726 (HCVW-1 p. 169)

2-4 **John Cocke, Jr.**; d. by 2 Oct 1699; m. 24 Nov 1696 Henrico Co. **Obedience Branch**; surety Richard Cocke & Thomas Edwards (QRH p. 92; MHC p. 20); Obedience d. by 17 Jun 1746; d/o John Branch of *Kingsland*, dec'd; she m/2 **Alexander Trent**; d. by 2 Aug 1703; m/3 **Thomas Turpin**; d. by 4 May 1724; Cocke children of Obedience:

   24-1 John Cocke
   24-2 Martha Cocke

1 Oct 1696; 1 Dec 1696; from Jane Gower of *Kingsland*, Henrico Co. & Parish, deed of gift to John Cocke, Jr. and his wife Obedience, eldest d/o my son John Branch, dec'd, the 100 ac. plantation give me by my father in law Christopher Branch, dec'd, where my son John dwelt on s. side of James River (HCVD-1 p. 97)

1 Dec 1697; 1 Dec 1697; quit claim from Thomas Branch to John Cocke and Obedience, dau. and co-heir of John Branch; for £5; 100 ac. Christopher Branch gave Jane, grandmother of sd. Obedience and wife of William Branch, s/o Christopher, and father of John (HCVD-1 p. 102)

2 Oct 1699; 27 Oct 1699; 1 Aug 1700; inventory of Mr. John Cocke; presented in Ct. by Obedience, relict and extx. of John Cocke (HCVW-1 p. 74)

1 Jun 1700 [recorded]; John Cocke of Varina Parish and Obedience his wife, d/o John Branch, release Thomas Edwards for all debts as ex. of John Branch or his dau. Obedience in right of Martha, our mother, w/o sd. Edwards (HCVD-1 p. 112)

Will of Obedience Turpin, widow, of Goochland Co.; "weak in body"; 26 Jan 1745/6; 17 Jun 1746
To son John Cocke, negro boy
To dau. Martha Friend, 5s
To grandsons William & Benjamin Moseley (at 18), & Alexander Trent, each a negro
To son Alexander Trent, 5s
To dau. Obedience Branch, 5s
To granddaus. Obedience Branch, Mary Goode, 1 negro each
To granddau. Obedience Turpin, 3 negroes, featherbed, items
To dau. Mary Goode, 5s

Ex: son Thomas Turpin, 3 negroes & remainder of estate
Wit: Benj. Mosby, Peter Bondurand, Ann Bailey (GCWD-3 p. 19, 20)

24-1 **John Cocke**; inherited negro boy from will of his mother
24-2 **Martha Cocke**; m/1 **Arthur Moseley**; d. by Feb 1736; m/2 **Edward Friend**; d. by 20 Jan 1761; as dau. Martha Friend, she inherited 5 shillings from the 1746 will of her mother Obedience Turpin (GCWD-3 p. 19); children in the order they are mentioned in Moseley's will:

242-1 **Arthur Moseley**, of age in 1735
242-2 **John Moseley**
242-3 **Richard Moseley**
242-4 **William Moseley**; inherited a negro from grandmother Obedience Turpin
242-5 **Edward Moseley**
242-6 **Thomas Moseley**
242-7 **Benjamin Moseley**; minor in 1746; not mentioned in will of Arthur Moseley, but the will of Obedience Turpin calls him grandson and leaves him a negro when he becomes 18
242-8 **Francis Moseley**; not mentioned in his father's will

Will of Arthur Moseley; Henrico Co.; 20 Jul 1735; Feb 1736
To son Arthur, 500 ac. plantation I live on after death or marriage of my wife Martha; also part of *Red Water Mill*, negroes, items; also 400 ac. on *Butterwood Creek*
To son John, 400 ac. on *Fighting Creek*, negroes, items
To son Richard, 400 ac. on *Butterwood Creek*, negroes, etc.
To son William, the other 400 ac. on *Butterwood Creek*, other land, negroes, etc.
To sons Thomas & Edward, each 400 ac. on *Fighting Creek*, negroes, etc.
To my 6 sons, my library of books equally, to be kept by Arthur until they are of age; sons to be of age at 18
To wife, negroes, rest of estate, use of *Redwater Mill*
Exs: wife Martha, bro. William, son Arthur
Wit: John James Fluornoy, Edward Haskins (HCVW-1, p. 213)
[Arthur Moseley; Henrico Co. Wills and Admns. (1662-1800) p. 599-600; will pro. Feb 1736, p. 611-612. Inv. & appr. rec. May 1737. Deeds and Wills, 1725-1737 (Reel 7a) (LOV)]

Mar Ct. 1742; Francis Moseley, orphan of Arthur Moseley, dec'd, his portion now in hands of Edward Friend (HCVW-2 p. 18)

Feb Ct 1744; motion of William and Arthur Moseley, exs. of Arthur Moseley, dec'd, informing the court that Edward Friend and Martha his wife, widow of dec'd, are making waste of the estate in their possession; the Friends came to court (HCVW-2 p. 24)

2 Jan 1761; Martha Friend, widow of Edward Friend, granted admn. of his estate (ChOB 3.98); 20 Jan 1761; inventory of Edward Friend; value £5.17 (ChWB 1.369); on motion of Edward Friend, ordered that Martha Friend, admx. of Edward Friend, make up an account (ChOB 3.186); accounts of estate of Edward Friend returned (ChOB 1.194)

3. **Elizabeth Cocke**, b. aft. 1646; she was to inherit £100 from will of her father at age 17 or marriage
4. **William Cocke**, of *Low Grounds,* b. ca 1657, age 24 on 29 Feb 1681 (QRH p. 149); d. by 1 Feb 1693; s/o Richard & Mary; possibly m/1 **Jane Flowers** or **Jane Clarke**; ml/2 16 Jun 1691 Henrico Co. **Sarah Dennis** (MHC p. 20); he was charged with 2 taxables in the 1678 list of Henrico Co.; d. by 1 Jun 1695; he inherited ½ "a dividend of land not disposed of" from the will of his father; known children:

> 4-1 William Cocke
> 4-2 Mary Cocke
> 4-3 Elizabeth Cocke

28 Feb 1684; from William Cocke to Giles Carter, both of Henrico Co. & Parish; for £25; 59 ac. on *Turkey Island Mill Run*; next to sd. William and his bro. John; Jane, w/o William, relinquished dower (HCVD-1 p. 28)

Will of William Cocke of the *Low Grounds*, Henrico Co.; 13 Oct 1693; 1 Feb 1693
To be buried beside my wife and children, dec'd
To son William, land I live on; daus. Mary and Elizabeth contingent legatees; one cow to each
To Mrs. Mary Clarke, 20s given me by my mother to buy each dau. a ring when they are of age
Children to stay with wife until of age or with my mother, Mrs. Mary Clarke
Extx: wife, remainder of estate
Wit: D. Clarke, Richard Cocke, Jr., Mary Horner, Mary Cocke (HCVW-1 p. 50)
1 Feb 1693; 1 Jun 1694; inv. of Mr. William Cocke (HCVW-1 p. 53)
1 Oct 1694; Sarah Cocke told Henrico Ct. she is selling William Cocke's estate at his dwelling house (TVF 7.231)
1 Jun 1695; Mrs. Sarah Cock, relict, gave inventory of William Cocke's estate (TVF 7.231)
[William Cocke; Henrico Co. Wills and Admns. (1662-1800) p. 452-453. Will pro. 1 Feb. 1693. p. 469-470. Adms. bond rec. 26 Apr. 1694. p. 490-491. Inv. & appr. rec. 1 June 1694. Deeds, Wills, Etc., 1688-1697 (Reel 5); Note p. 112. Accounts rec. 1 Aug. 1698. Deeds, Wills, Etc., 1697-1704 (Reel 6) (LOV)]

1 Jun 1695; recorded; inventory of Sarah Cocke; value 3,250# tobacco; presented by Capt. William Randolph (HCVW-1 p. 56)

4-1 **William Cocke**; 1 Nov 1701; William Cocke was named coroner in court of 1 Nov 1701 (HCVW-1 p. 78); d. young as the land left him in his father's will was sold by his sister Mary in 1734
4-2 **Mary Cocke**; minor in 1693; d. by 1 Apr 1754 Henrico Co.; m. bef. 1705 **Obadiah Smith**; d. by Jun 1746; known children from wills:

42-1 **John Smith**
42-2 **Obadiah Smith**; d. by Oct Ct. 1765 when his will was presented by Jacob Smith (HCVW-2 p. 91); Apr Ct. 1767; inventory returned (HCVW-2 p. 96)
42-3 **Jacob Smith**

42-4 **Elizabeth Smith**; m. _____ **Ellis**
42-5 **Mary Smith**; m. **William Smith**

   425-1 **Mary Smith** (TVF 7.233)

42-6 **Luke Smith**; left a will in Halifax Co. Mar 1758
42-7 **Ann Smith**
42-8 **William Smith**

6 Apr 1705; 1 Nov 1708; from Obadiah Smith & Mary his wife, of Henrico Co. and Lanstate (Lancelot) Woodward and Elizabeth his wife, of James City Co.; are seized in right of their wives a plantation inherited from their father, William Cocke; they have another plantation of 254 ac. in James City Co. inherited from their maternal uncle, John Flowers; Obadiah & Mary are to have the plantation on *Turkey Island Creek*, Henrico Co., adj. John Pleasants mill; the Woodwards to have the James City Co. plantation on *Chickahominy River* and *Warring Creek* (HCVD-2 p. 16); TVF 7.231)

2 Sep 1734; 3 Mar 1734; from Obadiah Smith and Mary his wife of Henrico Co. to George Flood of Charles City Co.; deeded 1 Apr 1723; for £80; 104 ac. on n. side of James River near *Turkey Island Creek*; plantation by will dated 13 Oct 1696 by William Cocke, dec'd, to daus. Elizabeth and Mary; doubt has arisen and deed conveyed for 20s (HCVD-2 p. 158)

Will of Obadiah Smith of Henrico Co.; 29 Oct 1744; Jun 1746
To son John, 300 ac. on *Miry Branch*; 20 ac. on *Cattail Creek*; water mill & 2 ac. & 2
   negroes
To son Obadiah, 300 ac. next to above; 1 negro
To son Jacob, 300 ac., remainder of above
To dau. Elizabeth Ellis, 400 ac. uppermost part of *Long & Hungry Branch*; 2 negroes
To dau. Mary Smith, 400 ac. part of afsd. tract; 2 negroes
To son Luke and dau. Ann, 1 negro each
To son William, ex., 300 ac. next to *Horse Swamp* on *Brook Road*; also 40 ac. of
   plantation where I now live and 3 negroes
Wit: Nathaniel Vandewall, John Pleasants, James Allen (HCVW-2 p. 29, 30)
21 Feb 1746/7; Mar 1746; inventory of Obediah Smith; value £137.15.0 (HCVW-2 p.
   33)
[Obadiah Smith; Henrico County Wills and Admns. (1662-1800) p. 155-156. Will pro. June 1746.
p. 243-244. Inv. & appr. rec. Mar. 1746. Deed Book, 1744-1748 (Reel 8) (LOV)]

Will of Mary Smith; 3 Jun 1753; 1 Apr 1754
To sons John & Luke Smith, £1 each to be paid by my son William
To son Obadiah Smith, 4 negroes
To son Jacob Smith, my writing desk
To dau. Elizabeth Ellis and Mary Smith, £1 each
To dau. Anne Smith, 1 negro
To granddau. Mary Smith; d/o William & Mary Smith, 1 negro, items
Ex: son William; he to inherit remainder of property
Wit: John Price, William Sneed, Nathaniel Bridgwater (HCVW-2 p. 63; TVF 7.233)
Apr 1754; 4 Jun 1754; inventory of Mary Smith; value £98.18 (HCVW-2 p. 63)

[Mary Smith; Henrico Co. Wills and Admns. (1662-1800) p. 1651-1654. Will pro. 1 Apr. 1754. Misc. Court Records, Vol. 5, [1747-1757] (Reel 3); p. 312-313. Will pro. Apr. 1754. p. 335. Inv. & appr. rec. 4 June 1754. Deeds, Wills, Etc., 1750-1767 (Reel 9) (LOV)]

4-3 **Elizabeth Cocke**; minor in 1693; m. by 1705 **Lancelot Woodward** of James City Co.

5. **John Cocke** of *Old Man's Creek*; m. 1685-1686 Henrico Co. **Mary Davis** (QRH p. 90; MHC p. 20); he was to inherit 4,000# tobacco from the 1666 will of his godfather Lt. Col. Walter Aston to be paid in 1668

1 Dec 1686; 1 Dec 1686; from John Cocke to Francis Clevely, both of Henrico Co. & Parish; 200 ac. adj. *Chickahominy Swamp*; Mary, w/o John, relinquished dower (HCVD-1 p. 35)

30 Oct 1701; 5 Nov 1701; 1 Nov 1701; from John Cocke of *Old Man's Creek*, Charles City Co. to Thomas Williamson; 552 ac. on n. side of James River; Giles Carter's part of dividend of 1,780 ac. which he sold to Cocke (HCVD-1 p. 118, 119)

6. **Richard Cocke**, the younger of *Old Man's Creek*, b. est. ca 1658; d. ca 1750 Charles City Co.; m. ____; from his father he inherited 1,750 ac. from patent taken up jointly by his father and John Beauchamp; possible children:

> 6-1 Richard Cocke, Jr.
> 6-2 Anne Cocke

1 Aug 1694; 1 Aug 1694; from Richard Cock, Jr. of *Old Man's Creek*, Charles City Co., planter, to Thomas Williamson; for £32; 125 ac. ac. on n. side of James River bounded by *Western Run*; part of 901 ac. patent of Lt. Col. Richard Cocke and John Beauchamp (HCVD-1 p. 84)

29 Oct 1696; Richard Cock granted 975 ac. Charles City Co. on n. side of James River on *Chickahominy Path* (LOP 9.67)

31 Oct 1707; from John Pleasants to Richard Cock of Waynoak Parish, Charles City Co.; for £15, 126 ac. on n. side of James River; also 500 ac on n. side of James River and both sides of *White Oak Swamp*; being part of a greater tract taken up by Richard Cocke, father of sd. Richard and bounded by him and his bros. Richard and Thomas Cocke, dec'd (HCVD-2 p. 9)

6-1 **Richard Cocke, Jr.** of Westover Parish; d. ca 1749; m. ____; possible children:

61-1 **Mary Cocke**; m. **Richard Epes** of Charles City Co.; in 1767 they sold the land her father gave her in 1735 (HCVD-4 p. 1010; TVF 11.46)
61-2 **Richard Cocke**; d. ca 1750

2 Jun 1735; 2 Jun 1735; from Richard Cocke of Westover Parish, Charles City Co. to Mary Epes, d/o sd. Richard Cocke; for 5s; 500 ac. being all my land in Henrico Co. (HCVD-2 p. 160)

6-2 **Anne Cocke**; she may have m. 27 Jan 1705/6 **Robert Bolling, Jr.**, b. 25 Jan 1681 Charles City Co.; d. ca 1749; s/o Robert Bolling and Anne Stith

7. **Edward Cocke**; d. by 1726 Charles City Co.; he was to inherit 6,000#
tobacco from the 1666 will of his godfather Walter Aston to be paid in 1669

Unplaced:
John Cocke; m. 22 Jul 1727 **Elizabeth** ____; d. bef. Jun 1746; widow of Edward Baxter:
Jun Ct. 1746; Richard Bland & Ann his wife, Edward Calwell & and Tabitha his wife,
Sarah Royall and Elizabeth Ragsdale vs. John Cocke:
Edward Baxter, bro. of Tabitha, Sarah, Elizabeth & uncle of Ann, d. in 1720 leaving
considerable estate; his will stated "I give to my wife the following slaves (listed), but
if my wife Elizabeth die, to my family"; exs. wife Elizabeth and William Royall.
Jul 1726; Charles City Co.; Elizabeth Baxter, widow, extx. of estate
Elizabeth Baxter [d. bef. Jun 1746] m. 22 Jul 1727 John Cocke of Henrico Co.
The court decided for the plaintiffs (HCVW-2 p. 44)
John Cocke of Goochland; mb. 21 Oct 1782 Powhatan Co. **Mary Branch**

THOMAS LIGON

Thomas Ligon, b. est. ca 1623, England; d. by 16 Mar 1675 Henrico Co.;
m. ca 1648-50 **Mary Harris**, b. ca 1625, age ca 64 on 2 Dec 1689 (HCVD-1 p.
152); d. by 1 Feb 1703/4 Henrico Co.; d/o Thomas & Adria Harris; sister of Maj.
Thomas Harris (LF&C); Thomas is said to have come to Virginia in 1641 at age
16, settling at *Neck of Land* near *Malvern Hills,* Henrico Co.; Lt. Col. Ligon is
said to have been passing the home of Dr. John Woodson when the Indians
made a sudden attack on the Virginia settlements on 18 Apr 1644; he helped
Sara Woodson defend the home against the Indians; he served in the House of
Burgesses, 1644-45; represented Henrico Co. in the House of Burgess in 1656;
was a Justice of Charles City Co. in 1657 and a member of the Henrico Co.
Militia by 1669; on the 2 Jun 1679 list of Henrico Co. "Mrs. Lygon" was
charged with 2 tithables; they may have had a son named Thomas as a patent
was granted to Thomas Ligon, Sr. on 18 Mar 1672/3; children:

        1. William Ligon, b. est. ca 1650
        2. Johan Ligon, b. ca 1653
        3. Richard Ligon, b. ca 1657
        4. Matthew Ligon, b. est. ca 1659
        5. Hugh Ligon, b. est. ca 1661
        6. Mary Ligon, b. est. ca 1663

5 Apr 1664; Thomas Liggon; 800 ac. at *Powells Creek* on the river next to Thomas
Jones; transport of 16 persons (PB 5.139 [6])

3 Oct 1664; Tho. Ligon & Capt. Wm. Farrar; 375 ac.; n. side of James River adj. Morgan Price; for transport of 8 persons (PB 5.376 [416]); sale mentioned 1699 (HCVD-1 p. 109)

3 Oct 1664; Capt. Wm. Farrar & Thomas Ligon (Liggon); 335 ac.; s. side of James River in *Mont Malada* (*Mount My Lady*) *field*; adj. *Proctors;* transport of 7 persons (PB 5.377)

29 Oct 1668; Lt. Col. Tho. Ligon & Maj. Wm. Ferrer; granted 300 ac. Henrico Co. (LOP 6.188)

18 Mar 1672/3; Thomas Ligon, Sr. granted 340 ac. Henrico Co. at head of *Ashen Swamp* on n. side of Appomatox River adj. Ligon's land at *Mount Malada* (LOP 6.447)

16 Mar 1675; will of Thomas Lygon, Gent., appointed his wife Mary executrix (HCVW-1 p. 6)
[Thomas Lygon; Henrico County Wills and Administrations (1662-1800) p. 35. Exors. bond rec. 16 Mar. 1675/76. Records, 1677-1692 (Reel 4) (LOV)]

"On August 20, 1678, division of the Estate of Mr. Thomas Lygon, Junior, decd., as it is presented by Mrs. Mary Lygon, and distributed amongst her children as follows, viz. : .... Richard Lygon, Mathew Lygon, Hugh Lygon, Mary Lygon" (Henrico Co. Orphan's Court, 1677-1739, 4.3)

17 Oct 1683; 1 Dec 1683; Mary Ligon & Tho. Chamberlayne; boundary agreement on *Sisemans Brook* (HCVD-1 p. 23)

2 Feb 1684/5; 2 Feb 1684; deed of gift from Mary Ligon, widow, to son in law Robert Hancock, horse & mare; to his dau. Sarah, mare; to his dau. Mary, the first foal (HCVD-1 p. 27)

29 Aug 1691; 1 Sep 1691; from Mary Ligon, Sr. to sons Richard & Hugh Ligon; 200 ac. at *Curles* part of a grant to Capt. Thomas Harris, dec'd given to his dau. Mary Ligon to be equally divided between Richard and Hugh (HCVD-1 p. 65)

23 Oct 1691; Mary Ligon had 166 ac. surveyed for her son Thomas Ligon; bounded as in will of Col. Thomas Ligon, dec'd; adj. land of William Ligon and Mathew Ligon, both dec'd (HCVD-1 p. 68)

Will of Mary Lygon, Sr.; 16 Apr 1702/3; 1 Feb 1703/4
To son Richard Lygon, 100 ac. *Curles* in Henrico Co.; adj. Richard Cocke, items
To son Hugh Lygon, 100 ac. adj. Richard, household goods
To grandson Thomas Farrar, items at age 21 or marriage
To son in law Thomas Farrar Indian boy Robin given his wife by her father
To grandson Henry Lygon, horse
To son Hugh Lygon and my dau. Hancock, all my sheep
Exs: son in law Robert Hancock & dau. Johan Hancock
Wit: Abra. Womack, John Hatcher, John Brown
Codicil: mentions son William Lygon d. before possessing abv. 200 ac. (HCVW-1 p. 86)
1 Feb 1703/4; probate granted Robert Hancock and Johan his wife on will of Mrs. Mary Lygon (HCVW-1 p. 88)
[Mary Ligon (Lygon), Senior; Henrico County Wills and Administrations (1662-1800) Note p. 366-367. Will pro. 1 Feb. 1703/04. p. 367. Codicil rec. 1 Feb. 1703/04. Deeds, Wills, Etc., 1697-1704 (Reel 6)]

1. **William Ligon**, b. est, ca 1650; d. by 1 Aug 1689 Henrico Co.; m. **Mary Tanner**; d. aft. 1721; d/o Joseph & Mary Tanner [later Mary Platt, widow of Gilbert Platt]; Mary, widow of William Ligon, m/2 aft. 1701 & by 1 Mar 1706/7 Henrico Co. as 2nd w/o **William Farrar** (QRH p. 93); in 1679 dau. Mary Ligon & husband William rec'd deed of gift from her mother Mary Platt & Mary was granted probate of her mother's will 1 Feb 1700 (HCVW-1 p. 77); Maj. Wm. Lygon was charged with 3 tithables in the list of 2 Jun 1679 Henrico Co.; 2 May 1709 George Robertson sued William Farrar for 20s, his fee for marrying him to Mary, relict of William Ligon; children's dates of birth est. from wills and other documents (not in order of estimated birth):

> 1-1 Thomas Ligon, b. est. ca 1672-82
> 1-2 William Ligon, b. est. ca 1682
> 1-3 John Ligon, b. aft. 1673
> 1-4 Joseph Ligon, b. est. ca 1670's-80's
> 1-5 Mary Ligon, b. est. ca 1680's
> 1-6 Lucretia Ligon, b. ca 1689

1 Apr 1680; Maj. William Lygon recorded a mare with foal for use of Martha Tanner, orphan (CRHC 4, Orphan's Ct. 1677-1739 p. 5)

20 Apr 1683; Mr. William Ligon did set upon the courthouse doors, according to law, intent of going to England (LF&C)

[undated]; William Lygon was committed to court [for a misdemeanor] and violently resisted arrest; fined 400# tobacco (CRHC 2.161); Mr. Richard Lygon and Mr. Robert Hancock made bond for themselves as surety for Mr. William Lygon's further good behaviour (CRHC 2.61)

Will of William Ligon; 21 Jan 1688; 1 Aug 1689
To sons Thomas & William; plantation I live on, equally divided
To son John, my part of *Ashen Swamp* land
To son Joseph & Thomas Farrar, Jr., equally land adj. Hancock's
To dau. Mary & child my wife goes with, land back of *Curles* at age 21 or if she
  marries to age 16
To each son, a gun at age
If wife remarries, children to be at their own disposeing at age 16
Ex: wife, remainder of estate during widowhood; if she remarries, ½ to wife and ½ to
  children
Overseers of will: Capt. Fra. Epes, Robert & John Worsham
Wit: John Worsham, Robert Hancock, Richard Ligon (HCVW-1 p. 37)
[William Ligon; Henrico County Wills and Administrations (1662-1800) p. 75-76. Will pro. 1 Aug. 1689. p. 96. Exors. bond rec. 20 Oct. 1689. Deeds, Wills, Etc., 1688-1697 (Reel 5) (LOV)]

1 Dec 1691; due 300 ac. to Mary Ligon, the younger, for importation William Ligon, William Hill, Anne Pullen, Will Shaw and negroes Robin & Bridget (HCVD-1 p. 143)

20 Aug 1692; 20 Aug 1692; from William Midgely to Mary Ligon, widow of William Ligon, both of Bristol Parish, Henrico Co.; 200 ac. on *Swift Creek* next to *Persimmon Branch* (HCVD-1 p. 72)

21 Aug 1692; Mrs. Mary Lygon, the younger, petitioned the county court as next of kin of her son Thomas Lygon, complaining of waste committed on her estate by Mrs. Mary Lygon, Sr. who claimed life interest in it from Col. Thomas Lygon, grandfather of sd. Thomas Lygon (LF&C)

1 Dec 1692; Mary Ligon, the younger, widow; purchased for 265# tobacco; ½ ac. lot #23 in town in Henrico Co. (HCVD-1 p. 74)

27 Nov 1694; 1 Dec 1694; Mary Lygon and Martha Haskins of Henrico Co., daus. of Joseph Tanner; agree on division of *Baldwins* left them by their father (HCVD-1 p. 86)

1 Jun 1696; Mary Lygon, widow of William Lygon, dec'd, of Henrico Co.; assigns to mother Mary Platt, widow of Gilbert Platt of Varina Parish; 200 ac. on *Swift Creek* (HCVD-1 p. 94)

1 Aug 1698; Court at Varina; Mary Ligon, the younger, and Thomas, her son, acknowledge lease and relinquishment of dower; Elizabeth, w/o Thomas, relinquished dower (CRHC 3.201)

26 Oct 1699; Mary Ligon, w/o William, dec'd, granted 385 ac. on n. side of *Proctor's Creek* for transport of 8 persons including William Ligon (PB 9.202)

Mrs. Mary Ligon; "Former wife of William Ligon decd." Virginia State Land Office. Patents 1-42, reels 1-41. Location: Henrico County. Description: On the north side of the great on main branch of Procters. Source: Land Office Patents No. 9, 1697-1706 (v.1 & 2 p.1-742), p. 242 (Reel 9) (LOP)

2 Mar 1701; 2 Mar 1701; deed of gift from Mary Ligon to son William Ligon 130 ac. of *Baldwins* given me by the will of my father Joseph Tanner and patented in my name also tract on n. branch of *Proctor's*; William Ligon, father of Thomas and William, granted ½ of his plantation to them equally; this gift to prevent suits between my two sons; William to give up his right to his portion to his bro. Thomas when he comes of age (HCVD-1 p. 121)

1-1 **Thomas Ligon**, b. est. ca 1672-82; d. by 2 Apr 1705; m1. 15 Mar 1697/8 Henrico Co. **Elizabeth Worsham**; d/o Capt. John Worsham (HCVW-1 p. 172); Elizabeth m/2 bef. 20 Aug 1706 **Alexander Marshall** (MHC p. 54); d. by Jul Ct. 1743 Henrico Co.; as Elizabeth Marshall she was one of the wit. to the will of Martha Brown 7 Aug 1721 (HCVW-1, p. 232; HCVW-2 p. 159); Thomas inherited livestock from 1700 will of his maternal grandmother Mary Platt; known children:

            11-1 Phebe Ligon, b. est. ca 1699
            11-2 Elizabeth Ligon, b. est. ca 1701
            11-3 Thomas Ligon, b. est. ca 1703
            11-4 Mary Ligon; b. ca 1704

1 Aug 1698; [fragment of record]; agreement or deed between Mary Ligon of Henrico Co. and Thomas Ligon regarding 60 ac.; 2 pages later Elizabeth Ligon, w/o Thomas, released dower to her mother in law Mary Ligon (HCVD-1 p. 105)

Apr 1705; Henrico Co. rent roll; Elizabeth Ligon, widow, & Mary Ligon, widow, held 1, 341 ac.

2 Apr 1705; administration granted Elizabeth Ligon on estate of her husband Mr. Thomas Ligon; Capt. John Worsham (HCVW-1 p. 92)

7 May 1705; 1 Jun 1705; inventory of Thomas Ligon; presented in court by Capt. John Worsham for his dau. Mrs. Elizabeth Ligon, relict & admx. (HCVW-1 p. 92)
[Thomas Ligon; Henrico County Wills and Administrations (1662-1800) p. 446-447. Inv. & appr. rec. 1 June 1705. Deeds, Wills, Etc., 1697-1704 (Reel 6) (LOV)]

1 Aug 1706; a document in the Varina Court includes the following "Mr. Alexander Marshall who lately had married Mrs. Elizabeth Ligon" (CRHC, Book 4, Orphans Ct. 1677-1739 p. 48)

Mar Ct. 1720; from Alexander Marshall to Henry Walthall, deed; Elizabeth, w/o Alexander, relinquished dower (HCVD-2 p. 192)

4 Dec 1733; 1ˢᵗ Mon Feb 1733; from Alexander Marshall to Thomas Friend, both of Bristol Parish, Henrico Co.; for £200; 2,250 ac. called *The Great Swamp* on both sides of *Swift Creek*; Elizabeth, w/o Alexander, relinquished dower right (HCVD-2 p. 150-, 151)

Jul Ct. 1743; will of Alexander Marshal presented by Alexander and William Marshal (HCVW-2 p. 19)
Aug Ct. 1743; inventory of Alexander Marshall recorded (HCVW-1 p. 20)

   11-1 **Phebe Ligon**, b. est. ca 1699; d. bef. 1756; m. ca 1716 **Henry Walthall**, b. 23 Oct 1690 (LF&C); d. May 1765; grandson of Richard Walthall and Ann Archer; Phebe was called granddau. in the 1700 will of her great-grandmother Mary Platt

   11-2 **Elizabeth Ligon**, b. est. ca 1701; m. **James Anderson**; he may have been the James Anderson who d. in Surry Co. in 1752; probably bro. of William Anderson who m. Mary Ligon and Elizabeth Anderson who m. Mathew Ligon

Jan Ct. 1723; from James Anderson and Elizabeth his wife to Alexander Marshall, deed (HCVD-2 p. 200)

1 Mar 1729; 1ˢᵗ Mon Aug; from James Anderson and Elizabeth his wife of Prince George Co. to Henry Walthall, Jr. of Henrico Co.; for £6.10; 66 ac. part of 200 ac., the 1/3 part on n. side of *Swift Creek* at *Persimmon Branch* adj. Capt. Henry Randolph (HCVD-2 p. 118, 119)

1 Oct 1733; 1ˢᵗ Mon Oct 1733; bond of £100 from James Anderson and Elizabeth his wife of Bristol Parish; to Alexander Marshall of Henrico Co.; re sale of 100 ac. called *Powells*; formerly owned by their father Thomas Ligon (HCVD-2 p. 149; ChDB 1.113, 193)

Sep Ct. 1740; from James Anderson and Elizabeth his wife to Henry Walthall, deed (HCVD-3 p. 87)

   11-3 **Thomas Ligon**, b. est. ca 1703; d. ca 1706 (Barton's Colonial Decisions, p. 150)
   11-4 **Mary Ligon**; b. ca 1704; d. bef. 1741; unmarried

1-2 **William Ligon**, b. est. ca 1682 (LF&C); d. 1764 Amelia Co.; m. bef. 1704
Elizabeth Batte, d/o Henry Batte and Mary Lound; they rec'd gift of land
on s. side of James River from Elizabeth's grandfather Henry Lound in
1703/4; his mother deeded her right in land inherited from her father to
William; he is not mentioned in 1700 will of his grandmother Mary Platt;
William, s/o William, age 59 years old, was a defendant in a lawsuit said to
have taken place ca 1741 (Barton's Colonial Decisions p. 150); presumed children:

> 12-1 Sarah Ligon
> 12-2 William Ligon, Jr.
> 12-3 Joseph Ligon

1 Dec 1694; deed of gift from Edward Haskins to William Ligon, s/o William Ligon,
dec'd; a cow now at *Powells*, the plantation of his mother Mary Lygon (HCVD-1 p. 87)

Jul Ct. 1721; Henrico Co.; William Ligon vs Mary Farrar, admx. of estate of William
Ligon, dec'd (LF&C)

11 Feb 1728; 1st Mon Apr 1729; from John Soan of Carolina to William Ligon and
Thomas Osborn, Jr. of Henrico Co.; for £30; 320 ac. *Wilminton* on s. side of James
River; Peter, Henry and Joseph Ligon wit. deed (HCVD-2 p. 116)

Jun Ct. 1742; from William Ligon to Benjamin Harris, Gent., deed; Elizabeth, w/o
William, relinquished dower (HCVD-3 p. 96)

6 May 1745; 1st Mon May 1745; from William Ligon to Richard Randolph, both of
Henrico Co.; for £150; 130 ac. called *Neck of Land* on s. side of James River in Dale
Parish patented by Henry Lound and conveyed to Ligon 1 Feb 1703/4; Elizabeth, w/o
William, relinquished dower (HCVD-3 p. 12)

Will of William Ligon of Prince Edward Co.; 22 Oct 1759; 27 Sep 1764
To wife Elizabeth Ligon, all my estate for her natural life
After her decease, to Martha Moseley, w/o Matthew Moseley, negro
To my dau. Sarah Ligon, w/o Henry, £10, furniture, livestock, after wife's decease
To grandson Joseph Ligon, livestock after decease of wife
To son William Ligon, remainder of estate
Ex: son William Ligon
Wit: Richard Burles, Wm. Ligon, Jessa Lewelling (AmWB 2x.75)
25 Sep 1765; 26 Sep 1765; William Ligon; appraisal value of estate £436.9.6 (AmWB
    2x.106)
[William Ligon, Senior; Amelia County Wills and Administrations (1734 - 1800) p. 75-76. Will
pro. 27 Sept. 1764. p. 106-107. Inv. & Appr. rec. 26 Sept. 1765. Will Book No. 2-X, 1761-1771
(Reel 28); Goochland County Wills and Administrations (1728 - 1800) p. 10-11. Inv. and Appr.
rec. Oct. 16, 1765. Deed Book No. 9, 1765-1769 (Reel 4); Cumberland County Wills and
Administrations (1749 - 1810) p. 332. Inv. & Appr. rec. 26 Oct. 1767. Will Book No. 1, 1749-
1769 (Reel 17) (LOV)]

> 12-1 **Sarah Ligon**; d. by Jan 1785; m. bef. 1734 cousin **Henry Ligon**; d.
>   by 14 Dec 1762; s/o Richard Ligon & Mary Worsham; they both d.
>   Prince Edward Co.

12-2 **William Ligon, Jr.**; d. ca 1796 Amelia Co.; m. by 14 Mar 1742 **Ann Rogers**; d/o Richard Rogers of Goochland Co. according to the will of Robert Rogers (GCWD-3 p. 3); children (LF&C):

> 122-1   Susanna Ligon, b. ca 1745
> 122-2   Martha Ligon
> 122-3   ____ Ligon (f)
> 122-4   William Ligon
> 122-5   Robert Ligon
> 122-6   Thomas Ligon
> 122-7   Joseph Ligon
> 122-8   Ann Ligon
> 122-9   Richard Ligon, b. 29 Jun 1773

20 Apr 1746; 16 May 1746; between William Ligon and Henry Ligon, both of Amelia Co.; William transfers to Henry 150 ac. on opposite side of *Sandy River* in Amelia Co. (AmDB 2.322)

20 Sep 1746; William Ligon, Jr. of Amelia Co. transfers to his father & mother, William and Elizabeth Ligon; 600 ac. on s. side of *Sandy River* Amelia Co. where William & Elizabeth now reside; also 50 adj. ac.; for their natural lives (AmDB 2.451)

12 Jan 1746; William Ligon, Jr. patented 800 ac. for 40s in Amelia Co. on both sides of *Saylor's Creek* (PB 28.57)

14 Jul 1749; between Henry Dawson and William Ligon, Jr.; 623 ac. on e. side of Appomattox River in Amelia Co. (AmDB 3.248)

26 Apr 1759; indenture of "feofment" between William Lygon & John Wright; Ann, w/o William relinquished dower (AmDB 5.231)

25 Jul 1759; between David Greenhill and William Ligon; both of Raleigh Parish, Amelia Co.; 593 ac. in Amelia Co., parish of Raleigh and Nottoway, in center of Appomattox River (AmDB 7.53)

12 Jun 1760; from William Ligon of Amelia Co. and Ann his wife to James Ligon of Chesterfield Co.; for £30; 30 ac. Prince Edward Co. on s. side of *Sandy River* (PEDB 2.23)

3 Oct 1760; from William Ligon of Amelia Co. to Samuel Goode of Prince Edward; for £335; 752 ac. on w. side of *Saylots Creek*; Ann, w/o William, waives dower (PEDB 2.28)

13 Jul 1762; from William Ligon to James Atwood; both of Amelia Co.; for £260; 970 ac. on s. side of *Sandy River*; Ann, w/o William, waives dower (PEDB 2.109)

19 Aug 1765; from William Ligon of Amelia Co. to Peter LeGrande of Prince Edward Co.; for £20; 300 ac on upper side of *Buffalo River* (PEDB 3.5)

6 Jul 1768; 20 Jul 1768; deed of gift; from William Ligon, Sr. to son William Ligon, Jr., both of Amelia Co.; 230 ac. formerly belonging to David Greenhill (AmDB 10.17)

6 Jul 1768; from William Ligon to Robert Ligon; transfer of 230 ac. on Appomattox River above *Ward's Ford* in Amelia Co. on *Franklin Creek* (AmDB 10.15)

15 Feb 1768; 20 Aug 1768; from William Ligon of Amelia Co. to John Wayles of Charles City Co.; for £150; 200 ac. on Appomattox River, Amelia Co.; being lower part of tract where sd. Ligon now dwells (AmDB 10.42)

22 Mar 1770; from William Ligon, Sr. of Amelia Co. to son Thomas Ligon; also 1 negro girl (AmDB 11.89)

20 Jul 1773; 22 Jul 1773; from William Ligon, Sr. to Robert Ligon, both of Raleigh Parish, Amelia Co.; for £50; 100 ac. on *Franklin Creek*, Amelia Co. (AmDB 12.87)

22 Jul 1773; 22 Jul 1773; from William Ligon to William Ligon, Jr., both of Raleigh Parish, Amelia Co.; for £30; 50 ac. on *Franklin Creek* (AmDB 12.87)

26 Feb 1795; from William Ligon to Joseph Ligon, both of Amelia Co.; sells 100 ac. on w. side of *Johnson Mill Creek* (AmDB 20.58)

16 Nov 1792; 16 Jul 1794; lease starting 25 Dec for 2 years of plantation from William Ligon to Philip Webber for the year 1793; for £28.3.8 ¾ (LF&C)

Will of William Ligon, Sr.; Amelia Co.; 22 Sep 1796; 27 Oct 1796
My debts to be paid out of crop of Brandy in hands of Joseph Ligon
I lend to Caroline Foster my land, plantation, negros, stock, etc. for her natural life
After the death of Caroline:
To son Joseph, land, plantation and 3 negroes
To dau. Martha Rogers, negroes, furniture
To grandsons John Webber and Benjamin Webber, negroes at age
Exs: James McGleason, Benjamin Chapman
Wit: John Henrick, Jr., John Wright, Polly Wright (AmWB 5.322)
26 Dec 1796; 17 Jul 1797; inventory; value £382.11.2 (AmWB 5.393)
31 Jul 1799; 27 Feb 1800; balance of estate; value £46.9.4.3 (AmWB 6.77)
[William Ligon, Senior; Amelia County Wills and Administrations (1734 - 1800) p. 322-323. Will pro. 27 Oct. 1796. p. 393-394. Inv. & Appr. rec. 27 July 1797. Will Book No. 5, 1793-1799 (Reel 30); Will Book No. 6, 1799-1803 (Reel 31) (LOV)

122-1 **Susanna Ligon**, b. ca 1745; d. bef. 1793; m. 22 Dec 1766 Amelia Co. **Samuel Williams**, b. ca 1746; d. 1823; s/o Thomas Williams; he m/2 **Mary Wright**; Samuel filed his will 2 Jul 1821, probated 1823 in Cumberland Co. (CuWB 7; LF&C)

122-2 **Martha Ligon**, b. est. ca 1747; m/1 **William Wright**; d. by 1789 Amelia Co.; m/2 **Mr. Rogers**; she inherited negroes and furniture from her father in 1796

122-3 ____ **Ligon** (f), b. est. ca 1749; m. ____ **Webber**; children:

1223-1 **John Webber**; to inherit negroes at age from his grandfather
1223-2 **Benjamin Webber**; to inherit negroes at age from his grandfather Ligon's will written in 1796

122-4 **William Ligon**, b. est. ca 1751; d. by 1805; m. **Susannah Woodson**, b. ca 1750; d. 7 Jan 1828 Laurens, SC, age 78 yrs. (tombstone); d/o John Woodson & Mary Miller (LF&C); as William, Sr. he sold land 24 Dec 1801 and Susanna relinquished dower (AmOB 25.59 – LF&C); children from family histories:

1224-1 **Polly Ligon**; m. **Jancy Holman**

1224-2 **Judith Ligon**; m/1 1801 Amelia Co. **Thomas Swann**; m/2 **Samuel Allen**

1224-3 **Susanna Ligon**; m. **Samuel Ward**

1224-4 **William Ligon**, b. ca 1772 Cumberland Co., VA; d. 25 Jun 1850 Laurens Co., SC; m/1 27 Sep 1794 Cumberland Co. **Martha Wright**, b. 10 Sep 1778; d. 11 Jun 1830 Laurens Dist., SC; m/2 **Elizabeth Burns**

1224-5 **Thomas Ligon**, b. ca 1775 VA; d. 20 Sep 1826 Laurens, SC; m/1 **Elizabeth Hill Beacham**; m/2 **Susannah** ____(poss. widow)

1224-6 **Woodson Ligon**; mb. 15 Dec 1823 Cumberland Co. **Elizabeth Allen**

1224-7 **John Ligon**, b. ca 1768; d. 28 Jul 1826 Richmond Co., GA; m. 19 Mar 1787 Prince Edward Co. **Rodith Marshall**

1224-8 **Elizabeth Ligon**; mb. 1802 Amelia Co. **Henry Johns**

1224-9 **Patsy Ligon**; mb. 22 Jul 1801 Amelia Co. **Anderson Stone**

1224-10 **Sally Miller Ligon**, b. ca 1790; d. 31 Aug 1815 Laurens Co., SC; m. **John Philips**

1224-11 **Miller Woodson Ligon**

1224-12 **Joseph M. Ligon**, b. 25 May 1790 Amelia Co.; d. 16 Feb 1857 Grenada, MS; m/1 **Sally** ____; m/2 24 Oct 1809 Cumberland Co. **Nancy Woodson**

122-5 **Robert Ligon**, b. est. ca 1753; m. **Edith Watkins**; 20 Apr 1797 he names bro. William trustee for his portion of father's estate (AmWB 6.78)

122-6 **Thomas Ligon**, b. est. ca 1755; d. by 1807; m. **Tabitha Ward**

122-7 **Joseph Ligon**, b. est. ca 1757; d. by 1830; m. **Nancy Keturah**

122-8 **Ann Ligon**, b. 24 Jun 1765; d. 30 Jun 1842; m. 5 Oct 1781 Amelia Co. **Harrison Jones**, b. 14 Oct 1757 Cumberland Co.

122-9 **Richard Ligon**, b. 29 Jun 1773; d. by 1844; m. 10 Sep 1797 Amelia Co. **Ann B. Webber**; d/o Philip Webber (see CuDB 8.133)

12-3 **Joseph Ligon**, b. ca 1704; d. by 1 May 1752 Chesterfield Co.; m/1 ____; m/2 **Judith Stewart (Stuart)**; d. 1784 Chesterfield Co.; she m/2 by 5 Jun 1761 **James Ligon** (ChWB 3.126); children from Joseph's will:

> Children of m/1:
> 123-1 Joseph Ligon, b. ca 1725-30
> 123-2 Mary Ligon
> 123-3 Martha Ligon
> Children of m/2:
> 123-4 John Ligon
> 123-5 Thomas Ligon

123-6 William Ligon
123-7 Judith Ligon
123-8 Elizabeth Ligon

10 Jan 1735; Joseph Ligon granted 169 ac. in Brunswick Co. on s. side of *Sandy River* for 25s (PB 16.515)

15 Mar 1735; Joseph Ligon granted 612 ac. in Brunswick Co. on both sides of *Sandy River* for £3.5 (PB 17.13)

28 Dec 1736; Robert Bowman and Joseph Ligon of Henrico Co. granted 238 ac. in Brunswick Co. on both side of *Sandy River* for 25s (PB 17.231)

18 Nov 1738; from Joseph Ligon of Henrico Co. to James Gravilet; for 5s; 100 ac. n. side *Sandy River* (AmDB 1.184)

20 Aug 1741; Joseph Ligon granted 469 ac. on lower side of *Sandy River* for 40s (PB 19.1098)

Aug Ct. 1744; from Joseph Ligon to Richard Randolph, deed (HCVD-3 p. 104)

11 Dec 1744; 1st Mon Jul 1745; from Thomas Eldridge of Prince George Co. and Martha his wife to Joseph Ligon of Henrico Co.; for £205; 640 ac. on s. side of James River at *Roxdale* (HCVD-3 p. 12)

25 Jul 1745; Joseph Ligon granted 183 ac. Henrico Co.; Robert Hancock d. seized of 625 ac.; resurvey showed 532 ac.; Margaret Hancock made suit and was granted 183 ac. which she assigned to Joseph Ligon (PB 25.138)

25 Jul 1746; Joseph Ligon granted 183 ac. Henrico Co. adj. his own land to head of branch called *Good Luck Spring* (LOP 25.138)

4 Apr 1748; 1st Mon Apr 1748; from Joseph Ligon of Dale Parish, Henrico Co. to Edward Folks; for £7; 75 ac. at *Rocksdale*; Judith, w/o Joseph, relinquished dower rights (HCVD-3 p. 54)

4 Nov 1751; 5 Jun 1752 from Joseph Ligon the younger of Dale Parish, Chesterfield Co. to Richard Randolph the younger of *Curles*; Joseph father of said Joseph for £250; 175 ac. tract *Warwick*; the elder Richard Randolph, dec'd, by his conveyed to his son Brett Randolph, infant under 21; Joseph Ligon the younger confirms land to sd. Richard (ChDB 1.426)

Will of Joseph Ligon; Dale Parish, Chesterfield Co.; 17 Nov 1751; [written]
To son Joseph, upper part of land testator lives on called *Roxdale*, negro, items
To son John, lower part of abv. land, colt, great Bible, gold ring
To son Thomas, 2 tracts; 800 ac. Amelia Co.; 469 ac. called *Acorn Ground*
To son William, 612 ac. Amelia Co. called *Island* (*Round Island*)
To William Baugh, Jr., 160 ac. called *Bolden*
To dau. Mary Moseley, negro Jammy now in possession of my father
To dau. Martha Ligon, 5 negroes
To daus. Judith Ligon & Elizabeth Ligon at age, 1 negro each
To wife 2 negroes for life, then to my 5 young children I had by my last wife
Other negroes divided between by 5 children, John, Judith, Thomas, William, Elizabeth

Extx: wife

Wit: Sarah Ward, Mary Stewart, Leonard Ward (ChWB 1.121)

6 Jun 1752; Joseph Ligon, appraisal of estate £616/2/ ½ (ChWB 1.125-7)

[undated]; inventory of Joseph Ligon; value £616.2 ½ (ChWB 1.125); inventory of
Joseph Ligon; value £294.10.2 (?in another county) (ChWB 1.127)

[Joseph Ligon; Chesterfield County Wills and Administrations (1754-1800) Will - dated 1751
Proved 1 May 1752 (O.B. 1, p. 184) Chesterfield Will Book 1, p. 121-124; Inv. & Appr. - undated
Returned 6 October 1752 (O.B. 1, p. 256) Chesterfield Will Book 1, p. 125-127; His orphan,
Martha Ligon, chose William Moseley as her guardian, 4 May 1753. (O.B. 1, p. 339); Orphan
children (not named). Their accounts returned by Judith Ligon, their guardian, 1 Aug. 1755. (O.B.
2, p. 114); Accts. for his orphans, John, Thomas, Judith and Elizabeth, returned by Judith Ligon,
their guardian, 5 Sept. 1755. (O.B. 2, p. 125); Accts. of his orphans, John, Thomas, Judith and
Elizabeth Ligon, returned by Judith Ligon, their guardian, 6 Aug. 1756. (O.B. 2, p. 209); Case
regarding his estate, his executrix having married James Ligon in the meantime, 5 June 1761.
(O.B. 3, p. 138); His orphans, Thomas and Elizabeth Ligon, to have John Ligon as their guardian,
5 March, 1762. (O.B. 3, p. 212); Division of slaves belonging to his estate. (NOTE: This is the
actual division naming heirs - not just the order for recordation of same.), 4 Oct. 1765. (O.B. 3, p.
699-700 (LOV)]

123-1 **Joseph Ligon, Capt.**, b. ca 1725-30 Henrico Co.; d. by 18 May
1780 Halifax Co.; s/o his father's m/1; m. ca 1754 **Judith Watts**; 11
May 1769 Joseph petitioned to establish a ferry from his land on the n.
side of the *Dan River* to the land of Alexander Roberts on the s. side
which was granted 5 Dec 1769; he was a Lt. in 1775; Capt. of VA
Militia in 1777; children from his will:

     1231-1   Blackman Ligon, b. ca 1757
     1231-2   John Ligon
     1231-3   Joseph Ligon, Jr.
     1231-4   Thomas Ligon
     1231-5   James Ligon
     1231-6   Obediah Ligon
     1231-7   Henry Ligon

17 Jun 1756; 13 Jul 1756; from Joseph Ligon to James Ligon, both of Chesterfield Co.;
for £100 and 10,000# tobacco; *The Round Island* in Prince Edward Co. on both sides
of the *Sandy River*; land was willed by Joseph Ligon of Chesterfield Co. to his son
William Ligon (PEDB 1.77)

13 Nov 1760; 5 Jun 1761; from Joseph Ligon and Judith his wife to William Walthall,
all of Chesterfield Co.; for £1,200; 470 ac. tract where sd. Joseph lives on James River
given him by his dec'd father in his will (ChDB 1756-1764, p. 32)

Will of Joseph Ligon; Halifax Co.; 27 Jan 1779; 18 May 1780

To son Blackman Ligon, land on w. side of *Wades Creek*, called *Peters Creek* in my
    patent; if he is dead or dies before he leaves the Army, the land to my son John &
    his heirs; also colt, etc.

To son Joseph Ligon, 150 ac. on *Wades Creek*, cattle, sheep; he shall act in all things
    as if he was actually 21 years of age

To son John Ligon, 100 ac.; if he inherits land given Blackman, then the 100 ac. to be
    sold and divided between Thomas, James, Obediah & Henry Ligon; also to John
    horse, guns, etc.

To wife Judith, choice of furniture, mare, etc.; to have 150 ac. for life including dwelling house, negro, etc., and 1/8th of household furniture and stock not before given

To my 6 sons, Blackman, John, Thomas, James, Obediah & Henry, negroes

Exs: John Flinn, Junr., Robert Jordan, Elizabeth Jordan (HaWB 1.309)

15 Jul 1780; 19 Oct 1780; Capt. Joseph Ligon; inventory & appraisement; value £34,972.12.0 (HaWB 1.320)

14 Aug 1782; 15 Aug 1782; Guardian Account; Joseph Liggon, Guardian; orphans Thomas, James, Obediah & Henry (HaWB 1.418)

> 1231-1 **Blackman Ligon**, b. ca 1757; d. 3 May 1831 Greenville district, SC in his 75th year; mb. 17 Jun 1782 Halifax Co. **Elizabeth Townes**, b. 28 Apr 1763 Amelia Co.; d. Oct 1842 SC; he was a Sgt. in the 5th Virginia Infantry, Revolutionary War
>
> 1231-2 **John Ligon**, b. 7 Mar 1761 Chesterfield Co.; d. Apr-Dec 1839 Smith Co., TN; mb. 12 Nov 1782 Halifax Co.; m. 6 Dec 1782 **Nancy Anderson Martin**, b. 15 Jul 1767; his pension application 4 Sep 1832 Smith Co., TN gives his date of birth

1 Feb 1781; John Ligon granted 135 ac. on *Rockey Branch*, Halifax Co. (LOP D.505)

5 Jun 1794; John Ligon granted 200 ac. Halifax Co. on *Difficult Creek* (LOP 30.139)

> 1231-3 **Joseph Ligon**; mb/1 10 Jun 1784 Halifax Co. **Lettice Sims**; mb/2 10 Apr 1790 Halifax Co. **Diana Coleman Clay**
>
> 1231-4 **Thomas Ligon**, b. ca 1761; d. ca 1795; mb. 7 Jan 1788 Granville, SC **Michel Stewart Moody**; she m/2 9 Dec 1799 Halifax Co. **Henry Stokes**

11 Apr 1795; 22 Jun 1795; inventory and appraisal estate of Thomas Ligon, dec'd; value £168.10.1½ (HaWB 3.168); 25 Jun 1804; appr. recorded by Michal S. Stokes, formerly Michal S. Ligon, admx. of Thomas Ligon total £335.5.11½ (HaWB 7.7)

> 1231-5 **James Ligon**; m. 25 Jun 1789 Halifax Co. **Judith Church**; they moved to Henderson Co., KY
>
> 1231-6 **Obediah Ligon**, b. ca 1772; d. ca 1823 Mecklenburg Co. VA; mb./1 16 Oct 1799 Halifax Co. **Anne Isbell**: mb/2 18 Sep 1802 Granville Co., NC **Fanny Stoval**
>
> 1231-7 **Henry Ligon**, underage in 1793

25 Nov 1758; 6 Jul 1759; mortgage from Joseph Ligon to James Deans, both of Chesterfield Co.; for £120.16.8; 470 ac. willed to sd. Joseph by his father Joseph Ligon, dec'd (ChDB 4.1); 12 Nov 1760; 5 Jun 1761; for £132.13.4 paid by sd. Joseph Ligon; mortgage released (ChDB 4.391)

13 Nov 1760; 15 Jun 1761; from Joseph Ligon and Judith his wife to William Walthall; for £1,200; 470 ac. on James River where sd. Joseph now lives; given him by his father Joseph Ligon by his will (ChDB 4.102)

7 May 1762; May 1762; from Thomas Clark and Jane his wife to Joseph Ligon, all of Chesterfield Co.; 60 ac adj. land where Ligon now lives (ChDB 4.313)

6 Jul 1764; Jul 1764; from Peter Edwards to Joseph Ligon, both of Chesterfield Co.; for £7.10; a ½ ac. lot #19 in town of *Gatesville*, Chesterfield Co. (ChDB 4. 697)

7 Dec 1764; Nov 1764; from Joseph Ligon and Judith his wife to John Hylton of Bermuda Hundred; for £550; two tracts; 425 ac. *Baldwyns* and 60 ac. adj. (ChDB 5.26); 17 Dec 1764; Joseph and John Ligon made bond to sd. John Hylton for £1,000 (ChDB 5.28)

17 Dec 1770; 18 Dec 1770; from Joseph Ligon of Halifax Co. to Thomas Scott of Prince Edward Co.; 358 ac. Prince Edward Co. on easternmost fork of *Sandy River* (PEDB 3.460)

Will of Joseph Ligon; Antrim Parish, Halifax Co.; 27 Jan 1779; 18 May 1780
To son Blackman Ligon, part of land on w. side of *Wade's Creek*; if he dies before he leaves the Army, land to return to my son John
To son Joseph Ligon, 150 ac. on *Cedar's Creek*, slave, livestock, etc.; son Joseph to act & dispose of his estate as if 21 years of age
To son Blackman "my young Rove Cote"
To son John 100 ac. I bought of Philmer Green & £350
Should son John inherit land given by my will to son Blackman, land to be sold and with the £350 to be divided equally among sons Thomas, James, Obediah and Henry Ligon
To wife Judith, choice of furniture, items, slaves, use of 150 ac. and dwelling House during widowhood; 1/8 part of furniture and stock not given
Remainder of plantation to sons Thomas, James, Obediah & Henry to be equally divided when Thomas comes to age 21; 6 negroes to be divided between my 6 sons when John comes of age
Exs: Judith Ligon, Blackman Ligon, Joseph Ligon (HaWB 1.309)
15 Jul 1780; 19 Oct 1780; inventory of estate; value £34,872.12.0 (HaWB 1.320)
[Joseph Ligon; Halifax County Wills and Administrations (1753-1800) p. 309-312. Will pro. 18 May 1780. p. 320-322. Inv. & Appr. rec. 19 Oct. 1780. Will Book No. 1, 1773-1783 (Reel 36) (LOV)]

123-2 **Mary Ligon**; m/1 bef. 1751 **William Moseley**; d. ca 1772 Chesterfield Co.; m/2 Mar 1799 Amelia Co. **Lewis Clark** (ChWB 2.142)
123-3 **Martha Ligon**, b. aft. 4 May 1732; m. **Matthew Moseley**; d. by Apr Ct 1769; children from his will; children not followed:

1233-1 **Blackman Moseley**
1233-2 **William Moseley**
1233-3 **Joseph Moseley**
1233-4 **Frances Moseley**
1233-5 **Martha Moseley**

Will of Matthew Moseley; Dale Parish, Chesterfield Co.; 9 Nov 1768; Apr Ct. 1769
To wife, use of plantation for life, then to son Blackman Moseley
To son Blackman Moseley, land where my father now lives & land on n. side of road, mare, livestock

To son William Moseley, all land on n. side of *Skinquarter Creek* & land I bought of
   Richard Robertson, mare
To son Joseph, remainder of land bought of Robertson
Mentions bro. William Moseley
Stock at *Skinquarter* to be divided between sons William & Joseph, excepting 3 cows
   apiece to daus. Frances & Martha
To daus. Frances & Martha, a negro each
To wife Martha, negroes for life
Remainder to be divided between my several children
Exs: wife & John Archer, Jr. (ChWB 2.139)

> 123-4 **John Ligon**, b. ca 1741; d. by 1 Apr 1774; m. Chesterfield Co.
> **Mary Moseley**; he was a legatee of his uncle John Stuart (Stewart) for
> whom he was probably named; his mother and step-father made £1,000
> bond on the estate in 1761 (HCVD-4 p. 751); children from John's will:
>
>> 1234-1 John Ligon
>> 1234-2 Thomas Ligon, b. 13 Oct 1744
>> 1234-3 Mary Ligon

Will of John Ligon of Dale Parish; 26 Dec 1773; 1 Apr 1774
To wife Mary, use of ½ *Acorn Ground* Prince Edward Co., negroes, ½ lower part of
   plantation I live on for life, horse, mare, items for widowhood
To my mother Judith Ligon, use of 6 hands on Cumberland Co. plantation for life
To son John, plantation and land I live on and land in Prince Edward Co. called *Acorn
   Ground*
To son Thomas, lands in Cumberland Co. at death of my mother; also *Mollons Tract* in
   Prince Edward Co. on *Sandy River*
To dau. Mary Ligon, negro
Remainder to be divided between my 3 children and wife
Exs. wife Mary, Arthur Moseley, William Walthall, Jr., Thomas Batte
Wit: Jo. Bass, John Stewart Radford, Benjamin Tomes (ChWB 2.301)
30 Sep 1774; John Ligon; estate in Cumberland Co.; value £231.8.6
3 Oct 1774; John Ligon; estate in Prince Edward Co.; value £1,084.15.8
18 Mar 1775; John Ligon; estate in Cumberland Co.; value 20.0 (ChWB2.304-310)
[John Ligon; Chesterfield Co. Wills and Admns. (1754-1800) Will - dated 1773 Proved 1 April
1774. (O.B. 6, p. 4) Chesterfield Will Book 2, p. 301-303; Inv. & Appr. of property in Prince
Edward Co. - dated 1774 Chesterfield W.B. 2, p. 304; Inv. & Appr. - dated 1774 Returned 7
October 1774. (O.B. 6, p. 57.) Chesterfield W.B. 2, p. 304-303; His estate, including estate in
Cumberland and Prince Edward Cos., to be appraised, 1 April 1774. Chesterfield O.B. 6, p. 4;
Inv. & Appr. of property in Cumberland Co. - dated 1775 Chesterfield W.B. 2, p. 310; Suit
concerning the division of his estate, 5 January 1777. Chesterfield O.B. 6, p. 119 (LOV)]

> 1234-1 **John Ligon**; d. by 11 Jun 1794 Chesterfield Co.; mb. 12 Nov
> 1789 Chesterfield Co. **Jane Dunavant**; sur. Richard Baugh; m. 24
> Nov Dale Parish Episcopal Church (MCC p. 78); d/o Thomas
> Dunavant; believe she m/2 20 Oct 1796 Dale Parish **William Dunn**
> of Prince George Co. (MCC p. 41)

23 Sep 1791; received from John Baugh, guardian of Jane Dunnivant, wife of John Ligon (at present), all accts. in full (ChDB 13.317); 6 Sep 1794; Dec Ct 1794; Jane Ligon discharges John Baugh, guardian (ChDB 13.318)

11 Jun 1794; 13 Apr 1795; inventory and appraisal estate of John Ligon, dec'd; value £895.11.5 (ChWB 4.654)

22 Apr 1796; 27 Apr 1797; from Jane Ligon, widow of John Ligon late of Chesterfield Co., to Thomas Ligon; lands Jane holds as heir to her late father Thomas Donnivant (AmDB 20.274)

> 1234-2 **Thomas Ligon**, b. 13 Oct 1744; m/1 15 Apr 1793 Prince Edward Co. **Elizabeth Perkinson**; d/o Caleb Perkinson; m/2 21 Dec 1829 Powhatan Co. **Judith Clarke**
>
> 1234-3 **Mary Ligon**

> 123-5 **Thomas Ligon**, b. est. ca 1748; d. bet. 9-25 Jun 1764; mb. 23 Apr 1764 Cumberland Co. **Betty Povall**, spinster; d/o Richard Povall of Cumberland Co.; she m/2 ____ **Howlett**; d. by 6 Aug 1784; ?child:
>
> 1235-1 **Chamberlayne Ligon**

Will of Thomas Ligon, Southam Parish, Prince Edward Co.; 9 Jun 1764; 25 Jun 1764
To wife Betty, part of tract in Prince Edward Co. bought of Morton
Remainder of my lands called *Acorn* to my heirs
If no issue, remainder of sd. land to my brother John Ligon
To my sister Elizabeth Ligon
Exs: Maj. Richard Povall, bro. John Ligon (CuWB 1.295)
[Thomas Ligon; Publication 1764 Cumberland Co. Wills and Admns. (1749 - 1810) Note p. 295. Will, pro. 25 June 1764. p. 297. Inv. Appr. rec. 24 Sept. 1764. W.B. No. 1, 1749-1769 (Reel 17) (LOV)]

Apr Ct. 1765; Chamberlayne Liggon, s/o Betty Liggon, bound out by the churchwardens of Henrico Parish (HCVW-2 p. 89)

16 Aug 1784; inventory of slaves from estate of Betty Howlett, formerly of estate of Thomas Ligon in Prince Edward Co.; value £540 (ChWB 3.460)

> 123-6 **William Ligon**; d. bef. 5 Sep 1755 Chesterfield Co.
> 123-7 **Judith Ligon**; m. by 4 Oct 1765 **Thomas Moody** (ChOB 3.699); d. by 22 May 1797 (CuWB 3.90); they are said to have had 11 children with the 1st 6 children named in his will
> 123-8 **Elizabeth Ligon**; m. **Samuel Pointer**; known child:
>
> 11238-1 **Judith Stewart Pointer**

1-3 **John Ligon**, b. aft. 1673; d. bef. 1757; m. ____; he inherited 200 ac. on *Swift Creek* from 1700 will of his grandmother Platt; children (LF&C):

> 13-1   Samuel Ligon
> 13-2   John Ligon
> 13-3   Elizabeth Ligon
> 13-4   ____ Ligon

At the Vestry St. John's Church; Richmond Town; Henrico Parish:
3 Jan 1757; 800 # tobacco for maintenance of John Liggon's wife and child
10 Dec 1758; 250# tobacco to Samuel Liggon for care of John Liggon's child; 1200#
tobacco to the Church Wardens for care of John Liggon's wife and child
4 Oct 1762; 1000# tobacco to Eliza Dalton for care of John Liggon's wife

    13-1 Samuel Ligon; d. by 6 Jun 1789 Henrico Co.; m. **Agnes** _____;
    children from will of their father & brother John:

            131-1 Samuel Ligon, Jr.
            131-2 Willis Ligon
            131-3 Elisha Ligon
            131-4 John Ligon
            131-5 Sherwood Ligon
            131-6 Agnes Ligon
            131-7 Bathsheba Ligon

5 Jul 1751; Samuel Ligon granted 179 ac. Henrico Co. on w. side of *Gilleys Creek*
(LOP 30.457)

9 Oct 1766; 3 Nov 1766; Deed of Gift from Samuel Liggon, Sr. to son John Liggon,
both of Henrico Co.; 89 ac. on *Gill's Creek*; part of tract sd. Samuel patented 5 Jul
1751 (HCVD-4 p. 989; TVF 11.42)

27 Nov 1769; 7 May 1770; from Samuel Liggon of Henrico Co. to John Williams of
Goochland Co.; for £60; 200 ac. (HCVD-4 p. 211; TVF 11. 177)

Will of Samuel Ligon; Henrico Co.; 11 Nov 1783; 6 Jun 1789
To wife Agnes, all land (179 ac.) for life
Sons: Samuel, Jr., Willis, Elisha, Sherwood
Daus.: Agnes, Bathsheba
Exs: wife Agnes, Isham Freeman, Richard Hooper
Wit: Lewis Buckner, James Hooper, William New (Henrico Co. Will Book 2.79)

    131-1 Samuel Ligon, Jr.; m. 22 Sep 1788 Henrico Co. **Bathsheba
    Harwood**; d. by 6 Feb 1792 Henrico Co.; children from her will:

        1311-1 **Patsy Allen Ligon**
        1311-2 **Rebecca Harwood Ligon**
        1311-3 **Bathsheba Harwood Ligon**

Will of Bathsheba Liggin; Henrico Co.; 6 Feb 1792; [probated]
To daus. Patsy Allen, Rebecca Harwood, Bathsheba Harwood, as their father's will
    directs
Wit: John Cocke, John H. Brazeal (Henrico Co. Will Book 2.222)
[Bathsheba Liggin; Henrico County Wills and Administrations (1662-1800) p. 222. Will pro. 6
Feb. 1792. Will Book No. 2, 1787-1802 (Reel 55) (LOV)]

    131-2 Willis Ligon; m. **Nancy Gaddy**; d/o David Gaddy; went to
      Hancock Co., GA by 1791
    131-3 Elisha Ligon

131-4 John Ligon; d. 1785-88 Henrico Co.; mentioned in the 1785 will
of his Uncle John, but not in his father's will of 1783

131-5 Sherwood Ligon; d. bef. 1827; m. **Tabitha** ____; he was entitled
to 2 draws in the 1803 lottery for Wolkes Co., GA

131-6 Agnes Ligon; she is called Agatha in will of her uncle John Ligon

131-7 Bathsheba Ligon

13-2 John Ligon; d. bet. 27 Aug - 8 Nov 1785, *Richmond*, Henrico Parish;
unmarried; following are two abstracts of his will; the 1st from TVF and
the 2nd from LF&C; they do not exactly agree, so both are included as the
original copy of the will was not examined

23 May 1769; 5 Feb 1770; from Alexander McCaul of *Town of Richmond*, Henrico Co.
& John Pride, Jr. of Amelia Co., to John Liggon of *Town of Richmond*, Henrico Co.;
for £57; lot number *G half F* in *Town of Richmond*; being collateral under deed of trust
(HCVD-4 p. 203; TVF 11.175)

Will of John Liggon, City of Richmond, Parish of Henrico; 27 Aug 1785; 8 Nov 1785
To be sold: lot & improvements in *City of Richmond*, reserving 50' in front and back;
also negroes
To bro. Samuel Liggon, £20
To nieces Agatha & Bushabe (sic) Liggon; to nephews Andrew Casler, Elitia Liggon;
Mrs. Ann Newland, Elizabeth Povel, Sarah Povel, my nieces and John Sampson
Povel, my nephew, £25 each
Lend nephew Samuel Liggon, Jr. the 40' ground in front & breath of lot where I live
for 5 years, then to return to purchaser
To nephews John Liggon & Sherwood Liggon, each 1s/3p
Remainder divided between, Samuel, Willis, Agatha, Bushabe, & Elitia Liggon; John
Caslen; Ann Newland; Elizabeth, William, Henry, John Sampson & Sarah Povel;
John Cock, s/o my niece Sarah Cock
Exs: Friends Richard Crouch, John Roper, John Clark, John Ellis (s/o Thomas Ellis)
Wit: Robt. Gilbert, Robt. Burns, Wm. Henry Wilson (HCVW-3 p. 253; TVF 7.47)

Will of John Ligon; Henrico Parish; 8 Nov 1785; [probate]
Brother Samuel Liggon's children: Agnes, Bethsheba, Elisha, Samuel, Jr., Sherwood
Nephews: Andrew Casler, John Casler, John Sampson Powell
Nieces: Mrs. Ann Nowland, Elizabeth & Sarah Powell, Sarah Cooke & her son John
Rest to be divided between: Samuel, Agnes, Bethsheba & Elisha Liggon, John Casler,
Andrew Casler, Ann Nouland, Elizabeth Powell & John Cooke, s/o my niece Sarah
Cooke
Exs: Richard Crouch, John Roper, John Clark, John Ellis (s/o Thomas Ellis) (Henrico
Co. Will Book 1.253 – LF&C)
[John Liggon (Leggon); Henrico County Wills and Administrations (1662-1800) p. 253-254. Will
pro. 8 Nov. 1785. Will Book No. 1, 1781-1787 (Reel 53) (LOV)]

13-3 Elizabeth Ligon; m. **William Powell**; [or Poval]; children (LF&C):

133-1 Elizabeth Powell, b. 2 Jul 1767; bapt. 15 Aug 1767

133-2 William Powell, b. 7 Aug 1769; bapt. 1 Oct 1769

133-3 John Sampson Powell, b. 25 Apr 1776; bapt. 2 Jun 1776

133-4 **Sarah Powell**; she may have been the niece who m. ____ **Cooke** or **Cocke**; son from will of her Uncle John Ligon:

1334-1 **John Cooke** or **Cocke**

133-5 **Henry Powell**

133-6 **Ann Powell**; possible child; she may have been the niece "Mrs. Ann Newland or Nowland" mentioned in the will of her uncle John.

13-4 ____ **Ligon**; m. **Mr. Casler**; from will of Uncle John Ligon:

134-1 **John Casler**

134-2 **Andrew Casler**

1-4 **Joseph Ligon**, b. est. ca 1680's

1-5 **Mary Ligon**, b. est. ca 1680's; m1/1 15 Jul 1698 Henrico Co. **William Anderson**; m/2 by 1 Jan 1716/7 **Peter Rowlett** of Bristol Parish; d. after 5 Jan 1749/50 when he wrote his will in Chesterfield Co.; children:

           15-1   Joseph Rowlett
           15-2   William Rowlett
           15-3   Martha Rowlett
           15-4   Sarah Rowlett

4 Jan 1716; from Peter Rowlet and Mary his wife of Bristol Parish, Henrico Co. to Benjamin Hopson of Henrico Parish; 100 ac. given Mary by will of her father William Ligon (HCVD-2 p. 60)

Will of Peter Rowlet; Dale Parish, Chesterfield Co.; 5 Jan 1749; [written]
To son Joseph, 190 ac. on *Old Town Creek*, furniture
To son William and heirs, 160 ac. plantation I now live on, furniture
To dau. Martha Cousins, household items
To dau. Sarah, furniture
Exs: sons Joseph & William; they to equally divide remainder of estate
Wit: George Willson, Sherman Nunnally (ChWB 1.8; LF&C)

15-1 **Joseph Rowlett**

[Joseph Rowlett; Chesterfield County Wills and Administrations (1754-1800) Will - dated 1773 Proved 1 April 1774. (O.B. 6, p. 3) Chesterfield Will Book 2, p. 335-336; Inventory - dated 1774 Returned 6 January 1775. (O.B. 6, p. 68) Chesterfield Will Book 2, p. 337 (LOV)]

15-2 **William Rowlett**

15-3 **Martha Rowlett**; m. ____ **Cousins**

15-4 **Sarah Rowlett**

1-6 **Lucretia Ligon**, b. ca 1689; d. aft. 1716, single, age ca 27; she was called granddau. in the 1700 will of Mary Platt

1 Jan 1716; by his will William Ligon [dec'd] bequeathed land equally to daus. Mary and child his wife "went with," known as Lucretia Ligon, now age 21; agreement to divide land; Mary to have southern half; consent of Peter Rowlett who m. Mary (HCVW-1 p. 140; HCVD-2 p. 60, 75)

4 Jan 1716; from Lucretia Ligon to Joseph Hopson, both of Henrico Co. & Parish; for £10; 100 ac. on back of *Curles* left her by her father (HCVD-2 p. 60)

2. **Johan Ligon**, b. ca 1653, age 30 in 1683 deposition (LF&C); d. by 7 Nov 1726; m. **Robert Hancock**; d. by 1 Mar 1708

3. **Richard Ligon**, b. est. ca 1657; age 36-37 in deposition 1 Dec 1693 (LF&C); d. by 2 Feb 1723 Henrico Co.; surveyor of Henrico Co.; m. ca 28 Aug 1678 **Mary Worsham**; d. by 1 Jan 1721; d/o Mrs. Elizabeth Eppes (HCVD-1 p. 11) & William Worsham; he inherited 100 ac *Curles* & his father's stone ring from his mother in 1703/4; he surveyed Henrico Parish, Henrico Co. Jun 1706-Jun 1708 (HCVD-2 p. 12); Richard was charged with 1 taxable in Henrico Co. in the list of 2 Jun 1679; he held 1,028 ac. of land in the Apr 1705 rent roll of Henrico Co.; [undocumented information on this family came from several family histories]:

> 3-1 Matthew Ligon
> 3-2 Henry Ligon
> 3-3 Sarah Ligon
> 3-4 Mary Ligon

10 Feb 1678/9; Richard Ligon, legatee of Thomas Harris whose will calls him cousin; Mary Lygon, Jr., and Richard Lygon wit. will (HCVW-1 p. 5)

28 Aug 1678; Richard Ligon marrying Mary Worsham, dau. & donee of Mrs. Eliz. Epes, dec'd, and Mr. John Worsham, also a donee of dec'd (HCVD-1 p. 11)

1 Aug 1689; due Mr. Richard Ligon; 200 ac. for import of 4 persons (HCVD-1 p. 141)

21 Apr 1690; Richard & Hugh Ligon and Samuel Newman granted 292 ac. in Bristol Parish Henrico Co. on n. side of *Swift Creek* adj. Newman's land (LOP 8.56)

29 Apr 1693; Richard Ligon and James Eakens, Jr. granted 285 ac. in Bristol Parish, at *Swift Creek* at mouth of *Poplar Branch* (LOP 8.304)

1 Jun 1703; from John Worsham & Francis Parram to Richard Liggon; 308 ac. in main for of *Proctors Creek* (HCVD-1 p. 127)

27 Oct 1704; division of land taken up by James Adkin, Jr. and Richard Ligon (HCVD-1 p. 135)

17 Mar 1707; from Richard Ligon, surveyor of Henrico Co., to John Curtis; 303 ac. on main fork of *Proctor's Creek*; Mary, w/o Richard, relinquishes dower (HCVD-2 p. 6)

1 Nov 1707; A series of lawsuits names Richard Ligon and his bro. Thomas and 200 ac. of land which descended to William, s/o Thomas which eventually involved Matthew, s/o sd. Richard; the land was lately in tenure of tenants placed there by Mrs. Mary Ligon, dec'd; William to get the upper half of the land and Matthew the lower half; [these bonds & deeds take up pages 4-9 in the 1706-1736 book of deeds] (HCVD-2 p. 1, 2)

1710; 1 Aug 1710; Richard Ligon appointed atty. for Elizabeth Chamberlayne (HCVD-2 p. 25)

1 Oct 1717; from Richard Lygon to James Aken; for £4; 142 ac. in Henrico Parish on s. side of *Cold Water Run*; being ½ of patent granted Lygon and Aken; Mary, w/o Richard, relinquished dower rights (HCVD-2 p. 68)

Mar Ct. 1723; Will of Richard Ligon presented by Matthew Ligon, ex. (HCVW-2 p. 168)

4 Apr 1724; 6 Apr 1724; inventory of Mr. Richard Ligon by court order of 2 Feb 1723; value £30.3.3.; appraised 4 Apr 1724; presented by Matthew Ligon (HCVW-1 p. 234)
[Richard Ligon; wills not listed in Virginia Wills & Admns., 1632-1800 (Torrence). Inv. - 1724 Henrico Co. Misc. Records. Vol. 2, p. 595; Henrico Co. Wills & Admns. (1662-1800) Note p. 595-596. Inv. & appr. rec. 6 Apr. 1724. Misc. Ct. Records, Vol. 2, [1718-1726] (Reel 1) (LOV)]

3-1 **Matthew Ligon,** b. ca 1680; d. bet, 21 Apr – 24 Sep 1764 Cumberland Co.; m. bef. 1710 Henrico Co. **Elizabeth Anderson**; she was probably the sister Elizabeth mentioned in the will of Mathew Anderson, Jr. and sister of William Anderson who m. Mary Ligon and James Anderson who m. Elizabeth Ligon; Matthew Ligon was appointed Constable of Henrico Co. 1 May 1710, serving 1 year, and 29 Jun 1724 he and Alexander Marshall were appointed to count the tobacco plants between *Swift Creek* and the lower branch of "the P'ish" (Parish); children (LF&C):

> 31-1 Richard Ligon
> 31-2 James Ligon
> 31-3 Matthew Ligon, Jr.
> 31-4 Thomas Ligon, b. 7 Feb 1724/5
> 31-5 Elizabeth Ligon, b. 9 Dec 1727
> 31-6 William Ligon
> 31-7 Francis Ligon

10 May 1708; Mathew Ligon held 280 ac. in Henrico Parish (HCVD-2 p. 13)

31 Jul 1710; 1 Aug 1710; from Richard and Matthew Ligon of Henrico Co.; for £14 to Richard Grills; 297 ac. on s. side of *Swift Creek*; Elizabeth, w/o Matthew, relinquished her dower rights (HCVD-2 p. 25)

Will of Mathew Anderson, Jr. of Bristol Parish, Prince George Co.; 25 Feb 1717/8; [written]
To brother William Anderson, plantation where I now live, items
To brother James Anderson, items
To sister Elizabeth Ligon, items
Remainder to be divided among 2 bros. and 1 sister
Ex: bro. James Anderson
Wit: James Thweatt, Buller Herbert (PGWD 1.232)

22 Jan 1718; Matthew Ligon and Richard Ligon, Jr.; granted 290 ac. Henrico Co. on s. side of *Swift Creek*; for 30s (LOP 10.409; HCPB 10.409)

5 Sep 1723; Matthew Ligon; granted 300 ac. Henrico Co. on s. side of James River on e. side of *Fine Creek*; for 40s (LOP 11.240; HCPB 11.240)

18 Jun 1728; 1 Jul 1728; from Matthew Ligon of Henrico Co. to William Price; for £5; 2 ac. on n. side of *Swift Creek*; Eliza., w/o Matthew, relinquished dower rights (HCVD-2 p. 110)

31 Oct 1728; from Matthew Ligon of Henrico Co. to William Pride; for £25; 100 ac. on *Swift Creek*; purchased from Richard Grills; adj. Matthew and Henry Ligon (HCVD-2 p. 115; HCRB-1 p. 219)

4 Nov 1728; from Matthew Ligon to George Farrar, both of Henrico Co.; 150 ac. on s. side of *Swift Creek* taken up by Richards Grills; mentions Matthew and his father Richard Ligon (HCVD-2 p. 116)

12 Jun1729; Matthew Ligon was granted the right to include 2 patents of 400 ac. each into one patent (LF&C)

17 Sep 1731; Matthew Ligon granted 1,100 ac. Goochland Co. on s. side of James River; for £4 (LOP 14.340; GCPB 14.340)

1 Sep 1737; 1st Mon Sep 1737; from Matthew Ligon of Goochland Co. to Henry Walthal of Henrico Co., both of St. James Parish; for £16; land that Thomas Ligon, dec'd willed 10 Jan 1675 to Richard Ligon who left said land to Matthew his son and heir (HCVD-2 p. 182; GCDB 3.296)

Mar Ct. 1738; from Mathew Ligon to his son Mathew Ligon, Jr. (HCVD-3 p. 81)

20 May 1740; from Mathew Ligon to Theodorick Carter, both of St. James Parish, Goochland Co.; for £21 (or £81 LF&C); 250 ac. on branches of *Fine Creek* and *Fighting Creek*; Elizabeth, w/o Matthew, relinquished dower right (GCWD-2 p. 40; GCDB 3.296)

18 Jun 1742; 20 Jul 1742; from Matthew Ligon to Richard Ligon, both of Goochland Co.; for £5; 300 ac. from mouth of *Great Branch* to *Fine Creek* (GCDB 4.544)

24 Sep 1750; deed of gift from Mathew Ligon of Southam Parish, Cumberland Co., to son James Ligon; 276 ac. (CuDB 1.225)

10 Nov 1756; 24 Jan 1757; from Mathew Ligon to son Richard Ligon, both of Cumberland Co.; for £80; 275 ac. plantation where Mathew now liveth (CuDB 2.319)

Will of Mathew Ligon of Southam Parish, Cumberland Co.; 21 Apr 1764; 24 Sep 1764
To sons James and Richard, 1 negro each, stock, cattle, household goods, etc.
Ex: son Richard
Wit: Thomas Ligon, William Ligon, Frances Ligon (CuWB 1.299)
[Matthew Ligon; Cumberland County Wills and Administrations (1749 - 1810) p. 299. Will, pro. 24 Sept. 1763. Will Book No. 1, 1749-1769 (Reel 17) (LOV)]

   31-1 **Richard Ligon**; d. by 18 Feb 1779 Powhatan Co.; m/1 ____; m/2
   Anne Ward; d/o Joseph Ward and Sarah Stewart; Ann was one of the
   contingent heirs of her bro. Leonard Ward (ChWB 3.55); children:

                    311-1 William Ligon, b. ca 1740-46
                    Children of m/2:
                    311-2 John Ligon
                    311-3 Thomas Ligon
                    311-4 Joseph Ligon, b. 24 Nov 1759

311-5 Leonard Seth Ligon, b. 1 Apr 1762
311-6 Authur Ligon

25 Jun 1750; Jun Ct. 1750; from Henry Stratton to Richard Ligon, both of Southam Parish, Cumberland Co.; for £37; 150 ac. Southam Parish on branches of *Fine Creek* (CuDB 1.175)

28 Jan 1760; 25 Feb 1760; from Isham Pruit to Richard Ligon, both of Southam Parish, Cumberland Co.; for £25; 80 ac. at fork of *Muddy Creek* Cumberland Co. (CuDB 2.537)

27 Sep 1762; 25 Oct 1762; from Joseph Chandler to Richard Ligon, both of Cumberland Co.; 150 ac. Cumberland Co. (CuDB 3.327)

25 Aug 1766; 17 Aug 1766; from Richard Eggleston to Richard Ligon, both of Cumberland Co.; for £50; 285 ac. Cumberland Co. (CuDB 4.95)

24 Dec 1770; 24 Dec 1770; from John Minter & Elizabeth his wife to Richard Ligon, both of Cumberland Co.; for £500; 116 ac. Cumberland Co. on James River (CuDB 4.46)

26 Jul 1772; 27 Jul 1772; from Jacob Michaux and Sally his wife to Richard Ligon; for £450; 125 ac. on s. side of James River in Southam Parish, Cumberland Co. adj. land purchased of Minter (CuDB 5.68)

17 Dec 1777; from Richard Ligon of Powhatan Co. to son John Ligon, land in Powhatan Co. adj. Mayo (PoDB 1.12)

Will of Richard Ligon, Southam Parish, Powhatan Co.; 6 Jan 1779; 18 Feb 1779
To wife Ann, I lend 973 ac. plantation where I live with all stock, plantation on James River with all negroes, etc., till my son Joseph is 21; he to get profits of plantation until death of his mother when it will be divided
To son John, slaves; also 492 ac. bounded by *Long Branch*, etc.
To son Thomas, slaves; also 500 ac. adj. his brother John; also lot in Town of *Scottsville*
To son Joseph, my 245 ac. plantation on James River adj. Netherland and Michaux
To son Seth, 973 ac. plantation where I live, after death of my wife
To sons Joseph and Seth, negroes after death of wife
To grandson William Ligon at age 21, 400 ac. on *Muddy Creek*
To granddau. Sarah Ligon, negro
Exs: Thomas Miller, George Radford, David Owen and my son John
Wit: Thomas Pollock, Nathaniel Harris
Codicil: 17 Jan 1779; my son Thomas, now being to the northward in the service; if he should die, his estate to my son John until death of my wife, then divided between John & Seth; *Scottsville* lot of Joseph and slaves divided (PoWB 1.22)
19 Mar 1779; 19 Mar 1779; Richard Ligon; inventory lists negroes (PoWB 1.28)
16 Nov 1786; Richard Ligon; account (PoWB 1.117)
[Richard Ligon; Powhatan County Wills and Administrations (1777-1800) p. 22-26. Will pro. 18 Feb. 1779. p. 28-30. Inv. & appr. rec. 19 Mar. 1779. p. 117-119. Accounts rec. 16 Nov. 1786. Will Book No. 1, 1777-1795 (Reel 15) (LOV)]

311-1 **William Ligon**, b. ca 1740-46; d. under age; m. ca 1762 **Frances Moseley**; m/2 ca 1767 **William Stratton, Jr.** of Powhatan Co.; minor children:

3111-1 **William Ligon**, b. 24 Nov 1762 Powhatan Co.; m. 27 Dec 1784 Powhatan Co. **Ann Davenport**; Samuel Steger, security; at age 21 he was to inherit 400 ac on *Muddy Creek* from the will of his grandfather Ligon; 17 Aug 1832 in Owen Co., KY he made application for his Revolutionary War Pension

3111-2 **Sarah Ligon**; m. ca 1779 **Edward Stratton**; s/o William Stratton of Powhatan Co.; she inherited negroes from grandfather Ligon

19 Feb 1765; Thomas Pleasants, Quaker, affirmed William Ligon died without a will (GCOB, beginning Jun 1765, p. 88); Sep Ct 1765; 3 Oct 1765; appraisal of estate of William Ligon (GCWB 9.10 – LF&C); 26 Oct 1767; William Ligon; estate appraisal of *Fighting Creek* plantation in Cumberland Co. (CuWB 1.332)

20 Sep 1767; 28 Dec 1767; from Mathew Moseley of Chesterfield Co. to Frances Liggon of Cumberland Co.; for £429; 330 ac. on n. side of Appomattox River in Cumberland Co.; at death of Frances Ligon, land to be transferred to her son William Ligon at age 21 (CuDB 4.203)

26 Oct 1767; Richard Ligon appointed guardian to William & Sarah Ligon, orphans of William Ligon, dec'd (CuOB 1767-1770 p. 56)

23 Nov 1767; 24 Nov 1767; guardians of William & Sarah Ligon vs Frances & William Stratton, Jr., adms. of William Ligon, dec'd (CuOB 1767-1770 p. 67, 288)

311-2 **John Ligon**, b. Powhatan Co.; d. by ca 1820; m/1 **Martha ____**; m/2 ca 1784 Powhatan Co. **Sally Saunders**; said to have had 3 children by Martha and 7 by Sally

311-3 **Thomas Ligon**; d. by 16 Jan 1779

311-4 **Joseph Ligon**, b. 24 Nov 1759; d. 1797 Powhatan Co.; mb. 5 Jul 1780 Powhatan Co. **Frances Netherland**; surety George Miller, m. 6 Jul 1780 Powhatan Co. Frances b. 15 Nov 1763; d. 25 Dec 1838 Nelson Co.; children:

3114-1 **Nancy Ann Ligon**, b. 7 Aug 1781
3114-2 **Richard Ligon**, b. 20 Aug 1784 Nelson Co.; d. by 28 Oct 1816
3114-3 **John Ward Ligon**, b. 15 Nov 1785
3114-4 **Seth Ward Ligon**, b. 28 May 1789; d. 3 Jan 1791
3114-5 **Seth Ward Ligon**, b. 10 Jun 1791
3114-6 **Littleberry Netherton Ligon** (twin), b. 22 May 1794 *Massies Mill*, Nelson Co.
3114-7 **Elizabeth Ligon** (twin), b. 22 May 1794 *Massies Mill*, Nelson Co.

311-5 **Leonard Seth Ligon**, b. 1 Apr 1762; d. 1809 Powhatan Co.; mb. 4 May 1789 Powhatan Co. **Jannett Mayo**; surety John Ligon; Jannett b. ca 1773 Powhatan Co.; d. ca 1862

311-6 **Authur Ligon**

31-2 **James Ligon**; d. ca 1764 Cumberland Co.; m. **Judith (Stuart) Ligon**;
d. by 5 Mar 1784 Chesterfield Co.; widow of **Joseph Ligon**; d. ca 1752
Chesterfield Co.; s/o William Ligon & Elizabeth Batte; children from his
will [infants under age 21 in 1765]:

> 312-1 Mary Ligon
> 312-2 James Ligon

29 Sep 1761; 6 Sep 1762; Bond of James Ligon and Judith Ligon his wife, to John
Ligon, s/o said Judith; for £1,000; by the death of John Stuart, late of Henrico Co., bro.
of sd. Judith Ligon, Sarah Ward & Mary Stuart, died possessed of 2 tracts, in Henrico
and Cumberland Co.; agreement to partition allotting land in Cumberland to Judith on
condition that she & her husband execute bond that land will descend to John Ligon
upon her death (HCVD-4 p. 751; TVF 10.185)

[Note: The will of Lewis Orange of Henrico Co. written 24 Aug 1734 (HCVW-1 p. 220) names
wife Mary & dau. "Judith Ligon" among his children.]

Will of James Ligon; Southam Parish, Cumberland Co.; 21 Jun 1764; 24 Sep 1764
To pay debts, land on *Fine* and *Fighting Creek*, Cumberland Co., to be sold
To son James, land on *Sandy River*, Prince Edward Co.
To wife Judith
To dau. Mary
Ex: Mathew Moseley, brother Richard Ligon
Wit: Richard Povall, Thomas Childrey, Joseph Mosely (CuWB 1.298)
25 Feb 1765; James Ligon; estate value Cumberland Co. £701.7.9; 1 Aug 1766; value
  £292.14.8 ¼; 25 Feb 1765; James Ligon; estate value Prince Edward Co. £245.1.6; 1
  Aug 1766; value £23.8.4 ½ (CuWB 1.303, 304)
[James Ligon; Cumberland Co. Wills and Admns. (1749 - 1810) p. 298. Will, Pro. 24 Sept. 1764.
p. 316. Acctt. current, rec. 25 Aug. 1766. p. 303-304. Inv. & Appr. rec. 25 Feb. 1765. p. 304-305.
Inv. Appr. rec. 25 Feb. 1765. W.B. No. 1, 1749-1769 (Reel 17); Chesterfield Co. Wills & Admns.
(1754-1800) Ordered that his slaves be divided, 4 Oct. 1766. Chesterfield O.B. 3, p. 786; His
orphan, Joseph Ligon, chose Matthew Mosely as his guardian, 6 Feb. 1767. Chesterfield O.B. 3,
p. 804 (LOV) [note: Weisiger's abstract says this is John, s/o John]

Will of Judith Ligon, Dale Parish, Chesterfield Co.; 2 Nov 1783; 5 Mar 1784
To grandson Thomas Ligon, my plantation on *Fighting Creek*, Powhatan Co., £100
To grandson John Ligon, £100
To 3 granddaus. Judith, Mery, Betty Ann Moody, 1/3 of stock and household goods
To dau. Elizabeth Pointer, 1/3 of stock and household goods
To dau. Mary Hilton, 1/3 of stock and household goods
To granddaus. Michal Stewart Moody, Judith Stewart Pointer, Elizabeth Cooke
    Hylton, each a negro
Exs: Samuel Pointer, John Hilton
Wit: Blackman Moseley, Baxter Folkes, Mathew Moody (ChWB 3.428)
7 Mar 1784; Judith Ligon; appraisal of estate; £278.16.10 (ChWB 3.457)
[Judith Ligon; Chesterfield Co.Wills and Admns. (1754-1800) Will - dated 1783 Proved 5 March
1784. (O.B. 6, p. 512) Chesterfield W.B. 3, p. 428-429; Inv. & Appr. - dated 1784 Returned 7
May 1784. (O.B. 6, p. 526) Chesterfield W.B. 3, p. 457-458 (LOV)]

312-1 **Mary Ligon**; m. **John Hylton**; d. aft. 7 Nov 1773 Chesterfield Co.

312-2 **James Ligon**; d. aft. 22 Jan 1802 Prince Edward Co. (PEWB 3.460); m/1 19 Feb 1774 **Sarah Holcomb**; d/o Philip Holcomb; m/2 **Mary Haskins**; d/o Thomas Haskins of Prince Edward Co.; James had children by both wives

31-3 **Matthew Ligon, Jr.**: d. by 1764 Cumberland Co.; m. **Susannah** ____; children (LF&C):

313-1 **James Ligon**

313-2 **Richard Ligon**, b. ca 1745; d. 1820 Nottoway Co.; mb. Mar 1765; ml. 28 Mar 1765 Amelia Co. **Mary Bagley**

6 Jan 1758; 7 Jul 1758; from Mathew Ligon, Jr. & Susannah his wife, to John Hylton, Gent., all of Chesterfield Co.; for £220; 200 ac. on n. side of Appomattox at mouth of *Size Moors Creek*; land devied by Richard Ligon, dec'd, to Mathew Ligon, father of sd. Mathew Ligon, Jr., by my father deeded to me (ChDB 3.282); Susannah, wife of Mathew Ligon, Jr., relinquished dower (ChDB 3.284)

Will of Matthew Ligon of Southam Parish; 24 Sep 1763 (probated)
Sons: James Ligon, Richard Ligon
Ex: son Richard Ligon
Wit: Thomas Ligon, William Ligon, Frances Ligon (CuWB 1.299)
[Mathew Ligon; Cumberland County Wills and Administrations (1749 - 1810) p. 299. Will, pro. 24 Sept. 1763. Will Book No. 1, 1749-1769 (Reel 17) (LOV)]

31-4 **Thomas Ligon**; b. 7 Feb 1724/5 Bristol Parish, Henrico Co.; m. **Ann** ____; by 1787 he sold land in Conwall Parish, Charlotte Co. (Charlotte Co. Deed Book 5.198); children (LF&C):

314-1 **Thomas Ligon, Jr.**; mb. 13 Dec 1780 Charlotte Co. **Fanny Bumpass**

314-2 **Elizabeth Ligon**; d/o Thomas Ligon; mb. 3 Sep 1770 Charlotte Co. **Sherwood Purson**

314-3 **Mary Ligon**; mb. 5 May 1772 Charlotte Co. **John Bridges**; surety James Sullivant

314-4 **Joseph Ligon**; m. ca 1788 **Mary Church**; moved to Clark Co. GA

314-5 **Obedience Ligon**; m. **John Owens**; in list of marriages by Baptist minister returned 11 Mar 1784 Lunenburg Co.

18 Dec 1760; 30 Mar 1761; from Robert Jones of Raleigh Parish, Amelia Co. to Thomas Ligon of Cornwall Parish, Lunenburg Co.; part of a tract on *Twitty's Creek* (LuDB 6.359)

31-5 **Elizabeth Ligon**, b. 9 Dec 1727 Bristol Parish, Henrico Co.

31-6 **William Ligon**; b. ca 1732; d. 9 Mar 1828 Cumberland Co. (CuWB 8.451); m. 1767 **Elizabeth East**; d. 18 Feb 1794 VA; children from his will:

316-1 **Elijah Ligon**; m. 26 Oct 1789 **Judith Carter**; Elijah witnessed a will and presented another in Henrico Co. in 1762 (HCVW-2 p. 175, 840)

316-2 **Susannah Ligon**, b. ca 1770; m. 4 Jan 1787 Powhatan Co. as 2nd wife of **Hugh Robertson**

316-3 **Sarah Ligon**; m. ____ **Wood**

316-4 **John Ligon**, b. 4 Oct 1778 Cumberland Co.; d. 1861; m. 12 Nov 1812 Charlotte Co. **Nancy Daniel**; he made oath on 12 Mar 1839 that he, age 62, recalled his father going with Hugh Robertson to the clerk in Cumberland Co. to obtain license for Hugh to marry his sister and they were later married by a minister in Powhatan Co.

316-5 **Frances Ligon**

316-6 **Elizabeth Ligon**

316-7 **Richard Ligon**, b. 10 Sep 1772; d. 14 Dec 1841 Nelson Co.

31-7 Frances Ligon

3-2 Henry Ligon, Sr.; d. ca 1762 St. Patrick Parish, Prince Edward Co.; m. bef. 1734 cousin **Sarah Ligon**; d. 1785 St. Patrick Parish, Prince Edward Co.; d/o William Ligon and Elizabeth Batte; children from Henry's will:

> 32-1   Henry Ligon, Jr.
> 32-2   Elizabeth Ligon
> 32-3   William Ligon
> 32-4   Sarah Ligon
> 32-5   ____ Ligon (f)

3 Feb 1734; 3 Feb 1734; from Henry Ligon to Henry Clay, both of Henrico Co.; for £13; 100 ac. on n. side of *Swift Creek*; bounded by land formerly Matthew Ligon's; Sarah, wife of Henry, relinquished dower (HCVD-2 p. 157; HCRB-1 p. 462)

9 Feb 1737; Henry Ligon granted 618 ac. Amelia Co. on both sides of *Mountain Creek* (LOP 17.504)

20 Jun 1740; from Samuel Hudson & wife to Henry Ligon; 186 ac. Brunswick Co. (AmDB 1.236)

Oct Ct. 1740; from Henry Ligon to William Moseley, deed; Sarah, w/o Henry, relinquished dower rights (HCVD-3 p. 88)

Jun Ct. 1742; from Henry Ligon to Benjamin Harris, Gent.; Sarah, w/o Henry, relinquished dower rights (HCVD-3 p. 96)

25 Jul 1746; Henry Ligon granted 400 ac. Amelia Co. on lower side of *Sandy River* (LOP 25.137)

13 Sep 1757; from Henry Ligon, Sr., and Sarah his wife, to Henry Ligon, Jr., all of Prince Edward Co.; for £55; 772 ac. "bearing date ye 9th day of Febr 1737" on *Mountain Creek* in Prince Edward Co. (AmOB 1.226); also mentions on both sides of *Mountain Creek* 25 Jul 1746 (LOP 25.269)

Will of Henry Ligon of St. Patrick Parish, Prince Edward Co.; 12 Nov 1759; 14 Dec 1762
To son Henry Ligon, 1 bed and furniture
To dau. Elizabeth Ligon, 1 bed and furniture
To son William Ligon, part of tract I now live on, negroes
To dau. Sarah Ligon, negroes, bed, furniture
To wife Sarah Ligon, remainder of slaves, movables, and lend of remainder of tract of land given William during widowhood; then whole tract to son William
Exs: wife Sarah Ligon, son Henry Ligon
Wit: Charles Anderson, Nathan Hall, Henry Lester (PEWB 1.52)
29 Jan 1763; 18 Apr 1763; estate value £2,521.5.3 (PEWB 1.55)
[Henry Ligon, Senior; Prince Edward County Wills and Administrations (1754-1800) p. 52-53. Will pro. 14 Dec. 1762. p. 55. Inv. & appr. rec. 18 Apr. 1763. Will Book No. 1, 1754-1785 (Reel 15) (LOV)]

Will of Sarah Ligon of Prince Edward Co.; 4 Jul 1784; Jan Ct. 1785
To son William Ligon, negro, ½ my stock & cattle and all my mill
To grandson John Turner Ligon, s/o William, furniture, negroes including Dianah
Dianah to be companion to John T. to take care of James Atwood to age 21
To dau. Sarah Atwood, personal property & chattels if she comes to this country to live
To grandson, William Ligon, s/o Henry, negro
To granddau. Sarah Holt, d/o son Henry, negro, etc.
To grandson Henry Ligon, s/o William, negro
To grandson James Atwood, negro
To granddau. Mary Mason, livestock, negro, etc.
To granddau. Elizabeth Ligon Atwood, negro
To granddau. Mary Atwood, negro
To son in law Thomas Ligon, 5s
To dau. in law Elizabeth Ligon, 5s
To dau. Sarah Atwood, furniture, negroes
Remainder to grandson John T. and Henry Ligon
Exs: grandson John T. Ligon
Wit: John Richards, Thomas Vaughan, George Foster, Abraham Foster (PEWB 1.55)
15 Feb 1793; 15 Jul 1793; Sarah Ligon; estate appraised and recorded (PEWB 2.193)
[Sarah Ligon; Prince Edward County Wills and Administrations (1754-1800) p. 351-353. Will pro. Jan. 1785. Will Book No. 1, 1754-1785 (Reel 15); Prince Edward County Wills and Administrations (1754-1800) p. 24-26. Inv. & appr. rec. 19 Dec. 1785. p. 193-194. Accounts rec. 15 July 1793. Will Book No. 2, 1785-1795 (Reel 15) (LOV)]

32-1 **Henry (Harry) Ligon, Jr.**; d. by 15 Aug 1778 Prince Edward Co.; m. bef.1756 **Elizabeth** ____; she is mentioned in will of her mother in law; children (LF&C):

321-1 **Sarah Ligon**; m. ____ **Holt**; legatee in will of her grandmother
321-2 **William Ligon**, b. ca 1756; said to have d. ca 1838 TN; m. **Sarah Herring** of Lunenburg Co.; d/o Arthur Herring of Lunenburg Co.; Henry was a legatee in will of his grandmother
321-3 **Phebe Ligon**; mb. 4 Jan 1792 Prince Edward Co.; m. 6 Jan 1792 **Stephen Dickerson Turner** of Charlotte Co.; s/o Keziah Turner; surety Robert Holt

321-4 **John Howson Ligon**, b. ca 1761; d. ca 1845 Wilson Co., KY; m.
23 Dec 1790 Prince Edward Co. **Elizabeth Guill**; d/o Alexander Guill

321-5 **Henry Ligon**; m. 16 Nov 1801 Prince Edward Co. **Elizabeth
Smith**

321-6 **Lucy (Lucinda) Ligon**, mb. 21 Jan 1793 Prince Edward Co.
Armistead Pamphin; surety Robert Holt; moved to Lincoln Co., TN

15 Aug 1778; 1779; Henry Ligon, Sr.; appraisal of estate signed by Elizabeth Ligon,
admx. (PEDB 2.165)

32-2 **Elizabeth Ligon**; m. ____ **Mason**

322-1 **Mary Mason**; called granddau. in will of grandmother Sarah
Ligon

32-3 **William Ligon**; d. ca 1788 Prince George Co.; m. 14 Nov 1759
Prince Edward Co. **Edith Turner**; d/o John & Mary Turner

323-1 **John Turner Ligon, Sr.**, b. 9 Sep 1760; d. 8 Apr 1822 Prince
Edward Co.; m. 13 Apr 1786 **Jane Haskins**; d. 21 Aug 1817; d/o
Benjamin & Phebe Haskins; John's obituary in the *Richmond Enquirer*
called him one of the heroes of 1776

323-2 **Henry Ligon**; d. ca 1809; mb. 21 Mar 1785 Prince Edward Co.;
m. Apr 1785 **Patty Wooten**; surety William Wooten

323-3 **William Ligon**, b. ca 1765; d. 1829 Prince Edward Co.; m. 28 Sep
1793 Prince Edward Co. **Sarah Leigh**; d/o John & Elizabeth Leigh

323-4 **Joseph Ligon**; d. ca 1808 Prince Edward Co.; m. 18 Jan 1796
Prince Edward Co. **Ann Clarke**; d/o Thomas and Agnes Clarke

Will of William Ligon; Prince Edward Co.; 21 Dec 1787; 21 Jan 1788
To son John Turner Ligon, part of land I live on
To son Henry Ligon, land on n. side of *Spring Branch*
To son William Ligon, part of land on road to *Sandy River Church*
To son Joseph Ligon, residue
Slaves to be divided among sons
Exs: sons Henry & William Ligon
Wit: Edmund D. Ford, Thomas Vaughan, George Foster (PEWB 2.44)
20 Jul 1791; William Ligon; inventory and appraisal; value £556.14.2 (PEWB 2.139)
[William Ligon; Prince Edward Co. Wills and Admns. (1754-1800) p. 44-45. Will pro. 21 Jan.
1788. p. 139-141. Inv. & appr. 20 July 1791. Will Book No. 2, 1785-1795 (Reel 15) (LOV)]

32-4 **Sarah Ligon**; m. ____ **Atwood**; children from will of grandmother
Ligon:

324-1 **James Atwood**

324-2 **Elizabeth Ligon Atwood**

324-3 **Mary Atwood**

32-5 ____ **Ligon**; ? d. bef. her mother's will was written in 1784; m.
Thomas Ligon; called son in law in that will

3-3 **Sarah Ligon**; m. **Richard Grills**; d. bef. 1729

3-4 **Mary Ligon**; d. bef. 14 Jul 1749; m. **John Coleman**; d. bef. 14 Jul 1749; s/o Robert Coleman of Prince George Co.; John held 200 ac. in the 1704 rent roll of Prince George Co.; child:

> 44-1 Mary Ligon Coleman, b. 18 Jul 1731

8 Jun 1714; from John Coleman to Robert Munford; for 1,400# tobacco and 10s; 10 ac. (PGDB 1713-28 p. 16)

10 May 1725 from John Coleman and Mary his wife of Prince George Co. and Robert Munford; 208 ac. on s. side of Appomattox in Bristol Parish; 3 Mar 1701 John bought 12 of the ac. and the residue was granted to Robert Coleman, father to John, 29 Sep 1668; /s/ John Coleman, Mary Coleman (PGDB 1713-28 p. 834)

14 Jul 1749; 14 Jul 1719; Michael, Irish servant of John Coleman, age adjudged; Jack, slave of John & Mary Coleman, b. 6 Feb 1726 Prince George Co. (LF&C)

34-1 **Mary Ligon Coleman**, b. 18 Jul 1731; bapt. 10 Aug 1731 Bristol Parish; m. 24 Sep 1750 Cumberland Co. **Thomas Bedford**; security Micajah Mosby; Thomas was s/o Stephen Bedford & Elizabeth Flippin

14 Oct 1749; Mary Ligon Coleman made a quit claim deed to Matthew Ligon, both of Cumberland Co.; James and Thomas Ligon as witnesses (CuDB 1.85)

4. **Matthew Ligon**, b. ca 1659 Henrico Co.; d. bef. 1 May 1689; unmarried (LF&C)

5. **Hugh Ligon**, b. est. a 1661; ml/1 16 Oct 1689 Henrico Co. **Elizabeth Walthall**, b. est. ca 1663; d/o William Walthall & Anne Archer; m/2 by 1713 **Jane Pew**; d/o Henry Pew and widow of **John Price**; Hugh rec'd 100 ac. adj. his bro. Richard of *Curles* from his mother in 1703/4, her household goods & ½ her sheep; the 1689/90 document which acknowledges receipt of Elizabeth's portion of her father's estate calls her husband Henry Ligon; believe this to be clerical error as all other documents give his name as Hugh including the Henrico Co. rent roll of Apr 1705 which shows Hugh held 150 ac.

23 Jan 1689/90; 1 Oct 1690; William, Richard & Henry Walthall, sons of William Walthall, and Henry Ligon in right of wife Elizabeth, d/o sd. dec'd have rec'd of our mother Anne Morris, widow, relict and extx. of dec'd all our portion due from dec'd (HCVW-1 p. 41)

2 Feb 1690/1; 2 Feb 1690; from Thomas Wells to Hugh Ligon, both of Bristol Parish Henrico Co.; for 8,080# tobacco; tract called *Northampton* on n. side of Appomattox River (HCVD-1 p.61)

25 Aug 1691; 1 Sep 1691; from Thomas Wells and Hugh Ligon of Bristol Parish, Henrico Co.; for 800# tobacco; 100 ac. called *Scury Hill* on s. side of *Flintons Swamp*; Elizabeth, w/o Hugh, relinquished dower (HCVD-1 p. 65)

4 Aug 1718; Hugh Ligon, Arthur Moseley, William Ligon; give bond for Hugh Ligon as guardian for Elizabeth Price, orphan (HCVW-1 p. 226)

7 Dec 1713; 7 Dec 1713; from Hugh Ligon and Jane his wife, relict of John Price, dec'd, to John, eldest s/o John Price; ½ tract where Henry Pew, father of Jane, formerly lived (HCVD-2 p. 39)

4 Jan 1713; 1 Feb 1713; a land swap describes tract swapped to James Cocke by Jno. Price as "50 ac. on n. side of James River in Henrico Co. given on 31 Jul 1688 by Henry Pew to his dau. Jane, then wife of John Price; on 7 Dec 1713 Hugh Ligon and sd. Jane his wife, conveyed to John Price, eldest s/o sd. Jane" (HCVD-2 p. 40)

7 Oct 1717; 7 Oct 1717; from Hugh Ligon of Appomattock Parish, Henrico Co., planter, and Jane his wife, to Pew Price; their right in 120 ac. John Price gave Pew Price after death of Jane, his mother (HCVD-2 p. 67, 68)

6. **Mary Ligon**, b. est. ca 1663; d. bef. 1685; m. **Thomas Farrar**, b. ca 1665; age ca 24 on 1 Apr 1689 (QRH p. 152); d. by 15 Jun 1742 Goochland Co.; he m/2 by 1686 **Katherine Perrin** (QRH p. 90)

SIMON LIGON

The will of Richard Ward written 18 Apr 1682 mentions Symon Lygon as one of his laborers and on 1 Dec 1687 Seth, s/o Richard Ward, claimed land for the transport of Simon Ligon (HCVD-1 p. 12, 141); Robert Thompson also claimed land for his transport 23 Apr 1688 (PB 8.303). Simon can be found in several court & land records of Henrico Co.; he was probably the husband of Mary Bridgewater.

____ **Ligon**; d. bef. 11712; m. **Mary Bridgewater**, b. ca 1686 Varina Parish; d. by 7 Jul 1712; d/o Samuel & Samuel Bridgewater; children [minors in 1711/2]:

1. Elizabeth Ligon
2. Peter Ligon; d. by Apr 1743
3. Simon Ligon
4. Ann Ligon
5. Mary Ligon
6. Martha Ligon

Will [oral] of Mary Ligon; 1 Feb 1711/2; 7 Jul 1712
My bro. Thomas Bridgewater to have care of my eldest dau. Elizabeth
William Kent to have care of my sons Peter & Simon Ligon
Ann Cardwell to have care of my dau. Ann Ligon
Ann Easly to have care of my dau. Mary Ligon
Martha Hudson to have care of my dau. Martha Ligon
Wit: James Cox, Edward Heathcott, Martha Hudson (HCVW-1 p. 120)
[Mary Ligon; Henrico County Wills and Administrations (1662-1800) p. 138. Nunc. will pro. 7 July 1712. Records, 1710-1714 (Reel 6) (LOV)]

1. **Elizabeth Ligon**
2. **Peter Ligon**; d. by Apr Ct. 1743; the 1745 will of Aaron Haskins mentions 332 ac. bought of Peter Ligon (HCVW-2 p. 31)

Apr Ct. 1743; Peter Ligon's estate, admn. David Bell (HCVW-2 p. 19)

3. **Simon Ligon**; wit. deed 15 Apr 1730 (HCVD-2 p. 126); he lived near Tuckahoe Creek in 1738 (GCWD-2 p. 26)
4. **Ann Ligon**
5. **Mary Ligon**
6. **Martha Ligon**; she may have been the following Martha:

Feb Ct. 1745; Churchwardens of Dale Parish bind Elizabeth and Francis mulattoes, children of Martha Ligon (HCVW-2 p. 43)

Thanks to
William Douglas Ligon of Birmingham, Alabama, for
sharing his research and assisting in sorting the Ligon family
Any and all mistakes are mine. EGJ

HENRY LOUND

Henry Lound, b. ca 1618, age 63 on 1 Feb 1681 (HCVD-1 p. 149); d. by 1 Dec 1708 Henrico Co.; many Henrico Co. deeds mention bounding his land; m. by 1703/4 **Ann** _____; children from wills:

1. Mary Lound
2. Anne Lound

24 Jul 1645; Michael Mastert claimed land in Bermodo Hundred for transport of Henry Lownee (PB 2.26)

Mar 1652; Henry Lowne claimed 300 ac. Henrico Co. n. side of Appomattox River beginning at *Conecock Brook*; for transport of 6 persons (PB 3.41; LOP 3.41)

26 Sep 1674; Henry Lowne granted 516 ac. Henrico Co. on s. side of James River beyond mouth of *Ushers Creek* (LOP 6. 530)

2 Jun 1689; Henrico Co.; Mr. Henry Lounds, tithable, 3

1 Apr 1680; Henry Lound guardian to children of Henry Hatcher (HCVD-1 p. 4)

19 Aug 1678; from Henry Lound of Varina Parish, Henrico Co. livestock to grandchildren Anne, Henry, Mary, William and Martha Hatcher at age 15; contingent heirs were heirs of Henry and Mary Batte; also dau. Anne Moody (HCVD-1 p. 139)
2 Apr 1690; 200 ac. due Henry Lound for transport of James Drake and Negroes Daniel, Besse and Tom (HCVD-1 p. 142)

1 Feb 1703/4; from Henry Lowne, planter of Henrico Co.; to great-grandson Henry Edloe at age 21, s/o granddau. Martha Edloe; to William Lygon and my granddau.

Elizabeth his now wife, 258 ac. on s. side of James River; ½ of my patent for 516 ac. dated 26 Sep 1674; Ann, w/o Henry relinquished dower right (HCVD-1 p. 129)

Will of Henry Lound; 2 Jul 1708; 1 Dec 1708
To dau. Mary Batte, 258 ac. ½ of patent (1/2 already disposed of by William Ligon
Dau: Anne Moody
Grandsons: Henry Hatcher, William Ligon
Granddaus: Anne Ward, Mary Tanner, Martha Blanks, Elizabeth Ligon
Wit: Thomas Chamberlayne, John Wooldridge, William Rollo, Charles Roberts
    (HCVW-1 p. 102)
1 Nov 1708; probate granted Mary Batte (widow) on will of her father Henry Lound
    (HCVW-1 p. 105)
[Henry Lound; Henrico County Wills & Administrations (1662-1800) Note p. 119. Will pro. 1
Nov. 1708. Records, 1706-1709 (Reel 6) (LOV)]

1. **Mary Lound**; m. **Henry Batte**; d. bet. 1682 & 1708

2. **Anne Lound**; m/1 **Henry Hatcher**; d. bef. 1 Sep 1677; m/2 by 1678 **Samuel Moody**; d. by 4 Oct 1727 Charles City Co.; he was said to have been the eldest son of Robert Moody who, under the law of primogeniture, took over the patent in Charles City Co. of his father; Moody child:

2-1 Samuel Moody, Jr.

26 Apr 1688; Samuel Moody; son and heir of Thomas Moody late of Wyanoak Parish, Charles City Co.; granted 82 ac. on n. side of James River in Wyanoak at edge of *Wyanoak Marsh* (LOP 7.656)

19 Dec 1711; Samuel Moody granted 94 ac. 3r. 12po. Charles City Co. at edge of *Wyanoak Marsh* next to James River (LOP 10.47)

[Samuel Moody; wills not listed in VA WA, 1632-1800 (Torrence). Further inventory taken 4 Oct. 1727 Returned Oct. 1727 Charles City Co. Deeds, Wills, etc., 1724/5-1731, p. 185 (LOV)]

2-1 **Samuel Moody, Jr.**; d. by 15 Dec 1737

Died- Last Thursday the 15th inst., Samuel Moody drowned when his canoe overturned in Moorcock Creek near Chicohominy Ferry. (p. 4, c. 2) Publication Friday, December 23, 1737. Gen. note From the marriage and obituary citations compiled by Bernard J. Henley from Virginia newspapers on microfilm at the Library of Virginia. Other Format Available on microfilm (Library of Virginia Film 11)
Samuel Moody & another white man, going a ducking in a very small canoe in *Moorcock Creek*, by *Chickahominy Ferry*, were upset and drowned the 15th instant. 1737

JOHN PLEASANTS

John Pleasants of *Curles*, Henrico Co. was, according to family histories, b. 27 Feb 1644/5 Norwich, England, s/o John Pleasants of St. Savior's, Norwich (VP p. 2290). He came to Virginia ca 1665; he was a merchant, a Quaker and a very large landholder in Virginia. His will identifies his brothers as Samuel, Benjamin and Thomas Pleasants, who are not found in the records of settlers of Henrico Co. His will designates a gift of £20 to his unnamed mother who is not identified further in the abstract.

    John Pleasants; d. ca 1690; m. by 1680 **Jane Larcome** (VP p. 2290); d. by 1709; widow of **Samuel Tucker** [their child, Mary Tucker m. John Woodson, Jr. (HCVD-1 p. 13)]. Jane and John Pleasants had 3 children, whom he identifies in each case where they are mentioned as "born of the body of my dear wife Jane, formerly extx. of Samuel Tucker, dec'd"; as "Mr. John Pleasants of James River in Virginia" atty. for Peter Paggen, merchant of London, he was "absent" on 30 Mar 1696 when another man was appointed atty. (HCVD-1 p. 95); children:

1. John Pleasants
2. Joseph Pleasants
3. Elizabeth Pleasants

2 Jun 1679; Ct. at Varina for Henrico Co.; Mr. John Pleasants, tithable 13; 1678 (TVF 1.191)

1 Oct 1679; 10 Feb1680; John Pleasants and John Haddellsey granted 548 ac. 3r. 20po. Henrico Co. on n. side of James River and main book of *Four Mile Creek* (LOP 7.12) (HCVD-1 p. 9, 15)

29 Nov 1680; 1 Aug 1681; Jane Pleasants, formerly wife and extx. of Samuel Tucker to Martin Elam; for 15,000# tobacco; 2 tracts in Bermuda Hundred given me by my husband Samuel Tucker in his will; total 63 ac. (HCVD-1 p. 12, 13)

1 Aug 1685; 1 Aug 1685; deed of gift from John Pleasants of *Curles*, Henrico Co., to my 3 children of my wife Jane, formerly extx. of Samuel Tucker; to son John, dau. Elizabeth & son Joseph, negroes and mares (HCVD-1 p. 30)

20 Dec 1691; John Pleasants granted 1,220 ac. Varina Parish Henrico Co. on n. side James River above *West Ham Creek* and mouth of *Tuckahow Creek* (LOP 8.173)

May 1692; 16 May 1692; from John Pleasants, deed of gift for life to James Cocke, s/o Thomas Cocke, Sr., of Henrico Co. who m. dau. Elizabeth Pleasants; 70 on *Curles Swamp* and 400 ac. purchased of Henry Rowen and Robert Woodson, Sr.; then to their oldest surviving son (HCVD-1 p. 69)

1d 4m 1693; from John Pleasants deed of gift to son Joseph Pleasants; several horses and mares (HCVD-1 p. 78)

Will of John Pleasants of Curles; 27 Sep 1690; 1 Oct 1690 (presented by testator prior to his death); d. by 1 Oct 1698
To son John (s/o Jane, formerly wife and extx. of Samuel Tucker, dec'd); 300 ac. *Curles*, 900 ac. *Timber Slash*; *Half Sink*, my ½ of 7,000 ac. taken up by John Woodson, Henry Rowing and myself

If John has no heirs, to son Joseph (s/o Jane); is he has no heirs to dau. Elizabeth (d/o
   Jane); if she has no heirs, to my brothers Samuel, then to Benjamin, then to Thomas
   Items to John, if he dies then to Elizabeth and Joseph to be divided when they reach 18
To dau. Elizabeth, 70 ac. bordering *Curles Swamp*; also 400 ac.
To son Joseph, *Turkey Island Point* on *Chickahominy Swamp* of 1,400 ac.; 100 ac.
   Colson's; 548 ac. bought of Abram Childers; 2,000 ac. jointly with Richard Ligon
   on *Westham Creek* to mouth of *Tuckahoe Creek*, partly islands; if no heirs, then to
   Joseph Woodson, s/o my wife's dau. Mary [wife of John Woodson, Jr.]
To 2 sons, John and Joseph, 2,600 ac. above *Four Mile Creek;* 11 ac. s. side of *Four
   Mile Creek*; corn mill and saw mill; wife to have profits from mill and rent from
   lands for life
To the Friends (Quakers) land for a meeting house and burying place
To daughter in law, Mary Woodson, £20
To mother £20
Extx: wife
Wit: John Butler, Alexander Makenny (HCVW-1 p. 40, 41)
3 May 1697; 1 Jun 1698; Codicil: land at *Tuckahoe* and *Colsons* has been sold; land
   given dau. Elizabeth in poss. of her and her husband; new tracts purchased [see will]
   to John and Joseph; mentions land to grandson Thomas Pleasants and son or dau. of
   my son John (HCVW-1 69, 70)
1 Oct 1698; Jane Pleasants granted probate of will of husband John (HCVW-1 p. 70)
[John Pleasants; Henrico Co. Wills and Administrations (1662-1800); p. 80-87 & p. 148-154;
Will prob. 1 Oct 1690 & 1 Jun 1698; codicil recorded 1 Jun 1698, Deeds, Wills, Etc. 1688-1697
& 1697-1704 (Reels 5 & 6) (LOV)]

Will of Jane Pleasants of *Curles*; 2 Jan 1708; 1 Jun 1709
Dau: Mary Woodson; granddau. Jane Woodson; son John Woodson; Joseph Woodson;
   grandsons Tucker and Benjamin Woodson
Son Joseph Pleasants; dau. Elizabeth Cocke, her children James & Elizabeth Cocke
   [both minors]
Dau: Dorothy Pleasants; grandsons Thomas and John Pleasant; granddaus. Anne, Jane
   & Dorothy Pleasants
Granddaus: Elizabeth, Jane; daus. of Joseph; grandson Joseph Pleasants; granddau.
   Martha Pleasants
Ex: son John
Wit: Robert ____, Nicholas Hutchins, William Porter, Jr. (HCVW-1 p. 106, 107)
1 Jun 1709; probate granted John Pleasants on will of Mrs. Jane Pleasants (HCVW-1 p.
   108)
[Jane Pleasants; Henrico Co. Wills and Administrations (1662-1800); p. 166-168; will pro. 1 Jun
1709; Records 1706-1709 (Reel 6) (LOV)]

1. **John Pleasants**, b. est. ca 1672; d. by 7 Jun 1714; bur. grounds of *Curles*
   Meeting House; m. by 1701 **Dorothy Cary** (Quaker); d/o Thomas Cary &
   Anne Milner (VP 2248); she m/2 9d/7m/1718 as 3rd w/o **Robert Jordon** of
   Nansemond Co., b. ca 1668; d. ca 1728; Dorothy is called "dau." in the will of
   her mother in law, Jane, and the abstract of Quaker records erroneously states
   she was the d/o John (QRH p. 9); from his father's will ca 1698 John inherited:
   300 ac. *Curles, 900* ac. *Timber Slash*, and *Half Sink*, ½ of 7,000 ac. taken up
   with others; with his bro. Joseph inherited 2,600 ac. above and 11 ac. on s.

side of *Four Mile Creek*, corn mill and saw mill; the will of John Woodson, Jr., who m. his half-sister Mary Tucker left him 400 ac. on *Four Mile Creek* in 1700; John held 9,669 ac. in the Apr 1705 rent roll of Henrico Co.; children b. est. 1695-1705:

        1-1 Thomas Pleasants
        1-2 John Pleasants, Jr.
        1-3 Anne Pleasants
        1-4 Dorothy Pleasants
        1-5 Joseph Pleasants
        1-6 Jane Pleasants

1 Feb 1698/9; 1 Feb 1698; from John Pleasants of Henrico Co. to bro. Joseph Pleasants; for 10,000# tobacco; 320 ac. called *Pecquenock* bought by father, dec'd, from Henry Wyatt on 1 Apr 1697; and 100 ac. purchased by father of Giles Webb 24 Mar 1696 (HCVD-1 p. 107)

1 Jun 1699; John Pleasants granted 732 ac. on *Chickahominy Swamp* at *Half Sink* (HCVD-1 p. 119); 1 Dec 1701; 1 Dec 1701; from John Pleasants to Hugh Jones; for 1,000# tobacco; 732 ac. granted 1 Jun 1699; Dorothy, w/o John, releases her dower rights through her atty. Joseph Pleasants (HVCD-1 p. 119)

6 Jun 1699; John Pleasants granted 3,087 ac. 3r. 24po. Henrico Co. on s. side of *Chickahominy Swamp* (LOP 9.236)

1 May 1700 [recorded]; rec'd of mother Mrs. Jane Pleasants my share of estate of dec'd father John Pleasants (HCVW-1 p. 73)

25 Apr 1701; John Pleasants granted 2,994 ac. 2t. 35po. Henrico Co. on s. side *Chickahominy Swamp*; part lies on n. side of James River on *Cattaile Run* (LOP 9.322)

28 Oct 1702; John Pleasants granted 331 ac. 3r. 24po. Henrico Co. on s. side James River on *Prockters Brook*; part of grant to Timothy Allen (LOP 9.489)

20 Sep 1704; John Pleasants and Joseph Pleasants granted 286 ac. Henrico Co. on head of *White Oak Creek* (LOP 9.627)

Surveys of Henrico Parish, Henrico Co.:29 Oct 1706; John Pleasants 1,385 ac.; 10 Nov 1706, 1,029 ac.; with John Woodson 3,090 ac.; 7 Apr 1708, 2,497 ac.; 20 Apr 1708, 540 ac. (HCVD-2 p. 12, 13)

31 Oct 1707; 1 Nov 1707; from John Pleasants of Henrico Co. to Richard Cock of Waynoak Parish, Charles City Co.; for £15; 126 ac. on n. side of James River; also 500 ac. on n. side of James River on both side of *White Oak Swamp*; /s/ John Pleasants, Dorothy Pleasants (HCVD-2 p. 9)

1 Nov 1708; from John Pleasants of Henrico Co. & Parish release mortgage to Benjamin, Thomas and William Bridgwater, sons of Samuel Bridgwater; land on n. side of James River near the falls which was mortgaged for 8,542# tobacco 7 Aug 1689 to my father John Pleasants, Sr.; except for privilege of building a mill on any part with 5 ac. (HCVD-2 p. 16)

16 Nov 1708; 1 Dec 1708; from John Pleasants of Henrico Co. to William Cocke; for 225# tobacco; 1,600 ac. on s. side of *Chickahominy Swamp*, excepting 100 ac. sold Humphry Smith; Dorothy, wife of Pleasants, relinquished dower (HCVD-2 p. 17)

13 Nov 1713; John Pleasants granted 1,385 ac. on n. side James River Henrico Co.; adj. John Woodson below mouth of *Beaverdam Creek* (LOP 10.94)

Will of John Pleasants; 5 Mar 1713; 7 Jun 1714
To son John Pleasants, lands, mills, etc. on s. side of James River
To son Thomas Pleasants, ½ mill on *Turkey Island Branch* & ½ land on *Turkey Island*
To son Joseph Pleasants, other half of that given Thomas
Wit: John Scott, Joseph Pleasants, Elizabeth Cocke (HCVW-1 p. 127; VP p. 1080)
7 Jun 1714; recorded & proved by Dorothy Pleasants (Quaker), relict of John (HCVW-1 p. 128)
7 Jun 1714; 2 Aug 1714; court order of inv.; appraisal; presented by Mrs. Dorothy Pleasants (HCVW-1 p. 128)
[John Pleasants; Henrico Co. Wills and Administrations (1662-1800); p. 227-230; Will pro. 7 Jun 1714; Misc. Court Records, Vol. 1, 1650-1717; Inv. & appr. rec. Aug 1714 (Reels 1 & 6) (LOV)]

15 Jul 1717; Dorothy Pleasants granted 463 ac. Henrico Co. on n. side of James River & e. side of *Wolf Pit*; adm. John Pleasants (LOP 10.329)

Ct. 3 Jul 1721; Robert Jordan and Dorothy his wife, admx. of John Pleasants vs. Ebenezer Adams (HCVW-2 p. 159)

9 Apr 1768; from Robert Pleasants of Henrico Co. to Wm. Royster; 463 ac. in Goochland [formerly Henrico] Co. granted Dorothy Pleasants and given by her to her son Joseph; he gave by deed to her 3 daus., Jane, Dorothy & Ann; same land which Robert Pleasants purchased of Wm. Davis and Dorothy his wife & Thomas Trotter who m. sd. Ann (VP p. 985, 986)

1-1 **Thomas Pleasants**, b. ca 1695; d. by Mar 1744; on 3/3/ 1718 Thomas requested clearance to marry and on 7/9/1718 a certificate was granted at Curles Meeting House (QRH p. 8); m/1 **Mary Jordan** (VP), b. 24 Dec 1699; d/o Robert Jordan, Sr. & his 2nd wife, Mary Belsen; d. bef. 17 Jun 1765; m/2 **Mary ____**; d. by 16 Oct 1797 Goochland Co.; Thomas inherited ½ mill on *Turkey Island Point* and ½ land on *Turkey Island* from will of his father; "Tho. & Mary" wit. a wedding 28/2/1722 (QRH p. 11); children from wills:

        11-1 John Pleasants
        11-2 Robert Pleasants
        11-3 Lydia Pleasants
        11-4 Mary Pleasants
        11-5 Thomas Pleasants
        11-6 Jane Pleasants
        11-7 Sarah Pleasants
        11-8 Elizabeth Pleasants

1 Jul 1714; 2 Aug 1714; from Thomas Pleasants, son and heir of John Pleasants lately dec'd, to Robert Blaws; for 6,000# tobacco; 100 ac. purchased by John Pleasants from Darby Enroughty; Thomas to cut down pines for sawmill; Dorothy, mother of Thomas, relinquished dower (HCVD-2 p. 44); 3 Dec 1716; same deed (HCVD-2 p. 57)

3 Dec 1716; 3 Dec 1716; Thomas Pleasants, eldest son and heir of John Pleasants, dec'd, to Thomas Williamson; for £50; 490 ac. on n. branch of *Usuum Brook*; part of 334 ac. purchased 16 Jul 1696 from James & Anthony Moore & John Field by John Pleasants grandfather of Thomas; other part purchased 20 Jan 1695/6 by same from James Lyle (HCVD-2 p. 58)

4 Dec 1716; 7 Jan 1716; from Thomas Pleasants, eldest son and heir of John Pleasants to John Watson; for £30; 541 ac on n. side of James River on *Usuum Brook*; patented to John Pleasants, dec'd (HCVD-2 p. 58)

7 Jan 1716; 7 Jan 1716; from Thomas Pleasants, eldest son and heir of John Pleasants, dec'd, to William Edwards; for 11,800# tobacco; 530 ac. on n. side James River; conveyed from Edward Jones to John Pleasants, Sr., dec'd, to John Pleasants, Jr., dec'd (HCVD-2 p. 58, 59)

7 Jan1716 [recorded]; from Thomas Pleasants, s/o John Pleasants, dec'd, of Henrico Co. & Parish; for £200; 300 ac. on s. side of *Chickahominy Swamp* (HCVD-2 p. 59)

7 Jan 1716; 7 Jan 1716; from Thomas Pleasants, s/o John Pleasants, dec'd, of Henrico Co. & Parish, to Obadiah Smith; for 10.000# tobacco; 600 ac on n. side of James River on *Cornelius Creek, Four Mile Creek, Fall of the James River*; obtained by Thomas' father John by deed of exchange 1 Nov 1705 (HCVD-2 p. 59, 60)

26 Jun 1717; 1 Jul 1717; from Thomas Pleasants, son and heir of John Pleasants, dec'd to Thomas Mathews; for £60; 600 ac on s. side of *Chickahominy Swamp*; it being all the land that John Pleasants died seized of on the lower side of *Boar Swamp* (HCVD-2 p. 66)

26 Jun 1717; 1 Jul 1717; from Thomas Pleasants, son and heir of John Pleasants, dec'd, to Richard Truman; for £3; 60 ac. on s. side of *Chickahominy Swamp* (HCVD-2 p. 66)

5 May 1729; 1st Mon May 1729; from Thomas Pleasants of Henrico Co. to Thomas Watkins; for 1,500# tobacco; 50 ac. on n. side of James River bounded by *White Oak Swamp* and land sold by Giles Carter to John Pleasants; Mary, wife of Thomas, relinquished dower rights (HCVD-2 p. 116)

5 Aug 1734; 1st Mon Nov 1734; from Thomas Pleasants of Henrico Co. to John Hales of Charles City Co.; for £10; 60 ac. [excepting 1 ac. where Quaker Meeting House stands]; on *White Oak Swamp*; Mary, wife of Thomas, relinquished dower rights (HCVD-2 p. 156)

7 Mar 1736; 1st Mon Apr 1737; from Thomas Pleasants, eldest son and heir of John Pleasants, late of Henrico Co., to Joseph Pleasants, eldest son and heir of Joseph Pleasants, late of Henrico Co.; for £100; 150 ac. on n. side of James River called *Turkey Island Point* (HCVD-2 p. 178)

Apr Ct. 1744; from Thomas Pleasants to son John Pleasants, deed [?recorded after Thomas' death] (HCVD-3 p. 103)

Will of Thomas Pleasants; 19 Nov 1743; Mar 1744
To wife profit from negroes; to build Thomas a house
To son Thomas, use of tobacco house; ½ track in Goochland, negroes, items
To son John, negroes, certain land in Goochland Co. for 21 yrs. on *Beaverdam Creek*

To son Robert, Goochland track if John dies; also ½ Goochland tract, negroes, items
To dau. Lydia Jordan, w/o Benjamin Jordan; land, negroes, items
To my sister Elizabeth Pleasants, widow of my bro. Joseph Pleasants
To my 4 unmarried daus: Mary, Jane, Sarah, Elizabeth, negroes, land in Nansemond
and Norfolk Cos.
Exs: wife and 3 sons
Trustees: bro. John Pleasants, his son Robert, my nephew John Crew
Wit: Henry Sharp, Benjamin Jordan, John Pleasants, Thomas Pleasants, Jr. (HCVW-2 p. 25)
Aug 1745; inventory of Thomas Pleasants; value £1098.5.6 (HCVW-2 p. 27)
[Thomas Pleasants; Henrico Co. Wills and Administrations (1662-1800); p. 155-162; Will pro.
Apr 1745 (p. 60-61b) & 3 Aug 1790; Will Book 2, 1787-1802 (Reel 55); Misc. Ct. Records, Vol.
4, 1738-1746 (Reel 2); inv. & appr. rec. Aug. 1745, Deed Book 1744-1748 (Reel 8) (LOV)]

5/7/1747; Sufferings: Curles: Mary Pleasants (QRH p. 24)

26 Dec 1751; 1st Mon Jun 1752; Re settlement of dispute between John Pleasants, son
and heir of Thomas Pleasants, dec'd, Mary and Jane Pleasants, daus. of sd. Thomas,
and surviving trustees of will of sd. Thomas Pleasants; dispute between estates of
Sarah & Elizabeth Pleasants, dec'd, sisters of afsd. John, Mary and Jane Pleasants;
Sarah & Elizabeth died under age; dispute being whether their estates should be vested
in their bro. John or their surviving sisters; agreement made that legacy is hereby
vested entirely among John, Mary & Jane; Thomas Pleasants, Robert Pleasants and
Benjamin Jordan each rec'd £8.6.8 on 8 Apr 1752 from John, Mary & Jane of the
divided estate of their deceased sister or half-sister (HCVD-4 p. 131; TVF 9.39)

4 Jul 1781; from Mary Pleasants of Goochland Co., deed to Mary Younghusband, her
dau.; 7 negroes (GCDB 13.254; VP p. 987)

19d/10m/1782; Mary Pleasants of Goochland Co.; deed emancipating 4 negroes
"Being fully persuaded that freedom is the natural right of all mankind" (GCDB 13.260;
VP p. 987)

Will of Mary Pleasants of Goochland Co.; 17 Jul 1797*; 16 Oct 1797*
To daus. Mary Younghusband and Jane Hunicutt, money
To son Thomas Pleasants, residue of estate
Ex: son Thomas Pleasants
Wit: James Venable, John Hunter, Benjamin Shepherd, Francis Peart
2 Jul 1788*; Thomas Pleasants qualified as wit Isaac W. Pleasants, sec. (GCWD 17.164;
VP p. 974)
[Note: These dates appear to be questionable; a will recorded 14 pages later in book #17 was rec.
by the court 15 May 1778; original document was not examined.]

11-1 **John Pleasants, Jr.,** b. est. 1720s; d. by Jul Ct. 1765; of *Bailey's;* m.
Elizabeth Scott; d. by Aug Ct. 1758; d/o Mourning Exum & William
Scott (see VP p. 2296 for discussion of ancestry of the Scott family); John inherited
land in Goochland from will of his father; children from John's will:

        111-1 Thomas Pleasants
        111-2 Sarah Pleasants
        111-3 John Pleasants
        111-4 Elizabeth Pleasants

111-5 Exum Pleasants

1 Apr 1745; 1st Mon Apr 1745; from John Pleasants, son and heir of Thomas Pleasants, dec'd, of Henrico Co. & Parish, to James Woodfin; for £7.10; 500 ac. in Henrico Parish (HCVD-3 p. 11)

1 Apr 1745; John Pleasants, Jr. ack. above deed; Mary, his mother, and Elizabeth, his wife, relinquish dower (VP p. 1020)

12 Dec 1754; 1 Dec 1755; from William Parker to John Pleasants, s/o Thomas Pleasants, both of Henrico Co.; for 50 pistoles, ½ part of 61 ac. with a water grist mill now out of repair by overflowing of water, on *Four Mile Creek*, being the land and mill devised by John Pleasants, first of the name in this colony, unto his son Joseph in joint partnership with John, his other son, which part was sold to John Redford the Elder by Thomas Pleasants, father of the party to this deed (HCVD-4 p. 441; TVF 9.253)

Aug Ct. 1758; John Pleasants, Jr.; guardian for Thomas, Sarah and John Pleasants, his children (HCVW-2 p. 74)

6 Dec 1762 [recorded]; from John Pleasants, heir at law of his father, Thomas Pleasants, dec'd, to John Pleasants, Charles Woodson, Robert Pleasants, Robert Pleasants, Junr., Thomas Pleasants, Junr., Thomas Bates, Charles Keesee, James Ladd, John Crew, Joseph Ellyson, David Johnson, Edward Stabler and Charles Woodson Junr., Trustees; for 5s, 1 ac. on s. side of *White Oak Swamp*, adj. land of James Binford and is remaining part of a tract sold to John Hales; the same whereon the Meeting House of the people called Quakers now stands; and also 2 ac. bought by John Pleasants, great grandfather to the said John and William Hatcher on James River near *Four Mile Creek*, being the same whereon the Curles Meeting House of the aforesaid people called Quakers now stands, and was given by said John Pleasants (dec'd) by his last will and testament in trust and for the use and convenience of the said people in the discharge of their publick worship and as a burying ground, now the trustees being dead, and said John Pleasants, as heir of his great grandfather and for the better promotion of the Christian religion and being one of the said Quakers does convey the 3 ac. to the said trustees forever; cites that when said trustees shall be reduced to three or less in number, they shall convey same parcels to 10 or more friends or trustees. (HCVD-4 p.758; TVF 10.186)

Jul Ct. 1765; will of John Pleasants, Jr. presented by Thomas Pleasants, Jr. and Robert Pleasants, Jr.; estate in Goochland Co. to be appraised (HCVW-2 p. 90)

Will of John Pleasants (s/o Thomas of Henrico Co.); 6 Jun 1765; re-recorded 3 Mar 1784; original destroyed by enemy

To son John, tracts in fork of *Four Mile Creek,* water grist mill, fishing land at *Turkey Island*

To son Thomas, slave bought with part of money left him by his uncle Exum Scott; lease of 50 ac. on *Four Mile Creek*

To dau. Sarah, slave bought with part of money left her by her uncle Exum Scott

To son Exum, land in Goochland Co. and 1/3 of 463 ac. on *Beaver Run Creek* now in possession of Robert Pleasants, s/o John; also £150

Land in Bedford, Halifax and Lunenburg Cos. to be sold to pay debts, then to children

Exs: son Thomas; bros. Thomas and Robert Pleasants [they to be guardians to children]

Wit: Thos. Pleasants, Eliz'a Pleasants, James Williamson, Martha Matthews, Mary
  Younghusband, Hannah White
Codicil: My part of my father's estate and mother's estate to be equally divided
  among my children (HCVW-2 p. 175; HCVW-3 p. 115; TVF 6.178)
Aug Ct. 1766; exs. of John Pleasants, Jr.; to make acct. of guardianship of his 3
  children: Thomas, John and Sarah Pleasants (HCVW-2 p. 93)
Aug Ct. 1767; Thomas Pleasants, one of the exs. of the estate of John Pleasants, Jr.,
  presents estate accts. (HCVW-2 p. 98)
[John Pleasants; Henrico Co. Wills & Administrations, 1662-1800, p. 310-312; Inv. & Appr. rec.
28 Oct 1765, p. 300-301; Will, pro. 28 Jan 1765; Will Book No. 1, 1749-1769 (Reel 17) (LOV)]

26 Aug 1765; 2 Sep 1765; Bond for £1,000, and report of Robert Pleasants, s/o John,
to Robert Pleasants, s/o Thomas, and Thomas Pleasants, Jr., s/o John, who take upon
them to act in behalf of Exum Pleasants, an infant, in resolving the claim of John
Pleasants, dec'd, late of *Bailey's*, Henrico Co., to 1/3 part of a tract of land in
Goochland Co., being the lands given by Dorothy Pleasants to her son Joseph
Pleasants by deed of gift 22 July 1718, the said John Pleasants bequeathing to his son
Exum Pleasants, an infant, his said right in the land before same was completed
(HCVD-4 p. 864; TVF 11.34)

111-1 **Thomas Pleasants, Jr.**; s/o John and Elizabeth Pleasants of
       Henrico Co.; m. intention 1/8/1767; m. 10d 9m 1767 at Curles Meeting
       House to [121-2] **Margaret Pleasants**, d/o Robert and Mary Pleasants
       of same (QRH p. 44, 45); [VP p. 2297 says Thomas d. 1796 unmarried]

111-2 **Sarah Pleasants**; m/1 ca 1767 [23-5] **Jacob Pleasants**; m/2 9 Sep
       1779 Curles Meeting House **Samuel Parsons**; children of both
       marriages listed under [23-5]

111-3 **John Pleasants**; inherited grist mill, land at *Four Mile Creek* &
       fishing rights at *Turkey Island* from his father

111-4 **Elizabeth Pleasants**; m. [123-1] **Samuel Pleasants** of *Fine Creek*,
       Powhatan Co.

111-5 **Exum Pleasants**; inherited land in Goochland and on *Beaver Run
       Creek* from his father

11-2 **Robert Pleasants**; d. by Dec 1791 Goochland Co.; m. **Susannah
      Webster** (VP); Robert inherited land in Goochland; his name appears as
      witness in several Goochland deeds; as Robert, s/o Thomas, dec'd, he
      was one of the exs. of the will of his friend Joseph Parsons, Sr. of Henrico
      Parish dated 6 Aug 1762 (HCVW-3 p. 149); children (VP p. 2298):

                        112-1 Isaac Webster Pleasants
                        112-2 Mary Pleasants
                        112-3 Elizabeth Pleasants
                        112-4 Robert Pleasants
                        112-5 Margaret Pleasants
                        112-6 Thomas W. Pleasants
                        112-7 Robert Cary Pleasants

4/4/1761; Susanna Pleasants, wife of Robert Pleasants, Jr., represents that she sometime ago requested to the monthly meeting at Nottingham in PA (in the verge where she was educated) for a certificate to join her to this meeting but has not received it, having her residence in this province for some time. (QRH p. 36)

> 112-1 **Isaac Webster Pleasants**; of *Pleasants Green* of Goochland Co.; d. by 16 May 1826; m. 19 Aug 1782 Goochland Co. [123-2] **Jane Pleasants**; children from his will (VP p. 978, 2298):

> > 1121-1 **Webster Pleasants**
> > 1121-2 **Ann R. (or Anna) Pleasants**; m. **Nicholas M. Vaughn**
> > 1121-3 **Susannah W. Pleasants**
> > 1121-4 **Isaac Pleasants**; m. **Susan Bradley**
> > 1121-5 **Emily Pleasants**
> > 1121-6 **Harriet J. Pleasants**
> > 1121-5 **Robert W. Pleasants**; m. **Mary Harris**

11 Jan 1787; from Isaac Pleasants and Jane his wife of Goochland Co.; deed to Thomas Pleasants of same; ½ of mill seat known as *Beaver Dam Mills*, Goochland Co.; containing 50 ac. (GCDB 13.350; VP p. 988)

8 Apr 1791; from Isaac W. Pleasants & Janey his wife to Richard Bedford; 140 ac. on *Beaver Dam Creek* (GCDB 15.497; VP p. 989)

Will of Isaac Webster Pleasants of *Pleasant Green*, Goochland
To wife, entire estate during her lifetime for support of herself and testator's daus. Susannah W., Emily and Harriet J. Pleasants
At death of wife estate to be sold and proceeds equally divided between testator's children Anne R. Vaughn and Susanna W., Emily, Harriet J. and Robert W. Pleasants
Nothing to representatives of dec'd son Isaac Pleasants or his widow
Ex.: wife, son Robert W. Pleasants & son in law Nicholas M. Vaughn (VP p. 978)

> 112-2 **Mary Pleasants**; m. [23-4] **Philip Pleasants**
> 112-3 **Elizabeth Pleasants**
> 112-4 **Robert Pleasants**
> 112-5 **Margaret Pleasants**
> 112-6 **Thomas W. Pleasants**
> 112-7 **Robert Cary Pleasants**; Cary, orphan of Robert, dec'd, chose Isaac W. Pleasants as guardian; Philip Pleasants, sec.; Dec Ct. 1791 (GCOB 19.27; VP p. 1015)

> 11-3 **Lydia Pleasants**; m. 6d 10m 1741 Henrico Co. **Benjamin Jordan** (QRH p. 22); d. aft. 10 Feb 1775; s/o Benjamin Jordan of Isle of Wight Co.; known children from their father's will:

> > 113-1 Robert Jordan
> > 113-2 Benjamin Jordan
> > 113-3 Thomas Pleasants Jordan

1 Apr 1773; from Benjamin Jordan, Sr. & Lydia his wife to William Gathright, s/o Ephraim, all of Henrico Co.; for £15; 16 ac. on n. side of *White Oak Swamp, Duck's Branch*, etc. (HCVD-5 p. 465; TFV p. 58)

Will of Benjamin Jordone, dated 10 Feb 1775; certified by Robert Jordone; refiled
To wife Lydia, whole estate
To eldest son Robert, *Streets,* tract where he lives in Hanover Co., 3 negroes
To 2nd son Benjamin, 2/3 of tract where he lives, remainder at death of his mother, 3 negroes
To 3rd son Thomas Pleasants Jordone, *Hambletts* adj. where I live, 3 negroes
To grandson, Pleasant Robertson Jordone, negro
Exs: friend George Woodson and my son Benjamin
Wit: James Binford, Elizabeth Binford, Francis Binford (HCVW-2 p. 142)
[Benjamin Jerdone (Jordone); Publication 1775. Henrico County Wills and Administrations (1662-1800) p. 102-103. Will dated 10 Feb. 1775 & rec. 9 July 1783. Records [Deeds, Wills, Etc.,] 1774-1783 (Reel 10) (LOV)]

113-1 **Robert Jordan**; he may have d. 1772 as Robert "Jr." to distinguish him from his uncle; m. 11d 1m 1764 Black Creek Meeting House, New Kent Co. to **Mary Ellyson** of New Kent Co.; d/o Joseph and Mary Ellyson
113-2 **Benjamin Jordan**
113-3 **Thomas Pleasants Jordan**

11-4 **Mary Pleasants**; d/o Thomas and his m/2; m. **Isaac Younghusband**, b. ca 1727; merchant age 55 living alone in Ward 3, City of *Richmond* in 1782, owner of 2 slaves; Mary married outside the Society; disowned 7 Jul 1753 (QRH p. 28); children from the will of their uncles and Mary's mother:

114-1 **Mary Younghusband**; m. **Roger Brooke**; children (VP p. 2292):

1141-1 **Sarah Brooke**; m. **Charles Farquhar**
1141-2 **Mary Brooke**; m. **John Hall**
1141-3 **Roger Brooke**; m. [2433-8] **Sarah Pleasants**
1141-4 **George Brooke**; m. **Eliza Jordan**

114-2 **Isaac Younghusband**; he may have been the Capt. Isaac Younghusband on the cruiser, *Muskito*, 13 Sep 1776 (Virginia Gazette)
114-3 **Pleasants Younghusband**; m. [235-2] **Elizabeth T. Pleasants**; widow of [115-3] **Thomas S. Pleasants**; Pleasants and his bro. Isaac were heirs in the will of their uncle Thomas Younghusband of Currituck, NC written 16 Oct 1787; children (VP p. 2292, 2292):

1143-1 **Caroline Younghusband**; m. ____ **Burffin**
1143-2 **Martha Younghusband**

11-5 **Thomas Pleasants**; b. est. ca 1720s; d. by 1804; m. 1761 **Elizabeth Brooke** (VP); Thomas inherited use of tobacco house and ½ of a tract in Goochland; children (VP):

- 115-1 James Brooke Pleasants
- 115-2 Deborah Pleasants
- 115-3 Thomas S. Pleasants
- 115-4 William Henry Pleasants
- 115-5 Mary Pleasants
- 115-6 Sarah Pleasants
- 115-7 Elizabeth Ann Pleasants
- 115-8 Henrietta M. Pleasants
- 115-9 Margaret Pleasants

Oct Ct. 1789; Mary Pleasants, d/o Thomas, chooses him as guardian; he is also appointed guardian of his children, Sarah, Henrietta and Margaret Pleasants; Thomas S. Pleasants, sec. (GCOB 18.256; VP p. 1014)

Will of Thomas Pleasants of Goochland Co.; 31 Dec 1803; 18___1804
Exs: sons James Brooks Pleasants & William Henry Pleasants; sons in law William & Edward Stabler
Land to be sold: 600 ac. called *Minters* on *Cary Creek* in Fluvanna Co.; 527 ac. on *Little Byrd Creek* in Goochland; 20 ac. on *Ginetos Creek*; 226 ac. on sd. creek in sd. county; also my 1/3 part of 157 ac. including mill seat near mouth of *Island Creek*, Buckingham Co.; also land in Maryland called *Brookes Piney Grove, Fair (?) Hill* after taking off 800 ac. to be given my 2 daus. Henrietta and Margaret Pleasants, supposed to contain 60 ac. on *Sinaca Creek* Montgomery Co.; all remainder of tract called *Brookes Addition, Dickinsons Delight & Brother's Content* after taking 550 ac. to be given my daus. Deborah & Mary Stabler; 172 ac. is mill seat; a tract called *Brookes Green* of 190 ac.; 40 ac. from tract called *Brookes Addition* on *Haulins River* below *Gathers Mill*
To son James Brook Pleasants, upper part of plantation where testator lives and ½ *Beaver Dam Mill*
To son William Henry Pleasants, lower half of plantation and *Beaver Dam Mill*
To dau. Deborah Stabler, 390 ac. on Patuxant River, mostly in Anne Arundel Co. [Md.]; also strip of 150 ac. on both side of river called *Brookes Addition*
To dau. Sarah Pleasants, 400 ac. adj. above 150 ac., including plantation where Elizabeth now lives
To dau. Henrietta Pleasants, 400 ac. on *Seneca Creek*, Montgomery Co., part of *Brooke Piney Grove, Fair Hill*, etc.
To dau. Margaret Pleasants, 400 ac. on *Seneca Creek* adj. Henrietta
To 2 sons James Brooke & Will Henry, £100 in trust for support of the poor of the Monthly Meeting of Cedar Creek
To niece Mary Younghusband, use of negro to lawful age, then to be freed
£100 to such children collectively who taken negro children, teaches them to read and write and enable them to earn a living and release them at lawful age
Annuity left by my mother Mary Pleasants to my sister Jane Hunnicut being paid up as far as her estate extended, my exs. to pay sd. Jane £10 during her life
To son William Henry, all household furniture and cattle at time of testators death
Remainder to my 7 children, equally

Wit: James Bryden, Micajah Crew, Margaret Crew
25 Aug 1806; William Henry Pleasants qualified as exs.; penalty $50,000 (GCWD
  19.40; VP p. 976-978)

115-1 **James Brooke Pleasants**; m. **Deborah Brooke**; children (VP p.
  2297):

    1151-1 **Hannah Pleasants**; m. **Henry Howard**
    1151-2 **Basil B. Pleasants**; m. **Phebe Ring**
    1151-3 **Mifflin Pleasants**

115-2 **Deborah Pleasants**; m. **William Stabler**; she received $500 from
  the 1826 will of her bro. William H. Pleasants (VP p. 978); children (VP
  p. 2297):

    1152-1 **Thomas P. Stabler**; m. **Elizabeth Brooke**
    1152-2 **Edward Stabler**; m. **Ann Gilpin**
    1152-3 **James P. Stabler**; m/1 **Elizabeth Gilpin**; m/2 **Sarah Briggs**
    1152-4 **Caleb Stabler**; m. **Ann Moore**
    1152-5 **William Henry Stabler**; m. **Eliza Thomas**

115-3 **Thomas S. Pleasants**; m. [235-2] **Elizabeth T. Pleasants**; she
  m/2 [114-3] **Pleasants Younghusband**; Pleasants child:

    1153-1 **Elizabeth S. Pleasants**

115-4 **William Henry Pleasants**; d. by 16 Oct 1826; m. **Mary Ladd** (VP
  p. 2297); children from his will:

        1154-1 Thomas S. Pleasants
        1154-2 Joseph J. Pleasants

Will of William H. Pleasants; Goochland Co.; 9d/2m/1823; 16 Pct 1826
To son Thomas S. Pleasants, 381 ac. where he now lives
To son Joseph J. Pleasants, 372 ac. Hanover Co., also $3,000
To sister Deborah Stabler, $500
To sister Elizabeth Ann Pleasants, claim on Nicholas M. Vaughn & Isaac W.
  Pleasants, Jr.
Exs: Thomas S. & Joseph J. Pleasants; they to have residue of estate
Wit: William Miller, Tarleton W. Pleasants (VP p. 978, 979)

    1154-1 **Thomas S. Pleasants**; m. **Eliza Brooke**; children (VP p. 2297):

        11541-1 **Caroline R. Pleasants**
        11541-2 **Brooke Pleasants**
        11541-3 **Mary L. Pleasants**
        11541-4 **John M. Pleasants**; m. **Laura T. Brichett**
        11541-5 **Eliza C. Pleasants**; m. **Joseph A. Rogers**

    1154-2 **Joseph J. Pleasants**; m. **Martha Bates**; children (VP p. 2297):

        11542-1 **Benjamin B. Pleasants**; m. **Marietta Carter**

11542-2 **Mary G. Pleasants**; m. **Philip B. Price**
11542-3 **William H. Pleasants**; m. **Eliza Janney**
11542-4 **George D. Pleasants**; m. [2342-3] **Martha J. Pleasants**
11542-5 **Ann Pleasants**
11542-6 **Margaret T. Pleasants**
11542-7 **Walter F. Pleasants**
11542-8 **Julia M. Pleasants**
11542-9 **Martha Ellen Pleasants**

115-5 **Mary Pleasants**; m. **Edward Stabler**; children (VP p. 2298):

    1155-1 **William H. Stabler**; m. **Deborah Hewes**
    1155-2 **Elizabeth Stabler**; m. **Joseph Bond**
    1155-3 **Robinson Stabler**
    1155-4 **Thomas S. Stabler**

115-6 **Sarah Pleasants**; m. [243-3] **Tarlton W. Pleasants**
115-7 **Elizabeth Ann (or B.) Pleasants**; a legatee of her bro. William (VP p. 978)
115-8 **Henrietta M. Pleasants**; m. **Benjamin Bates**
115-9 **Margaret Pleasants**; d. by Feb 1807 Goochland Co. (VP p. 978)

Will of Margaret Pleasants of Goochland Co.; 25 Aug 1806; 16 Feb 1807
To brother William Henry Pleasants, £10
To sister Deborah Stabler, £1,000
To 4 sisters, Deborah Stabler, Mary Stabler, Sarah Pleasants & Henrietta M. Pleasants, the residue of the estate
Ex: I. W. Pleasants, Mary Pleasants, Thomas Nucols
Codicil: To nieces Elizabeth Ann & Margaret Pleasants, £10 each (VP p. 977)

11-6 **Jane Pleasants**; d/o Thomas and his 2nd wife Mary; m. **Glaister Hunicutt** (VP); 7 Jul 1759 Jane Hunnicutt removed from *Curles* (QRH p. 34, 35)

Jun Ct. 1746; Jane Pleasants, orphan of Thomas Pleasants, dec'd, chooses her bro. John Pleasants, guardian; he was also appointed guardian to her sisters Sarah and Elizabeth (HCVW-2 p. 44)

11-7 **Sarah Pleasants**; d. bef. 26 Dec 1751, minor; mother not identified
11-8 **Elizabeth Pleasants**; d. bef. 26 Dec 1751, minor; mother not identified; m. **Joseph Pleasants** (VP p. 2292)

1-2 **John Pleasants**; Quaker; merchant of *Curles*; d. aft. 11 Aug 1771; m/1 **Margaret Jordan** (VP), b. 12 Apr 1702 Nansemond Co.; d. 5 Oct 1746; d/o Robert Jordan, Sr. & his 2nd wife Mary Belson; as John Sr. he m/2 2 Apr 1750 at White Oak Swamp Meeting House to **Mary Woodson**; alive Dec 1761 (VP p. 1814); d/o Tarlton Woodson of Chesterfield Co. (ChWB 1.496); m/3 21d/10m/1769 at Black Water Meeting, Surry Co., **Miriam Hunnicutt**,

widow (VP p. 2292); he inherited lands, mills on s. side of James River from
his father's will; children from John's will:

      12-1 Robert Pleasants, b. ca 1723
      12-2 Samuel Pleasants
      12-3 John Pleasants
      12-4 Mary Pleasants
      12-5 Elizabeth Pleasants
      12-6 Dorothy Pleasants
      12-7 Ann Pleasants
      Children of m/2:
      12-8 Mary Pleasants
      12-9 Jonathan Pleasants
      12-10 Thomas Pleasants

16 Jun 1714; John Pleasants granted 541 ac. on n. branches of *Upnim Brook* (LOP
10.157)

16 Aug 1715; John Pleasants granted 1,309 ac. on s. side of James River on river bank
1½ miles below mouth of *Fine Creek* (LOP 10.239)

16 Aug 1715; John Pleasants granted 258 ac. on adj. s. side of James River and land of
sd. Pleasants (LOP 10.238)

6 Apr 1750; 1st Mon Dec 1750; Marriage Contract between John Pleasants of Henrico
Co of the 1st part and Mary Woodson of Chesterfield Co. of the 2nd part; Henry &
David Turrill of Caroline Co., Wyke Hunicutt of Prince George Co. & John Pleasants,
s/o Thomas Pleasants, of the 3rd part; in consideration of marriage between the first
two; 200 ac. and dwelling house at mouth of *Four Mile Creek*, Henrico Co. and 600 ac.
in Cumberland Co. to belong to John Pleasants for life then to Mary, his intended wife
(HCVD-4 p. 43; TVF 8.166-7;1 VP p. 1027)

12 Dec 172; 25 Feb 1765; Deed of gift from John Pleasants of Henrico Co. to grandson
Charles Woodson, s/o Charles Woodson and my dau. Mary, dec'd; 100 ac.
Cumberland Co. (CuDB 4.5; VP p. 968)

7 Mar 1757; deed of mortgage from Abraham & Henry Childers of Henrico Co. to
John and Robert Pleasants, his son, merchants; for payment of £100 with interest on or
before 27 Aug 1763; collateral being 50 ac. of *Roundabout* and 77 ac. near *Gravelly
Hill* (HCVD-4 p. 488; TVF 10.41)

Will of John Pleasants, 3rd of the name in VA; date 20 Aug 1771; certified by Joseph
    Pleasants (Quaker) and John Brooke
[This will is very long and very complicated; therefore mainly only names of descendants and
    part of land locations are mentioned here]
Son: Robert Pleasants, land where I live, 319 ac.; 350 ac. purchased of Robert Blaws;
    land on *Licking Hole Creek* in Goochland Co.; 3 tracts on *Four Mile Creek*, etc.
Grandson: Samuel Pleasants; s/o my son who kept store in Cumberland Co.; land
    called *The Fine Creek Tract*
Son: Jonathan Pleasants; land on *Four Mile Creek* and in Cumberland & Charlotte
    Cos.; mentions his sister Jane Pleasants, etc.
Son: Samuel Pleasants, of Philadelphia; £3,000 (already rec'd $2,000), £200, items
Dau: Elizabeth Langley, w/o Robert Langley; land she lives on

Dau: Dorothy Briggs, w/o Gray Briggs; £195

Dau: Ann Atkinson; £520

Grandson: Charles Woodson, tract in Cumberland Co., £100, etc.

Son: Jonathan, 400 ac. Cumberland Co.; 360 ac.; all land in Charlotte Co. & upper side of *Four Mile Creek*, etc.

Son: Thomas Pleasants; land on *Deep, Muddy & Angola Creeks* in Cumberland Co., 2, 600 ac.; etc.

Granddau. Jane Pleasants, d/o son John, dec'd

Dau: Mary Pleasants; 300 ac. in Nansemond Co.; £500, slaves, etc.; mentions her brothers Jonathan and Thomas

Mentions: Elizabeth, w/o Joseph Pleasants; their dau. Ursula Johnson

Mentions: Robert Jordan and his sister Mary

Wife, land on *Fine Creek Tract* for life than to grandson Samuel Pleasants; livestock

Father in law Tarlton Woodson

Exs: Thomas Pleasants, Jr. & Sr., Robert Pleasants, Jr., Thomas Pleasants, Jr., John Crew, Charles Woodson, Jr.

Lastly exs: sons Robert and Jonathan, Charles Woodson and Thomas Pleasants

Wit: Peter Strathan, Robert Pleasants, Jr., John Downes

Codicil: "Elizabeth Bates and the rest of my dear wife's children be permitted to live in the house built for my son John on upper side of *Fine Creek*"

Wit: James Hill, Ro. Pleasants, Jr. (HCVW-2 p. 137-140)

[John Pleasants, Sr.; Henrico Co. Wills & Administrations, 1662-1800, p. 63-82; Will dated 11 Aug 1771; codicil dated 12 Aug 1771 & rec. 8 Mary 1783; Records (Deeds, Wills, etc.) 1774-1783 (Reel 10); Abstract of will 1771 Va. Journal of the House of Delegates, 1790, p. 58]

12-1 Robert Pleasants of *Curles*, b. ca 1723; d. 3d/4m/1801, in his 79th year; bur. *Curles Burying Ground*; from Black Water Meeting minutes (VP p. 1240); s/o John & Margaret Pleasants; m/1 **Mary Webster**; m/2 **Mary H.** ____ (VP); he inherited over 1,200 ac. from his father, £600, 1/3 of large cargo he was managing, etc.; he was one of the trustees of the will of his uncle Thomas in 1744; children of m/1 (VP p. 2292):

         121-1   Robert Pleasants
         121-2   Margaret Pleasants
         121-3   Mary Pleasants
         121-4   Ann Pleasants

7/9/1747; Robert Pleasants request a certificate to PA or MD signifying his clearness in marriage (QRH p. 24)

2/12/1758; Robert Pleasants, Jr., intending to the northward, requests certificate to PA and MD signifying his clearness in marriage (QRH p. 33); 7 Jul 1759; Robert Pleasants intends to travel northward and requests certificate to PA & MD (QRH p. 34)

25 Apr 1760; Certificate from West River Monthly Meeting, MD, for Mary, wife of Robert Pleasants (QRH p. 35, 36)

16 Jan 1773; Robert Pleasants, ex. of John Pleasants of Henrico, dec'd, surviving partner of John Pleasants of Cumberland Co., dec'd, to Thomas Morgan; all interest of his late father (John of Henrico) and bro. John (of Cumberland) to 50 ac. sold Thomas Morgan (CuDB 5.135; VP p. 369)

121-1 **Robert Pleasants, Jr.**; m. 15 Oct 1784 Goochland Co. **Elizabeth Randolph**; Robert and Eliza were dec'd by 7/5/1796 when Robert, their grandfather & guardian requested membership for the children (QRH p. 80); children:

1211-1 **Robert Pleasants**
1211-2 **Elizabeth Pleasants**
1211-3 **Ann Pleasants**
1211-4 **Mary Pleasants**; m. **John G. Mosby**; 2 of their children:

12114-1 **Virginia Mosby**; m. [2473-3] **Adair Pleasants**
12114-2 **Lydia Mosby**; m. [2473-4] **Matthew Pleasants**

1211-5 **Margaret Pleasants**

121-2 **Margaret Pleasants**; m. [111-1] **Thomas Pleasants, Jr.**
121-3 **Mary Pleasants**
121-4 **Ann Pleasants**

12-2 **Samuel Pleasants**, b. Oct 1737 *Curles*; d. 2 Nov 1807; m. **Mary Pemberton** (VP); he rec'd over £3,000 from his father's will; living in Philadelphia in 1771 when his father's will was written; children:

122-1 **Israel Pleasants** of *Philadelphia*, b. 20 May 1764; d. 26 Jun 1843; m. 6 Feb 1788 **Anne Paschall Franklin**; d. 8 Jul 1822; they had 14 children; he and his bro. John bankrupted their Baltimore stores in 1804
122-2 **John Pemberton Pleasants**, b. 16 Apr 1766 Philadelphia; d. 6 Aug 1825; m/1 14 Mar 1793 **Anne Cleves Armistead** of Hesse, Matthews Co., VA; d. 9 Jun 1801; 4 children; m/2 19 May 1816 **Mary Hall** of Harford Co., MD; 9 children; he inherited £1,000 from his uncle Jonathan
122-3 **Charles Pleasants**
122-4 **Joseph Pleasants**
122-5 **Robert Pleasants**
122-6 **James Pleasants**
122-7 **Sarah Pleasants**
122-8 **Samuel Pleasants**
122-9 **Elizabeth Pleasants**
122-10 **Mary Pleasants**
122-11 **James Pleasants**

[Note: Samuel Pleasants left Henrico Co. for Philadelphia sometime around 1 Feb 1762 when a certificate was requested to monthly meeting at Philadelphia respecting his unity and clearness from marriage engagements (QRH p. 36). While operating his successful mercantile firm in Philadelphia, he was also manager of the Pennsylvania Hospital 1779-1781. Samuel and his sons, individually and together founded several businesses in Philadelphia and Baltimore which are detailed in the J. Hall Pleasants Paper, 1773-1957, deposited in the Manuscript Section of the Maryland Historical Society, 300 W. Monument St., Baltimore, from which the above information was abstracted.]

12-3 John Pleasants, Jr. of Cumberland Co.; d. bef. 21 Mar 1765.; mb. 12 Jun 1759 Cumberland Co. **Anne Randolph** (widow of **Daniel Scott**), security John Scott; wit. Geo. Carrington, Jr. (VP p. 971); she was d/o Isham Randolph & Jane Rogers of *Dungeness* (VP p. 2303, 2295, 2298); Anne m/3 bef. 24 Jul 1770 [24-3] **James Pleasants**; this John may have been the John, minor of *Baleys*, who, for £60, sold 600 ac. on s. side of *White Oak Swamp* 4 Jun 1745 (HCVD-3 p. 13); he operated store in Cumberland Co.; children (VP p. 964-5, 2298):

> 123-1 Samuel Pleasants
> 123-2 Jane Pleasants
> 123-3 John Pleasants, b. 1765

Will of John Pleasant, Jr.; Cumberland Co.; 28 Jan 1765
To wife Ann, £300 and 3 negroes
To son Samuel Pleasants, 130 ac. adj. east end of tract where testator lives; also 50 ac. tract, 70 ac. tract and 265 ac. on *Jones Creek*, 3 negroes and 1/3 personal estate
To dau. Jane Pleasants, 1 negro, 1/3 personal estate
To child wife goes with, if a son the above 265 ac. 7 remainder of estate not given; if a dau. 1/3 part of estate
Exs: wife and kinsman James Pleasants
Guardian to children: bro. Robert Pleasants
Wit: James Pleasants, Joseph Pleasants, Judith Scott, Mary Turpin
Ann Pleasants & James Pleasants (both Quakers), qualified (CuWB 1.300; VP p. 964-5) 28 Oct 1765; 21 Mar 1765; John Pleasants, estate value £927.5.1 ¼ (CuWB 1.310-12; VP p. 965)

24 Jul 1770; Cumberland Co. Court; James Pleasants & Anne, his wife, widow of John Pleasants, Jr., dec'd, exs. of sd. John Pleasants, Jr.; defendants vs. John Hunt, plaintiff; re a debt (VP p. 971)

123-1 Samuel Pleasants; of *Fine Creek*, Powhatan Co.; d. ca May 1811 Powhatan Co.; m. [111-4] **Elizabeth Pleasants**; d. aft 1811; Samuel inherited land on *Jones Creek*, Cumberland Co. from his uncle Jonathan and *The Fine Creek Tract*, land on Appomattox River also land on *Hook* and *Hughes Creek* from the will of his grandfather John Pleasants which mentions store his father kept in Cumberland Co., etc.; children from original papers, Powhatan Chancery Ct. (VP p. 1168, 2298):

> 1231-1 **John Thomas Pleasants**; m. **Ann Maria Smith**; d/o Granville Smith & Ann Pasteur
> 1231-2 **Sarah (Salley) Pleasants**; m. **Edward Mayo**
> 1231-3 **Ann R. Pleasants**; not named in Chancery papers
> 1231-4 **Dr. Samuel Pleasants**; m/1 **Elizabeth ____**; m/2 ____ **Vandervort**
> 1231-5 **Eliza S. Pleasants**; m/1 **William Collier**; m/2 **Josiah Poore**

1231-6 **James Madison Pleasants**; under 21 in 1811
1231-7 **Robert Pleasants**; m. **Julia Woodson**; under 21 in 1811
1231-8 **William Pleasants**; under 21 in 1811

22 Jul 1765; from William Worley to Samuel Pleasants, an infant, 5 ac. on n. side of Buckingham Road, Cumberland Co. (CuDB 4.22; VP p. 968)

28 Oct 1765; from William Gaites to Samuel Pleasants, an infant, 200 ac. in Cumberland Co.; adj. Wm. Worley (CuDB 4.65; VP p. 968)

28 Dec 1768; from John Ware to Samuel Pleasants, an infant, son and heir of John Pleasants, late of Cumberland Co., dec'd; 275 ac. Cumberland Co. on *Jones Creek* (CuDB 4.344; VP p. 969)

123-2 **Jane Pleasants**; m. [112-1] **Isaac W. Pleasants**
123-3 _____ **Pleasants**, b. 1765 posthumously

12-4 **Mary Pleasants**; d. by 1746; d/o John Pleasants m. intent 12d/4m/1737 Henrico Meeting; m. 5d/1m/1737 **Charles Woodson**; s/o Tarlton Woodson of Henrico (QRH p. 19, 20); he m/2 1746 **Agnes** _____, widow of Samuel Richardson

12-5 **Elizabeth Pleasants** (d/o John); m. 5 Jul 1749 at dwelling house of John Pleasants, Henrico Co., to **Robert Langley** (VP p. 2292); s/o John Langley of Walsham, Old England (QRH p.25); children (VP p. 2292):

125-1 **Ann Langley**
125-2 **Margaret Langley**
125-3 **Elizabeth Langley**
125-4 **Mary Langley**

4 Mar 1749; Robert Langley, producing certificate from Winslit in Lincolnshire, announced intentions to marry (QRH p.25)

8 Feb 1755; Robert Langley, reports he and his family are prevented from attending meeting because of distance from his home. 9 Jun 1755; A subscription and collection is made for the use of Robert Langley (QRH p. 30)

1/11/1766; Robert Langley for himself and family and Ann Atkinson request to join the Blackwater Meeting (QRH p. 43)

12-6 **Dorothy Pleasants**; m. **Grag Briggs** (VP p. 1293); 4/2/1758; an inquiry to be made into the clearness of John Pleasants respecting the marriage of his dau. Dorothy m. by the priest to a person not of the Society (disowned) (QRH p. 32)

12-7 **Ann (Anna) Pleasants**; m. by 12 Jan 1753 outside society (QRH p. 29) **Roger Atkinson**; 3/5/1755; Ann Atkinson condemned her disorderly marriage [outgoing in marriage] (QRH p. 30; VP p. 2292); known children (QRH p. 65):

127-1 **Dorothy Atkinson**, b. 1 Jun 1756; d. 16 Jun 1767
127-2 **John Atkinson**, b. 2 Jan 1759

127-3 **Jane Atkinson**, b. 18 Feb 1762
127-4 **Roger Atkinson**, b. 28 Feb 1764
127-5 **Anne Atkinson**, b. 1 Oct 1766

12-8 **Mary Pleasants**; her father's will states she is live with her mother and to receive 300 ac. in Nansemond Co., 4 slaves, items and £500; is she dies to her brothers Jonathan and Thomas; she inherited land in Henrico Co. and on *Deep Creek* in Cumberland Co. from her brother Jonathan; she may have been a child of m/2 as her father's will mentions "lands of my late wife, which my daughter Mary is heir to."

12-9 **Jonathan Pleasants** (Quaker); d. bef. 1 May 1777 (VP p. 969-970); unmarried; he inherited land on *Four Mile Creek* and in Cumberland & Charlotte Cos. from his father; unmarried

Will of Jonathan Pleasants; dated 11 May 1776; certified by Robert Pleasants
Slaves to be taught to read and free at age 30
To sister Story* Pleasants, land on *Deep Creek* Cumberland Co.; all land in Henrico Co. and 2/3 of my slaves; if she die, to bros. Robert and Samuel and nephew Samuel Pleasants
To nieces Ann, Margaret, Elizabeth and Mary Langley, each a negro and £50
To niece Jane Pleasants, 3 negroes
To David Woodson, s/o Charles, and Ann Woodson, d/o Charles and Ann Woodson, 1 negro each
To kinsman Joseph Pleasants, 1 negro
To nieces Jane and Ann Atkinson, each £50
To bros. Robert and Samuel and nephew Samuel, remainder of negroes
Mentions: Mary Netherland
To nephew Samuel Pleasants, s/o bro. John, my land on *Jones Creek* Cumberland Co.
To nephew John Pleasants, s/o bro. Samuel of Philadelphia, £1,000
All my lands on *Wards Forte* in Charlotte Co., tract on *Muddy Creek* in Cumberland Co. to be sold to pay my debts; remainder to my brother Robert and sister Mary
Exs: bro. Robert, kinsman Thomas Pleasants, Jr., John Green (s/o John)
Wit: Isaac Sharp, Alex. McDonald, Abraham Sharp, Miner Redford (HCVW-2 p. 141, 142)
*should read "sister Mary"
4 Jan 1775; Sep Ct. 1778; re-recorded 3 May 1784; division of negroes from will of Joseph Pleasants of Henrico Co.; to bro. Robertson (sic), bro. Samuel, nephew Samuel Pleasants; 2/3 to sister Mary (86 in number); [names of negroes given] (HCVW-3 p. 127; TVF 6.180)
[Jonathan Pleasants; wills not listed in Virginia Wills and Administrations, 1632-1800 (Torrence). Note Abstract of will - 1776 Va. Journal of the House of Delegates 1790, p. 60; Henrico County Wills and Administrations (1662-1800) p. 127-128. Accounts rec. Sept. 1778 & 3 May 1784. Will Book No. 1, 1781-1787 (Reel 53); Henrico County Wills and Administrations (1662-1800) Note p. 92-96. Will dated 5 May 1776 & rec. 30 June 1783. Records [Deeds, Wills, Etc.], 1774-1783 (Reel 10) (LOV)]

12-10 **Thomas Pleasants**; d. bef. 22 Apr 1776; inherited land on *Deep, Muddy & Angola Creeks* in Cumberland Co. from his father; unmarried

Will (oral) of Thomas Pleasants; John Hall made oath that on 14 Dec 1775 Thomas Pleasants did give him a watch; to Peggy Hunnicutt, a negro girl, horse and saddle; affirmed Mariam Pleasants, Sarah Scott & John Hall (CuOB D, 1774-1778 p. 368; VP p. 970)

1-3 Anna Pleasants; m/1 **Joseph Jordan**, b. 18 Nov 1695 Nansemond Co.; d. 26 Nov 1735; m/2 **Thomas Trotter**; children (VP p. 2291):

    13-1 Sarah Jordan; m. **Joseph Robertson**
    13-2 Abigail Jordan; m. **James I. Scott**
    13-3 Thomas Trotter; m. **Elizabeth Robertson**
    13-4 Ann Trotter; m. **Charles Woodson**
    13-5 Elizabeth Trotter; m. **William Scott**

1-4 Dorothy Pleasants; m. **Matthew Jordan**; children (VP p. 1291):

    14-1 Joseph Jordan; m. **Mourning Ricks**
    14-2 Matthew Jordan

1-5 Joseph Pleasants; of Nansemond Co.; d. bef. Nov 1743; m. **Elizabeth Jordan**; he inherited ½ lands, mills, etc. on *Turkey Island Branch* and ½ *Turkey Island Point* from will of his father, but is not mentioned in the will of his grandmother Jane; therefore he may have been b. aft. Jan 1708/9 when her will was written; Elizabeth called "sister, widow of my bro. Joseph" in will of Thomas Pleasants; children (VP):

    15-1 Robertson Pleasants
    15-2 Joseph Pleasants
    15-3 Sarah Pleasants

1 Sep 1728; 1st Mon Sep 1728; from Joseph Pleasants to John Pleasants; for £100; 3 slaves (HCVD-2 p. 112)

22 Sep 1739; 15 Apr 1740; Jos. Pleasants of Nansamond Co. to John Pleasants of Henrico Co.; for £60; 463 ac. on n. side of James River & lower side of *Beaverdam Creek*; bounded by patent of Dorothy Pleasants (mother of Joseph & John) 15 Jul 1717, with all houses (GCWD-2 p. 38)

1-6 Jane Pleasants; m. **Robert Jordan** (VP p. 2291)

2. **Joseph Pleasants** (Quaker); b. est. ca 1670's; d. by 7 Feb 1725 Henrico Co.; m. 15 May 1699 Henrico Co. to **Martha Cocke** (QRH p. 92; MHC p. 67); d/o Richard Cocke & Elizabeth; Martha m/2 intention 3/10/1726 m. 5d 12m 1726 **Edward Bennett**; d. by May 1742 Henrico Co.; he having presented a certificate from Pennsylvania. (QRH p. 26) Joseph's father gave him negroes Kate and Tony and a mare in 1685 and several horses and mares in 1693 (HCVD-1 p. 30, 78); from his father's will he inherited 1,400 ac. on *Chickahominy Swamp*, new lands bought after *Colson's*, and *Tuckahoe* land was sold which appear to be 550 ac. at *Falling Creek*, 320 ac. at *Pequanocka* in Varina Parish, 470 ac. in Varina Parish on s. side of James River with

greater part on an island and 200 ac. on n. side of James River; he and his bro.
John inherited 2,600 ac. above and 11 ac. on s. side *Four Mile Creek*, corn
mill and saw mill; Joseph was an active Quaker holding the position of clerk
and actively involved in the Society; children b. early 1700s:

2-1 Elizabeth Pleasants
2-2 Jane Pleasants
2-3 Joseph Pleasants
2-4 John Pleasants
2-5 Richard Pleasants
2-6 Robert Pleasants
2-7 Thomas Pleasants
2-8 Martha Pleasants

26 Oct 1699; Joseph Pleasants granted 98 ac. Henrico Co. on *Chickahominy Swamp*;
known as John Bottoms Plantation (LOP 9.236)

1 May 1700; Joseph Pleasants ack. receipt of his portion of his father's estate from his
mother Jane Pleasants (HCVW-1 p. 72)

20 Oct 1704; Joseph & John Pleasants granted 286 ac. Henrico Co. (LOP 9.627)

Apr 1705; Henrico Co. rent roll; Jos. Pleasants, 1,709 ac.

30 Oct 1706; survey of Henrico Parish, Henrico Co.; Joseph Pleasants, 1,309 ac.
(HCVD-2 p. 12)

18 Nov 1706; will of Richard Cocke names grandchildren Joseph and Elizabeth
Pleasants and dau. Martha Pleasants (HCVW-1 p. 93)

31 Jul 1708; 2 Aug 1708; from Joseph Pleasants to John Alldridge of New Kent Co.;
for £50; 500 ac. in Henrico Parish on s. side of *Chickahominy Swamp*; tract given
Joseph by will of John Pleasants, Sr., but land had relapsed and was granted to John
Pleasants the younger by patent 6 Jun 1699 who sold it to said Joseph 1 Aug 1705;
Martha, w/o Joseph, relinquished dower (HCVD-2 p. 14)

1 Oct 1708; 1 Nov 1708; from Joseph Pleasants of Henrico Co. & Parish to Gilly
Groomarrin; 450 ac. on s. side of James River part of island above *Powhite Creek* and
The Falls sold John Pleasants, Jr. 1 Apr 1697 and descended to John, s/o John, Sr.,
who sold to Joseph 1 Aug 1705; Martha, w/o Joseph, relinquished dower (HCVD-2 p.
15)

13 Nov 1713; Joseph Pleasants granted 1,029 ac. on n. side of James River Henrico
Co. adj. John Pleasants (LOP 10.93)

7 Mar 1714; from Joseph Pleasants of Henrico Co. & Parish to Edward Good, Jr.; for
6,000# tobacco; 150 ac. on n. side of James River, n. side of *Four Mile Creek*, between
Eastern Run and a branch of sd. creek; 4 Apr 1715; Martha, w/o Joseph, relinquished
dower (HCVD-2 p. 48)

4 Apr 1715 [recorded]; from Joseph Pleasants of Henrico Co. to John Redford; for
4,000# tobacco; land on s. side of James River; Martha, w/o Joseph, relinquished
dower (HCVD-2 p. 48)

6 Jun 1715; 4 Jun 1716; from Joseph Pleasants of Henrico Co. & Parish to John
Pledge; for £30; 300 ac. part of grant to Pleasants 13 Nov 1713; Martha, w/o Joseph,
relinquished dower (HCVD-2 p. 53)

4 Jun 1716; 4 Jun 1716; from Joseph Pleasants of Henrico Co. & Parish to John Webb,
Sr.; 550 ac. on n. side of James River adj. patent to sd. Pleasants 16 Aug 1715; Martha,
w/o Joseph, relinquished dower (HCVD-2 p. 53)

16 Aug 1716; Joseph Pleasants granted 550 ac. on n. side of James River on n. side of
west branch of *Beaver Dam Creek* (LOP 10.254)

3 Nov 1718; Nov 1718; from Joseph Pleasants of Henrico Co. & Parish to Richard
Cocke; for £15; 150 ac. on n. side of James River bounded by *Beaverdam Creek* and
Buffalo Branch; Martha, w/o Joseph, relinquished dower (HCVD-2 p. 78)

Oct Ct. 1720; from Joseph Pleasants to Learner Bradshaw, deed; Martha, w/o Joseph,
relinquished dower (HCVD-2 p. 191)

Dec Ct. 1720; Martha Pleasants relinquished dower in land her husband Joseph sold to
Obadiah Smith (HCVD-2 p. 191)

Dec Ct. 1720; Joseph Pleasants to William Frogmorton, deed; Martha, w/o Joseph,
relinquished dower (HCVD-2 p. 191)

Will of Joseph Pleasants; 9 Sep 1725; 7 Feb 1725/6
To son Joseph, 300 ac. called *Pickanockey*, negroe, goods, chattells, cattle, mare,
    horse; should Joseph or his heirs disturb my son Robert in his possession of land, the
    bequest of land at *Pickanockey* to be void
To son John, 150 ac. above *Horse Swamp*, negro, goods, chattells, cattle, mare
To son Richard, 300 ac. adj. upper side of *Buffalo Branch*, negro, goods, chattells,
    cattle, mare
To son Thomas 200 ac. on branch of *Tuckahoe* called *Long and Hungry*, negro, goods,
    chattels, cattle, mare
To son Robert, 200 ac. adj. *Four Mile Creek*
To dau. Jeane, negro, goods, chattells, cattle, mare
To dau. Martha, negro, goods, chattells, cattle, horse
To wife Martha, sole extx., remainder and use of plantation for life; if she marries she
    gets 1/3, children 2/3; if she not marry, use & produce of estate during her natural
    life in consideration of her bring up children in their minority, paying debts, etc.
Wit: Thomas Pleasants, John Pleasants, Edward Bennett, John Cooke, Jr., Eliz. Morris
    (HCVW-1 p. 148)
11 May 1726; Nov 1728; inventory of Joseph Pleasants; value £420.18.2; presented in
    court Nov 1728 by Martha Bennett, extx. (HCWB-1 p. 169)
Apr 1729; accts. of Joseph Pleasants presented (HCVW-1 p. 171)
4 Nov 1732; accts. of Joseph Pleasants presented by Edward Bennett & recorded
    (HCVW-1 p. 185)

27 Feb 1727; Edward Bennett, 400# of tobacco suffering; also Edward Bennett, 240
lbs. of tobacco (QRH p. 15, 16); he was sued for trespass; case dismissed Jul Ct 1739
(HCWB-2 p. 5)

5/11/1734 Edward Bennett condemned his evil practices of taking the oath (QRH p. 18)

4 May 1742; Jun 1742; Edward Bennet, inventory (HCVW-2 p. 15, 109)

2-1 **Elizabeth Pleasants**, b. early 1700s; d. betw. 1709 & 1725; mentioned in will of her grandmother Pleasants, and the 1706 will of her grandfather Richard Cocke; not mentioned in her father's will or that of her sister Jane

2-2 **Jane Pleasants**, b. early 1700s; d. by 6 Feb 1726

Will of Jane Pleasants; 19 Sep 1726; 6 Feb 1726
To mother Martha Pleasants; the mare my grandmother Jane left to me
To sister Martha Pleasants, bros. Richard, Thomas, Robert, John, each a negro
To bro. Joseph , a silver tumbler
Exs: cousins Thomas and John Pleasants
Wit: Ann Redford, John Lankford, Elizabeth Burton (HCVW-1 p. 158; VP p. 1103)
[Jane Pleasants; Henrico County Wills and Administrations (1662-1800) p. 84. Will pro. 6 Feb. 1726. Deeds & Wills, 1726-1737 (Reel 7a) (LOV)]

2-3 **Joseph Pleasants**, b. early 1700s; eldest s/o Joseph; d. by Dec Ct. 1753; m/1 1726 **Sarah Goode**; m/2 5d 9m 1732 Henrico Co. **Elizabeth Woodson**; d. by Aug Ct. 1766; d/o John Woodson, dec., of Henrico Co. (QRH p. 17); he bought 150 ac. called *Turkey Island Point* from his cousin Thomas Pleasants in 1736; he inherited 300 ac. of *Pickamonckey* from the will of his father; he is named in the 1706 will of his grandfather Richard Cocke; suspected children [use with caution]:

> 23-1 William Pleasants
> 23-2 Joseph Pleasants
> 23-3 Martha Pleasants
> 23-4 Philip Pleasants
> 23-5 Jacob Pleasants
> 23-6 Jesse Pleasants

3/10/1726; Joseph Pleasants was disowned & condemned for taking a wife, not a member (QRH p. 15, 17)

1 Apr 1728; 1 Apr 1728; from Joseph Pleasants to John Pleasants, both of Henrico Co.; for £20; ½ of water grist mill on *Four Mile Creek* devised John & Joseph, dec'd, by their father's will; descended to Thomas & Joseph Pleasants as heirs of sd. John and Joseph; also ½ of 50 ac. purchased by John from Darby Enroughty; also ½ of 11 ac. below mill purchased by John of Abraham Childers; Sarah, w/o Joseph, relinquished dower rights (HCVD-2 p. 109)

22 Jul 1736; [recorded]; from Tarlton Woodson to Stephen Woodson, both of Henrico Co. & Parish; I, Joseph Pleasants make bond to indemnify myself harmless as heir at law of my dec'd father, Joseph Pleasants and Edward Benet & Martha his wife, exs. of my father; re contract with Samuel Tucker Woodson of Henrico Co., dec'd and his heirs, relating to 266 ac. in Goochland occupied by late Joseph Woodson, Sr., dec'd, granted to sd. Tarlton and Stephen (GCWD-1 p. 89)

Dec Ct. 1753; will of Joseph Pleasants presented by Elizabeth and Jesse Pleasants, exs. Dec Ct. 1753 (HCVW-2 p. 76); Jan Ct. 1759; inventory of Joseph Pleasants records

(HCVW-2 p. 76); Feb Ct. 1759; Elizabeth and Jesse Pleasants, exs. of Joseph Pleasants summoned to ct. by petition of sureties (HCVW-2 p. 77)

16 Nov 1761; Apr Ct. 1762; Bond of Joseph Pleasants to Elizabeth Pleasants, widow and extx. of his father, Joseph Pleasants, dec'd, for £480; upon rec't of negroes and various unnamed properties, including a mill and the *Greater Survey* near *White Oak Swamp, Turkey, Four Mile Creek,* the 394 ac. where Joseph Pleasants now lives called *The Eastern Run*; negroes not to be moved or sold out of Virginia (HCVD-4 p. 726; TVF 10.181); [comparable bond of Elizabeth to Joseph not abstracted]

Aug Ct. 1766; will of Elizabeth Pleasants presented by Jesse and Jacob Pleasants, exs. (HCVW-2 p. 93)
Aug Ct. 1767; inv. of Elizabeth Pleasants returned (HCVW-2 p. 98)

23-1 **William Pleasants**; he and his bro. Joseph were grandsons and legatees of the will of their grandfather Joseph Goode of Dale Parish according to his will dated 14 Aug 1761 (ChWB 1.II.371)

23-2 **Joseph Pleasants**; m. **Mary Aiken**; children (VP p. 2296):

232-1 **William Pleasants**
232-2 **Joseph Pleasants**
232-3 **Sarah Pleasants**

[A Joseph Pleasants, Quaker, s/o Joseph, m. 5 Oct 1747 Mary Woodson, d/o Stephen Woodson (QRH p. 94)]

23-3 **Martha Pleasants**; m. **Joseph Pleasants**
23-4 **Philip Pleasants**; of Goochland; d. by 18 Jul 1831; m. [112-2] **Mary Pleasants**; d. aft 1792; d/o Robert Pleasants; 16 Apr 1792; from Philip Pleasants & Mary his wife to Philip Lawson; 30 ¼ ac. Goochland; 29 Jan 1792; Mary gave power of atty. to her son Thomas Pleasants (GCDB 16.49, 65; VP p. 990); [*children named in his will (VP p. 979)]; others (VP 2294, 2295):

234-1 **Martha A. Pleasants***; m. **John A. Golsby**
234-2 **Joseph Edwin Pleasants***; m. **Elizabeth S. Davis**; children (VP p. 2295):

2342-1 **Margaret W. Pleasants**
2342-2 **Bettie D. Pleasants**
2342-3 **Martha J. Pleasants**; m. [11542-4] **George D. Pleasants**
2342-4 **Laura A. Pleasants**
2342-5 **J. Hebee Pleasants**
2342-6 **John T. Pleasants**
2342-7 **Mary C. Pleasants**; m. **Henry Reese**

234-3 **Mary Jane Pleasants**
234-4 **Henrietta M. Pleasants**
234-5 **Thomas W. Pleasants***; m/1 **Susan H. Goodman**; m/2 **Nancy** ____; children (VP p. 2296):

2345-1 **James E. Pleasants**
2345-2 **Mary E. Pleasants**
2345-3 **Joseph J. Pleasants**
2345-4 **Robert H. Pleasants**; m. **Martha Maskeny**
2345-5 **Thomas I. Pleasants**; m. **Sarah Rapp**
2345-6 **Philip R. Pleasants**
2345-7 **Isaac R. Pleasants**

234-6 **Margaret W. Pleasants***; m. as 3rd wife of [243-3] **Tarlton W. Pleasants**
234-7 **Harris T. Pleasants***; m. **Sally Rowsey**; child (VP p. 2296):

2347-1 **John T. Pleasants**

234-8 **Elizabeth Pleasants**; m. **Nicholas Bowles**
234-9 **Philip Sidney Pleasants***; m. [252-3] **Elizabeth Pleasants**; children (VP p. 2296):

2349-1 **Charles S. Pleasants**; m. **Iacintha Totty**
2349-2 **Endocia J. Pleasants**
2349-3 **Joseph R. Pleasants**; m. **Elizabeth Sutter**
2349-4 **Mary E. Pleasants**; m. **Sylvester P. Cocke**
2349-5 **Samuel H. Pleasants**

234-10 **L. C. Pleasants**
234-11 **Robert Lee [or S.] Pleasants***; m. [252-4] **Demaris Pleasants**; he is called Robert Lee in the Valentine chart; children (VP p. 2296):

234(11)-1 **Endocia J. Pleasants**
234(11)-2 **Martha H. Pleasants**
234(11)-3 **Joseph P. Pleasants**
234(11)-4 **Margaret A. Pleasants**
234(11)-5 **Mary E. Pleasants**; m. ____ **Ridd**
234(11)-6 **Lucins C. Pleasants**

23-5 **Jacob Pleasants**; d. aft. 8 Jan 1776; s/o Joseph and Elizabeth Pleasants late of Henrico Co., dec'd, m. intention 4/4/1767; m. 7d 5m 1767 Curles Meeting House [111-2] **Sarah Pleasants**, d/o John of *Baileys*, dec'd (QRH p. 44); she m/2 9 Sep 1779 Curles Meeting House, Henrico Co. **Samuel Parsons**; children:

235-1 John Scott Pleasants
235-2 Elizabeth T. Pleasants
235-3 Thomas Exum Pleasants
235-4 Sarah Pleasants
235-5 Samuel T. Parsons
235-6 Margaret P. Parsons

2 Dec 1766; 6 Jun 1768; Boundary settlement between John Pleasants and Jacob Pleasants respecting their lands on *Horse Swamp* at the main *Chickahominy Swamp* devised by Joseph Pleasants the Elder unto Joseph, father of the said Jacob and the said John, by his last will and testament, defined by arbitrators Thomas Pleasants and Robert Pleasants (HCVD-4 p. 59; TVF 11.103)

Will of Jacob Pleasants; dated 8 Jan 1776; re-filed 17 Dec 1784 by John Pleasants, Gent. & Philip Pleasants (Quaker)
To wife Sarah whole estate for widowhood until son John Scott Pleasants is of age
To John Scott Pleasants plantation I live on; he paying my son Thomas Uxum Pleasants £250
To son Thomas Uxum Pleasants, 2 lots (nos. 494, 495 drawn in lottery) in Town of *Richmond*
Remainder to be equally divided between my children John Scott, Thomas Uxum, Elizabeth
Exs: brothers in law Thomas and John Pleasants & uncles Thos. Pleasants & John Crew Pleasants & friend Samuel Parsons; [no witnesses] (HCVW-2 p. 143)
[Jacob Pleasants; Henrico County Wills & Administrations (1662-1800) p. 107-110; will dated 8 Jan 1776 & rec. 17 Dec 1784; Records (Deeds, Wills, Etc.) 1774-1783 (Reel 10)]

6/7/1799; Certificate from Cedar Creek Meeting for Samuel Parsons and wife Sarah and for their infant children, Samuel and Margaret; and for Sarah's dau., Elizabeth T. Pleasants (QRH p. 82)

   235-1 **John Scott Pleasants**; m. **Sarah Lownes**, b. 17 Aug 1766; their children from family histories:

     2351-1 **Sarah Lownes Pleasants**
     2351-2 **George Pleasants**
     2351-3 **Mary Hewes Pleasants**
     2351-4 **Frederick Woodson Pleasants**
     2351-5 **Eliza Ann Pleasants**
     2351-6 **Charles Scott Pleasants**
     2351-7 **Louisa Pleasants**
     2351-8 **James Pleasants**
     2351-9 **Fitzhenry Pleasants**
     2351-10 **Cyrus Rodalphus Pleasants**

6/10/1792; Certificates for John Scott Pleasants and Sarah his wife from Fairfax Monthly Meeting (QRH p. 76)

1/11/1794; John S. Pleasants and his wife Sarah and their children have removed within the limits of Cedar Creek Monthly Meeting (QRH p. 78)

5/9/1795; Certificate from Cedar Creek Meeting for John S. Pleasants has obstructions [later disowned]; a certificate also requested for his wife Sarah and their two children, Sarah L. and Mary Pleasants, to Cedar Creek Monthly Meeting (QRH p. 79)

5/12/1795. Women's minutes: A certificate for Sarah Pleasants [wife of John S. Pleasants] and her children, Sarah and Mary Pleasants was prepared to join them to Cedar Creek Monthly Meeting. (QRH p. 85)

235-2 **Elizabeth T. Pleasants**; m/1 [115-3] **Thomas S. Pleasants**; m/2 [114-3] **Pleasants Younghusband**
235-3 **Thomas Exum Pleasants**; 12 Jan 1792; certificate to Henrico Meeting from Cedar Creek for Thomas Exum Pleasants (QRH p. 77)
235-4 **Sarah Pleasants**
235-5 **Samuel T. Parsons**; m. **Elizabeth Ladd**
235-6 **Margaret P. Parsons**; m. **Caxton Lumpkin**

23-6 **Jesse Pleasants**; m.12 Jun 1759 Cumberland Co. **Elizabeth Smith**, d/o William Smith of Cumberland Co.; wit. George Carrington, Jr. (VP p. 971); children (VP p. 2296):

236-1 **Joseph Pleasants**
236-2 **Ann Pleasants**
236-3 **Mary Pleasants**
236-4 **Elizabeth Pleasants**

Jan Ct. 1769; Josiah Pleasants, orphan of John Pleasants, chooses Jesse Pleasants his guardian (HCVW-2 p. 104)

8 May 1769; Jessie Pleasants [s/o Joseph] married by a priest to a woman not of the Society [also suffered himself to pass through outward ceremony of water baptism] (disowned) (QRH p. 48)

Sep Ct. 1766; Mary Pleasants (Quaker) granted admn. of estate of husband Joseph Pleasants (HCVW-2 p. 93)
Nov Ct. 1766; inventory of Joseph Pleasants returned (HCVW-2 p. 94)

2-4 **John Pleasants** of *Picquinoque*, b. early 1700s; d. aft. 20 Aug 1776; m. 7d/ 9m/1731 **Susannah Woodson**; d/o Tarlton Woodson (QRH p. 17); John inherited 150 ac. above *Horse Swamp* from the will of his father; Susanna inherited ½ 598 ac. in Goochland & negroes from the will of her father written 4 Dec 1761 which leaves land to her sons James, Joseph, Matthew & Archibald (ChWB 1.II.496); children:

24-1 John Pleasants
24-2 Susanna Pleasants
24-3 James Pleasants
24-4 Ursula Pleasants
24-5 Joseph Pleasants
24-6 Archibald Pleasants
24-7 Matthew Pleasants
24-8 Tarleton Pleasants

Will of John Pleasants of Picquinoque; Henrico Co.; dated 9 Dec 1776
7 children: John, Susanna Storrs, James, Ursula Brooke, Joseph, Archibald and Matthew
To son Joseph tract where I live bounded by *Horse Swamp* & *Chickahominy River* if he pay my son John £100; if not tract to be divided between them
To grandchildren John Woodson Ellis and Catherine Ellis

Wit: Sarah Pleasants, Elizabeth Pleasants, Samuel Pleasants (HCVW-2 p. 140, 141; VP p. 1135)

[John Pleasants; Henrico County Wills and Administrations (1662-1800) p. 88-91. Will dated 29 Dec. 1776 & rec. 30 June 1783. Records [Deeds, Wills, Etc.], 1774-1783 (Reel 10) (LOV)]

24-1 **John Pleasants**; carpenter; m/1 **Agnes Woodson**; m/2 by 1764 **Sarah Cox**; d/o Stephen and Judith Cox; children:

> 241-1 Samuel Pleasants
> 241-2 Ursula Pleasants
> 241-3 John Pleasants
> 241-4 Elizabeth Pleasants
> 241-5 Judith Pleasants
> 241-6 Tarlton Pleasants
> 241-7 Mary Pleasants
> 241-8 Susanna Pleasants

2/2/2764; reported that John Pleasants, Jr. has acted very disorderly and taken Sarah Cox to wife contrary to the usual form amongst Friends (QRH p. 40)

7/4/1764. It appears that the woman John Pleasants, Jr., married, was with child, and that a meeting was appointed at Elizabeth Pleasants, attended by several friends and others, who witnessed a certificate of that marriage (QRH p. 40)

7/7/1764. John Pleasants, Jr., carpenter, confessed his disorderly conduct (QRH p. 40)

3 Aug 1767; 3 Aug 1767; deed of gift from John Pleasants to granddau. Susanna Pleasants (TVF 11.48)

3 Aug 1767; 3 Aug 1767; deed of gift from John Pleasants, carpenter, of Henrico Co. to his 2 daus. Mary & Susannah (TVF 11.49)

3/9/1768. Sarah Pleasants, wife of John Pleasants, carpenter, is received into membership (QRH p. 46)

3/5/1777; John Pleasants, carpenter, and wife requested to have their marriage certificate recorded although their marriage was conducted much to the displeasure of Friends yet it is considered that their request ought to be granted (QRH p. 55)

6/2/1779; reported that John Pleasants, carpenter, concerned in the sale of a Negro (QRH p. 58)

241-1 **Samuel Pleasants**; mb. 18 Jul 1795 **Deborah Lownes**, b. 19 Feb 1774; surety Jesse Thornton; Sally Hewes testifies Debby, d/o James Lownes, was 21 on 19 Feb 1795 (MHC p. 67); children (VP p. 2295):

> 2411-1 **Sally Anne Pleasants**; m. ____Christian
> 2411-2 **Charlotte Pleasants**; m. **William J. Armstrong**
> 2411-3 **Edwin C. Pleasants**; m. [2467-1] **Indiana Pleasants**
> 2411-4 **Samuel Pleasants**

241-2 **Ursula Pleasants**; d/o John Pleasants, carpenter, dec'd, has declined attendance of meeting, disowned 2/7/1791 (QRH p. 76)

241-3 **John Pleasants**

241-4 **Elizabeth Pleasants**

241-5 **Judith Pleasants**

241-6 **Tarlton Pleasants**; it has been reported that Tarlton Pleasants, s/o John Pleasants, carpenter, has married contrary to discipline – disowned 5/9/1789 (QRH p. 73)

241-7 **Mary Pleasants**; 10 Sep 1776 **Jessee Hargrave**

Mary Pleasants, d/o John and Agness Pleasants of Henrico Co. and Jessee Hargrave, s/o Samuel and Martha Hargrave of Caroline Co., married 10 da., 9 mo., 1776 at *Picquenocque*, Henrico Co. (QRH p. 55)

241-8 **Susanna Pleasants**

24-2 **Susanna Pleasants**; m. intent 6/2/1762; m. 7d 3m 1762 Hanover Co. to **Joshua Storrs**; d. aft. 18 Oct 1779; s/o William Storrs of Old England; 7 Apr 1761 a certificate from Brigghouse Monthly Meeting in Yorkshire for Joshua signifying his clearness of marriage engagement, having left that place clear of debt (QRH p. 36); 5 Jun 1786 Susanna has frequently taken to strong drink to excess; 6 Mar 1786 in visiting Susannah conducted herself in an unbecoming manner (QRH p. 70); children from their father's will:

> 242-1 Gervas Storrs
> 242-2 Hanna Storrs
> 242-3 Susanna Storrs

Will of Joshua Storrs, merchant; 18 Oct 1779; certified by Joseph Pleasants, one of the exs.

Land to be held jointly by wife Susanna [during widowhood] and son Gervis

To son Gervis, tenement on n. side of main street in *Richmond*

To 2 daus. Hanna & Susanna Storrs, tenement on s. side of same

Believing all men have an equal and just right to freedom, negroes to be freed

My son Gervis to be sent to Gervis and Mary Storrs in Leeds Town, England, to be educated

Wit: Martin Burton, More Bell, Samuel Bridgwater, Patrick Spicer, John Pleasants, Samuel Parsons (HCVW-2 p. 132)

[Joshua Storrs (Stoors); Henrico Co. Wills and Admns. (1662-1800) p. 30-32. Will dated 18 Oct. 1779 & rec. 14 Apr. 1783. Records [Deeds, Wills, Etc.,] 1774-1782 (Reel 10); p. 291-293. Will pro. Apr. 1780 & 8 Mar. 1786. Will Book No. 1, 1781-1787 (Reel 53); p. 328-329. Accounts rec. 4 Mar. 1795. p. 365-366. Accts. rec. 1 Feb. 1796. p. 401-402. Accts. rec. 11 Mar. 1797. W.B. No. 2, 1787-1802 (Reel 55) (LOV)]

242-1 **Gervas Storrs**; mb. 28 Oct 1791 [243-6] **Susannah Randolph Pleasants**; Gervas disowned 7/1/1792 for absenting himself from meetings (QRH p. 76)

242-2 **Hanna Storrs**; m. outside society; 3/2/1781 (QRH p. 60)

242-3 **Susanna Storrs**

24-3 **James Pleasants,** of *Contention*, Goochland Co.; d. by ca 1825; s/o John and Susannah; m/1 ca 1759 **Anne Randolph**; d/o Isham Randolph

& Jane Rozer; widow of **Daniel Scott**; d. 1755 & [12-3] **John Pleasants**; m/1 intentions 1/12/1764; as James, s/o John & Susannah of Henrico Co. m/2 10d 1m 1765 Henrico Co. to **Dorothy Jordan**, d/o Pleasants and Mary Jordan, late of Nansemond Co., dec. (QRH p. 41); James produced a certificate from Cedar Creek Monthly meeting 5/1/1765 (QRH p. 41); children from their father's will and Valentine Paper (VP p. 2294):

> 243-1 John L. Pleasants
> 243-2 Martha Woodson Pleasants, b. 2 Dec 1779
> 243-3 Tarlton Woodson Pleasants
> 243-4 Anna Scott Pleasants
> 243-5 Pauline Pleasants
> 243-6 Susanna Randolph Pleasants
> 243-7 James Pleasants, b. ca 1769

Will of James Pleasants, Goochland Co.; 27 May 1816; 21 Mar 1825
To son James, plantation where testator lives with all appurtenances on condition he pay the following to my children:
To dau. Ann S. Webster £1,000 and a negro
To dau. Paulina Pleasants, £1,000
To dau. Martha W. Pleasants, £1,000
To son Tarlton W. Pleasants, £30
To Granddau. Louisa P. Mosby, £10
Wit: Francis W. Royster, Henry M. Lane, William H. Pleasants, Marcellus Smith (GCWB 26.91; VP p. 977)

243-1 **John L. Pleasants**
243-2 **Martha Woodson Pleasants**, b. 2 Dec 1779; m. **Randolph Railey**
243-3 **Tarlton Woodson Pleasants**; m/1 [115-6] **Sarah Pleasants**; d/o Thomas Pleasants of Goochland; m/2 **J___ Crew**; m/3 [234-6] **Margaret W. Pleasants**; children (VP p. 2294):

> 2433-1 **J. Newton Pleasants**
> 2433-2 **Polly Pleasants**
> 2433-3 **Henrietta Pleasants**
> 2433-4 **Thomas L. Pleasants**; m/1 **Eloise Adams**; m/2 **Martha White**
> 2433-5 **T. C. Pleasants**
> 2433-6 **Edward S. Pleasants**; m. **Lucy C. Bates**
> 2433-7 **Walter H. Pleasants**
> 2433-8 **Sarah Pleasants**; m. [1141-3] **Roger Brooke**
> 2433-9 **Margaret Pleasants**
> 2433-10 **Elizabeth A. Pleasants**

243-4 **Anna Scott Pleasants**; m. **Isaac Webster**
243-5 **Pauline Pleasants**

243-6 **Susanna Randolph Pleasants**; mb. 28 Oct 1791 [242-1] **Gervas Storrs**

243-7 **James Pleasants**, b. ca 1769; d. 1836; of *Contention*; mb. 8 May 1790 Chesterfield Co. **Susanna Rose**, age 19, sur. Philip Turpin (MCC p. 97); he was a member of the House of Delegates 1796-1810; elected Clerk in 1803; US House of Representatives 1811-1810; US Senator 1819-1822; elected Gov. of Virginia in 1822 by the General Assembly; children (VP p. 2295):

2437-1 **Anna M. Pleasants**; m. **Dr. Elam**

2437-2 **Charles James Pleasants**

2437-3 **Hugh R. Pleasants**

2437-4 **Susanna Pleasants**; m. **Dr. John Morris**

2437-5 **Marcella Pleasants**; m. **Marcullus Smith**

2437-6 **John Hampden Pleasants**; m/1 **Ann Ervine**; m/2 **Mary Massie**

2437-7 **Caroline Pleasants**; m. **Thomas Curd**

2437-8 **Mary Anna Lilburne Pleasants**; m. **William Granville Smith**

24-4 **Ursula Pleasants**; m. intentions 6 Jul 1766; m/1 10d 7m 1766 at the Swamp Meeting House in Hanover Co. to **George Ellis**; d. aft. 21 Feb 1771; s/o John and Catherine Ellis of Old England; George came over from England as an apprentice, resided in the colony for several years and pretty diligently attends meeting for the most part request to be taken under the care of Friends (QRH p. 42); Ursula m/2 outside Society by 2/3/1776 to **John Brooke**; disowned (QRH p. 54); known children:

244-1 **John Woodson Ellis**

244-2 **Catherine Ellis**

2 Jul 1767; Swamp Meeting reports that the w/o George Ellis was delivered of a child about 6 mos. of marriage; he ack. and condemned the fact (QRH p. 43)

Will of George Ellis; dated 21 Feb 1771
To wife for life ½ of 250 acres where I live; then to son John Woodson Ellis at age 21
Dau. Catherine Ellis
Bros. William and Robert Ellis
Sisters Lydia and Catherine Ellis
Exs: wife and my bros. James and Joseph Pleasants
Presented in court by Ursula Ellis and Joseph Pleasants, ex. (HCVW-2 p. 124; TVF 6.101)
[George Ellis; wills not listed in Virginia Wills and Admns., 1632-1800 (Torrence). Will - 1772/3 Henrico Co. Misc. Records. Vol. 7, p. 2153; Henrico Co. Wills and Admns. (1662-1800) 'p. 103-104. Will pro. 3 Mar. 1772 & 4 Nov. 1783. W.B. No. 1, 1781-1787 (Reel 53); p. 2153-2154. Will pro. 3 Mar. 1772 Misc. Court Records, Vol. 7, [1770-1807] (Reel 3); Henrico Co. Wills and Admns. (1662-1800) p. 12-14. Accts. rec. 1 Oct. 1787. Will Book No. 2, 1787-1802 (Reel 55)

3 Feb 1776; Ursula Ellis (wife of George Ellis) disowned; being married by a priest (QRH p. 54)

24-5 **Joseph Pleasants**; s/o John of *Picquanocque* in Henrico Co.; intent to marry 1/10/1768; m. 10d 11m 1768 at Curles Meeting House Henrico Co. to **Elizabeth Jordan**, d/o Pleasants Jordan of Nansemond Co. (QRH p. 47); known children from his will:

> 245-1 Joseph Carlin Pleasants
> 245-2 Mahala Pleasants
> 245-3 Clementine Pleasants
> 245-4 Sophia Pleasants
> 245-5 Dorothy Pleasants
> 245-6 Jordan Pleasants

<u>Will of Joseph Pleasants; Henrico Co.; 8 May 1785; 4 Jul 1785</u>
To wife Elizabeth, during her natural life, land, appurtenances, personal estate for support & maintenance of children who are to have equal portion as they arrive at lawful age
To son Jordan Pleasants, land on James River, Goochland Co. & items; should he died before age, tract to be sold and land divided between daughters as they arrive at age or marriage
To son Joseph Carlin Pleasants, tract where I live after death of my wife
At death of wife, personal estate to be divided among daughters: Dorothy, Sophia, Clementine, Mahala
Exs: wife Elizabeth Pleasants, John Brooke, William Burton
Wit: Turner Southall, Jno. Russell, Isaac Sharpe, Tarleton Pleasants (HCVW-3 p. 222; TVF 7.42)
[Joseph Pleasants; Henrico County Wills and Administrations (1662-1800) p. 222-224. Will pro. 4 July 1785. Will Book No. 1, 1781-1787 (Reel 53) (LOV)]

245-1 **Joseph Carlin Pleasants**; m. **Susan Burton**; children (VP p. 2094):

> 2451-1 **William H. Pleasants**; m. **Rosa Smoot**
> 2451-2 **Martha Pleasants**
> 2451-3 **Joseph Pleasants**; m. **Harriet Smoot**
> 2451-4 **Susannah Pleasants**; m. **Charles L. Cocke**
> 2451-5 **Sophia M. Pleasants**; m. **John Murry**
> 2451-6 **Rebecca Pleasants**; m. **John O. Chiles**
> 2451-7 **Elizabeth Pleasants**; m. **Joshua Hollowell**
> 2451-8 **Daniel Pleasants**; m. **Julia Rezee**

245-2 **Mahala Pleasants**
245-3 **Clementine Pleasants**; m. **Martin Burton**
245-4 **Sophia Pleasants**; m. ____ **Woodfin**
245-5 **Dorothy Pleasants**; she married contrary to discipline (QRH p. 75)
245-6 **Jordan Pleasants**; m. **Elizabeth Tyler**

4/6/1791; It appears Jordan Pleasants (who has a birthright in our Society) has wholly declined the attendance of religious meetings; disowned (QRH p. 75)

24-6 **Archibald Pleasants**; d. by 19 Sep 1836; mb. 17 Jul 1775; m. 5 Aug
1775 St. James Northam Parish **Jane Woodson**; both of this parish; d/o
Col. John Woodson and Dorothea Randolph; he was "within the limits of
the Circular Monthly Meeting" 6 Apr 1768 (QRH p. 46); children from their
father's will (VP p. 979-980); others (VP p. 2294):

246-1 **Virginia Pleasants**
246-2 **Susanna Pleasants**
246-3 **Charles T. Pleasants**; not named in father's will
246-4 **Jane Pleasants**
246-5 **Frederick Pleasants**; d. bef. 1836; m. **Maria Eustace**; children:

  2465-1 **Carolina M. Pleasants**; m. **William Brent**
  2465-2 **Frederick W. Pleasants**; m. **Sally W. McCarthy**
  2465-3 **Sarah Maria Pleasants**; m. **George W. Gretter**; grandfather's
  will calls her Sarah M. & Valentine Chart calls her Maria (VP p. 2294)
  2465-4 **Warren Eustace H. Pleasants**
  2465-5 **Elizabeth Jane Pleasants**; m. **Archibald Pleasants**; will of
  her grandfather calls her Jane & the Valentine Chart calls her
  Elizabeth (VP p. 2294)

246-6 **Archibald Pleasants**; m. **Mary Brent**

  2466-1 **Albert C. Pleasants**

246-7 **John Woodson Pleasants**; m. **Elizabeth Coleman**; children (VP p. 2294):

  2467-1 **Indiana Pleasants**; m. [2411-3] **Edwin C. Pleasants**
  2467-2 **Emeline Pleasants**; m. **Alexander Mebane**

246-8 **Dorothy Pleasants**; not named in father's will
246-9 **Matilda Pleasants**

4/6/1768; Archibald Pleasants being within the limits of the Circular Monthly meeting,
certificates will be prepared (QRH p. 46)

Will of Archibald Pleasants, Goochland Co.; 29 Mar 1836; 19 Sep 1836
Daughters: Matilda, Jane, Virginia, Susanna
Sons: John W., Archibald
Grandchildren: Jane, Sarah M., Warren E., Carolina M. & Frederick W.; children of
  son Frederick (dec'd)
Exs: son Archibald Pleasants, dau. Virginia Pleasants
Wit: R. W. Pleasants, Henry Satterwhite, Saml. Cocke (GCWD 31.51; VP 979, 980)

24-7 **Matthew Pleasants**; he is said to have m. Feb 1784 **Anne Railey**;
reported 4/11/1780 by Swamp Meeting that Matthew is contributing
money for the purposed of hiring soldiers and attending muster; reported
3/2/1781 he has removed to Goochland and joined the militia; (disowned)
(QRH p. 60); children (VP p. 2294):

247-1 **Matthew Pleasants**
247-2 **Elizabeth Pleasants**; m. **William B. Young**
247-3 **Benjamin Franklin Pleasants**; m. **Isabella Adair**; children (VP p. 2294):

    2473-1 **Joseph R. Pleasants**; m. **Martha Bowles**
    2473-2 **George Pleasants**
    2473-3 **Adair Pleasants**; m. **[12114-1] Virginia Mosby**
    2473-4 **Matthew Pleasants**; m. **[12114-2] Lydia Mosby**
    2473-5 **Catherine Pleasants**; m. ____**Noble**

247-4 **Paulina Pleasants**; m. **Robert Johnson**
247-5 **Peyton R. Pleasants**
247-6 **Caroline Pleasants**; m. **William Mayo**
247-7 **Mary Pleasants**
247-8 **Susannah Pleasants**; m. **Warren Pleasants**

11 Jan 1787; from Matthew Pleasants & Ann his wife to Thomas Pleasants, all of Goochland Co.; 187 ac. part of tract where Matthew and Ann now live (GCDB 13.360; VP p. 1988)

4 Aug 1791; from Matthew Pleasants and Anna his wife of Goochland to Wm. Reynolds of New Kent Co.; 50 ac. on *Genito Creek* (GCDB 16.21; VP p. 1990)

30 Nov 1791; Anna Pleasants; w/o Matthew, relinquished dower in 187 ac. sold to Thomas Pleasants (GCDB 16.45; VP p. 990)

24-8 **Tarleton Pleasants**

2-5 **Richard Pleasants**, b. early 1700s; d. by 21 Sep 1778 Goochland Co.; m. by 1735 outside Society (QRH p. 19) **Ann Porter**; d/o William Porter whose will of Oct 1750 names daus. Ann Pleasants and Elizabeth Pleasants; he inherited 300 ac. adj. upper side of *Buffalo Branch* from the will of his father; circumstantial evidence suggests he was the father of this Richard; children:

    25-1 Richard Pleasants, Jr.
    25-2 Joseph Pleasants
    25-3 Martha Pleasants

Will of Richard Pleasants; Goochland Co.; 15 May 1778; 21 Sep 1778
To son Richard, 360 ac. near *Genito Creek*, bay mare
To son Joseph, 200 ac. on *Beaver Dam* and *Buffalo Creek* where testator lives; household & kitchen furniture after death of wife
To dau. Martha Watson
To granddau: Jane Pleasants, negro, bed & furniture
To granddau. Ann Watson, negro
To grandson: Reuben Pleasants, negro
Wife to have use of plantation, household furniture and 3 negroes for life
Remainder to be divided equally

Exs: wife Anne, sons Richard and Joseph
Wit: Archd. Pleasants (Quaker), John Guerrant (GCWD 17.178; VP p. 974, 975)
[Richard Pleasants; Goochland County Wills and Administrations (1728 - 1800) p. 178-179. Will pro. 21 Sept. 1778. p. 261 263. Inv. & Appr. rec. 19 July 1779. Deed Book No. 12, 1777-1779 (Reel 5) (LOV)]

25-1 **Richard Pleasants, Jr.**; m. 16 Jun 1762 St. James Northam Parish to **Ann (Jeanie) Laprade**, d/o John Laprade; Richard & Ann sold several tracts in Goochland in 1791 (VP p. 989); children (VP):

251-1 **Johanna Pleasants**
251-2 **Richard Pleasants**
251-3 **Union Pleasants**
251-4 **Samuel Pleasants**
251-5 **Temperance Pleasants**
215-6 **Robert Pleasants**
251-7 **Jane Pleasants**, b. 2 Nov 1763; m. 2 May 1785 Goochland Co. **Robert Blanks** (VP p. 1018)
251-8 **Martha Pleasants**, b. 26 Apr 1765; m. 1 Apr 1786 Goochland Co. **William Suddearth**
251-9 **John Pleasants**, b. 10 Jan 1767
251-10 **Nancy Laprade (Ann) Pleasants**

25-2 **Joseph Pleasants**; m. 21 Apr 1772 Goochland **Mary Guerrant**; children (VP):

252-1 **Joseph Pleasants**
252-2 **Samuel Pleasants**; m. **Elizabeth Holeman**; children :

2522-1 **Ellen Pleasants**
2522-2 **Elizabeth Pleasants**
2522-3 **Laura Pleasants**
2522-4 **Samuel B. Pleasants**
2522-5 **Francis A. Pleasants**
2522-6 **Addison Pleasants**
2522-7 **Mary J. Pleasants**; m. **William Knibb**
2522-8 **William H. Pleasants**; m. **Betsy Pulliam**

252-3 **Elizabeth Pleasants**; m. [234-9] **Philip Sidney Pleasants**
252-4 **Demaris Pleasants**; m. [234-11] **Robert Lee Pleasants**
252-5 **Endocia Pleasants**; m. **Hezekiah Puryear**
252-6 **Simeon Pleasants**
252-7 **Mary Pleasants**
252-8 **Daniel Pleasants**; m/1 **Ann Ormand**; m/2 ____ **Puryear**
252-9 **Reuben Pleasants**; m. **Samah Goutry**; child (VP p. 2293):

2529-1 **Joseph R. Pleasants**; m. **Martha Bowles**

25-3 **Martha Pleasants**; m. 17 Feb 1767 Goochland **William Watson**

2-6 **Robert Pleasants**, b. early 1700s; d. by Dec 1751; he inherited 200 ac. adj. *Four Mile Creek* from will of his father; Robert, s/o Joseph, disowned 1 Apr 1746/9 for lewdness and vanity and of whoredom with Sarah Nolton to the great scandal; 11 Mar 1748; informed that Robert Pleasants, s/o Joseph, has some time past lived with Sarah Nolton (QRH p. 25)

22 Nov 1751; Dec 1751; inv. of Robert Pleasants; value £101.7.9 (HCVW-2 p. 55)
[Robert Pleasants; Henrico Co. Wills & Administrations, 1662-1800, p. 101-102 & 11691670; Inv. & appr. rec. Dec 1751; Deeds Wills, etc., 1750-1767 (Reel 9); admns. bond 4 Nov 1751, Misc. Court Records, Vol. 5, 1747-1757 (Reel 3) (LOV)]

2-7 **Thomas Pleasants**, b. early 1700s; d. by 21 Aug 1775 Goochland; m. **Elizabeth Porter**; d/o William Porter; Thomas inherited 200 ac. on branch of *Tuckahoe* called *Long and Hungry* from the will of his father; known children:

> 27-1 Robert Pleasants
> 27-2 Thomas Pleasants
> 27-3 Ann Pleasants
> 27-4 Elizabeth Pleasants
> 27-5 Jesse Pleasants

5 Sep 1726; 5 Sep 1726; from John Watson to Thomas Pleasants, s/o Joseph Pleasants, dec'd; for £10; 200 ac. part of tract on n. side of James River bounded by *Long & Hungry Branch* (HCVD-2 p. 92)

4 Oct 1762; 4 Oct 1762; from Thomas Pleasants of Goochland Co., s/o Joseph Pleasants, the elder, dec'd, to John Staples of Henrico Co.; for £30; 300 ac. on *Long & Hungry Branch* granted John Watson 22 Feb 1724 and conveyed Thomas Pleasants 5 Sep 1726; Elizabeth, w/o Thomas, relinquished dower (HCVD-4 p. 746; TVF 10:184)

4 June 1768; 6 Jun 1768; from Thomas Pleasants and his wife Elizabeth, of St. James Northam Parish, Goochland Co., to Richard Adams of Henrico Co.; for £40; 340 a. granted unto George Riddell of the town and co. of York by patent dated 10 March 1756 and by him sold to said Thomas Pleasants and one Lewis Parham, deceased, late of Prince George Co., as joint tenants, by deed dated 30 April 1760 and recorded in the General Court (HCVD-4 p. 60; TVF 11.103)

Will of Thomas Pleasants, St. James Parish Notham, Goochland Co.; 8 Mar 1775; 21 Aug 1775
To son Robert, 15 ac. n. of the 50 ac. given him previously by deed
To son Thomas, 65 adj. Robert's land
To son Jesse, 65 ac. on s. side of testator's land, including house and plantation of testator; also a heifer
To daus. Ann Martin, Elizabeth Pleasants, each 1 heifer and furniture
Remainder divided equally between my 5 children, Robert, Thomas, Ann, Elizabeth, Jesse
Exs: bro. John Pleasants, nephew Joseph Pleasants of Goochland
Wit: Robert Shapart, Stephen Nowlin, William Rogers (GCWD 11.38; VP p. 973)
[Thomas Pleasants; Goochland County Wills and Administrations, 1728-1800; p. 38-40; will pro. 21 Aug 1775, p. 59-60; inv. & appr. rec. 16 Oct 1775; Deed Book no. 11, 1775-1777 (Reel 4)]

27-1　**Robert Pleasants**; m. **Ann Clarke**

27-2　**Thomas Pleasants**; miller; d. by 15 Apr 1776 Goochland; m. **Ann Parsons**; use with caution as this is very iffy; the Pleasants Chart in the Valentine Papers, p. 2293, names the 1st two children; the will of Thomas names only the child Sally; children:

272-1　**Thomas Pleasants**

272-2　**Ann Pleasants**

272-3　**Sally Pleasants**; minor in 1776; named in her father's will; she might have been the Sally who m. 12 Mar 1782 in Chesterfield Co. **James Aiken** (MCC p. 2)

Will of Thomas Pleasants, Goochland Co.; 15 Apr 1776; 3 Jul 1776

Land lying on *Buffalo Creek* adj. Joseph & Robert Pleasants, given him by his father to be sold

To wife Ann Pleasants & dau. Sally Pleasants, equal shares in residue after debts are paid; should Sally die before age, then to testator's wife

Wit: Hezh. Puryear, Chas. Jordan, Betty Pleasants (GCWD 11.103)

[Thomas Pleasants; Goochland County Wills and Administrations (1728 - 1800) p. 103-104. Will pro. 15 Apr. 1776. Deed Book No. 11, 1775-1777 (Reel 4)

27-3　**Ann Pleasants**; m. **Samuel Martin**

27-4　**Elizabeth Pleasants**; m. **Edward Carter**

27-5　**Jesse Pleasants**

2-8　**Martha Pleasants**; m. intent 7/10/1734 **Nathanell VanDerwall**, of London (VP p. 2291); he was disowned 4/10/1737 having been found in the practice of several vices, in particular drunkenness, and unwilling to condemn his practices (QRH p. 18, 19); children (VP p. 2291):

28-1　**Martha VanDerwall**; m. **Turner Southall**

28-2　**Mary VanDerwall**; m. **William Lewis**

3.　**Elizabeth Pleasants**; b. est. by 1675; m. 11 Jan 1691 Henrico Co. **James Cocke**; Capt. Thomas Cocke, Jr., & William Cocke, Jr., sureties (QRH p. 91); in May 1692 Elizabeth's father made deed of gift for life to James of 2 tracts of 79 ac. and 400 ac.

Unplaced:

Dec 1733; acct. of estate of John Pleasants by John Pleasants (HCVW-1 p. 191)

[John Pleasants; Henrico County Wills and Administrations (1662-1800) p. 422-423. Accounts rec. Dec. 1733. Deeds & Wills, 1725-1737 (Reel 7a) (LOV)]

15 Feb 1776; John Pleasants, Jr. & Margaret his wife of Henrico Co. to Thomas Pleasants of Goochland Co.; 469 ac. in Goochland on branches of *Genito* and *Beaver Dam Creek* (HCDB 11.97; VP p. 986)

Dr. JOHN WOODSON

Dr. John Woodson, b. ca 1586 Dorchester, Devonshire, England; d. 18 Apr 1644 in an Indian uprising either at Flowerdew Hundred or at *Curles*; m. **Sarah Winston**; she possibly m/2 _____ **Dunwell**; m/3 _____ **Johnson**; children:

1. John Woodson, Sr., b. ca 1632
2. Robert Woodson, b. ca 1634
3. Deborah Woodson

In the 16 Feb 1623 List of Living in Virginia, Dr. John Woodson and his wife Sarah were in Flowerdew Hundred of Charles City Co. The Jamestown City census of 20 Jan 1624 shows John Woodson, head of household, wife Sarah, in Piersleys Hundred, having arrived on the *George* in 1619. Dr. Woodson was killed in the 1644 Indian uprising and Sarah is said to have hidden their 2 sons, thus saving their life. By this time they were still in Flowerdew Hundred or had moved to *Curles*. Sarah is thought to have married twice more and the following inventory suggests this might be correct:

17 Jan 1660; [recorded]; inventory of Sara Johnson, widow, with distribution of property
List of good "disposed of a little before her death and by her order"
To Deborah Woodson, items
To John Woodson, a cow, with calves to be raised for Deborah Woodson
To Elizabeth Dunwell (?), a heifer and cow; calf to remain in hands of John Woodson until Elizabeth comes of age
To Robert Woodson, what tobacco he owed her (HCVW-1 p. 218)

1. **John Woodson, Sr.**; est. b. ca 1632; d. by 1 Oct 1684; of *Curles,* Henrico Co.; m. est. ca 1651 **Sarah** _____; d. 1 Oct 1704; widow of **John Brown**; John was tithable for 3 in 1678 Henrico Co.; he and his bro. Robert and others granted 470 ac. in Varina Parish 21 Oct 1687 (LOP 7.602); known children:

1-1 Robert Woodson, b. est. ca 1653
1-2 John Woodson, b. est. ca 1655

28 Sep 1681; Robert Woodson, John Woodson, Thomas East, Robert Clarke & Wm. Porter granted 531 ac. 1r. 4po. Varina Parish, Henrico Co. on s. side of *White Oak Swamp* (LOP 7. 102)

Will of John Woodson, Sr. of Henrico Co., planter; 26 Aug 1684; 1 Oct 1684
To son Robert, 60 ac. adj. my cozen John Woodson & 100 ac. on n. side of *Bayley's Creek*, servants
Remainder of estate:
1/3 to wife
1/3 to son Robert
1/3 to be divided: ½ to my son's children Jane and Samuel and the other ½ to my bro. Robert Woodson's 4 youngest children: Robert, Richard, Joseph and Benjamin
To my cozen John Woodson, the small parcel where his dwelling standeth
Son John, ex.; 1 hogshead of tobacco and remainder of land
Wit: John Mackmioll, George Steward, Tho. Charles (HCVW-1 p. 15)

[John Woodson, Sr.; Henrico Co. Wills & Admns. (1662-1800) p. 279-280. Will pro. 1 Oct 1684. p. 292. Exors. bond rec. 1 Dec 1684; Records, 1688-1692 (Reel 4) (LOV)]

Will of Sarah Woodson, widow; 4 Feb 1701/2; 1 Oct 1704
To Martha Batte, d/o Thomas Batte, negro
To granddau. Martha Batt, items in poss. of her father in law John Farrar, etc.
To grandsons: John Knibb, negro & items; Soll. Knibb, items
To Seth Ward's dau., goddau. of Mary Ragsdale, dec'd, item
To grandson John Farrar, negro
To grandson Thomas Knibb, negro, items; if he die then to my dau. Temperance Farrar
My sheep to be divided equally between grandchild. Martha Batte, John & Mary Farrar
Dau. Temperance Farrar, extx., my clothes, livestock, £3, items, remainder of estate
Wit: John Bolling, Arth. Mosely, F. Bondurant (HCVW-1 p. 90)
1 Nov 1704; probate granted Temperance Farrar on will of her mother (HCVW-1 p. 92)
[The Batte, Farrar & Knibb grandchildren were from Sarah's 1st marriage to John Brown – Ed.]
[Sarah Woodson; Henrico Co. Wills & Admns. (1662-1800 p. 427-428. Will pro. 1 Nov 1704. Deeds, Wills, Etc., 1697-1704 (Reel 6 (LOV)]

1-1 **Robert Woodson**; d. aft. 1684 Henrico Co.; Robert inherited 60 ac. adj. his cousin John Woodson & 100 ac. on *Bayley's Creek* from his father in 1684, plus 1/3 of the remainder of the estate; the will of his father leaves ½ of 1/3 of the estate to "my son's children" without designating which son; some family histories place these children, Jane and Samuel, as belonging to Robert. However, John had children of the same name mentioned in wills.

1-2 **John Woodson, Jr.**, b. est. ca 1655; d. by 1 May 1700; Quaker of Henrico Parish; m. est. ca 1677 **Mary Tucker**; d. by 1 Aug 1710 Henrico Co.; d/o Samuel Tucker & Jane Larcome [Jane m/3 John Pleasants of *Curles*]; John was tithable for 2 in 1678 Henrico Co.; he inherited the unspecified remainder of land and 1 hogshead of tobacco from the will of his father; Mary inherited £20 from the 1690 will of her step-father John Pleasants & a negro and items in 1708 from her mother; children from the will of their father and their maternal grandmother Jane (__) Tucker Pleasants:

> 12-1 Jane Woodson, b. est. ca 1678
> 12-2 Joseph Woodson, b. est. ca 1680
> 12-3 Samuel Tucker Woodson, b. est. ca 1682
> 12-4 Benjamin Woodson, b. ca 1698
> 12-5 Mary Woodson, b. ca 1700

20 Aug 1681; 15 Dec 1680 (sic); I, John Woodson, Jr., as marrying Mary Tucker, the orphan of Samuel Tucker, assign my right in tract in Bermuda Hundred; sold by Jane Pleasants, widow & extx. of Samuel Tucker, to Martin Elam; I release all claim to above land to John Pleasants as guardian of said Mary (HCVD-1 p. 12, 13)

23 Oct 1690; John Woodson, Jr. granted 1,385 ac. Henrico Co., Varina Parish; on n. side of James River; near Henry Price (LOP 8.83)

23 Oct 1690; John Woodson, Jr. granted 732 ac. on branches of *Chickahominy Swamp* at *Half Sink* (LOP 8.84)

1 Oct 1691; 1 Oct 1691; from John Woodson and Mary his wife of Henrico Co. & Parish; to freeholders of Charles City Co.; for 12,000# tobacco a 50 ac. parcel chosen in Bermuda Hundred Point to be laid out for a town in compliance with Act of Assembly of 16 Apr 1691 (HCVD-1 p. 65)

22 Feb 1698; 1 May 1700; rec'd of my mother Mrs. Jane Pleasants; our parts of legacy of dec'd father John Pleasants; /s/ John Woodson, Jr., Mary Woodson (HCVW-1 p. 73)

Will of John Woodson, Jr.; 1 Dec 1699; 1 May 1700
To wife Mary, ½ of plantation I live on, slaves, English goods in storehouse, items
To eldest and only dau. Jane at age or marriage, negro, livestock and 1/5 of money, merchandise, tobacco
To eldest son Joseph at age 21, 120 ac. next to my bro. John Pleasants, negro, 1/5 of money, etc., 100 ac. at *Claytons*, Henrico Co., items
To 2nd son Samuel Tucker Woodson at age 21, remainder of land where I live, 60 ac., 1/5 of money, etc., negro, 150 ac. on s. side of *Four Mile Creek*, all land in Bermuda Hundred
To 3rd son Benjamin Woodson at age 21, 200 ac. on the river, negro, items, 1/5 of money, etc.
To child my wife goes with, 100 ac., negro, 1/5 of money, etc.
To cozen John Woodson, Sr., 600 ac. adj. *Cornelius's*; he to manage my affairs
To bro. John Pleasants, 400 ac. on s. side of *Four Mile Creek*
Exs: John Pleasants, John Woodson, Sr.
Wit: Matthew Payson, Edward Hughs, Nathan Jordan (HCVW-1 p. 72, 73)
[John Woodson, Junior; Henrico Co. Wills & Admns. (1662-1800) p. 169-170. Will pro. 1May 1700. Deeds, Wills, Etc. 1697-1704 (Reel 6))LOV)]

Will of Mary Woodson, relict of John Woodson; 24 Sep 1709; 1 Aug 1710
To son Joseph Woodson, negroes, items
To dau. Jane Woodson, negro
To sons Tucker & Benjamin Woodson, negro & items each
To children of my dau. Jane Woodson, grandsons John & Joseph Woodson, granddau. Mary Woodson
To grandson Sandbourne Woodson, negro; if he die then to the child of my dau. Mary now goes with, w/o my son Joseph
To my own son Joseph Woodson, ex., remainder of estate
Wit: Hannah Townsend, C. (Charles) Evans (HCVW-1 p. 110)
[Mary Woodson; Henrico Co. Wills & Admns. (1662-1800) p. 19-20. Will pro. 1 Aug 1710. Records, 1710-1714 (Reel 6) (LOV)]

12-1 **Jane Woodson**; b. est. ca 1678, eldest and only dau.; d. bef. 1 Aug 1710; m. 1701 her 2nd cousin **Joseph Woodson**; s/o Robert Woodson (QRH p. 2); she inherited from the 1684 will of her grandfather Woodson, the 1700 will of her father & 1710 will of her mother & 100 ac. at *Dover* from the 1717 will of her brother Samuel

12-2 **Joseph Woodson**, b. est. ca 1680; of *Curles*; later of *Little Low Ground*; b. est. 1680's; d. 1756 Cumberland Co.; eldest son; [called Jr. in some records to distinguish him from his older cousin]; m/1 9d 11m 1706 Chuckatuck Monthly Meeting **Mary Sanborne**; consent given by her father; d/o Daniel Sanborne and Sarah Copeland; m/2 **Elizabeth Scott**; m/3 by 1734 **Elizabeth Murry**; Joseph inherited from his step-grandfather Joseph Pleasants in 1690 (HCVW-1 p. 40), from his father & mother, and in 1708 from his grandmother Jane Pleasants of *Curles*, & his brother Samuel in 1717 as well as from his son John in 1727; he inherited 170 ac. on *Four Mile Creek* at *Dover* from the will of his bro. Samuel in 1718; children:

Child of m/1:
122-1 Sanborne Woodson
Child of m/2:
122-2 Mary Woodson
Children of m/3:
122-3 John Woodson
122-4 Lucy or Snagg Woodson
122-5 Joseph Woodson
122-6 Samuel Woodson
122-7 Martha Woodson
122-8 Elizabeth Woodson

29 Jun 1714; 2 Aug 1714; Joseph Woodson, Jr., son and heir of Mary Woodson, dec'd, to Samuel Tucker Woodson; for £25; 25 ac. in Bermuda Hundred devised Samuel Tucker Woodson by John Woodson, Sr., father of this grantor and grantee by his will (HCVD-2 p. 44)

24 Dec 1715; from Joseph Woodson, Jr. to Richard Cocke, Jr., both of Henrico Co. & Parish; for £60; 114 ac. on n. side of James River bounded by line between sd. Joseph and his bro. Samuel Tucker Woodson; mentions *Marcum's Gutt* (HCVD-2 p. 53)

18 Feb 1722; Joseph, John & John Woodson, Jr. granted 400 ac. Henrico Co. (LOP 11.158)

3 Jun 1734; from Joseph Woodson & wife Elizabeth of Henrico Co. to Lewis Meacum of Upper Parish of Isle of Wight Co., cordwainer; for £10; 30 ac. in sd. Parish & county; from Joseph & Elizabeth, power of atty. to "our trusty and well beloved brother Thomas Murry" of Isle of Wight Co. (Isle of Wight DB 4.352; VP p. 2024)

Jun Ct. 1739; Elizabeth, w/o Joseph Woodson, relinquished dower right in land sold by her husband to John Pleasants 7 Dec 1719 (HCVD-3 p. 82) [deed not located]

1749; 5 Feb 1749; from Joseph Woodson of Henrico Co. & Parish to son Joseph Woodson; 100 ac. at mill run of *Four Mile Creek* to be retained by me for life (HCVD-3 p. 73)

122-1 **Sanborne Woodson**; d. by 1756 St. James Parish, Goochland Co.; s/o Joseph Woodson & Mary Sanborne; said to have m/1 **Elizabeth Hughes**; d/o Stephen Hughes whose will, proved 25 Jun 1753 in Cumberland Co., mentions dau. Elizabeth; m/2 **Charity ____**; she mb/2 28 Aug 1756 Cumberland Co. **John Burch**; sec. Benjamin Childrey of Goochland (VP p. 1850); Burch d. ca 1801 Surry Co., NC; Sanborne was named in 1710 will of his grandmother Mary Woodson; children from his will:

1221-1 Hughes Woodson
1221-2 Sarah Woodson

1221-3 Jane Woodson
1221-4 Jesse Woodson
1221-5 Mary Ann Woodson

20 Sep 1745; Sanburn Woodson granted 400 ac. Goochland Co. near Appomattox River above *Dry Creek* (LOP 24.151)

26 Jun 1748; Sanburn Woodson of Cumberland Co. to James Anderson; 400 ac. near Appomattox River; granted sd. Woodson 20 Sep 1745 (CuDB1.9; VP p. 1834)

30 Jan 1750; from Sanburn Woodson of Cumberland Co. to Geo. Owen; 50 ac. Cumberland Co. on branch *Little Deep Creek* being part of land where he now lives (CuDB 1.373; VP p. 1835)

Will of Sanbourn Woodson of Southan Parish, Cumberland Co.; 13 Nov 1755; 28 Jun 1756
To wife Charity for life, 150 ac. with plantation where I now live, then to son Hughes Woodson
To my 5 children Hughes, Sarah, Jane, Jesse & Mary Ann Woodson, each £25 when they are 21
To wife Charity, remainder of my estate
Extx: wife Charity Woodson
Wit: Ann Owen, William Taylor, Susannah Fips (CuWB 2.115; VP p. 1823)
20 May 1757; appraisement Sanborn Woodson; value £208.12.0 (CuWB 2.130; VP p. 1823)
[Sanburn Woodson; Cumberland Co. Wills & Administrations (1749-1810) p. 115-116. Will, pro. 28 Jun 1756. p. 130. Inv. & Appr. rec. 23 May 1757. WB No. 1, 1749-1769 (Reel 17) (LOV)]

1221-1 Hughes Woodson

28 Feb 1774; from Hughes Woodson of Cumberland Co. to James Woodsy; 30 ac. in Cumberland Co. (CuDB 5.240; VP p. 1840)

21 Jun 1792; from David Susberry to Hughes Woodson of Powhatan Co.; 26 ac. in Powhatan Co. on s. side of Buckingham Road (PoDB 1.703; VP p. 2030)

1221-2 **Sarah Woodson**
1221-3 **Jane Woodson**
1221-4 **Jesse Woodson**
1221-5 **Mary Ann Woodson**

122-2 **Mary Woodson**; d/o Joseph Woodson & Elizabeth Scott; m. **William Pierce**; d. bef. 1767; children [John Woodson was guardian]:

1222-1 **Robert Pierce**
1222-2 **Joseph Pierce**
1222-3 **Ann Pierce**

122-3 **John Woodson**; d. by 2 Oct 1727 Henrico Co.; unmarried

Will of John Woodson; 3 Jan 1726; 2 Oct 1727
To bro. Samuel Woodson, 221 ac. from Matthew Gage and 93.5 ac. from Stephen Butler
To sister Martha Woodson, silver spoon

To cuzen Judith Woodson, 30s
Remainder to father Joseph Woodson, ex.
Wit: Thomas Atkinson, Jacob Michaux, Judith Woodson (HCVW-1 p. 164)
[John Woodson; Henrico Co. Wills & Admns. (1662-1800) p. 136. Will pr. 2 Oct 1727. Deeds &
Wills, 1726-1737 (Reel 7a) (LOV)]

122-4 Lucy Woodson

122-5 **Joseph Woodson**; d. by ca 1752 Henrico Co.; m. **Susanna** ___ ;
d. by Jan Ct. 1757 Henrico Co.; the will of John Pleasants written in
1771 mentions the land of the "late Joseph Woodson" (HCVW-2 p. 139);
children:

    1225-1 John Woodson
    1225-2 Joseph Woodson

Sep 1752; inventory of Joseph Woodson; value £255.19.5; presented by Susannah
Woodson (HCVW-2 p. 57)
[Joseph Woodson; Henrico Co. Wills & Admns. (1662-1800) p. 161. Inv. & Appr. rec. Sep 1752.
Deeds, Wills, Etc., 1750-1767 (Reel 9); p. 1769-1770. Accounts rec. 6 Nov 1758. p. 1979-1980.
Accounts rec. 1 Sep 1766. Misc. Court Records, Vol. 6, [1758-1769] (Reel 3 (LOV)]

Jan Ct. 1757; will of Susanna Woodson presented by Mary Sharp, extx. (HCVW-2 p. 71)
[Susanna Woodson; Goochland Co. Wills & Admns. (1728-1800) p. 209-210. Will pro. 15 Nov
1757; p. 296-297. Inv. & Appr. rec. 18 Jul 1758. Deed Book No. 7, 1755-1759 (Reel 3) (LOV)]

Jan Ct. 1757; John Woodson appointed guardian to John & Joseph Woodson, orphans
of Joseph; Charles Woodson, security; also appointed administrator (HCVW-2 p. 71)
Aug Ct. 1758; guardian, returned accts. for John & Joseph Woodson, orphans
of Joseph Woodson (HCVW-2 p. 75); Sep Ct. 1760; guardian to John & Joseph
Woodson, returns accounts (HCVW-2 p. 79)

1225-1 **John Woodson**; of *Carter's Ferry*; d. by 26 Aug 1793
Cumberland Co.; m. bef. 1746; **Elizabeth Hughes**; d. by 13 Sep
1805 Cumberland Co.; d/o Stephen Hughes of Cumberland Co.;
children:

    12251-1 John Hughes Woodson
    12251-2 Nancy Hughes Woodson
    12251-3 Mary Woodson
    12251-4 Judith Woodson
    12251-5 Elizabeth Woodson
    12251-6 Sarah Woodson

18 Mar 1746; 19 Mar 1746; from Stephen Hughes to John and Elizabeth Woodson, his
son in law & dau.; 438 [or 488] ac. in Goochland and Albemarle Co. (GCWD-3 p. 52;
GCRB 5.197; VP p. 1893)

May 1750; from Stephen Hughes to John Woodson and Elizabeth his wife, d/o Stephen
Hughes; at their decease to their dau. Judith, the part of her mother in Goochland Co.
(GCRB 6.54; VP p. 1897)

Will of Stephen Hughes of Cumberland Co.; to dau. Judith Cox; to dau. Elizabeth
Woodson, 5s; dated 6 Jul 1749 (CuWB 2.60; VP p. 1822-3); probated 25 Jun 1753 (LOV)

22 Aug 1766; from John Woodson, Sr. to John Woodson, Jr., both of Cumberland Co.; 225 ac. Cumberland Co. part of a tract granted to Joseph Woodson 6 Jul 1741 (CuDB 4.169; VP p. 1839)

20 Jan 1767; 20 Jan 1767; from John Woodson & Elizabeth his wife of Cumberland Co., to David Walker of Goochland Co.; 76 ac. Goochland Co. (GCRB 9.56; VP p. 1903)

18 Jan 1790; from John Woodson & Elizabeth his wife, Cumberland Co., to William Reynolds of City of Richmond; 400 ac. Goochland Co. (GCRB 15.337; VP p. 1907)

6 Nov 1792; John Woodson & Elizabeth his wife of Cumberland Co. to Elisha Meredith; lot #20 in Cartersville (CuDB 7.213; VP p. 1845)

Will of John Woodson of *Carter's Ferry* of Cumberland Co.; 9 Apr 1793; 26 Aug 1793; further proved 25 Sep 1793
Profits of my ferry, *Carter's Ferry*, and Woodson's tobacco warehouse adj. *Cartersville*, and the tavern being erected by me in *Cartersville* to pay my funeral expenses and debts
To wife Elizabeth Woodson, loan of slaves, my carriage, furniture, etc., profits from lands on s. side of James River in Cumberland Co. including lands where I live
To son John 600 ac. on n. side of James River in Goochland Co., ferry landing and 2 ac. on s. side of river after death of wife and debts paid; also furniture, horse, negro, etc.
To dau. Nancy Hughes Woodson, tract where I dwell, adj. tract, lot No. 1 in *Cartersville*, items
To dau. Mary Woodson, 300 ac. land in Cumberland Co. after death of wife, Woodson's warehouse, adj. lot, items
Having given to daus. Judith, late wife of Orlando Jones, Elizabeth wife of John Kennon and Sarah, late wife of Thomas Overton as much of my estate and I have "disined" for them, to Elizabeth, 1s; to representatives of sd. Judith & Sarah, dec'd, each 1s
Residue of estate to be divided among my son John and daus. Nancy and Mary at death of wife
Extx: wife Elizabeth, son John Woodson, Joseph Carrington, Mayo Carrington
Wit: Randolph Harrison, Frank B. Dean, Thos. M. Dean (CuWB 3.16; VP p. 1830-2)
[John Woodson of Carter's Ferry; CuWA (1749-1810) p. 16-18. Will, pro. 26 Aug 1793. WB No. 3, 1792-1810 (Reel 18) (LOV)]

Elizabeth Woodson of *Carter's Ferry*; Cumberland Co.; 23 Jun 1802; 13 Sep 1805; will mentions her former husband, John Woodson; son John Woodson, dau. Nancy H. Deane and grandchildren Francis, Elizabeth & John Deane (VP p. 1832-3)

    12251-1 **John Woodson**; d. by 28 May 1832 Cumberland Co.; calls himself "John Woodson of *Bear Garden*, Buckingham Co., s/o John Woodson of *Carter's Ferry*" and leaves his estate to his sister Nancy Dean, nephew Frances B. Deane, niece Elizabeth, w/o Robert Irving, and children of his dec'd sisters, Sally Overton and Elizabeth Kennon; unmarried

12 Aug 1794; from trustees of *Cartersville* to John Woodson of Cumberland Co.; lot #33 in *Cartersville* (CuDB 7.328; VP p. 1845)

12251-2 **Nancy Hughes Woodson**; m. **Francis B. Deane**; children from will of their grandmother Woodson:

122512-1 **Frances Deane**
122512-2 **Elizabeth Deane**
122512-3 **John Deane**

1790; from James & Thomas Deane of Cumberland Co. to Nancy H. Woodson, devisee of John Woodson & trustees of *Cartersville*; certain land in *Cartersville* (CuDB 7.386; VP p. 1845)

20 Mar 1794; from trustees of *Cartersville* to Nancy Hughes Woodson, devisee of John Woodson, dec'd; lot #1 in sd. town occupied by Wade Mosby's tavern (CuDB 7.313; VP p. 1845)

12251-3 **Mary Woodson**
12251-4 **Judith Woodson**; d. bef. 1793; m. **Orlando Jones**; child:

122514-1 **Lain Jones**

5 Feb 1789; 16 Feb 1789; from Lain Jones & Elizabeth, his wife, Albemarle Co., to John Woodson, Cumberland Co.; Stephen Hughes of Goochland, dec'd, did on 16 May 1750 deed 200 ac. Goochland Co. to Elizabeth, w/o John Woodson, on n. side of *Carter's Ferry* with remainder to Judith, d/o John & Elizabeth Woodson, and her heirs; Judith later m. Orlando Jones and died leaving issue, sd. Lain Jones (GCRB 15.196; VP p. 1906-7)

12251-5 **Elizabeth Woodson**; d. bef. 1832; mb. 10 Feb 1779 Cumberland Co. **John Kennon** of NC; John Woodson, security (VP p. 1848); they moved to Sparta, GA; one source says she m. William Kennon
12251-6 **Sarah Woodson**; d. bef. 1832; m. **Thomas Overton**

1225-2 **Joseph Woodson**; d. ca 1752; m. ____; possible children:

12252-1 **John Woodson**; in 1752 his grandfather Woodson made a deed of land on *Four Mile Creek* to John calling him "son and heir of my son Joseph, dec'd"
12252-1 **Joseph Woodson**

122-6 **Samuel Woodson**; he inherited 314.5 ac. from his bro. John in 1727

19 Aug 1729; 19 Aug 1729; from Mathew Oge [Age] of King William Parish, Goochland Co. to Samuel Woodson (s/o Joseph Woodson of *Little Low Ground*) of St. James Parish, being land in King William Parish where Oge did dwell on the river (GCWD-1 p. 15; GCRB 1.281; VP 1886)

122-7 **Martha Woodson**; she inherited from her bro. John in 1727
122-8 **Elizabeth Woodson**

12-3 **Samuel Tucker Woodson**, b. est. ca 1682; d. by 7 Jul 1718; 2nd son; he inherited from his grandfather Woodson, his mother &150 ac. on *Four*

Mile Creek from his father also he was one of the legatees in the 1708 will of his grandmother Jane Pleasant of *Curles*; unmarried

3 Dec 1715; 2 Jan 1715; from Samuel Tucker Woodson to Capt. Isham Epes; for £27; 25 ac. in Bermuda Hundred devised Samuel by his father John, Jr., dec'd, and confirmed 29 Jun 1714 by Joseph, bro. of Samuel (HCVD-2 p. 52)

Will of Samuel Tucker Woodson of Henrico Parish; 9 Dec 1717; 7 Jul 1718
To bro. Joseph Woodson, land on *Four Mile Creek*, 170 ac. at *Dover*
To sister Jane Woodson, 100 ac. at *Dover*
To bro. Benjamin Woodson, negroes, household goods, etc.
To cousin Tarlton Woodson, land at *Curles* that I bought of my bro. Joseph
Ex: brother Benjamin
Wit: Thomas Wadley, Charles Holmes, Martha Hatcher, Tarlton Woodson (HCVW-1 p. 146)
[Samuel Tucker Woodson; Henrico Co. Wills & Admns. (1662-1800) p. 341-342. Will dated 9 Dec 1717; p. 259-260. Will pro. 7 Jul 1718. Deeds, Wills, Etc., 1714-1718 (Reel 7) (LOV)]

Ct. 3 Oct 1720; exs. of William Irby, dec'd, vs. Benjamin Woodson, ex. of Samuel Tucker Woodson, dec'd; estate is to be attached (HCVW-2 p. 156)

12-4 **Benjamin Woodson**, b. ca. 1695; d. by 3 Sep 1778 Fluvanna Co.; 3rd son; said to have m. ca 1720 New Kent Co. **Frances Napier**, b. 5 Feb 1694/5 New Kent Co.; d/o Mary Perrin and Robert Napier; Benjamin lived in the area of Henrico which became Goochland Co.; he inherited 200 ac. on the river from his father and was mentioned in the will of his mother and 1708 will of his grandmother Jane Pleasants of *Curles* & the 1717 will of his brother Samuel; children:

    124-1 Booth Woodson, b. est. ca 1720's
    124-2 Benjamin Woodson, Jr., b. est. ca 1720's
    124-3 Mary Perrin Woodson, b. est. ca 1720's
    124-4 Rene Woodson, b. est. ca 1720-30's
    124-5 Frances Woodson, b. est. ca 1730's
    124-6 John Woodson, b. est. ca 1730-40's
    124-7 Patrick Woodson, b. est. ca 1740's

23 Sep 1730; Benjamin Woodson granted 400 ac. Goochland Co. on *Wildboar Branch* of *Lickinghole Creek* (LOP 13.538)

25 Aug 1731; Benjamin Woodson granted 200 ac. Goochland Co. on s. side *Rivanna* (LOP 14.261; VP p. 1813)

11 Apr 1732; Benjamin Woodson, Jr. and William Woodson granted 1,500 ac. Goochland Co. (LOP 14.440)

24 Mar 1734; Benjamin Woodson granted 400 ac. Goochland Co. in fork of James River on both sides of *Cary Creek* (LOP 15.475)

20 May 1749; Benjamin Woodson granted 394 ac. Goochland Co. among branches of *Cary Creek* on s. side *Rivanna River* (LOP 27..150 & 200)

16 Aug 1756; Benjamin Woodson granted 379 ac. Albemarle Co. on s. side *Rivanna River* (LOP 33.121)

16 Aug 1756; Benjamin Woodson granted 400 ac. Albemarle Co. on both sides of *Cary Creek* near head of *Rivanna* (LOP 33.299)

10 Aug 1760; from Benjamin Woodson of Albemarle Co. to Benjamin Woodson, Jr., of Goochland Co.; for £20; 200 ac. Albemarle Co. in fork of James River part of 400 ac. tract called *Raccoon*; adj. Woodson on *Little Raccoon* (AIDB 2.311: VP p. 1808)

10 Sep 1760; from Benjamin Woodson to Rene Woodson, both of Culpeper Co.; for £20; 400 ac. in fork of James River on branches of *Cary Creek* & *Little Breamor Creek* (AIDB2.313; VP p. 1809)

9 Nov 1761; from Benjamin Woodson of St. Ann's Parish, to his grandson Benjamin Fitzpatrick, both of Albemarle Co.; deed of gift; 200 ac. on head of *Cary Creek* Albemarle Co., part of 400 ac.; the other part of the land to son Benjamin Woodson, Jr. to be equally divided with Benjamin Fitzpatrick (AIDB 3.134; VP p. 1809)

8 Mar 1774; from Benjamin Woodson to Benjamin Anderson, both of Albemarle Co.; for goodwill; 200 ac. part of upper tract where Geo. Anderson lives (AIDB 6.264; VP p. 1810)

Will of Benjamin Woodson of Fluvanna Co.; 25 Oct 1777; 3 Sep 1778
To son Benjamin Woodson, Jr., part of my estate he now possesses
To son John Woodson, portion of my estate now in his possession; he to pay William
    Fitzpatrick £15 & giving Rene Napier right to 100 ac. on *Lickinghole Creek*,
    Goochland Co.
To son Rene Woodson; negro man plus what I have given him
To son Patrick Woodson, portion of my estate in his possession except 2 slaves I lend
    to my wife Frances during her life
To dau. Mary Perrin Fitzpatrick, negros
To dau. Frances Anderson and son in law George Anderson; 100 ac. and the plantation
    where they live for life, then to George Anderson, Jr.; also loan for life, 4 negroes,
    then to their children then living equally, excepting Benjamin Anderson
To granddau. Elizabeth Bouth Woodson, negro
Exs: sons Benjamin, Rene & Patrick and wife Frances
Wit: George Clough, Sr., Archbill Sneed, George Clough, Jr. (FIWB 1. 9; VP p. 1850)
[Benjamin Woodson; Fluvanna Co. Wills & Admns. (1777-1800) p. 9-11. Will pro. 3 Sep 1778.
WB 1, 1777-1808 (Reel 11) (LOV)]

124-1 Booth Woodson, b. est. ca 1720's; d. by 19 Jul 1757 Goochland; m. **Tabitha Cocke**; d/o James Cocke, Sr.; she m/2 **John Winston**; her father's will identifies the Winston children; the will of Rene Napier proved 19 Nov 1751 mentions "cousin Booth Woodson"

21 Jan 1734; [recorded]; deed from Adam Buttrey (Britteny) of Goochland Co.; to godson Bouth Woodson; s/o Benjamin and Frances Woodson; for £10 paid by his father; 120 ac. on s. side of then. fork of James River (GCWD-1 p. 65; VP p. 1886)

Will of Bouth (Booth) Woodson; Goochland Co.; 14 Nov 1756; 19 Jul 1757
If my wife Tabitha be with child and sd. child lives, the child & estate to stay with my
    wife until she marries; if child died without heirs, estate to be equally divided
    between my 4 bros. or their heirs

If there is no child, my wife to have her fortune that came by her and I lend her the plantation where I now live and 2 negroes so long as she is a widow; she to pay John Harris £20

To my mother my other two negroes for life

Then to my brother Renee Woodson, plantation in Albemarle Co. & negro; he to pay my sister Anderson's 2 sons, Benjamin & George £15

To bros. John & Patrick Woodson, 400 ac. called *Middle Strip* equally; them paying my sister FitzPatrick's 2 eldest sons each £15

To bro. Patrick, negro boy

Exs: To bro. Benjamin, George Anderson, bro. John and my father Benjamin Woodson

Wit: Bouth Napier, Elizabeth Napier, Bouth Woodson (GCRB 7.179; VP p. 1857)

11 Oct 1757; 17 Jul 1759; Booth Woodson; inventory value £53.15.6 (GCRB 8.28; VP p. 1877)

[Bouth (Booth) Woodson; Goochland Co. Wills & Admns. (1728-1800) p. 28. Inv. & Appr. rec. 17 Jul 1759. Deed Book No. 8, 1859-1765; (1728-1800) p. 179a-179b. Will pro. 19 Jul 1757. Deed Book No. 7, 1755-1759 (Reel 3) (LOV)]

Jun Ct. 1757; motion of Tabitha Woodson, widow & relict of Bouth Woodson, dec'd; ordered that Benjamin Woodson, heir at law of sd. Bouth, Geo. Anderson, Benjamin Woodson, Sr. & Frances Woodson ordered to appear next court and produce will of sd. Bouth (GCOB 8.2; VP 1938)

124-2 **Benjamin Woodson, Jr.**, b. est. ca 1720's; d. by 25 Apr 1808 Fluvanna Co.; m/1 bef. 4 Dec 1757 Goochland Co. **Rebecca Cocke**; sister of Tabitha; m/2 20 Sep 1783 Fluvanna Co. **Frances (Franky) Jordan**, by Wm. Moore (VP p. 1853); William Barnet made a deed of land 18 Oct 1742 to Benjamin Woodson, s/o Benjamin (GCWD-3 p. 33); he was given 200 ac. in Albemarle Co. by his father in 1761; children from St. James Northam Parish and their father's will:

        1242-1   Elizabeth Woodson
        1242-2   William Woodson
        1242-3   Booth Woodson, b. 4 Dec 1757
        1242-4   Frances Woodson, b. 17 Dec 1759
        1242-5   Tabitha Woodson, b. 11 Jul 1763
        1242-6   Rebecca Woodson, b. 29 Mar 1766
        1242-7   Sarah (Sally) Woodson, b. 6 Jul 1768
        1242-8   Benjamin Woodson; b. 8 Jul 1770

7 Aug 1777; from Benjamin Woodson to son Patrick Woodson, both of Fluvanna Co.; 100 ac. upper part of tract I now live on (FIDB 1.12; VP p. 1851)

4 Sep 1777; from Benjamin Woodson, Sr. & Frances his wife to their grandson George Anderson, Jr. of Fluvanna Co.; 100 ac. part of 400 ac. tract Fluvanna Co.; 200 ac. previously conveyed Ben Anderson (FIDB 1.31; VP p. 1852)

Will of Benjamin Woodson of Fluvanna Co.; 8 Oct 1807; 25 Apr 1808

To dau. Elizabeth Napier, 3 negroes for life; to be equally divided between her children at her decease

To son William Woodson, 300 ac. formerly given him in Fluvanna Co. on *Little Cary Creek*, 2 negroes

To son Bouth Woodson, what I have previously given, with land I now live on after my wife's death or marriage, also negro

To dau. Tabitha Napier, I lend 100 ac. during her life where she now lives then to her son William Napier; also 3 negroes for life, then divided between her children

To dau. Sally Williams, loan of 7 negroes during life, then to her children

To my wife Franky Woodson, negro woman and her increase during life, then to her children; also horse, furniture, 5 head of cattle; loan of house and land where I now live & negro so long as she remains a widow, then land to my son Bouth, negro to my son William; also sheep, hogs, etc.

Plantation not to be rented or leased

To grandson Benjamin Woodson Napier, negro, mare

Remainder of estate to be divided equally between my 2 sons and 3 daus.

Exs: William , Bouth, & Samuel T. Woodson

Wit: Frankey Woodson, Jane Woodson, Martha Woodson (FIWB 1.338; VP p. 1850-1)

> 1242-1 **Elizabeth Woodson**; m. 29 Sep 1776 St. James Northam **Patrick Napier**, in this parish (DR)
>
> 1242-2 **William Woodson**; inherited land Fluvanna Co. from father
>
> 1242-3 **Booth Woodson**, b. 4 Dec 1757; bapt. 25 Jul 1758 (DR); not mentioned in his father's will
>
> 1242-4 **Frances Woodson**, b. 17 Dec 1759; bapt. 24 Jun 1760 (DR); m. 22 May 1783 Fluvanna Co. **Richard Adams**; by W. Moore (VP p. 1853); not mentioned in her father's will
>
> 1242-5 **Tabitha Woodson**, b. 11 Jul 1763; 30 Oct 1763 (DR); said to have mb. 5 Jan 1786 Flauvanna Co. **Renier Napier**
>
>> 12425-1 **William Napier**; named in will of grandfather Woodson
>
> 1242-6 **Rebecca Woodson**, b. 29 Mar 1766; bapt. 15 Jun 1766 (DR); not mentioned in her father's will
>
> 1242-7 **Sarah (Sally) Woodson**, b. 6 Jul 1768; 27 Jan 1769 (DR); m. ____ **Williams**
>
> 1242-8 **Benjamin Woodson**; b. 8 Jul 1772; bapt. 27 Sep 1772 (DR); not mentioned in his father's will

> 124-3 **Mary Perrin Woodson**, b. est. ca 1720's; said to have m. **Joseph Fitzpatrick**, b. Ireland; child from will of grandfather Woodson:
>
>> 1243-1 **Benjamin Fitzpatrick**; in 1761 his grandfather Woodson made him a deed of gift for 200 ac. Albemarle Co.
>>
>> 1243-2 **Joseph Fitzpatrick**

> 124-4 **Rene Woodson**, b. est. ca 1720-30's; m/1 **Mary Thompson**; d. 1759 in childbirth; Rene "in Albemarle" m/2 2 Feb 1775 St. James Northam Parish **Martha Johnson** "in Louisa"; children [see 1814 will of Rene Woodson in Fluvanna Co. for more descendants]:
>
>> 1244-1 **Elizabeth Booth Woodson**, b. 16 Feb 1759; bapt. 2 May 1759 (DR); she inherited cattle from her grandfather Woodson in 1778

1244-2 Frances "Fanny" Woodson, b. 23 Aug 1780; bapt. 26 Aug 1781 (DR)

13 Jun 1764; from Rene Woodson of Albemarle Co. to Anthony Minter of Cumberland Co.; for £120; 400 ac. Albemarle Co. in fork of James River on branches of *Cary Creek & Little Bramer Creek*; granted Benjamin Woodson by patent 24 Mar 1734; Rene purchased of Benjamin (AIDB 3.455; VP 1809)

19 Mar 1768; from Rena Woodson to Roger Thompson, both of Albemarle Co.; for £100; 125 ac. called *Broken Island*; sd. tract conveyed to him by his bro. Booth Woodson (AIDB 4.497; VP p. 1809)

20 Oct 1797; from Rene Woodson to James Logon, both of Fluvanna; for £20; 60 ac in Fluvanna on *Little Raccoon Creek*; part of land I now live on (FIDB 1.535)

124-5 Frances Woodson, b. est. ca 1730's; m. by 1753 **George Anderson**; children:

1245-1 Susannah Anderson, b. 22 Sep 1753 Albemarle Co. (DR)

1245-2 Benjamin Anderson; mentioned in will of grandfather Woodson

1245-3 George Anderson, Jr.; mentioned in will of grandfather Woodson

124-6 John Woodson, b. est. ca 1730-40's; d. bef. 25 Oct 1803 Goochland Co.; mb. 18 Mar 1760; John "of Albemarle" m. 20 Mar 1760 St. James Northam **Mary Mimms** in this parish (DR; VP p. 1949); d/o David Mimms; sec. Charles Christian; wit. Val. Wood; children:

1246-1 Jane (Jennie) Booth Woodson, b. 25 Oct 1760; bapt. 19 Jul 1761 (DR); mb. 22 Sep 1779; m. 23 Sep 1779 Goochland **Richard Clough**; child:

12461-1 Mary Clough, b. 9 Mar 1782 Goochland

1246-2 Elizabeth Woodson, b. 22 May 1764; bapt. 12 Aug 1764 (DR)

1246-3 Samuel Tucker Woodson, b. Sep 1769; bapt. 31 Oct 1770 (DR); m. **Elizabeth** ____

1246-4 Booth Woodson, b. 28 Aug 1771; bapt. Sep 1773 (DR)

1246-5 John Woodson

25 Oct 1803; Samuel Tucker Woodson and Elizabeth his wife, Richard Clough and Jane B. his wife, Elizabeth Woodson, Bouth Woodson, John Woodson and Mary, widow of John Woodson the elder, make agreement for division of estate of John Woodson, dec'd (GCDB 19.412; VP p. 1914)

124-7 Patrick Woodson, b. est. ca 1740's; d. Fluvanna Co.; m. **Nancy Cloof**; [his name also given as Fitzpatrick]; children:

1247-1 Molly Woodson, b. 25 Jul 1771; bapt. 21 Oct 1781 (DR)

1247-2 Nancy Woodson, b. 16 Aug 1781; bapt. 21 Oct 1781 (DR)

12-5 Mary Woodson, b. ca 1700; b. after the death of her father; not mentioned in will of her grandmother Jane (__) Tucker Pleasants

2. Robert Woodson, b. ca 1634, age 46 on 1 Jun 1680 (HCVD-1 p. 148); d. aft. 1707 Varina Parish; m. **Elizabeth Ferris**; d/o Richard Ferris of *Curles*, Henrico Co.; Robert held 1,494 ac. when the survey of Henrico Parish was done 11 Feb 1706 (HCVD-2 p. 13); children:

> 2-1 John Woodson, b. est. 1658
> 2-2 Robert Woodson, b. est. ca 1660
> 2-3 Richard Woodson, b. est. ca 1662
> 2-4 Joseph Woodson, b. est. ca 1664
> 2-5 Benjamin Woodson, b. 21 Aug 1666
> 2-6 Mary Woodson, b. est. ca 1668
> 2-7 Sarah Woodson, b. est. ca 1670
> 2-8 Elizabeth Woodson, b. est. ca 1672
> 2-9 Judith Woodson, b. est. ca 1674

26 Jun 1670; Robert Woodson granted 1,192 ac. 3r. 32po. on n. side of James River along Ludwell line (LOP 6.287)

21 Oct 1687; Robert Woodson, Sr., John Woodson, Sr., Wm. Lewis, Thomas Charles, granted 470 ac. Varina Parish Henrico Co. on n. side of James River on a western branch of *Deep Run* (LOP 7. 602)

21 Oct 1687; Robert Woodson, Sr., Giles Carter, Wm. Ferris & Roger Cummins [Comeings] granted 1780 ac. Verina Parish, Henrico Co. on n. side of James River at *White Oak Swamp* (LOP 7.601); 2 Jun 1690; William Ferris never paid & relinquished; Comeings died and never paid; tract fell to Woodson (428 ac.), Carter (552 ac.) and Richard Ferris (600 ac.) (HCVD-1 p. 57)

1 Jan 1694; 1 Jun 1694; deed of gift from Robert Woodson, Sr. to son Robert Woodson, both of Henrico Co.; 250 ac. on s. side of *White Oak Swamp* (HCVD-1 p. 84)

30 Apr 1707; 1 May 1707; from Robert Woodson, Sr. of Henrico Co. to grandsons William & Joseph Lewis, 450 ac. patented by me and Ferris, Carter, Harris & Commins on 21 Oct 1687 on *White Oak Swamp* (HCVD-2 p. 5)

2-1 John Woodson; b. est. ca 1658; d. by 5 Dec 1715; Quaker of Henrico Co.; wheelwright, carpenter, merchant; m. bef. 30 Mar 1689 **Judith Tarleton**; d. aft. 1712; d/o Stephen Tarlton & Susannah Bates; he inherited the small tract where his house stood from the 1684 will of his uncle John; children from their father's will:

> 21-1 Tarleton Woodson
> 21-2 Jacob Woodson
> 21-3 John Woodson
> 21-4 Robert Woodson, Jr.
> 21-5 Josiah Woodson
> 21-6 Stephen Woodson
> 21-7 Judith Woodson
> 21-8 Elizabeth Woodson

30 Mar 1689; 1 Apr 1689; from John Woodson, Sr. to William Randolph, both of Henrico Co. & Parish; 400 ac. part of 1,800 ac. on *Chickahominy River*; Judith, w/o John, relinquished dower (HCVD-1 p. 49)

30 Mar 1689; 30 Mar 1689; from John Woodson to Benjamin Hatcher, both of Henrico Co.; 200 ac. on s. side of *Chickahominy Swamp*; Judith, w/o John, relinquished dower (HCVD-1 p. 49)

2 Jun 1690; from John Woodson, wheelwright, to bro. Robert Woodson, Jr., both of Henrico Co.; 106 ac.; 1/5 of a patent to Robert Woodson, Sr., John Woodson, Thomas East, William Porter and Robert Clark on s. side of *White Oak Swamp* (HVCD-1 p. 58)

1 Feb 1698/9; John Woodson Sr. of Henrico Co., for 2,000# tobacco paid by my father Robert Woodson, Sr. for use of my brother Robert Woodson, 180 ac. on s. side of *Chickahominy Swamp* (HCVD-1 p. 107)

25 Sep 1701; John Woodson, Sr. granted 1,020 ac. Varina Parish in *Rawsonsey Neck* (LOP 9.321)

30 Jul 1703; 2 Aug 1703; from John Woodson, merchant, to Hugh Jones, planter; for 200 ac. conveyed him by Jones, Woodson conveys 500 ac on n. side of James River next to *Half Cinque*; part of a tract granted him 25 Apr 1701; Judith, wife of John relinquished dower (HCVD-1 p. 127)

3 Feb 1706; survey of Henrico Parish; John Woodson, 1,596 ac. (HCVD-2 p. 12); 9 Apr 1708; John Woodson, 850 ac. (HCVD-2 p. 13)

1 Mar 1712; from John Woodson of Henrico Co. & Parish to John Pirant of New Kent Co.; for £40; 290 ac. on *Chickahominy Swamp* near *Half Sink*; part of Woodson's patent; Judith, w/o Woodson, relinquished dower (HCVD-2 p. 37)

Will of John Woodson; 25 Nov 1715; 5 Dec 1715
To son Tarlton, *Neck of Land* and 1,000 ac. at *Dover* on n. side of James River next to Charles Fleming, *Beaver Dam Creek*, etc.
To son Jacob, land at *Dover*, next to his bro. Tarlton; also 348 ac. tract opposite *Elk Island*
To son John, land next to his bro. Jacob, except 100 ac. given Josiah Paine (s/o George and Mary Paine); also tract with my corn mill & part of *Sabot Island*
To son Robert, land below his bro. John's land, including sawmill & part of *Sabot Island*; he and his bro. Josiah to divide equally land at *Half Sink* on *Chickahominy Swamp*, less 150 ac.
Above 4 sons each ½ (sic) *Elk Island*
To son Josiah, land below his bro. Robert on the river
To son Stephen, tract down river below his bro. Josiah & remainder *Sabot Island*
To dau. Judith, tract down river below her bro. Stephen next to Womack
To dau. Elizabeth, tract down river below her sister Judith
To each child, slaves; personal estate equally between 8 children
Tarlton to confirm land at *Chickahominy Swamp* to my bro. Benjamin Woodson
Exs: sons Tarlton, John, Robert and Jacob
Wit: Arthur Markham, Edward East, Barth. Newcome, Mathew Dod (HCVW-1 p. 136)
23 Apr 1716; 7 May 1716; inventory of John Woodson appraised value £381.1.49; presented in court by Tarlton Woodson, Quaker (HCVW-1 p. 138)

7 Jan 1722; Tarlton, John, Robert & Jacob Woodson, exs. of their father John Woodson of Henrico Co. to Jean Jouany; 200 ac. on s. side of James River part of 500 ac. survey (HCVD-2 p. 82); John & Robert Woodson, Jr. to Jean Jouanil , deed (HCVD-2 p. 197; VP p. 1951)

Oct 1733; accounts of estate of John Woodson by Tarlton Woodson (HCVW-1 p. 188) 1 Sep 1735; accounts of estate of John Woodson by Tarlton and John Woodson, exs. (HCVW-1 p. 205)

[John Woodson; Henrico Co. Wills & Admns. (1662-1800) p. 56-59. Will pro. 5 Dec 1715. p. 81-85. Inv. & appr. rec. 7 May 1716. Deeds, Wills, Etc. 1714-1718 (Reel 7); p. 410-411. Accounts rec. Oct 1733. Deeds & Wills, 1725-1737 (Reel 7a) {LOV}]

21-1 **Tarleton Woodson**; d. by Apr 1763 Chesterfield Co.; m. 3d/6m/1710 New Kent Co. meeting to **Ursula Fleming**, d/o Charles Fleming of New Kent Co. (QRH p. 6; VP p. 2046); he inherited land at *Curles* from his cousin Samuel Tucker Woodson; also tracts at *Neck of Land, Dover, Beaver Creek Dam*, etc., from his father's will; children from various records:

        211-1   Susannah Woodson
        211-2   Charles Woodson
        211-3   Tarleton Woodson
        211-4   Sarah Woodson
        211-5   Judith Woodson
        211-6   Mary Woodson
        211-7   Jacob Woodson
        211-8   George Woodson
        211-9   Frederick Woodson

17 Apr 1710; after Tarlton Woodson and Judith (sic) Fleming proposed their marriage, meeting discussed whether marriages to 1st cousins were agreeable according to scripture (QRH p. 5)

4 Jun 1716; 4 Jun 1716; from Tarlton Woodson of Henrico Co to William Howl, Jr. of New Kent; for £10; 220 ac. being 1/6 part of 1,324 ac. grant to John Woodson, Sr. on s. side of *Chickahominy Swamp*; ack. Ursula, w/o Tarlton, relinquished dower rights (HCVD-2 p. 53)

1 Nov 1716; 5 Nov 1716; from Tarlton Woodson, eldest son and heir of John Woodson, dec'd, of Henrico Co. & Parish, to Charles Evans of Westopher Parish, Charles City Co., writer, for £40; 100 ac on n. side of James River at *Dover* a mile above *Genito Creek*; part of a larger tract; Ursula, w/o Tarlton, relinquished dower (HCVD-2 p. 56, 57)

7 Jan 1716; 7 Jan 1716; from Tarlton Woodson to Benjamin Woodson, the elder, both of Henrico Co.; for 5,000# tobacco paid to his father John Woodson, dec'd, sells to Benjamin 500 ac. on s. south of *Chickahominy Swamp* being part of a patent to John Woodson, dec'd (HCVD-2 p. 59)

7 Oct 1717; [recorded]; from Tarlton & John Woodson, sons of John Woodson, of Henrico Co. to John Thornton of New Kent Co.; for £80; 1,278 ac. of *Elk Island* granted Charles Fleming and John Woodson 16 Jun 1714 (HCVD-2 p. 68)

6 Apr 1719; from William Womack of Henrico Parish, to Tarlton and John Woodson, 2 of the exs. of John Woodson; for £50; 450 ac. lower part of 550 ac. tract where Womack dwells (HCVD-2 p. 79)

5 Jun 1727; Jun 1727; from Tarlton Woodson to William Randolph; for £5; 20 ac. on n. side of James River conveyed by deed 8 Jan 1674 by Nathaniel Bacon to Robert Woodson, grandfather of Tarlton (HCVD-2 p. 100)

17 Apr 1736; 20 Apr 1756; from Tarlton Woodson of Henrico Co. to Col. John Fleming of Goochland Co.; 1,292 ac. part of 3,090 ac. patent called *Licking Hole Survey* dated 11 Jul 1719; 1.798 ac. sold in several parcels by John Woodson, Sr. & Tarleton (GCRB 3.3197)

1 Aug 1737; 1st Mon Sep 1737; from Tarlton Woodson to Joseph Hobson, both of Henrico Co.; for £10; __ ac. part of patent to Robert Woodson, the elder (HCVD-2 p. 183)

18 Feb 1739; 19 Feb 1739; from Tarlton Woodson of Henrico Co. to John Woodson of Goochland Co.; for £20; 600 ac. of 892 ac. formerly granted John Woodson, dec'd, on branch of *Jenetoe* and *Indian Graves Creek*; Tarlton stands seized of as ex. of his father John Woodson (GCWD-2 p. 37; GCRB 3.269; VP p. 1890)

24 Oct 1745; 19 Mar 1745; from Tarlton & Stephen Woodson of Henrico to Tucker Woodson of Goochland; 260 ac. Goochland Co. where Goochland Court House now stands (GCRB 5.58; VP p. 1895)

4 May 1747; 19 May 1747; from Tarlton Woodson to Robert Pleasants; 630 ac. on n. side James River, Goochland Co.; part of 3,090 ac. granted Tarlton (GCRB 5.246)

27 Oct 1750; from Tarlton Woodson Chesterfield Co. to son Jacob Woodson; 100 ac. where he now lives in Goochland Co. at *Poddom Bottom* near *Beaver Dam Creek* (GCRB 6.118; VP p. 1896)

Will of Tarleton Woodson, Chesterfield Co.; 4 Dec 1761; Apr 1763

To son Tarleton Woodson for life, 500 ac. Goochland Co., adj. Fleming, James River, Pleasants, & land of my son Jacob Woodson, dec'd; should he die without issue, to testator's grandsons James & Joseph Pleasants; should they die to testator's grandson George Cheadles

To son Tarleton for life, 213 ac. Goochland Co.; land given in will of Roger Powell to Matthew Pleasants, grandson of testator, to be given to testator's dec'd son Jacob; if Tarleton die without issue to testator's grandson Matthew Pleasants for life, entail as above

To grandson Matthew Pleasants for life, 212 ac. in Goochland Co. near *Jinto Creek*; shd. he die without issue to testator's grandson James Pleasants

To dau. Susanna Pleasants and her son Archibald Pleasants as joint tenants for life then to Archibald's issue if any, if not to testator's grandson Matthew Pleasants; 299 ac. in Goochland near *Beaver Dam Creek* where testator's son Jacob Woodson lived

To dau. Judith Cheadle and her son George Cheadle as joint tenants for life, then to the issue of sd. George Cheadle; if no issue to testator's grandson Thomas Cheadle [land not described]

To son Charles Woodson; 2 tracts in Chesterfield and Henrico Cos.

To John Cannon, testator's right to 100 ac. in will of testator's father

To son Tarleton Woodson, 3 negroes

To dau. Judith Cheadle's four youngest children, 4 negroes
To dau. Sarah Terrill, horse
To testator's 6 children: Charles and Tarleton Woodson, Susanna Pleasants, Sarah
　Terrill, Mary Pleasants, Judith Cheadle, 19 negroes
Exs: testator's 6 children
Wit: John Townley, Ed. Folkes, Ed. Folkes, Jr., John Sharp (ChWB 1.496; VP p. 1813-4)
1 Apr 1763; will of Tarleton Woodson, dec'd; will proved (ChOB 3.399; VP 1819)

> **211-1 Susannah Woodson**; d/o Tarlton of Henrico Co. m. 7d/9m/1731
> **John Pleasants**; s/o Joseph Pleasants of Henrico Co. (QRH p. 17)
>
> **211-2 Charles Woodson**; Quaker of *Curles* Henrico Co.; d. by 18 Feb
> 1796 Powhatan Co.; s/o Tarlton; intent to marry 4/12/1737; m/1
> 5d/1m/1737 at house of John Pleasants Henrico Co. **Mary Pleasants**
> (VP p. 2050); d/o "old" John Pleasants & his 1st marriage; m/2 marriage
> intent 1/10/1744; m/2 1d/10m/1744 intent; m/2 16d/12m/1744 Henrico
> Co. **Agnes Parsons**; d/o Joseph Parsons & widow of **Samuel**
> **Richardson**; d. by 1742 (QRH p.23, 94; HCVW-2 p. 110; VP p. 2052); Agnes'
> children of m/1 were George Richardson, b. 10 Jun 1740 & Samuel
> Richardson, b. 20 Nov 1741; children:

> > 2112-1　Charles Woodson
> > 2112-2　David Woodson
> > Children of m/2:
> > 2112-3　Agnes Woodson, 14 Dec 1745
> > 2112-4　George Woodson, b. 4 May 1747
> > 2112-5　Sarah Woodson, b. 4 Aug 1749
> > 2112-6　Caroline Matilda Woodson, 17 Oct 1751
> > 2112-7　Tarleton Woodson, b. 18 Mar 1754
> > 2112-8　Frederick Woodson, b. 24 Mar 1756
> > 2112-9　Ursula Woodson, b. 30 Jan 1760

[undated]; from Charles Woodson of Henrico Co. deed of gift to son George Woodson;
Neck of Land on s. side of James River in Chesterfield Co. (ChDB 6.383; VP p. 1817)

Aug 1745; accts. of Samuel & George Richardson, orphans of Samuel Richardson, by
Charles Woodson, guardian (HCVW-2 p. 46)

5 May 1746; 1st Mon May 1746; from Charles Woodson and Agnes his wife to John
Williamson, both of Henrico Co. & Parish; for £100; 273 ac. in Henrico Parish near
Uppam Brook granted Samuel Richardson 10 Sep 1735 which he devised to his wife
Agnes by his will (HCVD-3 p. 26)

Sep 1747; accounts of George & Samuel Richardson, orphans of Samuel Richardson;
mentions quit rents paid to sheriff of Goochland Co.; recorded by Charles Wilson,
guardian of orphans (HCVW-2 p. 36); Aug Ct. 1758; Charles Woodson, guardian of
George & Samuel Richardson, orphans of Samuel Richardson, returns accounts
(HCVW-2 p. 75); Aug Ct. 1760; Charles Woodson guardian for George and Samuel
Richardson (HCVW-2 p. 78)

17 Mar 1764; 24 Mar 1764; from Charles Woodson, eldest son & heir of Tarlton
Woodson, late of Chesterfield Co., dec'd, to bro. Tarlton Woodson, 2nd son of sd.
Tarlton Woodson, dec'd, who many years ago (upwards of 21 yrs. ago) put his son

Tarlton in possession of 500 ac. on James River and 213 ac. about ¾ miles from first tract with a promise to convey to sd. Tarlton his son; Charles his bro. conveys tracts (GCRB 8.390; VP p. 1900-1)

19 Feb 1765; from John Toms of Chesterfield Co. to Charles Woodson of Henrico Co.; for £25 in Chesterfield Co.; being land deed to sd. Toms by Tarleton Woodson, father of sd. Charles (ChDB 5. 477; VP 1817)

16 Mar 1775; from Charles Woodson to his son Tarleton Woodson; 200 ac in Cumberland Co. at head of *Solomon's Creek* (CuDB 5.342; VP p. 1840)

23 Mar 1778; from Charles Woodson of Powhatan Co. to son Charles Woodson; 100 ac. land in Powhatan Co.; mentions *Fine Creek* (PoDB 1.29; VP p. 2028)

24 Mar 1778; 25 Jun 1778; from Charles Woodson, Powhatan Co., to his son Charles Woodson; 200 ac. in Goochland Co. (GCRB 12.135; VP p. 1903)

23 Mar 1778; from Charles Woodson to son Frederick Woodson; 500 ac. in Powhatan on upper branch of *Solomon's* & *Fine Creek*; adj. Charles Woodson, Jr. (PoDB 1.80; VP. 2028)

9 Dec 1782; from Charles Woodson of Powhatan Co. to son Tarleton; 4 negro slaves (PoDB 1.226; VP p. 2029)

20 Mar 1783; from Charles Woodson deed of gift to son George Woodson; 200 ac. in Chesterfield Co. called *Tims*; formerly purchased by Tarleton Woodson, father of sd. Charles from John Soane 21 Aug 1728 (ChDB 11.102; VP p. 1818)

24 Mar 1783; from Charles Woodson to son Frederick; 8 negro slaves (PoDB 1.285)

14 Jan 1786; from Charles Woodson to sons George & Tarleton Woodson; power of atty. to sell his slaves and pay his debts (PoDB 1.353; VP 2030)

14 Jan 1786; from Charles Woodson of Powhatan Co. to Tarleton Woodson of Prince Edward Co.; 3 negro slaves; also 3 negro slaves to son George Woodson; and 4 negro slaves to son Frederick Woodson (PoDB 1. 460, 461; VP p. 2030)

6 Oct 1792; from Charles Woodson of Powhatan Co. to son Frederick Woodson; 42 ac. in Powhatan Co. adj. Charles Woodson (PoDB 2.28; VP p. 2030)

19 Dec 1793; from Charles Woodson of Powhatan Co. to dau. Ursula Woodson; 2 negro slaves (PoDB 2.50; VP 2031)

10 Jul 1795; from Charles Woodson to son George Woodson; receipt to him as agent for sd. Charles (PoDB; VP p. 2031)

[Charles Woodson, Sr.; Powhatan Wills & Admns. p. 189-190. Will pro. 18 Feb 1796. p. 222. Inv. & Appr. rec. 21 Apr 1796. p. 222. Inv. & Appr. of estate in Henrico Co. rec. 21 Apr 1796. DB No. 2, 1792-1800 (Reel 1) (LOV)]

> **2112-1 Charles Woodson, Jr.**; d. by 15 Oct 1789 Powhatan Co.; s/o Charles Woodson [& Mary Pleasants] of Henrico Co.; intent to marry 5/12/1767; 6/2/1768 marriage of Charles Woodson, Jr. accomplished; m. 2d/1m/1768 at Curles Meeting House **Ann Trotter** (VP p. 2056); d. by 18 Jun 1806 Powhatan Co. (PoWB 2.432; VP p. 2027-8);

d/o Thomas Trotter of Nansemond Co. (QRH p. 45, 46); Charles was ex. of the 1771 will of his grandfather John Pleasants from whom he inherited 100 ac. in Cumberland Co where he now lives; Charles & wife Ann within limits of Circular Monthly Meeting (QRH p. 47); he may have been the Charles Woodson of Wyanoak Meeting which reported that he had absented himself from his wife for several years and taken to strong drink [disowned] (QRH p. 56); children from his will:

21121-1 **Ann Woodson**; mb. 10 May 1792 Powhatan Co. **William Pope**; Frederick Woodson, security; consent of Ann Woodson to dau. Ann Woodson's marriage (VP p. 2032); as Ann, d/o Charles and Ann, she inherited a negro from the 1776 will of Joseph Pleasants of Henrico Co. (HCVW-2 141)

21121-2 **Mary Woodson**

21121-3 **Elizabeth Woodson**

21121-4 **Sarah Woodson**

5 Feb 1765; from John Pleasants of Henrico Co.; deed of gift to grandson Charles Woodson, s/o Charles Woodson and my dau. Mary his wife, dec'd; 400 ac. Cumberland purchased 12 Dec 1752 (CuDB; VP p. 1838)

19 Jun 1780; 20 Nov 1780; from Charles Woodson, the younger of Powhatan Co., & Ann his wife, to William Royster; 200 ac. Goochland Co.; part of tract granted Tarlton Woodson, late of Chesterfield Co, dec'd, who sold it to his son Jacob Woodson 9 Jun 1756; he died without issue and sd. land descended to Charles Woodson the elder who conveyed it to Charles Woodson the younger (GCRB 13.47; VP p. 1904)

Will of Charles Woodson, Jr., Powhatan Co.; 7 Jun 1789; 15 Oct 1789; 17 Dec 1789
To wife Ann during life, plantation where I now live; then to my dau. Elizabeth
To dau. Mary, plantation called *Cold Comfort*; also 100 ac. given me by my father adj. sd. plantation; also 2 lots in town of Manchester
To dau. Sarah, land in Hanover and Goochland Cos.
To dau. Ann, land in Powhatan Co. recently purchased of my bro. Frederick
To wife all slaves she brought me by marriage; also 2 slaves for life then to be divided amongst all my children; personal estate to be equally divided amongst same; estate to be maintained for 6 years, then divided
Exs. wife Ann and brother Frederick Woodson
Wit: James Bryden, Peter Pollock, Batt. Stovall, Tarleton Woodson (PoWB 1.170; VP p. 2025)
[Charles Woodson, Jr.; Powhatan Wills & Admns. (1777-1800) p. 167-169. Inv. & Appr. rec. 18 Feb 1790. p. 170-171. Will Pro. 15 Oct 1789 & bond rec. 17 Dec 1789. WB No. 1, 1777-1795 (Reel 15); Powhatan Wills & Admns. (1777-1800) p. 470-474. Accounts Rec. 19 Jul 1798. p. 373-478. Estate division rec. 19 Jul 1798. DB No. 2, 1792-1800 (Reel 1) (LOV)]

2112-2 **David Woodson**; s/o Mary Pleasants; he, as s/o Charles, inherited a negro from the 1776 will of Jonathan Pleasants (HCVW-2 p. 141)

29 Oct 1778; from David Woodson of Rowan Co., NC to Uriah Squires of Bedford Co.; for £75; 100 ac. on s. branches *Goose Creek* (BeDB F6.162; VP p. 1814)

2 Nov 1778; from David Woodson of Rowan Co., NC to William Ferrell of Bedford
Co.; for £1,100; 1,400 ac. on *Stony Fork*, s. branch of *Goose Creek* Bedford Co. (BeDB
F6.167; VP p. 1814)

> 2112-3 **Agnes Woodson**, 14 Dec 1745; d/o Charles; intent to marry
> 4/4/1772; m. 2d/5m/1772 at Curles Meeting **John Ellyson**, s/o
> Robert Ellyson of New Kent Co. (QRH p. 49, 50; VP p. 2056); m/2
> **Alexander Bolling** of Campbell Co.
>
> 2112-4 **George Woodson**, b. 4 May 1747 (Bates Bible); d. 18 Oct 1800
> Chesterfield Co. (ChDB 15.177; VP p. 1818); m. 5 Sep 1783 **Sarah
> (Sally) Friend**; d/o Thomas Friend of Chesterfield Co.; surviving
> children from his will and family histories:
>
>> 21124-1 Charles F. Woodson
>> 21124-2 Caroline Woodson
>> 21124-3 Margaret Woodson

10 Jul 1775; George and Frederick Woodson among those disowned by Curles
Meeting for enlisting as soldiers (QRH p. 53)

5 Mar 1785; George Woodson qualified as Justice of the Peace (ChOB 7.97; VP p. 1820)

1787; George Woodson, owner of the sloop *Flat Dolphin* of 28 Hhd. burden; Randolph
Spence, skipper with 3 fore men & 5 slaves; registered in court (ChOB 7.542; VP p. 1820

1792; George Woodson, gent., Sheriff of Chesterfield Co.; gives bond for the year
1792 (ChOB 9.530; VP p. 1820)

Will of George Woodson, Chesterfield Co.; 27 Jul 1800; [probated]; similar will
written 1 Mar 1799
To son Charles Woodson, plantation where testator lives called *Neck of Land*; also 2
tracts in of 200 ac. & 22 ½ ac.; also 272 ac. Botetourt Co.; also 156 ½ ac.; all cattle,
furniture, etc. belonging to plantation
To dau. Maria Woodson, 300 ac. Henrico Co. on James River and *Four Mile Creek*;
also 50 ac. Henrico Co. called *Baileys* which was devised John Scott Pleasants by
his uncle Thomas Pleasants; also cattle, tools, etc. on the plantation; slaves to be
maintained during their life
To son Charles Woodson and dau. Maria Woodson all slaves to be equally divided; no
man and wife nor child and mother to be separated
In case of death of both children with no issue alive to inherit, estate to be equally
divided between testator's brothers Tarleton and Frederick Woodson, they paying as
follows:
To children of: testator's brother Charles Woodson, $300 and testator's sister Agnes
Ellison, $500; to testator's sister Sarah Clark £30 annually for life; to testator's sister
Caroline Matilda Bates, £500 secured so as not to be subject to her husband's debts
Exs: brothers Tarleton Woodson, Frederick Woodson (ChWB 5.321; VP p. 1816-7)
Charles F. Woodson qualifies as admn. of will of George Woodson (ChWB 9.225; VP p.
1817)
[George Woodson; Chesterfield Co. Wills & Admns. (1754-1800) Will, codicil & second will –
dated 1799, 1800 & 1800. ChWB 5, p. 321-326 (LOV)]

21124-1 **Charles F. Woodson**; m. **Ann Thomas Watson**; d/o Dr. Goodridge Watson, Sr. of Prince Edward Co.; they moved to MO; children:

211241-1 **George Woodson**
211241-2 **Goodridge Woodson**
211241-3 **Sarah Woodson**; m. **Julian Bates**; s/o Edward Bates
211241-4 **Virginia Woodson**
211241-5 **Elizabeth Woodson**
211241-6 **Ellen Woodson**; m. **Richard Bates**
211241-7 **Julia Woodson**; m. **Isaac Newton Stoutemyer**
211241-8 **Mary Woodson**; m. **Alexander Harris**

21124-2 **Caroline Woodson**
21124-3 **Margaret Woodson**; this may have been the dau. called Maria in his will

2112-5 **Sarah Woodson**, b. 4 Aug 1749 (Bates Bible); m/1 **James Clarke**; m/2 **Archibald Bolling** of Campbell Co.; she was disowned for marrying outside Society 6 Jan 1771 (QRH p. 49); she wrote a letter from Greenock, Scotland, dated 22 Mar 1774 to her sister Caroline Matilda Bates (Mrs. Mary C. Benagh, dec'd)

8 Oct 1784; from Charles Woodson to his dau. Sarah, w/o James Clarke; 8 negro slaves (PoDB 1.275; VP p. 2029)

2112-6 **Caroline Matilda Woodson**, b. 17 Oct 1751 (Bates Bible); m. intent 6d/7m/1771; m. 3d/8/1771 **Thomas Fleming Bates** (VP p. 2056); children:

21126-1 **Edward Bates**; atty.-general of the US from MO
21126-2 **Frederick Bates**
21126-3 **James Woodson Bates**
21126-4 **Tarleton Bates**
21126-5 **Charles Bates**
21126-6 **Fleming Bates**

2112-7 **Tarleton Woodson**, b. 18 March 1754 (Bates Bible); s/o of Charles, late of Henrico Co.; m/1 **Anne Van der Veer** of NY; m/2 30 Oct 1794 **Ann Friend** (VP 1821); 4 Jan 1775 moved within limits of Circular Monthly Meeting; later learned he had enlisted as a soldier; disowned (QRH p. 25, 53); he was a Major in the Continental line taken prisoner in New York; settled Prince Edward Co. which he represented in the Virginia Legislature ; the will of Thomas Friend written 4 Nov 1797 mentions sisters Ann Woodson and Sarah Woodson (ChWB 5.142); children:

21127-1 **Charles Woodson**, b. ca 1781; d. 1838; m. **Nancy Jackson** of Prince Edward Co.

211271-1 Charles Van der Veer Woodson

Letter written by Charles Van der Veer Woodson to Mr. R. A. Brock of Richmond: I have a looking-glass framed in walnut bearing the inscription: This glass belonged to Stephen Tarleton, my great-grandfather who d. in 1687. I have had the present frame put on it this 14 Dec 1794; /s/ Charles Woodson (Richmond Standard, 17 Jan 1880, by Mr. R. A. Brock)

21127-2 Tarleton Woodson

8 Nov 1783; from Tarleton Woodson & Anne his wife of Prince Edward Co. to Edmund Toney; 196 ac. Powhatan Co.; sold by John Pleasants to Charles Woodson who made deed of gift to Tarleton in Cumberland Co. (PoDB 1.227; VP p. 2029)

8 Sep 1794; from Thomas Shelton, Mary his wife and Elizabeth his mother, to Tarleton Woodson, all of Albemarle Co.; for £100; 96 ac. Albemarle Co. (AIDB 11.280; VP p. 1811)

3 Apr 1798; from Philip Airy and Elizabeth his wife, to Tarleton Woodson, all of Albemarle Co.; for £62; 122 ac. Albemarle Co. (AIDB 12.403; VP p. 1811)

2112-8 Frederick Woodson, Capt., b. 24 Mar 1756 (Bates Bible); as a 1st Lt. Va. Regiment, he took the oath of allegiance at *Valley Forge* in the spring of 1777

21 Apr 1785; Frederick Woodson, Gent., Maj. of Militia of this country, produced his commission and took oath of Fidelity to the state and of office (PoOB 2.115)

15 Apr 1789; from Frederick Woodson to Charles Woodson, Jr., both of Powhatan Co.; 457 ¾ ac. in Powhatan on *Solomon's Creek & Fine Creek*; given Frederick by his father Charles Woodson; 16 Apr 1789; Charles, Jr. conveyed same land to Frederick (PoDB 1.504, 505; VP p. 2030)

Mar 1794; Frederick Woodson presented commission appointing him Capt. of Light Dragoons; took oath of fidelity to the Commonwealth and of office (PoOB 4.369; VP 2032)

2112-9 Ursula Woodson, b. 30 Jan 1760 (Bates Bible); m. Francis Luddington; [some histories call him Travis, others Travers]

19 Jul 1797; from Ursula Woodson, Goochland Co., to George Woodson, Chesterfield Co.; bill of sale of 7 negro slaves (GCRB 17.142; VP p. 1911)

211-3 Tarleton Woodson, Jr.; he may have been the one who d. in 1774 with an inventory of £816.4.0 (GCRB 10.493; VP p. 1779-80); m. ____; son:

2113-1 John Woodson; d. by Nov Ct. 1779 Albemarle Co.; m. 24 Dec 1754 Elizabeth Bailey, both in this parish (DR); as Elizabeth Woodson, widow, she mb/2 13 Feb 1782 Joseph Crockett of Montgomery Co. (VP p. 1811); children:

21131-1 Susannah Woodson, b. 11 Feb 1756; bapt. 30 May 1756 (DR); m. Micajah Wheeler
21131-2 Tarlton Woodson, b. 22 Mar 1758 (DR)

6 Jul 1754; from John Woodson & Elizabeth his wife of Cumberland Co. to John Noell; 400 ac. in Cumberland Co. (CuDB 2.145)

Will of John Woodson of Albemarle Co.; 18 Jun 1779; Nov Ct. 1779
To wife Elizabeth Woodson, loaned during her natural life, negroes, furniture, stock, plantation where we now live
To son Tarleton Woodson, negroes, land where we now live
To dau. Susannah Wheeler during life, then to her children, negroes
At death of my wife, furniture, stock, utensils to be divided between my 2 children
To kinsman Pleasant Bailey Oglesby, 200a c. Fluvanna Co. on waters of the *Byrd*
Exs: son Tarleton Woodson, son in law Micajah Wheeler, Augustine Shepherd
Wit: Robert Lague, Anna Wheeler, Annis Woodson (AIWB 2.383; VP 1807)
[John Woodson; Albemarle Co. Wills & Admns. (1748-1800) p. 383. Will pro. No. 1779. p. 385. Inv. & appr. rec. Feb 1780. WB 2, 1752-1785 (Reel 34) (LOV)]

Elizabeth Woodson, widow, of Albemarle Co. mb. 13 Feb 1782 Joseph Crockett of Montgomery Co., Edward Moore, security (VP p. 1811)

> 211-4 **Sarah Woodson**; d/o Tarlton; intent to marry 5/3/1744; m. 3d/4m/1744 Henrico Co. **Henry Terrell** of Cedar Creek Meeting; s/o William Terrell, dec'd, of Hanover Co. (QRH p. 23; VP p. 2051); Sarah was 2nd w/o Terrill; they had 6 children (TVF 5.222)
>
> 211-5 **Judith Woodson**; d/o Tarlton; intent to marry 7/9/1747; m. 3d/11m/1747 White Oak Swamp Meeting **Thomas Cheadle**; s/o John Cheadle of Caroline Co. (QRH p. 24, 25; VP p. 2053); child from his grandfather Woodson's will:
>
>> 2115-1 **George Cheadle**
>> 2115-2 **Thomas Cheadle**
>
> 211-6 **Mary Woodson**; d/o Tarlton of Chesterfield Co.; m. 7d/2m (April)/1750 at White Oak Swamp meeting house **John Pleasants, Jr.** of Henrico Co. (QRH p. 26; VP p. 2053)
>
> 211-7 **Jacob Woodson**; no descendants

9 Jun 1756; 17 Aug 1756; from Jacob Woodson of Goochland Co. to Tarlton Woodson, Sr. of Chesterfield Co.; 100 ac. where Jacob now lives in Goochland; same land as deed of gift from Tarleton to his son Jacob; same date Tarlton conveyed Jacob 200 ac. in Goochland (GCRB 7.109, 110; VP p. 1898)

17 Aug 1756; from Jacob Woodson, Goochland, to his father Tarlton Woodson; 3 negroes (GCRB 7.112; VP p. 1898)

> 211-8 **George Woodson**; no descendants
> 211-9 **Frederick Woodson**; no descendants

> 21-2 **Jacob Woodson**; d. by 5 Aug 1728; unmarried

4 Dec 1725; 1 Aug 1726; from Jacob Woodson to Samuel Burk, both of St. James Parish, Henrico Co.; for £100; 348 ac. at *The Bird* in St. James Parish bounded by *Bird Creek* (HCVD-2 p. 91)

Will of Jacob Woodson; 4 Jul 1726; 5 Aug 1728
To 2 bros. Josiah & Stephen Woodson, exs., all my land at *Dover* on *Jennoto Creek*
Bros. to make over to Samuel Burk 348 ac. in Henrico Co.
Wit: Edward Stratton, Ann Stratton, Henry Cox (HCVW-1 p. 168)
[Jacob Woodson; Henrico Co. Wills & Admns. (1662-1800) p. 190. Will pro. 5 Aug 1728. Deeds
& Wills, 1725-1737 (Reel 7a)

   21-3 **John Woodson, Maj.**; d. by 21 May 1754 Goochland Co.; m. 14 Feb
   1735/6 **Susannah Fleming**, b. 23 Oct 1688 New Kent Co.; d. by Jan Ct.
   1757 Goochland; d/o Charles Fleming & Susanna; widow of **John Bates**
   [d. 1722 York Co.]; children from her will:

                213-1 Charles Bates
                213-2 Fleming Bates
                213-3 John Bates
                213-4 James Bates
                213-5 Hannah Bates

24 Mar 1725; John Woodson granted 400 ac. Henrico Co. on n. side of James River on
heads of the river, branches which goes out against *Elk Island* (LOP 12.393)

24 Mar 1725; John Woodson granted 300 ac. Henrico Co. on s. side of James River
and e. side of *Stovall Creek* (LOP 12.393)

13 Oct 1727; John Woodson granted 4,934 ac. Henrico Co. on n. side of James River
beginning at *Jenitoe Creek* (LOP 13.196)

19 Nov 1728; 17 Dec 1728; from John & Robert Woodson of St. James Parish,
Goochland to Thomas Randolph; for £432.12.6; 1,300 ac. on n. side of James River
bounded by mouth of *Dover Mill Branch*, the main road, river, and *Mill Creek*;
patented to their father John Woodson who devised it to his sons John & Robert
(GCWD-1 p. 7)

28 Sep 1730; John Woodson granted 1,250 ac. Goochland Co. on n. side of James
River (LOP p. 13.538)

4 Dec 1730; from John Woodson of Goochland Co., Gent., to Phillip Lightfoot; for
£67.4; 160 ac. on n. side of James River on *Jenitoe Creek* being land John Woodson,
dec'd, gave his son Jacob, dec'd, with all houses, etc.; Susannah, w/o John,
relinquished dower right (GCWD-1 p. 26; GCRB 1.228; VP p. 1887)

11 Apr 1732; John Woodson granted 1,050 ac. Goochland Co. on n. side of
James River on *Stovals Creek* (LOP 15.26)

4 May 1732; 20 Mar 1733; from John Woodson of Goochland Co. to Benjamin
Woodson, Jr., Joseph Woodson (s/o Benjamin Woodson, dec'd), John Woodson, Jr.
and Robert Woodson, Jr.; 650 ac. on e. side of *Tabors Horse Pen Branch* of *Deep
Creek*; patented 11 Apr 1732 (GCRB 1.386; VP p. 1888)

20 Mar 1733; 20 Mar 1733; from John Woodson of Goochland Co. to Phillip Lightfoot
of York Co.; for £44; land on n. side of James River granted Josiah Woodson 24 Feb
1729 (GCWD-1 p. 53; GCRB 1.485; VP p. 1888)

14 Feb 1735; 17 Feb 1735; from John Woodson of Goochland Co. to Stephen Bedford;
for £52.10; 350 ac. on s. side of James River on *Deep Creek*; part of 1,000 ac. granted

Woodson 11 Apr 1735; 17 May 1737 Susannah, w/o John, relinquished dower rights on sale of 250 (sic) ac. sold Bedford by her attorney George Payne (GCWD-1 p. 81; GCWD-2 p. 5; GCRB 3.34, 163; VP p. 1889, 1890)

21 Feb 1735; 16 Nov 1746; from John Woodson (?); whereas my father died possessed of *Dover*, he gave to his several children, John, Robert, Josias, Stephen, Judith, Elizabeth this tract which was to be resurveyed; the council granted me a patent for the surplus land which I dispose of as follows to be claimed at my death: the land devised my brother Robert sold to Col. Thomas Randolph, to the heirs of sd. Randolph; to heirs of my brother Josias, to Stephen, Judith & Elizabeth; remainder of my estate, real & personal to my wife Susanna Woodson; exs. Susanna Woodson and Fleming Bates (GCRB 6.365; VP p. 1856)

18 Feb 1739; 19 Feb 1739; from John Woodson of Goochland Co. to Tarlton Woodson of Henrico Co.; for £20; 600 ac. called *Licking Hole Survey*; all my right in patent of 3,090 ac. granted Tarleton (GCWD-2 p. 37; also see GCRB 5.257; VP p. 1894)

20 Jul 1741; 21 Jul 1741; from John Woodson of Goochland Co. to Hon. Philip Lightfoot of York Co.; for £80; 558 ac. part of 892 ac. patent to John Woodson, dec'd; bounded by William, Robert & Jonathan Woodson [among others], *Jennytoe Creek*, *Indian Graves Creek* (GCWD-2 p. 58; GCRB 3.426; VP p. 1891)

Will of John Woodson, Goochland Co.; 3 Jan 1748; 21 May 1754
John Woodson, my dec'd father, died possessed of *Dover* tract which he willed to his
    several children John, Robert, Josias, Stephen, Judith & Elizabeth; resurvey showed
    a quantity of surplus land which was granted me by patent; I give this land devised
    my bro. Robert which he sold to Col. Thomas Randolph to the heirs of Col. Thomas;
    to bro. Josias's heirs; to Stephen, Judith & Elizabeth same
Remainder of my estate real & personal to my wife Susanna Woodson
Exs: wife Susanna Woodson, Fleming Bates
Wit: Stephen Sampson, David Layton, John Bates (GCRB 6.365; VP p. 1856)
11 Jun 1754; 18 Jun 1754; John Woodson; inventory value £392.15.5 (GCRB 6.376; VP p. 1875)
[John Woodson; Goochland Co. Wills & Admns. (1728-1800) p. 333-335. Accounts rec. 17 May 1763. Deed Book No. 8, 1759-1765; (1728-1800) p. 365-366. Will pro. 21 May 1754; p. 376-378. Inv. & Appr. rec. 18 Jun 1754. Deed Book No. 6, 1749-1755 (Reel 3) (LOV)]

21 Sep 1756; 21 Sep 1756; from Susanna Woodson to Joseph Evans, both of Goochland Co.; 40 ac. e. side of *Dover Creek* Goochland Co. (GCRB 7.119; VP p. 1898)

Will of Susanna Woodson, Goochland Co.; 4 May 1757; 15 Nov 1757
To son Charles Bates, 1s
Estate to be sold at public auction and money equally divided among my other 4
    children, Fleming, John & James Bates; and Hannah Easly
Exs: Fleming, John & James Bates
Wit: John Gordon, Judith Scott, George G. West (GCRB 7.209; VP p. 1858)

213-1 Charles Bates

8 Dec 1739; from John Woodson to Charles Bates, both of Goochland Co.; 350 ac. Goochland Co. (GCRB 3.253; VP p. 1890)

213-2 Fleming Bates; m. 5d/1m.1737 at house of John Pleasants, Henrico Co. to **Sarah Jordon**; d/o Benjamin Jordon, dec'd, of Nansemond Co. (VP p. 2050)

213-3 John Bates

213-4 James Bates

213-5 Hannah Bates; m. 23 Dec 1744 or 1745 Goochland Co. **Robert Easley**; sec. Roderick Easley; wit. James Bates, Henry Woods; certificate of consent from Susannah Woodson, mother of Hannah Bates; wit. Roderick Easley, James Bates

21-4 Robert Woodson, Jr.; d. by 17 Jun 1729 Goochland; m. **Sarah Womack**; no descendants

11 Apr 1729; 17 Jun 1729; from Robert Woodson, Jr. to Col. Thomas Randolph, both of St. James Parish, Goochland Co.; for £400; plantation in St. James Parish below *Dover Mill*; 2nd parcel on *Sabbott Island* bounded by John Woodson; 450 ac.; Sarah, widow and relict of Woodson, relinquished dower right (GCWD-1 p. 13; GCRB 1.105; VP p. 1887)

Will of Robert Woodson, Jr. of St. James Parish, Goochland; 12 Apr 1729; 17 Jun 1729
To wife Sarah, labor of all my negroes for life then to be divided between my brother Josiah Woodson and sister Elizabeth Woodson; money due me from Thomas Randolph to be divided between wife, brother & sister
Wit: Jno. Dandridge, Job Moore, James Smith (GCWD-1 p. 12, 13; GCRB 1.104; VP p. 1853)
[Robert Woodson, Senior; Henrico Co. Wills & Admns. (1662-1800) p. 260-261. Will pro. Feb 1729. Deeds& Wills, 1725-1737 (Reel 7a); Goochland Co. Wills & Admns. (1728-1800) p. 104-105. Will pro. 17 Jun 1729. Deeds, Etc., Vol. 1, 1728-1724 (Reel 1) (LOV)]

21-5 Josiah Woodson; d. by 16 Nov 1736 Goochland Co.; m. **Mary Royall**; d. by 20 Sep 1757; d/o Joseph Royall, Jr.; she m/2 **Joseph Farrar**; d. by 21 Nov 1749; Josiah was one of the legatees of his bro. Robert Woodson in 1729; children:

> 215-1 John Woodson
> 215-2 Joseph Woodson
> 215-3 Elizabeth Woodson

24 Feb 1729; Josiah Woodson and Stephen Woodson granted 110 ac. Goochland Co. on n. side of James River adj. John Woodson (LOP 13.433)

16 Dec 1730; 1st Mon Sep 1731; Josiah Woodson to Joseph Parsons, both of Goochland Co.; for £40; 232 ac. on s. side of *Chickahominy Swamp* at *Half Sink*; Mary, w/o Josiah, relinquished dower (HCVD-2 p. 133)

Will of Josiah Woodson, St. James Parish, Goochland Co.; 21 Feb 1735; 16 Nov 1736
To son John, plantation I live on left me by will of my father John Woodson, dec'd; plus my part of *Sabott Island*
To wife Mary, 1/3 of sd. land including dwelling and 1/3 my part of *Sabott Island* for life; 3 negroes
To son Joseph, 157 ac. on *Jones Creek* purchased from Joseph Parsons, also negro

To dau. Elizabeth, negroe
Money to be equally divided
If my children die under age, then estate to my bros. Tarlton & John Woodson
Exs: wife, bros. John and Tarlton, and Joseph Royall
Wit: James Barret, Tarlton Woodson, Jr., Michael Rice, Robert Atkinson, Thomas
    Tilman (GCWD-1 p. 93; GCRB 2.267; VP p. 1855-6)
8 Jan 1736; 17 May 1737; inventory of Josiah Woodson, dec'd; value £167.3.6;
appraised by George Payne [among others] (GCWD-2 p. 5) (£178.4.6; GCRB 3.35; VP p.
1873)
[Josiah Woodson; Goochland Co. Wills & Admns. (1728-1800 p. 267-268. Will pro. 16 Nov
1736. Deed Book No. 2, 1734-1736; p. 35 Inv. & Appr. rec. 17 May 1737; p. 120. Accts. rec. 16
May 1738. Deed Book No. 3, 1737, 1742 (Reel 1) (LOV)]

> 215-1 **John Woodson, Col.**; minor in 1735; d. 2 Dec 1789 Goochland;
> mb. <u>28</u> Oct 1751 Goochland; m. <u>14</u> Oct 1751 (DR) **Dorothea (Thia;
> Bethia) Randolph**; security Tarleton Woodson, Jr.; she d. 2 or 3 Feb
> 1794; d/o Col. Isham Randolph of *Dungness*; [her sister Jane was the
> mother of Pres. Thomas Jefferson];a notation in the Douglas Register
> states "Of Col. John Woodson's family I have baptized 12 and married
> 4, he is now dead 15 Deb 1790"; he inherited a tract on *Willis Creek*
> from the will of his step father, Joseph Farrar, in 1749; and from the
> will of his mother, Mary Farrar; children:

            2151-1   Jane Randolph Woodson
            2151-2   Elizabeth Woodson, b. Nov 1756
            2151-3   Josiah Woodson, b. 16 Jan 1758
            2151-4   Isham Woodson, b. Sep 1760
            2151-5   Susannah Woodson, b. 26 Jun 1761
            2151-6   John Woodson, 28 Feb 1763
            2151-7   Martha Woodson, b. 6 Jul 1764
            2151-8   Judith Woodson, b. 16 Feb 1767
            2151-9   Lucy Woodson, b. 13 Oct 1768
            2151-10 Sarah Woodson, b. 14 Nov 1770
            2151-11 Anna S. (Nansie) Woodson
            2151-12 Mary Woodson

8 Sep 1778; 15 Feb 1779; from John Woodson, Goochland Co., to son Josiah
Woodson; 100 ac. both sides *Stoney Creek*, Goochland Co. (GCRB 12.222; VP p. 1903)

14 May 1785; 16 May 1785; from Col. John Woodson & Dorathea Woodson to
Matthew Woodson, all of Goochland Co.; adj. Matthew Woodson & others (GCRB
14.158; VP p. 1905)

19 Dec 1785; 17 Jul 1786; from John Woodson & Dorathea, his wife, Goochland Co.,
to Francis Harris; 110 ½ ac. in Goochland Co. (GCRB 14.294; VP p. 1905)

Will of John Woodson, Goochland Co.; 2 Nov 1789; 18 Jan 1790

Trustees: Mattw. Woodson, Archib. Pleasant, John S. Woodson and my 2 sons Isaiah
    Woodson & John Woodson; to sell 150 ac. *Sabot Island* to pay debts; also land
    where my bro. Jos. Woodson now lives to be sold
To wife Dorathea for live, manor house, land, cattle, furniture, etc. for relinquishing
    her dower rights in my estate

To son Isaiah Woodson, tract where I live including part to my wife at her decease, also 2 negroes, furniture, mare, cows
To dau. Sarah Woodson, 2 negroes, furniture, horse, 2 cows, saddle
Children not previously named: Jane Pleasants, Ann S. Woodson, Elizabeth Cheadle, Susanna Railey, Jno. Woodson, Martha Railey and Judith Railey; all negroes and other property now in their possession from my estate
To dau. Judith in addition to what she had, furniture
Residue after debts paid, to be equally divided among my children including my wife's dower at her death
Exs: sons Isaiah Woodson and John Woodson, friend Matthew Woodson
Wit: James Bryden, Matthew Pleasants, John Gordon, John Utley (GCRB 15.335; VP p. 1860)
11 Mar 1790; Col. John Woodson; inventory value £796.11.2 (VP p. 1782-4)
[John Woodson; Goochland Co. Wills & Admns. (1728-1800) p. 335-336. Will pro. 18 Jan 1790. p. 357-360. Inv. & Appr. rec. 17 Mar 1790. DB No. 15, 1788-1791 (Reel 6) (LOV)]

> 2151-1 **Jane Randolph Woodson**; mb. 12 or 17 Jul 1775; m. 5 Aug 1775 St. James Northam Parish **Archibald Pleasants**; s/o John Pleasants & Susannah Woodson; both of this parish; she was bapt. by Rev. Douglas
>
> 2151-2 **Elizabeth Woodson**, b. Nov 1756; bapt. 19 Dec 1756 (DR); m. **John Cheadle**
>
> 2151-3 **Josiah Woodson**, b. 16 Jan 1758; bapt. 9 May 1758 (DR); mb. 22 Nov 1778 Goochland; m. 3 Dec 1778 (19 year old) **Elizabeth (Betsie) Woodson**, b. ca 1759 (DR); children:
>
> > 21513-1 **Mary Woodson**
> > 21513-2 **Elizabeth Woodson**
> > 21513-3 **Caroline Woodson**
> > 21513-4 **Martha Woodson**

22 Jan 1791; from Josiah Woodson, to Joseph Woodson, both of Goochland Co.; 25 ac. Goochland Co. adj. land sold Anderson Peers (GCRB 15.547; VP p. 1908)

16 Apr 1792; from Josiah Woodson & Elizabeth his wife, Goochland Co., to David McAllister; 27 ac. Goochland Co. adj. Josiah Woodson, Matthew Woodson (GCRB 16.58; VP p. 1908)

16 Apr 1792; from Josiah Woodson & Elizabeth his wife to John Crouch, all of Goochland Co.; 351 ¾ ac. Goochland; with condition that Maj. Joseph Woodson, have life estate in 25 ac. subject to dower of Sarah, w/o sd. Joseph (GCRB 16.61; VP p. 1908)

> 2151-4 **Isham Woodson**, b. Sep 1760; bapt. 30 Mar 1760 (DR); d. unmarried
>
> 2151-5 **Susannah Woodson**, b. 26 Jun 1761; bapt. 21 Feb 1762 (DR); mb. 17 Sep 1784 Goochland Co. **Isham Randolph Railey**; consent of John Woodson to his daughter's marriage (DR; VP p. 1950); child:
>
> > 21515-1 **John Woodson Railey**, b 18 Jul 1785 Goochland

2151-6 **John Woodson**, 28 Feb 1763; bapt. 15 May 1763 (DR); m. 30 Mar 1786 Hanover Co. **Mary Lightfoot Anderson** (DR); they had unnamed daus.; sons:

    21516-1 **Isham Woodson**
    21516-2 **Richard Woodson**

2151-7 **Martha Woodson**, b. 6 Jul 1764; bapt. 9 Sep 1764 (DR); m. 12 Dec 1786 Cumberland Co. **Thomas Railey**

2151-8 **Judith Woodson**, b. 16 Feb 1767; bapt. 10 Apr 1767 (DR); m. 17 Apr 1789 **William Railey**

2151-9 **Lucy Woodson**, b. 13 Oct 1768; bapt. 26 Mar 1769; d. by Feb Ct. 1796 when Josiah Woodson was appointed admn. of her estate (GCOB 20.202; VP 1947); unmarried

2151-10 **Sarah (Sally) Woodson**, b. 14 Nov 1770; bapt. 26 Dec 1773 (DR); m. 3 Oct 1790 Goochland Co. **Philip Woodson**; s/o Martha Woodson

2151-11 **Anna S. (Nansie) Woodson**; mb. 9 Oct 1777; m. 12 Oct 1777 **John Stephen Woodson** (DR); s/o Matthew Woodson & Elizabeth LeVillain

2151-12 **Mary Woodson**; mb. 10 Aug 1778 Goochland Co. **Col. Nathaniel G. Morris** of the British Army

215-2 **Joseph Woodson**; alive 1 Nov 1789 when his bro. wrote his will; m. **Sarah (Sally) Crouch**; d/o Richard; child:

    2152-1 **LaFayette Woodson**, b. 12 Oct 1783; bapt. 6 Nov 1783 (DR)

26 May 1783; from Joseph Woodson & Sally his wife of Cumberland Co. to Thomas Walton; 612 ac. in Cumberland Co. on both side *Little Muddy Creek*; same conveyed Joseph from Wm. Ronald (CuDB 6.143; VP p. 1841)

3 Oct 1783; from Joseph Woodson & Sally his wife of Cumberland Co. to George Nicholas of Albemarle Co.; for £100; 200 ac. on branches of *Meadow Creek*, Albemarle Co. (AIDB 8.103; VP p. 1811)

15 Apr 1794; from Stephen Woodson & Sally his wife to John Gray (admn. of James Dixon, dec'd); 97 ac. Goochland (GCRB 16.329; VP p. 1910)

15 Oct 1798; from Stephen Woodson & Sarah his wife, Goochland Co., to James Manteloe, Hanover Co.; 230 ac. on *Horsepen Creek*, branch of *Beaver Dam Creek*; land where sd. Stephen Woodson now lives (GCRB 17.297; VP p. 1912)

215-3 **Elizabeth Woodson**; mb. 21 Aug 1753 Goochland; m. 24 Aug 1753 St. James Northam **Alexander Sallee** (DR); mb. 21 Aug 1753 (VP p. 1949)

21-6 **Stephen Woodson**; d. by 30 Jul 1736 Goochland Co. (Bible says he d. 18 Jan 1735/6); m. 2 Nov 1730 **Elizabeth Branch**; d. 7 Nov 1789 (Bible); d/o Matthew Branch of *Warwick*; she m/2 **Charles Bates**, b. ca 1718; d.

16 May 1790; Stephen inherited tract below his bro. Joseph at *Sabot's Island* from his father's 1715 will; children:

> 216-1 Matthew Woodson, b. 25 Feb 1731/2
> 216-2 Elizabeth Woodson, b. 19 Mar 1734
> 216-3 Stephen Woodson, b. 25 Sep 1735

28 Sep 1730; Stephen Woodson granted 353 ac. Goochland Co. on s. side of James River and w. side of *Fine Creek* adj. Joseph Woodson (LOP 14.137)

4 Dec 1730; from Joseph & Stephen Woodson of Goochland Co. to Philip Lightfoot; for £160.10; 292 ac. on n. side of James River bounded by *Jenitoe Creek*; John Woodson by his will dated 25 Nov 1715 gave this tract to his son Jacob, who, by his will dated 4 Jul 1726, conveyed the land to Josiah and Stephen; Mary, w/o Josiah, and Elizabeth, w/o Stephen, relinquished their dower rights (GCWD-1 p. 27; GCRB 1.225; VP p. 1887)

20 Oct 1730; 2 Nov 1730; from Stephen Woodson to Joseph Parsons, both of Goochland Co.; for £40; 232 ac. on s. side of *Chickahominy Swamp* at *Half Sink* adj. *Turner's Run* (HCVD-2 p. 127)

Will of Stephen Woodson, St. James Parish, Goochland Co., House Carpenter; 14 Jan 1735; 30 Jul 1736
To wife Elizabeth, plantation I live on for life, bounded by *Maxfields Gut, Lewis's Gut, Sabbots Island*; then to son Matthew
To dau. Elizabeth Woodson, land on *Fine Creek*, when of age or married; also £40
If my two children die under age, then estate to my 2 bros. John and Josias Woodson
To Daniel Branch, s/o Matthew Branch, the elder, £18
To bro. Josias, slaves and ½ my tract in Goochland
Exs: wife, bros. John & Josias Woodson, Joseph Parsons
Wit: Edward Scott, John Lewis, Thomas Dickins (GCWD-1 p. 90; GCRB 2.249; VP p. 1854-5)
13 Nov 1736; 17 May 1737; inv'y of Stephen Woodson, dec'd; value £173.4.6 (GCWD-2 p. 5; GCRB 3.75; VP p. 1874)
[Stephen Woodson; Goochland Co. Wills & Admns. (1728-1800) p. 249-251. Will pro. 20 Jul 1736. Deed Book No. 2 1734-1736; (1728-1800) p. 35-36. Inv. & Appr. rec. 17 May 1737. Deed Book No. 3, 1737-1742 (Reel 1) (LOV)]

15 Mar 1754; 21 May 1754; from Charles Bates & Elizabeth is wife, relict of Stephen Woodson, late of Goochland Co., dec'd, to Matthew Woodson; conveying all right of dower in estate of Stephen Woodson, dec'd (GCRB 6.366; VP p. 1897)

216-1 **Matthew Woodson**, b. 25 Feb 1731/2 (Woodson Family Bible); d. 23 Oct 1794 St. James Northam, Goochland Co.; mb. 22 Nov 1753 Cumberland Co. **Elizabeth (Betty) LeVillain,** Jacob Woodson, sec. (VP p. 1849); m. 28 Nov 1753 *Manakin Town*; d/o John Peter Levillain and Phillipe Dupuy; children; [also said to have been 3 more sons: Matthew, Tarlton and Benjamin not mentioned in his will]:

> 2161-1 John Stephen Woodson, b. 17 Aug 1757
> 2161-2 Elizabeth Woodson, b. 12 May 1759
> 2161-3 Samuel Woodson, b. 24 Jul 1761
> 2161-4 Mary Woodson, b. 28 May 1763

2161-5 Frances Woodson, b. 22 Oct 1764
2161-6 Jacob Woodson, b. 25 May 1766
2161-7 Philip Woodson, b. 7 Aug 1767
2161-8 Daniel/David Woodson, b. 29 Apr 1769
2161-9 Thomas Woodson
2161-10 Jane Woodson
2161-11 Tabitha Woodson

15 Mar 1762; 16 Mar 1762; from Matthew Woodson to bro. Stephen Woodson, both of Goochland Co.; negro (GCRB 8.213; VP p. 1900)

Will of John Le Villain of King William Parish, Cumberland Co. to my dau. Elizabeth Woodson, 120 ac. in Chesterfield Co. after death of wife Phillipe 6 Jan 1765; 22 Feb 1768 (CuWB 2.336; VP p. 1824)

14 Mar 1768; from Philipe Levillain, widow of John Peter Levillian, dec'd, to her son in law Mathew Woodson and Elizabeth his wife, all negroes, stock and personal property devised by sd. John Peter Levillian to her his widow (CuDB 4.260; VP p. 1839)

20 Oct 1777; 20 Oct 1777; from Matthew Woodson & Elizabeth his wife of Goochland Co. to Joseph Sea, Amelia Co.; 95 ac. on *Money Creek* Goochland Co. (GCRB 12.54; VP p. 1903)

17 Mar 1780; 20 Mar 1780; from Matthew Woodson & Elizabeth his wife, Goochland Co., to John Ellis, Jr., Henrico Co.; 25 ac. on branches *Tuckahoe Creek*, Goochland Co. (GCRB 13.31; VP p. 1904)

18 Aug 1779; from Matthew Woodson & Elizabeth his wife of Goochland Co. to his son John Stephen Woodson; 320 ac. in Powhatan Co. in *Manikan Town*, except the grave yard walled in brick; beginning on bank of James River (PoDB 1.104; VP p. 2028)

14 Oct 1779; 18 Oct 1779; from Matthew Woodson & Elizabeth his wife, to William Webber, all of Goochland Co.; 141 ac. Goochland Co. on *Broad Branch* of *Tuckahoe Creek* (GCRB 12.295; VP p. 1904)

18 Apr 1791; from Matthew Woodson to son Samuel Woodson, both of Goochland Co.; tract on *Deer Pen Branches*, Goochland Co., Matthew purchased of Joseph R. Farrar; one known as *Glebe Tract* and adj. tract of 50 ac. (GCRB 15.498; VP p. 1908)

7 Aug 1793; from Matthew Woodson & Elizabeth his wife, Goochland Co. to David Ross & James Currie of *City of Richmond*; 90 ac. Goochland Co. near *Addams Coal Pits* (GCRB 16.219; VP p. 1910)

Will of Matthew Woodson of Goochland Co.; Feb 1794; 17 Nov 1794
To wife Elizabeth Woodson, land & plantation I live on; mentions *Lewis' Gutt, Adams Coal Pits*; also 72 ac. on e. side of meeting house road I purchased of John Woodson; at her decease to son Thomas Woodson; also 14 negroes for life then to descend to my children
To son John Stephen Woodson, tract where he now lives in Manakin Town, negros, stock, etc.
To son Samuel Woodson, land where he lives *The Out Glebe* with 50 more ac., with negroes, stock, etc.
To grandson John Levillian Woodson, negro

To son Philip Woodson, land below *Lewis' Gutt* including *Manakin Ferry*, etc., with negroes, stock, etc., he has in his possession

To son Daniel Woodson, land in Henrico Co. with negroes in his possession, furniture, cattle, etc.

To son Thomas Woodson, negroes, furniture, cattle, etc.

To dau. Elizabeth Woodson, negroes, stock, etc. now in her possession

To dau. Mary Rudd (Redd?), negroes, stock, etc. now in her possession

To dau. Jane Woodson, negroes, horse, furniture, cattle, etc.

To dau. Tabitha Woodson, negroes, horse, furniture, cattle, etc.

All money from my coal lease & money due on bonds from Jesse Rudd (Redd) to be equally divided between my 5 daus.: Elizabeth, Mary, Frances, Jane & Tabitha yearly

Bond against David Ross & James Curie, £160.13.4, to wife and friend William Webber, minister

To wife Elizabeth during life, my part of *Sabbot Island* then to my son Thomas Woodson

To wife Elizabeth all my estate not given for life then equally divided among my 11 children: John Stephen, Samuel, Jacob, Philip, Daniel, Thomas, Elizabeth, Mary, Frances, Jane & Tabitha

Exs: sons Samuel Woodson, Philip Woodson

Wit: John Utley, Josiah Utley, Elizabeth Utley (GCRB 16.338; VP p. 1861)

Jul Ct. 1795; Elizabeth Woodson qualified as administratrix of will of Matthew Woodson, dec'd (GCOB 20.133; VP p. 1947)

[Matthew Woodson; Goochland Co. Wills & Admns. (1728-1800) p. 338-339. Will pro. 17 Nov 1794. p. 480-481. Inv. & Appr. rec. 21 Sep 1795. DB No. 16, 1791-1796 (Reel 6) (LOV)]

15 Feb 1796; from Samuel Woodson, Goochland Co., to Philip Woodson, trustee deed to secure £46 to Elizabeth Woodson, guardian of Tabitha Woodson (GCRB 16.518; VP p. 1911)

22 Feb 1798; from Elizabeth Woodson, relict of Matthew Woodson, dec'd, Thomas Woodson & Sarah his wife, to Obediah Utley; 26 ac. Goochland Co. (GCRB 17.204; VP p. 1911)

Will of Elizabeth Woodson, Goochland Co.; 27 Nov 1802; 20 Jun 1803

To dau. Tabitha Brown, 1 negro

Two old negroes left me by my husband to live with my children as they choose

Balance of slaves (named) to be divided between my 3 sons, Jacob, Samuel & David and my 3 daus. Frances, James & Tabitha; each dau. to have twice as much as a son

Balance of estate to be divided among my 11 children [John S. Woodson, Samuel, Elizabeth, Jacob, Philip, Mary, Frances, David, Thomas, Jane & Tabitha] agreeable to my husbands will

Exs: Elder William Webber and my sons Samuel and David (GCRB 8.568; VP p. 1862)

2161-1 **John Stephen Woodson**, b. 17 Aug 1757; bapt. 25 Sep 1757 (DR); m. 9 Oct 1777 Goochland Co. to **Anna (Nancy) Woodson** (DR); sec. Joseph Woodson; witn. Joseph Watkins; letters of consent from Matthew Woodson, father of John Stephen and from Col. John Woodson, father of Anna; m. 12 Oct 1778 (DR & VP p. 1950); he inherited land in *Mannakan Town* from his father; children:

21611-1 **Matthew Woodson**

21611-2 **Benjamin Woodson**
21611-3 **George Woodson**
21611-4 **John Woodson**
21611-5 **Stephen Woodson**
21611-6 **Mary R. Woodson**; mb. 21 Nov 1793 Powhatan Co. to
    William Porter; John S. Woodson, gives consent to his daughter's
    marriage (VP p. 2032)
21611-7 **Dolly Woodson**
21611-8 **Nancy Woodson**

30 Nov 1797; from John Stephen Woodson & Ann his wife of Powhatan Co. to
Thomas Harris; 328 ac. Powhatan Co. (excepting grave yard walled in brick); same
land given by Matthew Woodson and Elizabeth his wife to sd. John Stephen 18 Aug
1789 (sic) Powhatan Co., being tract where John Levilion, father of Elizabeth
Woodson lived & died possessed (PoDB 2.412; VP p. 2031)

2161-2 **Elizabeth Woodson**, b. 12 May 1759; 17 Jun 1759 (DR); mb.
    22 Nov 1778 both in Goochland; m. 3 Dec 1778 **Josiah Woodson**, b.
    16 Jan 1758; s/o Col. John Woodson
2161-3 **Samuel Woodson**, b. 24 Jul 1761; bapt. 16 Sep 1761 (DR); m.
    Goochland **Sarah Mills (Miler)**; he inherited *The Out Glebe* tract
    from his father; children:

    21613-1 **William Fontain Woodson**, b. 30 Jan 1785; bapt. 9 Feb
        1785 (DR)
    21613-2 **John LeVillain Woodson**, b. 30 Jan 1785; bapt. 9 Feb
        1785 (DR)
    21613-3 **Spotswood Woodson**
    21613-4 **Samuel Woodson**
    21613-5 **Matthew Woodson**
    21613-6 **Daniel Woodson**
    21613-7 **Elizabeth Woodson**
    21613-8 **Maria Woodson**
    21613-9 **Sally Fountain Woodson**
    21613-10 **Tabitha Woodson**

5 Jan 1798; from Samuel Woodson & Sarah his wife, Goochland Co., to Benjamin
Ellis of Henrico Co.; 25 ac. Goochland Co. (GCRB 17.206; VP p. 1911)

2161-4 **Mary Woodson**, b. 28 May 1763; bapt. 26 Jun 1763 (DR); mb.
    20 Nov 1785 Goochland **Jesse Redd**; Matthew Woodson, sec. (VP p.
    1950)
2161-5 **Frances (Fanny) Woodson**, b. 22 Oct 1764; bapt. 2 Dec 1769
    (DR); m. 19 Aug 1782 **Robert Farrar**; Matthew Woodson, sec. (VP p.
    1950)
2161-6 **Jacob Woodson**, b. 25 May 1766; bapt. 22 Jun 1766; m. 13
    Jun 1791 Goochland **Dorothy Pears**; consent of Anderson Pears to

his daughter's marriage (VP p. 1950); Pears' will probated 30 Dec 1792 names them as dau. & son in law (GCRB 16.176); children:

21616-1 **Addison Woodson**
21616-2 **Nancy Woodson**
21616-3 **Virginia Woodson**

18 Apr 1791; from Jacob Woodson, Goochland Co., to David McAllister; 130 ac. *Stoney Creek*, Goochland Co. (GCRB 16.60; VP p. 1908)

8 Feb 1795; from Jacob Woodson and Dorathy his wife, Fayette, KY, to John Graham, Henrico Co.; 312 ac. on James River Goochland Co. (GCRB 16.457; VP p. 1910)

2161-7 **Philip Woodson**, b. 7 Aug 1767; bapt. 6 Sep 1767 (DR); m. 3 Oct 1790 **Sarah (Sally) Woodson**; d/o Col. John & Dorothea Woodson; children:

21617-1 **Philip M. Woodson**
21617-2 **Tarlton Woodson**
21617-3 **Paulina (Pollina) Woodson**

2161-8 **Daniel Woodson**, b. 29 Apr 1769; bapt. 28 May 1769 (DR); m. 25 Nov 1793 Miss **Nancy Gathright** of Henrico Co.; sur. Obadiah Gathright (VP p. 2023); son:

21618-1 **Marshall Woodson**

25 Nov 1793; I do certify my daughter Nancy Gathright is above age 21 and a resident of Henrico Co.; /s/ William Gathright (VP p. 2023)

25 Nov 1793; I do certify I am willing the Clerk of Henrico should issue license for matrimony for myself and Mr. Daniel Woodson; /s/ Nancy Gathright (VP p. 2023)

2161-9 **Thomas Woodson** m. 15 Feb 1796 Goochland Co. to **Sally Saunders**; Ro. H. Sanders, sec.; consent of Ro. H. Saunders to his niece Sally's marriage (VP p. 1951); son:

21619-1 **Robert Woodson**

2161-10 **Jane Woodson**

Jul Ct. 1795; Jane Woodson & Tabitha Woodson chose their mother, Elizabeth Woodson, widow of Matthew Woodson, dec'd as guardian (GCOB 20. 133; VP. p. 1947)

2161-11 **Tabitha Woodson**; m. 6 Feb 1798 **John Brown**; Elizabeth's consent to her dau. Tabitha's marriage (VP p. 1951)

216-2 **Elizabeth Woodson**, b. 19 Mar 1734 (Bible); mb. 1 Jan 1753 Goochland Co. to **Alexander Trent**; sec. John Woodson; witn., Will Pryor, H. Wood; certificate of consent from Charles Bates, guardian for sd. Elizabeth , d/o Stephen Woodson, dec'd; wit. Matthew Woodson, Samuel Branch (VP p. 1949)

Nov Ct. 1751; Elizabeth & Stephen Woodson Trent chose Charles Bates, Gent., their guardian (GCOB 7.87; VP p. 1936)

216-3 **Stephen Woodson**, b. 25 Sep 1735 (Bible); m. 9 May 1758 Goochland to **Lucy Farrar**, both of this parish; d/o Joseph Farrar and Mary Royall; children:

> 2163-1 Stephen Woodson, b. 11 Jan 1759
> 2163-2 Mary Woodson, b. 27 Oct 1760

28 Mar 1791; from Stephen Woodson, Sr. to his son, Stephen Woodson, Jr., both of Cumberland Co.; 50 ac. in the branches of *Willis's River* adj. *Moddle Bear Creek* & Stephen Woodson, Sr., etc. (CuDB 7.59; VP p. 1844)

2163-1 **Stephen Woodson**, b. 11 Jan 1759; bapt. 25 Mar 1759 (DR); d. by 25 Mar 1795; m. **Mary Holman**; two of their children:

21631-1 **Henry Woodson**
21631-2 **Judith Tarlton Woodson**

Will of Stephen Woodson, the younger, Cumberland Co.; 9 Aug 1794; 25 Mar 1795
To wife Mary, full possession of all my estate during life, at her death to be equally divided among all my children or their legal representatives
Residue consisting of horses and small parcel of land to my father
Exs: my father, Alex. Trent, Willis Wilson (CuWB 3.47)

[Stephen Woodson; CuWA (1749-1810) p. 64. Inv. & Appr. rec. 23 Nov 1795. p. 47 Will, pro. 23 Mar 1795. WB No. 3, 1792-1810 (Reel 18) (LOV)]

2163-2 **Mary Woodson**, b. 27 Oct 1760; bapt. 8 Feb 1761 (DR)

21-7 **Judith Woodson**; d. by 28 Nov 1774 when her will was probated in Cumberland Co. (CuWB 2.156); m. **Stephen Cox**; d. by 1759 Cumberland Co. when Judith sold land as extx. of her dec'd husband (CuDB 2.484); s/o William Cox and Sarah ____

21-8 **Elizabeth Woodson**; m. 5d/9m/1732 **Joseph Pleasants** of *Pickanocka*; s/o Jos. Pleasants dec'd of Henrico Co. (QRH p. 17; VP p. 2049)

2-2 **Robert Woodson, Sr.**; Henrico Co., b. est. ca 1660; d. by Feb 1729; said to have m/1 ca 1681 **Elizabeth Lewis**; m/2 1691 **Sarah Lewis** (QRH p. 91); d. ca 1710; d/o John Lewis (HCVW-1 p. 38); m/3 cleared to marry 12d/10m/1710 **Rachel Watkins** (QRH p. 6; VP p. 2046); Robert was one of the legatees of uncle John Woodson in 1684; he calls himself "Sr." in his will to distinguish himself from his nephew, Robert Woodson, Jr.; children from wills and family histories:

> Children of m/1:
> 22-1 Stephen Woodson, b. est. ca 1682
> 22-2 Joseph Woodson, b. est. ca 1685
> 22-3 Robert Woodson, b. est. ca 1687
> 22-4 Elizabeth Woodson, b. est. ca 1789
> Children of m/2
> 22-5 Sarah Woodson, b. est. ca 1692

22-6 Agnes Woodson, b. est. ca 1697
Children of m/3:
22-7 Jonathan Woodson, b. ca 1711
22-8 Elizabeth Woodson, b. ca 1713
22-9 Judith Woodson, b. ca 1715

1 Dec 1696; I, Robert Woodson, Jr., ack. receipt from my brother in law William
Lewis, my full share of what is due my wife Sarah, one of the orphans of John Lewis,
dec'd (HCVW-1 p. 61)

20 Oct 1704; Robert Woodson granted 171 ac. Henrico Co. on n. side *Ufnom Brook*
(LOP 9.629)

23 Dec 1714; Robert Woodson, Jr. granted 1,494 ac. on n. side of James River on
branches of *Mill Creek* and *Jenitoe Creek* (LOP 10.237)

4 Mar 1716; 4 Mar 1716; deed of gift from Robert Woodson to my cousins Obadiah,
John & Joseph Woodson, all of Henrico Co., sons of Richard Woodson, dec'd; 498 ac.
divided equally; on n. side of James River at *Dover* on branches of *Genytoe* and *Mill
Creek* (HCVD-2 p. 62)

4 Mar 1716; 4 Mar 1716; deed of gift from Robert Woodson of Henrico Co. to cousin
Richard Woodson, s/o Richard Woodson, dec'd; 85 ac. upper part of land granted me
by patent 20 Oct 1704 on n. side of James River on branch of *Usuum Brook* (HCVD-2
p. 62)

3 Mar 1717; 3 Mar 1717; deed of gift Robert Woodson, Sr. to dau. Sarah, now w/o
Joseph Passon, all of Henrico Co.; 158 ac. near *Dover* on a branch of *Genitoe Creek*;
part of a patent to me 3 Dec 1714 (HCVD-2 p. 72)

3 Mar 1717; 3 Mar 1717; from Robert Woodson to Benjamin Woodson, both of
Henrico Co.; for £5; middle 1/3 of tract at *Dover* (HCVD-2 p. 72)

<u>Will of Robert Woodson, Sr.; Henrico Co.; 6 Jul 1729; Feb 1729</u>
To son Stephen, land that came into my possession by marriage with his mother; also
    50 ac.
To son Joseph, parcel on w. side of *Jennitoe Creek* up *Rocky Branch* in Goochland
    Co., negro, items
To son Robert, the residue of and in Goochland on *Jennitoe Creek*
To son Jonathan at age 18, land near *White Oak Swamp*
To daus. Elizabeth & Judith, negro, items each; to dau. Agnes negro
Remainder to be divided by Stephen & Thomas Watkins, exs., between Joseph,
    Robert, Jonathan & Judith
Wit: William Porter, Jr., Theodorick Carter, Giles Davis, Tarlton Woodson (HCVW-1 p.
    173)

22-1 **Stephen Woodson**, b. est. ca 1695; of Henrico Co.; d. 1761 Henrico
    Co.; m. **Mary Woodson**, b. ca 1706; d/o Joseph & Jane Woodson;
    children:

221-1 Stephen Woodson
221-2 Elizabeth Woodson

20 Oct 1730; from Stephen Woodson to Joseph Parsons, both of Goochland Co.; for £40; 232 ac. on s. side of *Chickahominy Swamp* at *Half Sink* bounded by *Turners Run* (HCVD-2 p. 127)

5 Apr 1736; [recorded]; from John Lewis of Goochland Co., s/o William Lewis, dec'd, to Stephen Woodson, s/o Robert Woodson of Henrico Co. & Parish; for £150; 52 ac. bounded by Robert Woodson, *Cattail Swamp* and adj. where Stephen now lives near *Malvern Hills* (HCVD-2 p. 168)

20 Aug 1745; 20 Aug 1745; land swap between Stephen Woodson of Henrico & John Lewis of Goochland; a tract in Henrico near branches of *Turkey Island Creek* on back of *Manborne Hills* already recorded from Lewis to Woodson in Henrico Ct.; Woodson conveys to Lewis 200 ac. on branches of *Beaver Dam Creek*, deed recorded in Goochland GCRB 5.19; VP p. 1895)

2 Apr 1759; from Stephen Woodson of Henrico Co. to his grandchildren, Samuel & Mary Bell, children of George Bell the younger of Louisa Co.; 2 slaves now in possession of George Bell (HCVD-4 p. 579; TVF 10. 110)

May Ct. 1761; will of Stephen Woodson presented by Mary Woodson, extx. (HCVW-2 p. 80)

     221-1 **Stephen Woodson**; d. by 6 Aug 1770; 2/7/1768 incapable of managing his affairs; 6/8/1768 changes his mind and asks for court appointed guardian (QRH p. 46); unmarried

Oct Ct. 1762; Stephen Woodson, orphan of Stephen Woodson, chooses Joseph Parsons as guardian (HCVW-2 p. 83)

30 Oct 1769; Power of Attorney from Stephen Woodson of Henrico Co. to my trusty friend, Benjamin Johnson of Hanover Co. (HCVD-5 p. 188; TVF 11.188)

4 Sep 1768; 6 Aug 1770; Stephen Woodson of Henrico Co.; for 5s and good will and affection to William, Josiah, Woodson, Sarah, Mary, Ursley, Elizabeth, Agnes and Judith Parsons, my whole estate, real & personal; 100 ac. at *Piconoquey* to Woodson Parsons and my land at *Malbon Hills* equally to William, Woodson & Josiah Parsons; Woodson to have 1st choice; remainder of estate, 20 negroes, livestock, household furniture to be equally divided between them (HCVW-2 p. 145; HCVW-3 p. 224; TVF 11. 179)

     221-2 **Elizabeth Woodson**; d/o Stephen of Henrico Co.; m. 1d/9m/1753 at Curles Meeting House **George Bell**, the younger, of Louisa Co.; s/o George Bell of Hanover Co. (QRH p. 28; VP p. 2054); children who rec'd gift from their grandfather Woodson:

        2212-1 **Samuel Bell**
        2212-2 **Mary Bell**

     221-3 **Mary Woodson**; m. intent 12 Jul 1746 **Joseph Parsons, Jr.**; at a meeting 5 Apr 1747 near White Oak Swamp, they did declare themselves to be husband and wife (HCVD-4 p. 365; QRH p. 24)

   22-2 **Joseph Woodson**, b. est. ca 1685; d. ca 1757; m. est. ca 1710 **Elizabeth Mattox**; d/o John Mattox & Margaret Kent; the will of

Joseph's father in 1729 left him land on *Genito Creek*; they had several children according to family histories possibly including:

      222-1 Joseph Woodson
      222-2 William Woodson

Jun Ct. 1757; inventory of Joseph Woodson, recorded (HCVW-2 p. 72)
Oct Ct. 1758; John Woodson returned accts. of Joseph Woodson, dec'd (HCVW-2 p. 76)

222-1 Joseph Woodson of *Genito*, b. est. ca 1710-1720's; d. by 21 Jun 1784; m. **Elizabeth Parsons**; d. aft. 1792; children from Joseph's will dated 1783, some years after most if not all of the children were married, yet all the girls are called by their maiden name except Sarah:

      2221-1 Joseph Woodson, b. aft. 1748
      2221-2 Sarah (Sally) Woodson, b. aft. 1742
      2221-3 Mary (Molly) Woodson
      2221-4 Judith Woodson
      2221-5 Ann (Nancy) Woodson
      2221-6 Ursula Woodson
      2221-7 Agnes Woodson
      2221-8 Susannah Woodson
      2221-9 Elizabeth Woodson

[Note: In the following will Joseph Woodson names all his daus. except Sarah by their maiden names, yet most were known to have been married prior to 1783; see documents following will.]

Will of Joseph Woodson, Sr., Goochland Co.; 2 Oct 1783; 21 Jun 1784
To wife Elizabeth Woodson, 3 negroes and use of plantation where I live for support of
    herself and my youngest children
To son Joseph Woodson, negro, furniture
To dau. Nanny Woodson, furniture
To dau. Ursly Woodson negro, furniture
To dau. Agnes Woodson, negro, furniture
To granddau. Mary Woodson, furniture
To dau. Sarah Ellis, negro, furniture now in her possession
To dau. Susanna Woodson, 2 negroes, furniture
To dau. Judith Woodson, negro, furniture, mare & saddle
Three negroes to be equally divided among my living daus. after wife's decease
Residue to my wife
Exs: Thomas Pleasants, Joseph Watkins, my son Joseph Woodson
Wit: Thomas Watkins, Peter Prime (GCRB 14.25; VP p. 1858, 1759)
21 Jun1784; Joseph Woodson; inventory value £356.3.7 (GCRB 14.41; VP p. 1780-1)
[Joseph Woodson, Sr.; Goochland Co. Wills & Admns. (1728-1800) p. 25-26. Will dated 2 Oct 1783. p. 41-42. Inv. & Appr. rec. 21 Jun 1784. Deed Book No. 14, 1784-1788 (Reel 5) (LOV)]

25 Oct 1790; from Joseph Knight & Judith his wife, Granville Co., NC; Archer Pledge & Anna his wife, Goochland Co.; John Redford & Unita his wife, Henrico Co.; Pleasant Turner & Agatha his wife, Halifax Co.; Perrin Redford & Susannah his wife, Goochland Co.; Thomas Woodson & Mary his wife, Goochland Co. (daus. of Joseph Woodson of *Genito* and their husbands) to Joseph Woodson, son & heir of Joseph Woodson of *Genito*; 325 ac. on *Beaver Dam Creek* Goochland Co.; to correct error in

Joseph Woodson's will; he intended to give son Joseph the 325 ac. of land (GCRB 16.79; VP p. 1909)

22 May 1792; from Elizabeth Woodson to her son Joseph Woodson, both of Goochland Co.; her dower interest in 225 ac. land on *Jenito Creek* Goochland Co. (GCRB 16.97; VP p. 1909)

8 Oct 1812; Judith Knight, widow & relict of Jonathan Knight of Granville, NC; whereas Joseph Woodson, the elder, late of *Jenito Creek*, Goochland Co., did by his will dated 7 Oct 1783 bequeath unto his daughters then living, all residue of his estate including all real estate consisting of 325 ac. on *Jenito Creek* and branches of *Beaver Dam*; being sensible; it was always the intent of my father that his real estate should descend to his son Joseph; defect in the will due to default of the writer; do grant the sd. land to Joseph Woodson, son and heir of Joseph Woodson (GCWB 21.361; VP 1915, 1916)

     2221-1 **Joseph Woodson, Jr.**; of *Genito*, b. aft. 1748 [not 21when his father gave consent for his marriage]; mb. 30 Dec 1769 Goochland; m. 2 Jan 1770 **Mildred Redford**, both of this parish (DR); d/o Mildred Redford; sec. David Maddox; Joseph Woodson's letter of consent to his son's marriage; consent of Stoakes McCaul, guardian of sd. Milly Redford (VP p. 1949); children:

         22211-1 **Robert Woodson**
         22211-2 **William Woodson**
         22211-3 **Joseph Woodson**
         22211-4 **Milner Woodson**; this name came from the Redford family
         22211-5 **Edward Woodson**
         22211-6 **George Woodson**
         22211-7 **Frederick Woodson**
         22211-8 **Mary (Polly) Woodson**; m. 25 Jul 1794 Goochland to **William Downer**; Richard Redford, sec.; consent of Joseph Woodson to his dau. Polly's marriage
         22211-9 **Elizabeth Woodson**
         22211-10 **Sarah Woodson**

13 Oct 1797; from Joseph Woodson, Goochland Co., only s/o Joseph Woodson, the elder, dec'd, to Joseph Watkins; 3 ac. on w. side *Rocky Fork* of *Genito Creek* Goochland Co. (GCRB 17.154; VP p. 1911)

17 Apr 1797; from Joseph Woodson to William Woodson, both of Goochland Co.; 100 ac. land on *Genito Creek* (GCRB 17.92; VP p. 1911)

May 1800; from Joseph Woodson & Mildred his wife, to Philip Pleasants, all of Goochland Co.; 300 ¾ ac. Goochland bounded by road from *Dover Mills* to *Bever Dam Church* (GCRB 18.11; VP p. 1912)

20 Apr 1801; from Joseph Woodson (Jenito) & Mildred his wife to Robert Woodson, all of same county; 150 ac. Goochland Co. in fork of *Jenito Creek* (GCRB 18.166; VP p. 1912)

2221-2 **Sarah (Sally) Woodson**, b. aft. 1742 [not 21 in 1763]; she may
have d. fairly young as she is not mentioned in the 1790 document
with her sisters; mb. 9 Mar 1763 St. James Northam **Jesse Ellis** (DR);
d. by 5 May 1783 Henrico Co.; s/o Thomas Ellis; letter of consent
from Sarah's father, Joseph Woodson , of *Jenito*; sec. John Crouch;
wit. Hezekiah Holland; Thomas Ellis's letter of consent for his son
Jesse (VP p. 1949); children from Jesse's will:

22212-1 **John Ellis**; minor in 1779
22212-2 **Susannah Ellis**

Will of Jesse Ellis of Henrico Parish & County; Planter; Sep 1779; 5 May 1783
To wife Sarah, all of my estate until son John Ellis is 21; then he to get ½ of estate
To dau. Susannah Ellis at marriage, ½ of estate
To Susannah at wife's death, negroes and all my part of my father's estate [torn] –in-
law Joseph Woodson
If dau. married Samuel Woodward, s/o John, of Goochland Co. she is to be cut off with
10s and her part of estate to her brother John
To son John, all of my land in Henrico, the *Coal Pitts*, my land in Goochland Co.;
negroes, furniture
If wife remarries, she to take a negro from each child's part and may live on
Goochland property for life
Exs: John Ellis, s/o John; Stephen Ellis, s/o Joseph; Joseph Woodson, s/o Joseph
Wit: [torn off]
Proved by John Lewis and Edward Valentine, witnesses; John Ellis, s/o Thomas, &
Thomas Ellis, security (HCVW-3 p. 68; TVF 6.98)

2221-3 **Mary (Molly) Woodson**; m. 27 Sep 1758 **Thomas Woodson**
(DR); lived Goochland
2221-4 **Judith Woodson**; m. 24 Feb 1757 Goochland **Jonathan
Knight** of Lunenburg Co. (DR); d. by 12 Mar 1772 Lunenburg Co.;
he is called Joseph in the 1790 document; lived Granville, NC
2221-5 **Anna (Nanny) Woodson**; mb. 21 Feb 1775; m. 2 Mar 1775
Goochland **Archer Pledge**, both of this parish (DR; VP p. 1950); lived
Goochland Co.; child:

22215-1 **Archer Pledge**, b. 1 Jan 1782; bapt. 16 Jun 1782 (DR)

2221-6 **Ursula Woodson**; m. 27 Apr 1775 Goochland **William
Pledge**, both of this parish (DR); she may have m/2 **John Redford**;
the court case of 25 Oct 1790 names "John Redford and wife Unita"
in the list of daus. of Joseph Woodson; children:

22216-1 **William Pledge**, b. 4 Mar 1776; bapt. 31 Aug 1776 (DR)
22216-2 **Francis Pledge**, b. 15 Aug 1781; bapt. 21 Feb 1782 (DR)

2221-7 **Agnes Woodson**; mb. 11 Oct 1781 Goochland Co. **Pleasant
Turner**; lived Halifax Co.; she is called Agatha in the 1790
document

2221-8 **Susanna Woodson**; mb. 19 Jul 1784 Goochland Co. **Perrin Redford**; lived Goochland Co.

2221-9 **Elizabeth Woodson**, b. aft. 1750 [not 21 in 1771]; she may have d. bef. 1783 as she is not mentioned in her father's will or in the 1790 document; mb. 16 Nov 1771 Goochland **William Jordan**; letters of consent from Joseph Woodson, father of Elizabeth, and Charles Jordan, father of William; son Woodson Jordan, b. 27 Dec 1772

222-2 **William Woodson**; m. 18 Sep 1795 Henrico Co. **Milly Redford** of Henrico Co.; surety John Redford, father of Milly (VP p. 2023)

[undated]; Sir, Please to Grant my son William Woodson a License to marry Milly Redford the daughter of John Redford in my name; Joseph (x) Woodson; wit. Wm. Pledge, Richard Redford, Robert Woodson (VP p. 2024)

[undated]; Sir; You have my permission to issue a license for a marriage intended with Mr. Wm. Woodson of Goochland Co. & my dau. Milly Redford of Henrico Co.; to The Clerk of Henrico Co., I am Sir, yours, John Redford (VP p. 2024)

26 Dec 1804; 26 Dec 1804; from William Woodson and Mildred his wife to William Johnson; 5 1/8 ac. on Jenito Creek (GCDB 19.251; VP p. 1914)

22-3 **Robert Woodson**, b. est. ca 1687; no descendants

12 Mar 1739; Robert Woodson granted 400 ac. Goochland Co. among branches of *Treasurers Run* (LOP 19.623)

22-4 **Elizabeth Woodson**, b. est. ca 1689; d. bef. 1766; m. ca 1710 **John Povall**; d. 10 Oct 1749

22-5 **Sarah Woodson**, b. est. ca 1693; m. 17 May 1718 **Joseph Parsons** (QRH p. 93); d. ca 1770 Henrico Co.; 3 Mar 1717/8 her father gave Sarah, wife of Joseph, 158 ac. near *Dover* on a branch of *Genitoe Creek*; their daughter:

225-1 **Elizabeth Parsons**, b. est. ca 1719; m. ca 1737 **Joseph Woodson**; s/o Joseph Woodson & Elizabeth Mattox

22-6 **Agnes Woodson**, b. est. ca 1697; m. ca 1720 **Richard Williamson**; d. by 2 Apr 1774 Henrico Co. (HCVW-2 p. 122); children from his will which also names several grandchildren not included here:

226-1 **Thomas Williamson**
226-2 **Agnes Williamson**; m. ____ **McCaul**
226-3 **Lucy Williamson**; m. ____ **Ross**
226-4 **Mary Williamson**; m. ____ **Stone**
226-5 **Ann Williamson**; m. ____ **Netherland**
226-6 **Elizabeth Williamson**; m. **Robert Spiers**
226-7 **Sarah Williamson**; m. ____ **Lewis**

Children of m/2 Rachel Watkins:

22-7 Jonathan Woodson, b. est. ca 1711

5 May 1735; from Jonathan Woodson to Thomas Benford, both of Henrico Co. & Parish; for £4; 372 ac. in same parish on n. side of James River and s. side of *White Oak Swamp*; part of a greater tract given me by my father, Robert Woodson, deeded him by Robert and John Woodson, 2 of the patentees (HCVD-2 p. 159)

1 Mar 1743; Jonathan Woodson granted 230 ac. Goochland Co. adj. Capt. Hudson (LOP 22.40)

Jonathan Woodson swore an oath in open Court; fined 5s (AIOB 1744-48, p. 92; VP p. 1811)

22-8 Elizabeth Woodson, b. est. ca 1713; d. ca 1784; m. **John Knight**; d. ca 1772 Lunenburg Co.; they are said to have had 10 children including a son named Woodson

22-9 Judith Woodson, b. est. ca 1715; m. **John Cox** [name also given as Cooke and Cocke]

22-10 Mary Woodson; m. **Stephen Sampson**; listed in some family histories

2-3 Richard Woodson, b. ca 1662; d. by 1716; m. ca 1695 **Ann Smith**, b. ca 1677; d/o Obadiah Smith & Mary Cocke; Richard was one of the legatees of his uncle John in 1684; children:

          23-1 Richard Woodson
          23-2 John Woodson
          23-3 Elizabeth Woodson
          23-4 Judith Woodson
          23-5 Joseph Woodson
          23-6 Mary Woodson
          23-7 Agnes Woodson
          23-8 Obadiah Woodson
          23-9 Robert Woodson

23-1 Richard Woodson, b. est. ca 1696; of *Poplar Hill*; m. **Anne Madeline Michaux**, b. 17 May 1693; d/o Abraham Michaux; Richard was one of the ex. of the will of Jacob Michaux dated 13 Dec 1744 (GCWD-3 p. 11, 12); his uncle Robert Woodson gave him 85 ac. on *Upham Brook* in 1716; children:

   231-1 **Agnes Woodson**; m. **Francis Watkins** of Prince George Co.
   231-2 **Elizabeth Woodson**; m. **Nathaniel Venable**

Sep Ct. 1739; from Richard Woodson to Rebeccah Elmore, deed; Ann, w/o Richard, relinquished dower right (HCVD-3 p. 83)

30 Jun 1743; Richard Woodson granted 364 ac. Amelia Co. on both sides of *Bryer Creek* (LOP 20.526)

12 Jan 1746; Richard Woodson granted 400 ac. Brunswick Co. on both sides of *Wallis's Creek* (LOP 25.236)

20 Sep 1748; Richard Woodson granted 1,152 ac. Amelia Co. on both sides of *Bryer River* (LOP 28.432)

1 Jun 1750; Richard Woodson granted 175 ac. Amelia Co. on n. side of *Bryer River* (LOP 29.231)

14 Feb 1756; Richard Woodson granted 1,629 ac. on both side of *Briery River* (LOP 32.672)

  23-2 **John Woodson**, b. est. ca 1698; d. by 25 Mar 1793 Cumberland Co.;
  m. **Elizabeth Anderson**, b. ca 1707; d/o Agnes Gannaway and Thomas
  Anderson of Albemarle Co. whose will probated 9 Mar 1758 calls his
  dau. Elizabeth Woodson (AIWB 2.38); children from their parents' wills:

             232-1 Anderson Woodson
             232-2 Martha Woodson
             232-3 Ann Woodson
             232-4 John Woodson
             232-5 Drucilla Woodson
             232-6 Sarah Claiborne Woodson

26 Sep 1751; from John Woodson of Southam Parish, Cumberland Co., to Samuel Hancock, Jr. of Nottoway Parish, Amelia Co.; for £50; 400 ac. Amelia Co.; part of patent granted sd. Woodson by patent 20 Sep 1748 (AmDB 4.77; (VP p. 1812)

6 Jul 1754; from John Woodson & Elizabeth his wife of Cumberland Co. to John Noell; 400 ac. in Cumberland Co. (CuDB 2.145; VP p. 1836)

9 May 1772; Apr Ct. 1773; from John Woodson, Jr. of Cumberland Co. to Samuel Richardson of Prince Edward Co.; for £218.15; 175 ac. near *Four Mile Creek* (HCVD-4 p. 451; TVF 12.55)

Will of John Woodson, Cumberland Co.; 24 Aug 1791; 25 Mar 1793
To wife Elizabeth Woodson, lend to all lands, stock, plantation, furniture, all slaves, etc.
Exception negro with s. side of *Dry Creek* furniture and an equal part of my other
  children and plantation tools to son John; also 2 ac. on n. side of *Drie Creek*
To son Anderson Woodson, land on n. side of *Drie Creek* excepting abv. 2 ac.
To dau. Martha Ganaway, furniture
Ann Lumpkin, Martha Ganaway, Drucilla Walker, Anderson Woodson & John
  Woodson to return slaves lent them; at death of live everything to be equally divided
  amongst my children
Exs: Samuel Williams, John Woodson, Peter & Richard Allen
Wit: Richard Allen, Elizabeth Overstreet, Freeman Lewellen, John G. Robins, William
  O. Robbins, John Woodson (CuWB 3.10; VP p. 1829)
[John [D. W.] Woodson; CuWA (1749-1810) p. 44-45. Inv. & Appr. rec. 26 Jan 1795. p. 10. Will,
pro. 25 Mar 1793. WB No. 3, 1792-1810 (Reel 18) (LOV)]

  232-1 **Anderson Woodson**; of Buckingham Co.

10 Jan 1795; from Anderson Woodson, John Woodson, Wm. Walker & Drusilla his wife, Ann Lumpkin, John Ganaway & Martha his wife to John Woodson, planter; Anderson, John, Drusilla, Ann & Martha are children of John Woodson (D. W.),

dec'd; 100 ac. in Cumberland Co. on *Dry Creek* part of tract on which John Woodson (D. W.) lived (CuDB 7.399; VP p. 1845-6)

18 Jan 1798; from Daniel Gurrant of Cumberland Co. to Anderson Woodson of Buckingham Co.; 22 ac. on *Dry Creek* Cumberland Co. (CuDB 8.135; VP p. 1847)

18 Jan 1798; from Anderson Woodson of Buckingham Co. to Daniel Guerrant; 9 ½ ac. Cumberland Co. (CuDB 8.135; VP p. 1843)

     232-2 **Martha (Patty) Woodson**; mb. 14 Apr 1773 Cumberland Co. **John Gannaway**; Moore Lumpkin, sec.; consent of John to his daughter's marriage (VP p. 1849)

     232-3 **Ann Woodson**; mb. 14 Apr 1773 Cumberland Co. **Moore Lumpkin**; John Gannaway, sec.; consent of John Woodson to his daughter's marriage (VP p. 1849)

     232-4 **John Woodson**; mb. 5 Nov 1772 Cumberland Co. to **Ann Davenport**, d/o Thomas, Jr. of Littleton Parish; Norvel Dunivant, security; consent of Thomas Davenport to daughter's marriage (VP p. 1849); possible children:

         2324-1 **Joseph Woodson**; from family history

         2324-2 **Elizabeth Woodson**; mb. 30 Mar 1793 Cumberland Co. to **William Wright**; Seymour Wright, security; consent of John Woodson, father of Elizabeth (VP p. 1849)

Will of Thomas Davenport of Cumberland Co. leaves dau. Ann Woodson land on upper side of *Myre Creek* in Halifax Co., negroes; grandson Joseph Woodson, 1 negro; son in law John Woodson one of the exs.; 19 Mar 1777; 27 Nov 1780 (CuWB 2.268; VP p. 1827-8)

     232-5 **Drucilla Woodson**; m. **William Walker**

     232-6 **Sarah Claiborne Woodson**; named in the will of her grandfather Thomas Anderson written 9 Mar 1758 (AIWB 2.38)

    23-3 **Elizabeth Woodson**; m/1 **Edmond Goode**; m/2 **Thomas Morton**

    23-4 **Judith Woodson**; m. **Jacob Michaux**, b. 11 Nov 1695

    23-5 **Joseph Woodson**; not included in some family histories

    23-6 **Mary Woodson**; m. **Richard Turner** or **Truman**

    23-7 **Agnes Woodson**, b. 27 Feb 1710/1; d. 10 Mar 1802; m. as 2nd w/o **Joseph Morton**, b. ca 1709; d. 25 Jun 1782; children:

     237-1 **Josiah Morton**, b. ca 1737; d. 17 Nov 1783

     237-2 **Judith Morton**, b. ca 1739

     237-3 **William Morton**, b. ca 1743; d. 1820; m. 29 Oct 1764 **Susan Watkins**; d/o Thomas Watkins of *Chickahominy*; they had 12 children

     237-4 **Jane Morton**, b. ca 1745

     237-5 **Agnes Morton**, b. ca 1747; m. **Col. Joel Watkins**

     237-6 **Little Joe Morton**

     237-7 **Jacob Morton**

     237-8 **Elizabeth Morton**

23-8 **Obadiah Woodson**; d. by 21 Apr 1767 Prince Edward Co.; m. ca
1734 **Constant Watkins**; d. by Nov 1774 Prince Edward Co.; d/o John
Watkins [a tray-maker] (HCVW-2 p. 113; VP 1951); Obadiah was a land
dealer, acquiring great tracts of unsettled land; child:

238-1 Obadiah Woodson

30 Mar 1743; Obadiah Woodson granted 378 ac. Brunswick Co. on both sides *Buffalo
Creek* (LOP 21.254)

20 Sep 1745; Obadiah Woodson granted 300 ac. Goochland Co. on both sides of *Dry
Creek* of Appomattox River (LOP 22.502)

25 Sep 1746; Obadiah Woodson granted 800 ac. Amelia Co. on lower side *Buffalo
River* (LOP 24.460)

20 Jul 1748; Obediah Woodson granted 285 ac. Albemarle Co. on Appomattox River
(LOP 26.524)

27 Mary 1751; from Obediah Woodson and Constant his wife of Cumberland Co. to
John Richardson; 800 ac. on n. branches of Appomattox on both sides of *Dry Creek* in
Cumberland Co. (CuDB 1.337; VP p. 1835)

5 Jul 1751; Obediah Woodson granted 2,000 ac. Lunenburg Co. on both sides of
Stanton River adj. Matthew Talbott (LOP 29.442)

5 Jul 1751; Obediah Woodson granted 850 ac. Lunenburg Co. on both side of *Snow
Creek*, adj. William Owen (LOP 30.442)

9 Jun 1752; Obediah Woodson granted 1,250 ac. Lunenburg Co. on upper side of
Buffalo Creek (LOP 31.105)

10 Sep 1755; Obediah Woodson granted 400 ac. Lunenburg Co. on both sides of *Crab
Tree Fork* of *Snow Creek* adj. Randolph (LOP 32.624)

25 Jun 1765; from Obadiah Woodson of Prince Edward Co. to Richard Stith and
Benjamin Howard of Bedford Co.; for £100; 2,800 ac. in Bedford Co. on both side of
n. fork of *Little Otter River* granted sd. Woodson Aug 1764 (BeDB B2.479; VP p. 1814)

Sep 1766; 21 Apr 1767; Prince Edward Co.; will of Obadiah Woodson appointed wife
Constant his extx. and left her the plantation whereon he lived (PEWB 1.90; TVF 4.225-
226)
[Obadiah (Obediah) Woodson; PEWB (1754-1800) p. 94-95. Will pro. 21 Nov 1767. p. 102-102.
Inv. & Appr. rec. Apr. 1768. p. 107. Accounts rec. Oct 1769. p. 154-255. Accounts, undated. WB
No. 1, 1754-1785 (Reel 15) (LOV)]

Jul 1773; Nov 1774; Prince Edward Co.; will of Constant Woodson (PEWB 1.160; TVF
4.225-226)
[Constant Woodson; Prince Edward Wills & Admns. (1754-1800) p. 160-162. Will pro. 15 Nov
1773. p. 179. Inv. & appr. of estate in Bedford Co. rec. Dec 1774. p. 244-245. Inv. & Appr. rec.
Nov 1774. WB #1, 1754-1785 (Reel 15) (LOV)]

238-1 **Obadiah Woodson**; d. by Nov 1776 Prince Edward Co.

[Obadiah Woodson; Prince Edward Wills & Admns. (1754-1800) p. 199-200. Will pro. Nov
1776. p. 420-421. Exors. bond rec. 18 Nov 1776. WB No. 1, 1754-1785 (Reel 15) (LOV)]

23-9 **Robert Woodson**; not included in some family histories; he may have been the following Robert

[Robert Woodson; Goochland Co. Wills & Admns. (1728-1800) p. 469. Will pro. 18 Jul 1774. DB No. 10, 1769-1775 (Reel 4) (LOV)]

2-4 **Joseph Richard Woodson**, b. est. ca 1664 Henrico; d. by 15 Oct 1734 Goochland Co.; m. 6d/4m/1701 to 2nd cousin **Mary Jane Woodson**, b. est. ca 1682-5; d/o John Woodson, Jr. (QRH p. 2; VP p. 2044-5); Joseph was one of the legatees of his uncle John in 1684; he may have been the Joseph appointed to receive what money is in Tarlton Woodson's land belonging to this meeting (QRH p. 9); children from 1710 will of Jane's mother, Mary Woodson:

> 24-1 John Woodson, b. ca 1704
> 24-2 Mary Woodson, b. ca 1706
> 24-3 Joseph Woodson, b. ca 1709
> 24-4 Judith Woodson, b. ca. 1712
> 24-5 Martha Woodson, b. ca. 1716
> 24-6 Tucker Woodson, b. ca 1718

Oct Ct. 1723; from Joseph Woodson, Jr. to Tarlton Woodson, deed (HCVD-2 p. 199)

Will of Joseph Woodson of Goochland Co.; 25 Jan 1733; 15 Oct 1734
Lend to wife Jean 4 slaves
If negro woman has children, to be divided between my 2 daus Judith & Martha
To 2 granddaus. Elizabeth and Mary Woodson, negro, etc.
To son Tucker Woodson, land I live on, negroes after death of my wife also negro, mare
If he dies estate to be divided between his sisters Judith & Martha
Exs: Tucker Woodson, Stephen Woodson, John Pleasants
Wit: Thomas Carter, Joseph Woodson, Alexander Cunningham, Richard Curd (GCWD-1 p. 60, 61; GCRB 2.14; VP p. 1854)
20 Nov 1734; 18 Mar 1734; inventory of Joseph Woodson, Sr., dec'd; value £209.1.0; presented by Tarlton Woodson (GCWD-1 p. 68; VP p. 1873)
[Joseph Woodson; Goochland Co. Wills & Admns. (1728-1800) p. 14-15. Will, pro. 15 Oct 1734; p. 73-74 Inv. & Appr. rec. 18 Mar 1735-1735; Deed Book No. 2, 1734-1736 (Reel 1); (1728-1800) p. 41-43;Accts. rec. 20 Jul 1742; p. 264-265. Accts. rec. 16 Nov 1743; Deed Book No. 3, 1741-1745 (Reel 2); (LOV)]

> 24-1 **John Woodson**, b. ca 1704; d. ca 1727; he inherited 2 silver spoons from the 1708 will of great-grandmother Jane Pleasants of *Curles*; named in 1710 will of grandmother Mary Woodson
> 24-2 **Mary Woodson**, b. ca 1706; m. **Stephen Woodson**; s/o Robert Woodson & Elizabeth Lewis; she inherited 1 silver spoon from the 1708 will of great-grandmother Jane Pleasants of *Curles*; named in 1710 will of grandmother Mary Woodson; 2/7/1732 Mary, d/o Joseph of Henrico Co., disowned 5d/9m/1732 for marrying outside the Society (QRH p. 17; VP p. 2049)
> 24-3 **Joseph Woodson**, b. ca 1709; named in 1710 will of grandmother Mary Woodson; he is said to have d. young

6 Jul 1741; Joseph Woodson granted 423 ac. Goochland Co. on both sides of *Green Creek* of Appomattox River (LOP 19.1019)

23 Mar 1749; from Joseph Woodson to John Woodson, both of Cumberland Co.; 211 ½ ac. in Cumberland Co.; being ½ tract granted sd. Joseph 6 Jul 1741 on *Green Creek* and Appomattox River (CuDB 1.125; VP p. 1835)

28 Aug 1749; from Joseph Woodson to John Woodson, both of Cumberland Co.; 50 ac. where Joseph now dwells, conveyed to him by deed 27 Aug 1749 from Wm., John Jr. and Robert Woodson, Jr.; on branches of *Letalone Creek* (CuDB 1.48; VP p. 1835)

1 Mar 1757; from Joseph Woodson to John Woodson, both of Cumberland Co.; 274 ac. on *Green Creek* Cumberland Co.; 211 ac thereof part of 400 ac. granted sd. Joseph 6 Jul 1741; 63 ac. the residue granted sd. Joseph 20 Aug 1748 (CuDB 2.325; VP p. 1836)

24-4 **Tucker Woodson** of Goochland, b. ca 1718; d. by 21 Sep 1795 Goochland Co.; mb/1 18 Mar 1741 Goochland Co. **Sarah Hughes**; sec., John Cannon; wit., H. Wood; certificate from Stephen Woodson, guardian to Tucker Woodson, and stating her father, Robert Hughes, is agreed; witn., John Cannon, John Woodson; mb/2 22 Feb 1762 Cumberland Co. **Mary Netherland** of Cumberland Co., Wade Netherland, security (VP p. 1849); Tucker was heir & ex. of 1733 will of his father; Mrs. Tucker Woodson's funeral 12 Dec 1775, St. James Northam; the will of Robert Hughes probated in Cumberland Co. 22 Sep 1755 mentions dau. Sarah Woodson; children:

       244-1   Tucker Woodson
       244-2   Samuel Woodson
       244-3   Robert Woodson
       244-4   Joseph Woodson
       244-5   Jane Woodson
       Children of m/2:
       244-6   Tarleton Woodson, b. est. ca 1763
       244-7   Sarah Woodson, 22 Sep 1764
       244-8   John Pleasants Woodson, b. 21 May 1766
       244-9   Benjamin Woodson, b. 21 Aug 1768
       244-10   Henry Macon Woodson, b. 22 Mar 1770
       244-11   Wade Netherland Woodson, b. 22 Mar 1770

16 Sep 1740; 17 Sep 1746; from Robert Hughes to Tucker Woodson, 200 ac. Goochland Co.; ½ Hughes' patent dated 16 Sep 1740 (HCWD-3 p. 51; GCRB 4.180; VP 1893)

2 Mar 1755; 22 Sep 1755; Will of Robert Hughes of Cumberland Co.; names eldest dau. Sarah Woodson (CuWB 1.105; VP p. 1821-2)

10 Sep 1755; Tucker Woodson granted 430 ac. Lunenburg Co. on both side of *Mimicking Creek* (LOP 31.559)

10 Sep 1755; Tucker Woodson granted 400 ac. Lunenburg Co. adj. Nicholas Scott and on *Elhorn Creek* (LOP 32.632)

10 Sep 1755; Tucker Woodson granted 400 ac Lunenburg Co. on both sides of *Mimicking Creek* adj. his own line (LOP 32.635)

16 Jun 1756; Tucker Woodson granted 1,530 ac. Lunenburg Co. on both sides of *Mimikin Creek* (LOP 33.19)

17 Nov 1760; 18 Nov 1760; from Tucker Woodson, Goochland Co., to dau. Jane Lewis, w/o Robert Lewis; 10 negro slaves (GCRB 8.110; VP p. 1900)

19 Apr 1763; from Wade Netherland, Goochland Co., to Tucker Woodson & Mary his wife; 8 negro slaves; Mary was d/o Wade Netherland (GCRB 8.326; VP p. 1899)

Will of Wade Netherland of Cumberland Co.; 28 Jun 1764; 24 Apr 1769
To dau. Frances Macon, £5
To grandson Wade Netherland Woodson, £10 at age 21
Re my agreement with Tucker Woodson prior to his marriage with my dau. Mary; 8
  slaves for the life of Tucker and Mary; then to Mary's children; if none to my son
  Wade
To dau. Mary Woodson, £5
To Mary Lightfoot, orphan of James Lightfoot who was a brother of my late wife, £10
Residue of estate to my son Wade Netherland, ex.
Wit: Thos. Fleming, Wm. Fleming
11 Aug 1765; Codicil revoking £10 to grandson Wade Netherland Woodson; instead
  gives him negro girl, cows, cattle, etc. at age 21
25 Apr 1767; Codicil; to grandson Wade Netherland Woodson, negro, colt, items
  (CuWB 2.124; VP p. 1824-5)

12 Nov 1773; 25 Apr 1774 Will of Wade Netherland of Henrico Co.; mentions 5
children of sister Mary, wife of Tucker Woodson: Wade, John, Benjamin, Henry and
Sarah Woodson (CuWB; VP p. 1826)

Will of Tucker Woodson of Goochland Co.; 20 Nov 1792; 21 Sep 1795
Milly, Jule, Lewis, Lidy my negro to be free at my death & all my furniture, etc. in the
  hands of Samuel Woodson to be equally divided between my sons
Sons, Wade N. Woodson, Ben. Woodson, Henry Woodson, Tarlton Woodson & John
  P. Woodson
Wit: Roderick Payne, Mary Pollock, Margaret Payne (GCRB 16.384; VP p. 1861)
19 Sep 1796; 18 Sep 1797; Tucker Woodson, estate value £0.31.0 (GCRB 17.141; VP p.
  1885)
Apr Ct. 1796; Samuel Woodson, s/o Tucker Woodson, dec'd; summoned to take admn.
  of estate (GCOB 20.262; VP 1948)
[Tucker Woodson; Goochland Co. Wills & Admns. (1728-1800) p. 484-485. Will pro. 21 Sep
1795. DB No. 16, 1791-1796 (Reel 6); (1728-1800) p. 140-141. Inv. & Appr. rec. 18 Sep 1797.
DB No. 7, 1796-1800 (Reel 7) (LOV)]

244-1 Tucker Woodson; d. by May Ct. 1779 Albemarle Co.; m.
Elizabeth Moon; children from Tucker's will:

2441-1 Tucker Woodson
2441-2 Samuel Woodson

Will of Tucker Woodson, Jr. of Albemarle Co.; 16 Nov 1779; May Ct.1779
To my wife, all my negroes during her natural life or widowhood; is she shd. marry,
  1/3 part at her disposal among my children

To son Tucker Woodson "Minr." plantation where my father now lives; he paying to
Sam'l Jr. £7,500
To son Samuel Woodson, Jr. all my lands in Albemarle Co.
If my wife should be with child & same be male, sd. boys Tucker & Sam'l [pay]
£1,500 per peace, and if female £500 per peace
My stock to be divided among my children and debts paid
Exs: Friends Robert Lewis and Nicholas Lewis, my bro. Samuel Woodson and John
Henderson
Wit: John Gilmer, Hastings Marks, Jo. Woodson (AlWB 2.374; VP p. 1806)
[Tucker Woodson, Junior; Albemarle Wills & Admns. (1748-1800 p. 374. Will pro. May 1779.
pp. 416-417. Inv. & Appr. rec. Mar 1784. WB 2, 1752-1785 (Reel 34) (LOV)]

2441-1 **Tucker Moore Woodson**; mb. 11 Mar 1799 **Martha Eppe Hudson**; Matthew Henderson, security (VP p. 1811)

4 Mar 1799; Albemarle Co.; Sir, you are hereby otherwise to grant a License to Mr.
Tucker Woodson to be married to my Daughter Martha Eppe Hudson; /s/ Chas.
Hudson (VP p. 1812)

2441-2 **Samuel Hughes Woodson**; the following may belong to this Samuel

10 Sep 1798; Jun 1799; from Samuel Hughes Woodson of Fayette Co., KY; power of
atty. to Tucker Moore Woodson of same; 500 ac. in Albemarle Co., adj. Charlottesville
left me by will of my father; empower T. M. Woodson to sell (VP p. 1811)

244-2 **Samuel Woodson**; d. aft. 12 May 1810 Goochland Co.; mb. 12 Jun 1777 Goochland Co.; mb. 12 Jun 1777 Goochland Co., 19 Jun 1777 **Elizabeth Payne**, b. 19 Sep 1760, both of ye parish (DR; VP p. 1950); d/o George Payne the elder, sec. Nathaniel G. Morris; children from their father's will:

2442-1 **Robert Hughes Woodson**; d. bef. 1810; m. **Maria** ____; she m/2 **William F. Carter** (GCDB 26.105; VP 1921); children:

24421-1 **Deborah Woodson**
24421-2 **Mary Woodson**

2442-2 **Sally Pleasants Woodson**; m. 7 Jun 1798 Goochland **Warner Lewis**
2442-3 **Judith Woodson**
2442-4 **George Tucker Woodson**
2442-5 **Samuel Woodson**
2442-6 **Fielding Woodson**
2442-7 **Elizabeth Woodson**

27 Jan 1792; from Samuel Woodson & Elizabeth his wife of Goochland, Co. to David
Boyce; 80 ac. on James River Powhatan Co. (PoDB 1.662; VP p. 2030)

11 May 1792; Agreement between Samuel & Tucker Woodson; re. transfer in trust deed
lately obtained from Joseph Woodson re debts against Tucker Woodson; to pay

unto sd. Tucker £50 during his natural life, etc. for himself and his son Tarlton; Tucker conveyed all land on which sd. Samuel now lives (GCRB 16.70; VP 1908-9)

7 Feb 1798; from Samuel Woodson of Goochland Co. to Sackville King of Campbell Co.; for £50; 150 ac. Fluvanna Co. on both sides of s. fork of *Cary Creek* (FIDB 3.368; VP p. 1852); 21 Jul 1800 Samuel Woodson and Elizabeth his wife perfect title to this land (FIDB 1.551; VP p. 1852)

1 Mar 1799; from Samuel Woodson, Goochland Co., to Tucker Woodson of State of KY; mortgage to secure £700 due sd. Tucker; conveying tract on James River adj. tract whereon the Court House now stands conveyed Tucker, the elder (the tract where he lived and died) unto sd. Samuel; sd. Tucker releasing his claim to sd. land in consequence of a supposed marriage contract in favor of the abv. mentioned Tucker Woodson's father, Tucker Woodson, and the dismissing of a Chancery Court suit (GCRB 17.382; VP p. 1912)

Will of Samuel Woodson, Goochland Co.; 12 May 1810
Wife Elizabeth
Children: Sally P. Lewis, Judith Woodson, George Tucker Woodson, Samuel
    Woodson, Fielding Woodson & Elizabeth Woodson
Grandchildren: Deborah and Mary Woodson, daus. of dec'd son Robert H Woodson
Exs: son in law Warner Lewis, friends Isaac Curd, William Miller
Wit: Jno. Curd, Tho. Curd, Arched Pledge (VP p. 1862, 1863)

    244-3 **Robert Woodson**; no descendants
    244-4 **Joseph Woodson**, b. est. ca 1740-1750's Goochland; d. by 1817
          Goochland; m. 24 Sep/Nov 1779 St. James Northam **Sarah Hughes** in
          Cumberland Co.; [use with caution]; children:

       2444-1 **Joseph B. Woodson**
       2444-2 **Sally Hughes Woodson**; m. **Richard Goode**
       2444-3 **Jane Tucker Woodson**
       2444-4 **Judith Nevels Woodson**
       2444-5 **Mary Woodson**
       Children of Mary Ann Alvis and Joseph Woodson:
       2444-6 **John Woodson Alvis**
       2444-7 **Matthew Woodson Alvis**
       2444-8 **Robert Woodson Alvis**

11 Jul 1792; from Joseph Woodson, s/o Tucker Woodson, Goochland Co., to son Joseph Woodson; 300 ac. on s. side of road from Goochland Court House to *Carters Ferry*; reserving life estate (GCRB 16.499; VP p. 1911)

Will of Joseph Woodson; Goochland Co.; 2 Dec 1815; 17 Feb 1817
Having rec'd information to a certainty of the death of my only legitimate son (Joseph)
    and all my daus. have married except one and I suppose she has by this time entered
    into wedlock; all of whom have had so much as I could give and are moreover
    independent and wealthy, I shall only give them each a dollar out of my estate
To my natural of unlawful sons, John W. Alvis, Matthew W. Alvis & Robert W. Alvis
    (all begotten of the body of Mary Ann Alvis), the whole of my estate real and
    personal

Mentions family burying ground at Goochland Old Court House (GCWB 22.243; VP 1864, 1865)

244-5 **Jane (Jean) Woodson**; mb. 19 Feb 1760 Goochland Co.; m. 20 Feb 1760 **Mr. Robert Lewis**, both in this parish (DR); sec. Thomas Bolling

244-6 **Tarleton Woodson**, b. est. ca 1763; unmarried

244-7 **Sarah (Sally) Woodson**, b. 22 Sep 1764; bapt. 28 Dec 1764 (DR); m. ca 1781 **William Macon**; s/o Henry Macon of Cumberland Co. & Rebecca Mayo; children:

2447-1 **Henry Macon**, b. 2 Mar 1782; bapt. 17 Jun 1782 (DR)
2447-2 **Mary Mayo Macon**, b. est. ca 1784

244-8 **John Pleasants Woodson**, b. 21 May 1766; bapt. 29 Dec 1766 (DR)

18 Mar 1786; Frances Macon, sister of John Pleasant Woodson's mother, had no children of her own; she raised John Pleasant Woodson from infancy; she left him part of her estate including all of the negroes left her by her late husband, Henry Macon (CuDB 6.359; VP p. 1843)

Will of Frances Macon, relict of Henry Macon, of Cumberland Co.; leaves slaves to John P. Woodson, s/o Tucker Woodson 24 Oct 1785; 26 Jun 1786 (CuWB 2.406; VP p. 1828)

244-9 **Benjamin Woodson**, b. 21 Aug 1768; bapt. 23 Nov 1768 (DR)

244-10 **Henry Macon (Harry) Woodson** (twin), b. 22 Mar 1770; bapt. 4 May 1770 (DR); m. **Elizabeth Burton**; children:

244(10)-1 **Mary Woodson**
244(10)-2 **William Woodson**

3 Nov 1790; from Charles Allen & wife to Henry Woodson of Cumberland Co.; 100 ac. Cumberland Co. (CuDB 7.95; VP p. 1844)

21 May 1791; from Henry Woodson & Elizabeth his wife of Cumberland Co. to William Womack; 100 ac. Cumberland Co. (CuDB 7.107; VP p. 1844)

244-11 **Wade Netherland Woodson** (twin), b. 22 Mar 1770; mb. 27 Feb 1792 Powhatan Co. to **Mary Elizabeth Josepha Harris**; Thomas Turpin, Jr., security; consent of John Harris to his daughter's marriage (VP p. 2032); d/o Col. John Harris and Obedience Turpin; children:

244(11)-1 **Thomas Jefferson Woodson**
244(11)-2 **John Woodson**
244(11)-3 **Jordan Woodson**
244(11)-4 **Wade Woodson, Jr.**
244(11)-5 **Silas Woodson**; became Governor of Missouri
244(11)-6 **Emily Woodson**; m. **Francis Markham**
244(11)-7 **Mary Woodson**; m/1 **James Scott**; m/2 **Col. James Thornton**

244(11)-8 **Caroline Woodson**
244(11)-9 **Charlotte Woodson**; m. **John Woodson**; s/o William

19 Jun 1788; Wade N. Woodson admitted as deputy of the court of Powhatan Co.; 16 Dec 1790 qualified at atty. at law (PoOB 2.321; 3.624; VP p. 2032); 1793; Wade Woodson, Gent.; qualifies as an atty. at law (ChOB 10.76; VP p. 1820)

1 Oct 1795; from Seth Ligon to Wade N. Woodson of Powhatan Co.; 200 ac in Powhatan; adj. lands of Wm. Randolph & sd. Ligon on Buckingham Road; 15 Oct 1795 Woodson conveyed tract back to Seth Ligon (PoDB 2.151, 150; VP p. 2031)

22 Mar 1800; from Wade N. Woodson & Mary his wife to William Turpin; 397 ac. bounded by *Muddy Creek*; land where Woodson resides in Cumberland Co. (CuDB 8.329; VP p. 1848)

12 May 1800; from Wade N. Woodson of Cumberland Co. and Frances Harris, from John Harris of Powhatan; one undivided moiety of 6, 900 ac. Lincoln Co., KY on *Cumberland River & Stinking Creek* (PoDB 2.650; VP p. 2031)

24-5 **Judith Woodson**, b. aft. 1710;m. **Charles Christian**; she was named in the 1733 will of her father
24-6 **Martha Woodson**, b. aft. 1710; m. **John Cannon**; she was named in 1733 will of father; they were in Buckingham Co. in 1766

2-5 **Benjamin Woodson**, b. 21 Aug 1666; d. by 5 Aug 1723; St. James Parish, Henrico Co.; m. 12d/5m/1700 **Sarah Porter**; d. ca 1762; d/o William Porter, Jr. of Henrico Co. (QRH p. 1; VP p. 2044); Benjamin one of the legatees of his uncle John in 1684; an interesting historical note: several family histories state the outlaw Jesse Woodson James was a descendant of this Benjamin; children:

    25-1 Benjamin Lewis Woodson
    25-2 John Woodson
    25-3 William Woodson
    25-4 Elizabeth Woodson
    25-5 Robert Woodson
    25-6 Sarah Woodson
    25-7 Joseph Woodson

3 Dec 1707; 2 Feb 1707; from Benjamin Woodson of Henrico Co. to James Batts of Charles City Co., both planters; 125 ac. Henrico Parish on n. side of James River bounded by *Turkey Island Creek* (HCVD-2 p. 9)

6 May 1717; 6 May 1717; from Benjamin Woodson of Henrico Co. to Richard Allen of New Kent Co.; for £30; 200 ac. on s. side of *Chickahominy Swamp*; Sarah, w/o Woodson, relinquished dower (HCVD-2 p. 64)

6 May 1717; 6 May 1717; from Benjamin Woodson, Sr. to Thomas Harding, both of Henrico Co.; for £10; 150 ac. on s. side of *Chickahomy Swamp* next to Richard Woodson; Sarah, w/o Woodson, relinquished dower (HCVD-2 p. 64)

22 Jun 1722; Benjamin Woodson granted 178 ac. on n. side of James River on Rocky Run on line of John Woodson (LOP 11.110)

Ct. 5 Aug 1723; will of Benjamin Woodson, Henrico Co. presented by William Woodson, one of the exs.; John Woodson, Nowel Burton, sec. (HCVW-2 p. 167)

1762; by his will dated 19 Nov 1722 Benjamin Woodson of Henrico Co. directs that after the death of his wife, his personal estate be divided among his surviving children; Joseph Woodson, one of the survivors has possession of the estate and John Woodson, another of the survivors, for 5s, acquits sd. Joseph from any demands on the said estate; /s/ John Woodson (CuDB 3.317; VP p. 1837)

25-1 **Benjamin Woodson**, b. ca 1702; d. by 16 Sep 1735 Goochland Co.; said to have m. **Elizabeth Watkins**, b. 1712; d. 1802; d/o Thomas Watkins & Elizabeth Pride; said to have m/2 **William Daniel**; children from their father's will which makes no provision for a wife and includes a wit. named Elizabeth Daniel; use with caution:

> 251-1 Thomas Woodson
> 251-2 Jacob Woodson
> 251-3 Susannah Woodson

9 Feb 1724; Benjamin Woodson, Jr. and William Woodson; granted 400 ac. Henrico Co. (LOP 12.126)

11 Feb 1733; 19 Feb 1733; from Benjamin Jr., Joseph, John, Jr. & Robert Jr. to John Tabor, all of Goochland Co.; for £32; 200 ac. on *Tabor's Horsepen Branch* of *Deep Creek*; part of 582 ac. patent dated 11 Apr 1732; bounded by Matthew, *Licking Branch* (GCWD-1 p. 51; GCRB 1.451; VP p. 1888)

13 Feb 1733; Benjamin Jr., Joseph, John Jr., & Robert Woodson, Jr. of Goochland to George Michal Wolf; for £34; 359 ac. on *Tabors Horsepen Branch* of *Deep Creek*; part of abv. patent; next to Maj. John Woodson and Nicholas Cox (GCWD-1 p. 52)

Will of Benjamin Woodson of St. James Parish, Goochland Co.; 19 Aug 1735; 16 Sep 1735
To son Thomas, 200 ac. I now live on
To son Jacob, my land on *Deep Creek*
Wit: Sam. Allen, Elizabeth Daniel
Codicil: Rest of my estate to my daughter Susannah
Wit: Sam. Allen, Elizabeth Daniel, Hannah Daniel, Sarah Woodson (GCWD-1 p. 77; GCRB 3.135; VP p. 1853)
6 Aug 1738; [recorded]; accounts of estate of Benjamin Woodson, Jr.; mentions 460 ac. of land and 3 levys (GCWD-2 p. 21)
[Benjamin Woodson; Goochland Co. Wills & Admns. (1728-1800) p. 133. Will, pro. 19 Aug 1735, Addendum to will, pro. 16 Sep 1735. Deed Book No. 2 1734-1735; (1728-1800) p. 160 Settlement of estate rec. 16 Aug 1738. Deed Book No. 3, 1737-1742 (Reel 1) (LOV)]

251-1 **Thomas Woodson**; of *Janito*; d. by 30 Jun 1803 when his inventory was valued at £335.8.0 (GCRB 18.582); m. 27 Dec 1758 St. James Northam **Mary Woodson**; bapt. 9 Aug 1761 (DR); both in Goochland; children:

> 2511-1 **Elizabeth Woodson**, b. 3 Jun 1758; bapt 22 Oct 1758 (DR); m. ____ **Hull**

2511-2 **Jacob Woodson**, b. 29 Mar 1761; bapt. 9 Aug 1761 (DR); m.
Susannah Brooks

2511-3 **Stephen Woodson**, b. 2 Nov 1768; bapt. 19 Mar 1769 (DR)

2511-4 **Judith Woodson**, b. 7 Mar 1771; bapt. 19 Nov 1771 (DR)

251-2 **Jacob Woodson**; ?d. by 1762; he may have been the following
Jacob:

22 Jul 1751; from William, Joseph & John Woodson, surviving patentees of 1,500 ac.
granted 1 Apr 1732 to Jacob Woodson, son & heir of Benjamin Woodson, dec'd; 260
ac. part of 1,500 ac. in Cumberland Co. (CuDB 1.389; VP p. 1835)

26 Jun 1762; 16 Mar 1762; Jacob Woodson; inventory value £345.0.2 ½ (GCRB 8.203;
VP p. 1877-8)
[Jacob Woodson; Goochland Co. Wills & Admns. (1728-1800) p. 203-205. Inv. & Appr. rec. 16
Mar 1762. DB No. 8, 1759-1765 (Reel 3) (LOV)

251-3 **Susannah** or **Elizabeth Woodson**; possibly m. a Hubbard or Hull

25-2 **John Woodson**, b. ca 1706; d. 1790; mb. 10 Aug 1731 Lancaster Co.
Mary Miller, b. ca 1710; d 12 Dec 1775; d/o William Miller of Lancaster
Co.; children:

> 252-1 Miller Woodson
> 252-2 John Woodson
> 252-3 Anne Woodson
> 252-4 Sarah Woodson
> 252-5 Mary Woodson
> 252-6 Judy Woodson
> 252-7 Susanna Woodson

16 Mar 1723; John, William & Benjamin Woodson granted 400 ac. Henrico Co. on n.
side of James River (LOP 11.340)

11 Apr 1732; John Woodson granted 1,000 ac. Goochland Co. on s. side of James
River on *Deep Creek* (LOP 14.423)

10 May 1762; 15 Jun 1762; from John Woodson & Mary his wife, to William Stamps
of Bedford Co.; 100 ac. on branches of *Genito Creek*, Goochland Co., left him by his
father John Woodson (GCRB 8.253; VP p. 1901)

252-1 **Miller Woodson**; m. **Mary Degraffenriedt**, eldest d/o Tscharner
Degraffenriedt, late of Lunenburg Co.; Mary's ancestor Baron
Christopher De Graffenreidt (wife Regina Tscharner) was the founder
of New Berne, NC; Miller was clerk of Cumberland Co. in 1788;
children:

2521-1 **Tschaner Woodson**; deputy clerk in 1788, 1792; d. 1829
Cumberland Co.; will names several children

2521-2 **Blake B. Woodson**

2521-3 **Miller Woodson**

2521-4 **Christopher Woodson**

2521-5 **Mary Woodson**; m. **Jacob Michaux**
2521-6 **Sally Woodson**; m. **Creed Taylor**
2521-7 **Patsy Woodson**
2521-8 **Nancy Woodson**
2521-9 **Rutha Woodson**
2521-10 **Lucy Woodson**
2521-11 **Virginia Woodson**

18 Jan 1772; from Henry Patillo of Province of North Carolina to Miller Woodson of Prince Edward Co.; 100 ac. Cumberland Co. (CuDB 5.74; VP p. 1839)

22 Nov 1784; Miller Woodson, appointed & sworn as clerk of Court (CuOB 1784-6 p. 182; VP p. 1848)

Mar 1795; from Miller Woodson to Blake B. Woodson; 191 ac. on *Badluck Creek* Cumberland Co. (CuDB 7.390; VP p. 1845)

20 Dec 1796; Mary Woodson, eldest d/o Tscharner Degraffenriedt, late of Lunenburg Co., dec'd, now w/o Miller Woodson; made oath that Baker Degraffenriedt was the eldest son of Tscharner Degraffenriedt; that Vincent of Parsons, North Carolina, is the eldest s/o Baker (CuDB 7.501; VP p. 1846)

2521-1 **Tschaner Woodson**; his will in Cumberland Co. was dated 15 Oct 1829; he bought several tracts of land in Cumberland Co. 1796-7, one of 160 ac. on s. side of *Andlea Creek* (VP p. 1846, 1847)

Jan 1798; from Tscharner Woodson of Cumberland Co. to John Wright; 300 ac on *Angola Creek* Cumberland Co.; purchased by Woodson of Bauldwin Pearce (CuDB 8.178; VP p. 1848)

2521-2 **Blake B. Woodson**
2521-3 **Miller Woodson**
2521-4 **Christopher Woodson**
2521-5 **Mary Anne Elizabeth Miller Woodson**; mb. 23 Oct 1788 Cumberland Co. to **Jacob Michaux**; Wm. DeGraffenreidt, security (VP p. 1849)
2521-6 **Sally Woodson**; m. **Creed Taylor**
2521-7 **Patsy Woodson**
2521-8 **Nancy Woodson**
2521-9 **Rutha Woodson**
2521-10 **Lucy Woodson**
2521-11 **Virginia Woodson**

252-2 **Judy Woodson**, b. 26 Mar 1746; m. 9 Oct 1761 **Jacob Michaux**
252-3 **John Woodson**; m/1 **Susannah Booker**; m/2 **Elizabeth Raine Venable**, a widow; children:

2523-1 **Booker Woodson**
2523-2 **Peter Woodson**
2523-3 **Benjamin Woodson**
2523-4 **Joseph Woodson**

2523-5 James Woodson
Child of m/2:
2523-6 Betsy Woodson

252-4 Anne Woodson; m. **William Early** or **Worsham Easley**
252-5 Sarah Woodson; mb. 13 Jan 1756 Cumberland Co. **Frederick Hatcher**; John Woodson, security (VP p. 1849)
252-6 Mary Woodson; mb. 18 Sep 1752 Cumberland Co. **Francis McGraw**; Thompson Swann, security (VP p. 1848)
252-7 Susanna Woodson, b. ca 1750; d. 7 Jan 1828 Laurens, SC, age 78 (tombstone); m. **William Ligon**, b. est. ca 1751; d. by 1805

25-3 William Woodson; d. by 27 Jun 1785 Cumberland Co.; m. **Sarah Allen**; children from William's will [said to have been others]:

        253-1 Drury Woodson
        253-2 Jesse Woodson
        253-3 Shadrack Woodson
        253-4 William Woodson

15 Mar 1735; William Woodson granted 400 ac. Goochland Co. at head of *Soak-Arse Run* of *Willis's River* (LOP 17.34)

21 Jun 1737; 21 Jun 1737; from William Woodson of St. James Parish, Goochland Co., to Tandy Walker of Henrico Co.; for £40; 460 ac. part of 1,500 patent on s. side of James River to William, Benjamin, Jr., Joseph, Jr., John & Robert Woodson; Sarah, w/o William, relinquished dower rights (GCWD-2 p. 5; GCRB 3.38; VP p. 1890)

18 Aug 1752; 18 Aug 1752; from William Woodson, Albemarle Co., to Drewey Woodson, s/o William of Goochland; 200 ac. on *Jenito Creek*, Goochland Co. (GCRB 6.239; VP p. 1896)

17 Nov 1759; from William Woodson and Sarah his wife of Albemarle Co. to Wm. Roughton; 200 ac. Cumberland Co.; 200 ac. part of 400 ac. on both sides of *Soak Arse Run* granted sd. William Woodson and James Daniel by patent 15 Mar 1735 (CuDB 3.2; VP p. 1836)

17 Mar 1783; William Woodson, late of Buckingham, now of Cumberland Co.; made a gift to son Drury of 200 ac. on Branches of *Randolphs Creek* in Buckingham Co. [now in possession of John Bagby]; [confusing] agreement between Drury, Jesse and Shadrack, sons of William (CuDB 6.149; VP p. 1841-2)

<u>Will of William Woodson of Cumberland Co. ; 24 Jul 1784; 27 Jun 1785</u>
To son Jesse Woodson, part of my estate; remainder to be divided between my
   grandson Drury Woodson, s/o Drury, and grandson William Woodson, s/o Shadrack
To Drury and William, 125 ac. part of tract that I give Shadrack Woodson
Ex: Drury Woodson
Wit: Saml. Taylor, William Harris, Mary Woodson (CuWB 2.369; VP p. 1828)
[William Woodson; Cumberland Co. Wills & Admns. (1749-1810) p. 369. Will, pro. 27 Jun 1785. WB No. 2, 1769-1792 (Reel 17) (LOV)]

253-1 **Drury Woodson**; d. by 24 Nov 1788 Cumberland Co.; m. **Lucy Christian**; d/o Charles Christian & Judith Woodson; children from Drury's will:

> 2531-1 Charles Woodson
> 2531-2 Judith Woodson
> 2531-3 Nancy Woodson
> 2531-4 Mary Woodson
> 2531-5 Elizabeth Woodson
> 2531-6 Drury Woodson
> 2531-7 Martha Woodson

19 Aug 1760; 19 Aug 1760; Drewry Woodson, Albemarle Co., to William Royster, Goochland Co.; 200 ac. Goochland Co. on branches of *Genito Creek*; bounded by Thomas Woodson, etc.; Sarah Woodson, mother of sd. Drewry, and Lucy, wife sd. Drewry, both relinquish dower rights (GCRB 8.97; VP p. 1900)

28 Apr 1783; from Drury Woodson to Charles Woodson, both of Cumberland Co.; 253 ac. in Cumberland Co. (CuDB 6.137; VP p. 1841)

Will of Drury Woodson of Cumberland Co.; 7 May 1788; 24 Nov 1788
To wife Lucy Woodson, loan for life of 6 negros and land where I now live with all
    estate real and personal not otherwise given to my children; then to be equally
    divided among my children
Rest of estate to equally divided among all my children except Judith Johnson and
    Charles Woodson after my wife's decease
To dau. Judith Johnson, negro
To son Charles Woodson, 5s
To dau. Mary Woodson, 2 negroes
To dau. Nancy King, 2 negroes
To son Drury Woodson, 3 negroes and land where I live
To dau. Elizabeth Woodson, 2 negroes
All legacies to be rec'd as children come of age, except that given son Drury at death
    of wife
Exs: wife Lucy Woodson, son Charles Woodson
Wit: Jesse Talley, Agness Talley, Susana Foster (CuWB 2.442; VP p. 1828-9)
[Drury Woodson; CuWA (1749-1810) p. 161 Account Current, rec. 24 Nov 1800. WB No. 3,
1792-1810 (Reel 18); CuWA (1749-1810) p. 441-442 Will, pro. 24 Nov 1788. p. 453-454. Inv. &
appr. rec. 27 Apr 1789. WB No. 2, 1769-1792 (Reel 17) (LOV)]

> 2531-1 **Charles Woodson**; mb. 23 Sep 1780 Goochland Co. **Judith Leake**; d/o Joseph Leake; George Christian, sec.; consent of Drury to marriage of his son Charles (VP p. 1950)
>
> 2531-2 **Judith Woodson**; mb. 27 Dec 1773 Cumberland Co., Samuel Sanders, security (VP p. 1850)
>
> 2531-3 **Nancy Woodson**; mb. 22 Apr 1788 Cumberland Co. to **Philip King**; Creed Taylor, security; consent of Drury Woodson, father of Nancy (VP p. 1849)
>
> 2531-4 **Mary (Polly) Woodson**; m. 2 Mar 1789 **William King** of Buckingham Co.
>
> 2531-5 **Elizabeth Woodson**; m. **Charles Gilliam**

2531-6 **Drury Woodson** of Cumberland Co.; mb. 3 Mar 1800
Powhatan Co. **Sally Stovall**: Jesse Stovall, sec.; consent of Jesse
Stovall to daughter's marriage (VP p. 2032)

12 Aug 1794; from Edward Numan & wife to Drury Woodson of Cumberland Co.;
100 ac. adj. sd. Woodson in Cumberland Co. (CuDB 7.381; VP p. 1845)

20 Jan 1796; from Drury Woodson of Cumberland Co. to Charles Gilliam; 50 ac. land
Cumberland Co. adj. sd. Woodson (CuDB 7.444; VP p. 1846)

2531-7 **Martha Woodson**; unmarried

253-2 **Jesse Woodson**; d. bef. 24 Oct 1808 Cumberland Co.; m. **Mary
Ann** ____; his will names his wife Mary Ann and sons of his brother
Shadrack (VP p. 1833)

28 Oct 1776; from Isaac Bates to Jesse Woodson; bond re valuation of certain negroes
"which sd. parties become heirs to under their wives" (CuDB 6.30; VP p. 1840)

Caswell County, North Carolina; 7 Mar 1781
To Mr. Jessey Woodson, in Bucking; County:
Dear Loveing Uncle Jessey: This comes to inform you that we are all well and in about
fifteen miles from our grand army, and now are informed the enemy are surrounded by
our army. We expect to join the grand army by the 10th of this month, and I do no (not
known) when I shall be back if ever; pray if I never come, sell as much as will pay my
debts and the remains I desire shall be given to my sister Polly, and I never return I bid
you all farewell, for if I dy the hotest will be my portion; therefore beg to intrust in
your prayer and remember my love to Mary Ann Price. So no more at present, but
remaining your loving friend. /s/ Joseph Woodson (VP p. 1826-7)

This would have been a s/o Drury or Shadrack:
Will of Josiah Woodson, Cumberland Co.; 28 Mar 1781; Ct. compared handwriting on
letter to will and accepted will (CuWB 2.271; VP p. 1827)

253-3 **Shadrack Woodson** of Buckingham Co.; d. by Oct 1795 Franklin
Co.; m. 14 Aug 1766 St. James Parish **Susanna Walker**; d/o David
Walker, Jr. of Goochland (GCRB 10.283); St. James register calls her
Susanna Walker; the will of her grandfather, David Walker, Sr. leaves
her £20, proved 16 May 1774 (GCRB 10.435; VP p. 1871-2); children:

2533-1 **David Woodson**, b. 8 Apr 1770; bapt. 23 Apr 1770 (DR);
named in the will of his grandfather Watkins & uncle Jesse Woodson
2533-2 **Sally Woodson**; named in the will of her grandfather Watkins
2533-3 **Jesse Woodson**; named in will of uncle Jesse Woodson
2533-4 **Shadrack Woodson**; named in will of uncle Jesse Woodson
2533-2 **William Woodson**

14 Nov 1780; from Shadrack Woodson & Susannah his wife of Buckingham Co. to
Isaac Bryant; 220 ac. in Buckingham & Cumberland Co.; same conveyed Shadrack by
his father William Woodson on record in Buckingham Co. (CuDB 6.94; VP p. 1841)

[Shadrach Woodson; Franklin Co. Wills & Administrations (1786-1800) p. 154-156. Inv. &
Appr. rec. Oct 1795. Will Book No., 1786-1812 (Reel 18) (LOV)]

253-4 **William Woodson**; d. by 27 Jun 1785 Cumberland Co.; m. ____;
son:

2534-1 **Jesse Woodson**

25-4 **Elizabeth Woodson**; m. **James Daniel**
25-5 **Robert Woodson**; b. ca 1702; d. 1748-50; said to have m. ca 1720
Cumberland Co. **Rebecca Pryor**; d/o John Pryor; she inherited 5s from
the will of her father (GCRB 7.77; VP p. 1866); children from Robert's will:

> 255-1 John Woodson
> 255-2 James Woodson
> 255-3 Benjamin Woodson
> 255-4 Robert Woodson
> 255-5 Elizabeth Woodson
> 255-6 Mary Woodson
> 255-7 Sarah Woodson

Will of Robert Woodson of Goochland Co.; 7 May 1748; 19 Sep 1750
To son John Woodson upper portion and son James Woodson lower portion; equally,
land and plantation where I now dwell
To other 5 children, Benja., Robert, Eliza., Mary & Sarah, residue of real & personal
estate, equally; sons at age 21; daus. at age 18
Son James to continue with his uncle Joseph Woodson until he is of age
Sons to be taught to read and write & daus. taught to read
Exs: brothers William & Joseph Woodson
Wit: John Wright, Thomas Wright, William Christian (VP p. 1857)
16 Nov 1750; 20 Nov 1750; Robert Woodson; estate value £113.12.3 (GCRB 6.106; VP
p. 1874-5)
[Robert Woodson; Goochland Co. Wills & Admns. (1728-1800) p. 100-101. Will Pro. 19 Sep
1750. p. 106. Inv. & Appr. rec. 10 Nov 1754. Deed Book No. 6, 1749-1755 (Reel 3) (LOV)]

255-1 **John Woodson**; he inherited negroes and residue of estate of his
grandfather John Pryor of Goochland

19 Aug 1754; 17 Dec 1754; from John Woodson to f, both of Goochland Co.; 160 ac.
Goochland Co. on w. side of Western fork of *Beaver Dam Creek* where Rebecca
Woodson now lives; land devised John Woodson by his father Robert Woodson by his
will dated 19 Aug 1754; recorded 17 Dec 1754; Rebecca Woodson, widow & relict of
Robert Woodson, dec'd, relinquishes her dower rights in sd. land (GCRB 6.407; VP p.
1898)

255-2 **James Woodson**; mb. 23 Jul 1754 St. James Northam, Goochland
to **Elizabeth Whitlock (Whitelock)** (DR); their children said to have
left Goochland and settled in Union Co., SC:

2552-1 **James Woodson**, b. 10 Mar 1758; bapt. 30 Apr 1758 (DR)
2552-2 **Jeanie (Jennie) Booth Woodson**, b. 2 May 1760; bapt. 27
Aug 1760 (DR)
2552-3 **Gillie Woodson**, b. 13 Jan 1763; bapt. 17 Feb 1765 (DR)
2552-4 **Thomas Woodson**, b. 28 Feb 1767; bapt. 17 May 1767 (DR);
he may have been the Thomas Woodson of Goochland who mb. 20

Jul 1798 Henrico Co. **Elizabeth Redford**; surety John Redford, her father (VP p. 2023)

    2552-5 **Sally Woodson**, b. 25 May 17__; bapt. 6 Aug 1769 (DR)

    2552-6 **Cary Woodson**, b. 11 May 1771; bapt. 11 Aug 1771 (DR)

26 May 1756; 16 Nov 1756; from James Woodson & Elizabeth his wife to John Payne, all of Goochland Co.; 155 ac. Goochland Co. on w. fork *Beaver Dam Branch*; being part of tract Robert Woodson, dec'd, father of sd. James, formerly lived and devised by his will to son James; Rebecca Woodson, mother of sd. James, relinquishes her dower right (GCRB 7.134; VP p. 1899)

12 Sep 1776; from James Woodson and Elizabeth his wife to Jaell Perkins; for £55; 150 ac. Albemarle Co. (AlDB 8.44; VP p. 1810)

    255-3 **Benjamin Woodson**

    255-4 **Robert Woodson**; d. by 18 Jul 1774 Goochland

Will of Robert Woodson, St. James Northam Parish, Goochland; 20 Jan 1774; 18 Jul 1774
To brother Benja. Woodson, ex., all estate real and personal
Wit: Turner Roundtree, John Albritton (GCRB 10.469; VP p. 1858)

    255-5 **Elizabeth Woodson**; m. 24 May 1760 **Shadrack Mims** (DR)

    255-6 **Mary Woodson**

    255-7 **Sarah Woodson**; mb. 20 Aug 1766 St. James Northam **Turner Rountree**, both of this parish in Goochland (DR)

   25-6 **Sarah Woodson**; m. **John Allen**

2 Sep 1749; rec'd of Robert Woodson, one of the exs. of Benjamin Woodson, dec'd; £5; being in full satisfaction of my wife's part of estate of sd. Benjamin Woodson, Cumberland Co; /s/ John Allen (CuDB 3. 316)

   25-7 **Joseph Woodson**; d. by 15 Sep 1791 Powhatan Co.; m. 1726 **Susanna Watkins**; d/o Thomas Watkins & Elizabeth; daughter:

          257-1 Mary Woodson

1 Oct 1782; from Joseph Woodson of Powhatan Co. to grandson Benjamin Mosby; 150 ac. Powhatan Co.; part of land where Joseph resides (PoDB 1.182; VP p. 2029)

16 Apr 1785; from Joseph Woodson of Powhatan Co. to grandson Joseph Mosby; 50 ac. in Powhatan Co. part of tract where Joseph resides (PoDB 1.336)

Will of Joseph Woodson of Powhatan Co.; 4 Jul 1791; 15 Sep 1791
Mentions dau. Mary Mosby; grandson Benjamin Mosby [his son John]; grandson Joseph Mosby [his son Robert]; granddau. Mary Ann Hobson; granddaus. Elizabeth Mosby, Clarrissa Mosby; grandson Poindexter Mosby, granddaus. Sarah Mosby, Siller Mosby
Mentions Father and Mother, Poindexter Mosby and Mary his wife
Ex: grandson Joseph Mosby
Wit: Miller Woodson, Mathew Sanderson, Dancy McCraw, Benj. Hobson, Joseph Davis (PoWB 1.206; VP p. 2026-7)

[Joseph Woodson; Powhatan Wills & Admns. (1777-1800) p. 206-207. Will pro. 15 Sep 1791. p. 209. Inv. & Appr. rec. 15 Dec 1791. WB No. 1, 1777-1795 (Reel 15) (LOV)]

257-1 **Mary Woodson**; m. **Poindexter Mosby**; children:

2571-1 **Benjamin Mosby**; his grandfather gave him 150 ac. in Powhatan Co. in 1782
2571-2 **Joseph Mosby**
2571-3 **Mary Ann Mosby**; m. ____ **Hobson**
2571-4 **Elizabeth Mosby**
2571-5 **Clarissa Mosby**
2571-6 **Poindexter Mosby**
2571-7 **Sarah Mosby**
2571-8 **Siller Mosby**

2-6 **Mary Woodson**; m. bef. 30 Oct 1705 Goochland Co. **George Payne**, b. ca 1680; d. ca 1744 Goochland; known children:

26-1 Josias Payne, b. 30 Oct 1705
26-2 George Payne, b. 21 Nov 1707
26-3 Robert Payne, b. 16 Nov 1709
26-4 John Payne, b. 4 Dec 1713

Will of George Payne of St. James Parish, Goochland Co.; 3 Dec 1744; 15 Jan 1744
To wife Mary, all my land and estate for widowhood
To son John, land I dwell on at my wife's death; 200 ac. on head branches of *Stony Creek*; negro; my books, papers and accounts
To son Josias, negro
To son George, negro, cooper kittle; also 400 ac. on *Lickinhole Creek* now in his possession
To sons Josias and George and grandson Augustine, 800 ac. on branch of *Little Bird*, equally
Grandchildren: Agnes, Augustine, Jesse, negroes
To wife, remainder of estate
Exs: three sons: Josias, George and John
Wit: Will'm Miller, Charles Jordan, James Bates (GCWD-3 p. 13)

26-1 **Josias Payne**, b. 30 Oct 1705 (DR)
26-2 **George Payne**, b. 21 Nov 1707 (DR); m. **Judith Burton**; known children:

262-1 **Joseph Payne**, b. 23 Mar 1758 (DR)
262-2 **Elizabeth Payne**, b. 19 Sep 1760 (DR) m. 19 Jun 1777 **Samuel Woodson**
262-3 **Richard Payne**, b. 29 Apr 1765 (DR)

26-3 **Robert Payne**, b. 16 Nov 1709 (DR)
26-4 **John Payne**, b. 4 Dec 1713 (DR)

17 Dec 1754; 17 Dec 1754; from John Payne to John Woodson, both of Goochland Co.; 225 ac. in Goochland on both side of *Little Creek*; exchange for 150 ac. to be conveyed Payne by sd. John Woodson & Rebecca Woodson (GCRB 6.430; VP p. 1897)

5 Sep 1777; 20 Oct 1777; from John Payne to Joseph Woodson, Goochland Co.; 200 ac. Goochland Co. (GCRB 12.55; VP p. 1903)

2-7 **Sarah Woodson**; m/1 by 1689 **Edward Moseby**, carpenter; Quaker; children:

    27-1 **John Moseby**
    27-2 **Robert Moseby**
    27-3 **Benjamin Moseby**
    27-4 **Joseph Moseby**
    27-5 **Agnes Moseby**
    27-6 **Hezekiah Moseby**
    27-7 **Jacob Moseby**
    27-8 **Richard Moseby**

1 Jun 1689; 1 Jun 1689; deed of gift from Robert Woodson, Sr. of Henrico Co. to dau. Sarah, w/o Edward Moseby; 100 ac. on s. side of *White Oak Swamp* purchased of Robert Clark (HCVD-1 P. 52)

1 Jun 1689; 1 Jun 1689; from Robert Woodson, Sr., for 20 days carpenter work, to Edward Moseby; 50 ac. next to 100 ac. given this date to Sarah, w/o Edward (HCVD-1 p. 52)

Edward Moseby was to work on meeting house 9/3/1701; on 10/5/1702 Edward Mosby asked to finish meeting house without delay (QRH p. 2, 3); 19/4/1709 Friends appointed to visit Edward Mosby for not attending meetings (QRH p. 5); 5/1/1724 Edward Moseby disowned (QRH p. 13)

2-8 **Elizabeth Woodson**, b. est. ca 1670's; d. ca 1740 Goochland; m. **William Lewis**; d. by 1 May 1707; children:

    28-1 **John Lewis**
    28-2 **William Lewis**
    28-3 **Joseph Lewis**

Will of William Lewis (oral will); Henrico Co.; 24 Dec 1706; 1 May 1707
To eldest son John, the plantation where I live, 100 ac. on n. side of *White Oak Swamp*
To 2 sons, William and Joseph Lewis, 200 ac. at *Three Runs*, with parcel on White Oak Swamp and *Deep Run* to be divided
Remainder to wife, since children are hers as well as his, he knew she would do well for them
Wit: spoken in presence of George Paine & Elizabeth Johnson
Presented in court by Elizabeth Lewis, relict (HCVW-1 p. 97)
1 May 1707; administration of nuncupative will of William Lewis granted to Elizabeth Lewis, his relict (HCVW-1 p. 97)

2-9 **Judith Woodson**; m. **William Cannon**; children:

INDEX

John, 31
Nancy, 31
Bailey, Temperance, 101
Thomas, 101
Baileys Creek, 36, 201, 202
Baileys, 36, 171, 180, 188, 221
Baker, John, 91, 98
Sarah, 91
Thomas, 97
Baldwins, 135, 144
Ball, Valentine, 79
William, 60
Ballad, Edm'd, 114
Ballow, Charles, 122
Leon, 69
Leonard, 122
Bannister River, 84, 85
Bannister, John, 34, 36, 113
Barbadoes, 47, 48
Barnet, William, 211
Barrett, James, 72, 228
Lucy, 72
Sarah, 72
Barrow, 105
Bass, ____, 67
Ann, 57, 58
Archud, 30
Christopher, 57, 58
Ciceley, 57, 58
Edward, 57, 58, 65
Elizabeth, 57, 58
Frances, 57
Jo., 62, 145
Joseph, 57, 58
Mary, 57, 62
Obedience, 64
Sarah, 57, 58
Sissanah, 57
Stella, 58
Thomas, 58
William, 57, 58, 62
Bate, Chambling, 39
William, 39
Bates, Benjamin, 176
Caroline Matila, 221, 222
Charles, 54, 222, 225, 226, 230, 231, 235, 236
Edward, 222

Elizabeth, 178, 231
Fleming, 222, 225, 226, 227
Frederick, 222
Hannah, 225, 227
Henry, 36
Isaac, 109
James Woodson, 222
James, 225, 226, 227, 262
John, 225, 226, 227
Julian, 222
Lucy C., 193
Martha, 175
Richard, 222
Susannah, 214
Tarleton, 222
Thomas Fleming, 222
Thomas, 170
Batt, Dorothy, 33
Henry, 36
Michael, 33
William, 34
Batte, Amy, 34, 35, 40
Ann, 36, 37
Chamberlayne, 38, 39, 40
Elizabeth C., 39
Elizabeth Chamberlayne, 38
Elizabeth, 35, 36, 38, 39, 40, 137, 155, 157
Henry, 33, 35, 36, 37, 38, 39, 137, 162, 163
John, 33, 36, 37, 38, 40
Margaret Jones, 39
Margaret, 39
Martha, 34, 35, 36, 37, 113, 202
Mary, 34, 35, 36, 37, 38, 39, 162, 163
Peggy Jones, 39
Rachel, 36, 37
Richard B., 39
Richard Baugh, 38
Richard, 38, 39
Robert, 37, 38
Sarah, 34, 35, 36, 37
Temperance, 35
Thomas, 33, 34, 35, 36, 38, 39, 40, 113, 145
William, 33, 34, 36, 37, 38, 39
Batts, Henry, 34, 36

Elizabeth, 196
John, 160
Mary Ligon, 160
Mary, 160
Robert, 160
Susannah, 108
Coles Run, 76
Coles, Walter, 126
Collier, William, 180
Colson, Jacob, 89
Colson's, 165, 183
Comeings, Roger, 214
Compton, John, 93, 94
Conecock Brook, 162
Conjurer's Field, 34
Contention, 192, 194
Cooke, ____, 149
John, 42, 149, 185, 243
Thomas, 104
Copeland, Sarah, 203
Cornelius Creek, 70, 168
Cornelius' Run, 122
Cornelius's, 203
Cousins, ____, 149
Amy, 19
Ann, 19, 99, 100
Charles, 12, 14, 19
Elizabeth, 14, 19
George, 19
John, 19
Judith, 19
Margery, 12
Martha, 149
Mary, 19
Robert, 19
Rose, 19
William, 19
Cowley, Abraham, 119
Theodosia, 119
Cox, ____, 75
Edith, 123
Elizabeth, 123
George, 39, 40
Henry, 39, 225
James, 161
John, 243
Judith, 123, 191, 206
Martha, 123, 124

Mary, 38, 123
Prudence, 123
Richard, 79
Sarah, 75, 76, 122, 191, 236
Stephen, 123, 191, 236
William, 70, 123, 236
Crab Tree Fork, 246
Craddock, Robert, 88
Crawley, see Crowley
Crew, J., 193
John, 169, 170, 178
Margaret, 175
Micajah, 175
Crockett, Joseph, 223
Crook, Solomon, 115
Cross Swamp, 20, 62
Crouch, John, 229, 241
Richard, 148
Sally, 230
Sarah, 230
Crowley, Ann, 56, 57
John, 56
Crump Creek, 61
Crumpton, John, 93
Mary, 93
Cumberland River, 253
Cummins, Roger, 214
Cunneecock, 35
Cunningham, Alexander, 247
Curd, Isaac, 251
John, 251
Richard, 247
Thomas, 194, 251
Cureton, John, 37
Curles Burying Ground, 178
Curles Swamp, 116, 125, 164, 165
Curles, 101, 116, 123, 133, 134, 141,
150, 160, 164, 165, 178, 201, 202,
203, 204, 209, 214, 216, 218, 247
Currie, James, 232, 233
Curtis, John, 150

D., Thomas, 19
Dabbs, Joseph, 109
Dalton, Eliza, 147
Daly, Josiah, 38
Damril, Rich'd, 116
Dan River, 142

Mary, 64
Tabitha, 64
Thomas, 64, 68, 137
William, 44, 45
Osbornes, 17
Otter Dam Swamp, 33
Otter River, Little, 246
Out Glebe, The, 232, 234
Overby, ____, 19
Ann, 19
Overstreet, Elizabeth, 244
Overton, Sally, 207
Sarah, 207
Thomas, 207, 208
Owen, Ann, 205
Geo., 205
David, 153
William, 246
Owens, John, 156

Packers, 38
Paggen, Peter, 164
Paine, George, 215
Josiah, 215
Mary, 215
Pamphin, Armistead, 159
Pankey, Martha, 93, 96
Mary Ann, 48
Polly, 96
Samuel Hardin, 97
Samuel, 93, 96, 97
Stephen, 48, 53, 97
Parham, James, 37
Lewis, 199
Molly, 67
Rachel, 37
Sarah, 37
William, 66, 67
Parish, David, 118
Martha Holland, 118
Parker, ____, 33
Katherine, 32, 85
Martha, 32, 33
Mary, 32, 33, 85
Matthew, 32
Will, 32, 85
William, 32, 33, 170
Parram, Francis, 150

Parsons, Agnes, 218, 238
Ann, 200
Elizabeth, 238, 239, 242
Joseph, 171, 227, 231, 237, 238, 242, 263
Josiah, 238.
Judith, 238
Margaret, 189
Mary, 238
Samuel, 171, 188, 189, 192
Sarah, 189, 237, 238
Ursley, 238
William, 238
Woodson, 238
Passon, see Parsons
Pasteur, Ann, 180
Patrum, Fanney, 15
Pattillo, Henry, 256
Pattison, David, 51
Joseph, 12, 35
Payne, ____, 72
Ann, 71
Augustine, 262
Charles, 91
Elizabeth, 71, 72, 250, 262
George, 72, 226, 228, 250, 262, 263
John, 261, 262, 263
Joseph, 72, 262
Josias, 262
Kiturah, 71
Margaret, 249
Mary, 262
Richard, 72, 262
Robert Burton, 72
Robert, 71, 262
Roderick, 249
Payson, Matthew, 203
Pearce, Bauldwin, 256
Pears, Anderson, 229, 234
Dorothy, 234
Peart, Francis, 169
Pecquenock, 166
Peirce, Fra., 32
Will, 32
William, 33
Pemberton, Mary, 179
Pequanocka, 183
Perdue, Ezekiel, 16

Mary, 130, 131
Mrs., 102
Obadiah, 110, 129, 130, 168, 185, 243
Richard, 114
William Granville, 194
William, 87, 130, 190
Smoot, Harriet, 195
Smythe, Thomas, 104
Sneed, William, 130
Snelling, Ann, 91
Aquilar, 91
Alexander, 24
Snow Creek, 246
Soakarse Run, 83, 257
Soakarse, 84
Soane, John, 219, 137
Judith, 19
Solomon's Creek, 219, 223
Southall, Turner, 117, 200
Spence, Randolph, 221
Spicer, Patrick, 192
Spiers, Robert, 242
Spring Branch, 119, 159
Spring Gardens, 34
Spring Run, 5
Squire, 86
Squires, Uriah, 220
Stabler, Caleb, 175
Deborah, 174, 175, 176
Edward, 170, 174, 175, 176
Elizabeth, 176
James P., 175
Mary, 176
Robinson, 176
Thomas P., 175
Thomas S., 176
William H., 176
William Henry, 175
William, 174, 175
Stamper, Susannah, 78
Stamps, William, 71, 255
Staples, John, 199
Stark, John, 81
Thomas, 81
Staunton River, 109, 246
Steger, Samuel, 154
Steuart, Steward see Stewart

Stewart, Charles, 49, 51
George, 201
John, 89, 90, 98, 100, 145, 155
Judith, 140
Mary, 142, 155
Sarah, 152
Stiles, Richard, 19
Stinking Creek, 253
Stith, Anne, 131
Richard, 246
Stokes, Henry, 143
Michal S., 143
Stone, ____, 242
Anderson, 140
Stony Creek, 11, 15, 16, 48, 228, 235, 262
Stony Fork, 221
Stony Hill Run, 108
Storrs, Gervas, 192, 194
Hanna, 192
Joshua, 192
Mary, 192
Susanna, 190
William, 192
Stoutemyer, Isaac Newton, 222
Stovall Creek, 225
Stovall, Bar., 100
Batt., 220
Fanny, 143
George, 125
Jesse, 259
Sally, 259
Straham, Peter, 178
Stratton, Ann, 37, 225
Edward, 37, 154, 225
Elizabeth, 38
Frances, 154
Henry, 153
John, 39, 40
Martha, 12, 37
Mary, 37
Thomas, 21
William, 153, 154
Strattons, 38
Streets, 173
Stuart, see Stewart
Sublet, Abraham, 93, 94

Heritage Books by Elise Greenup Jourdan:

The Greenup Family

Abstracts of Charles County, Maryland Court and Land Records:
Volume 1: 1658–1666
Volume 2: 1665–1695
Volume 3: 1694–1722

Colonial Records of Southern Maryland:
Trinity Parish and Court Records, Charles County;
Christ Church Parish and Marriage Records, Calvert County;
St. Andrew's and All Faith's Parishes, St. Mary's County

Colonial Settlers of Prince George's County, Maryland

Early Families of Southern Maryland:
Volume 1 (Revised) and Volumes 2-10

Early Settlers of Tidewater Virginia:
Volumes 1-4

Settlers of Colonial Calvert County, Maryland

Settlers of Colonial St. Mary's County, Maryland

The Land Records of Prince George's County, Maryland:
1702–1709
1710–1717
1717–1726
1726–1733
1733–1739
1739–1743

with Francis W. McIntosh

1840 to 1850 Federal Census: Tazewell County, Virginia

1860 Federal Census: Tazewell County, Virginia

1870 Federal Census: Tazewell County, Virginia